FINLAND

Land of
Natural Beauty

Oy Valitut Palat – Reader's Digest Ab   Helsinki

EDITORIAL COMMITTEE

Veikko M. Neuvonen,
puheenjohtaja
Seppo Vuokko
Dick Forsman

AUTHORS

(referred to by their initials at the
end of the articles)

Anja Finne (AF)
Dick Forsman (DF)
Antti Haapanen (AH)
Martti Hario (MH)
Eero Helle (EH)
Timo Helle (TH)
Pekka Helo (PH)
Heikki Henttonen (HH)
Olavi Hildén (OH)
Pertti Hiltunen (PHu)
Carl-Adam Hæggström (C-AH)
Jouko Högmander (JH)
Urpo Häyrinen (UH)
Olli Järvinen (OJ)
Asko Kaikusalo (AK)
Kari Kaila (KK)
Pertti Kalinainen (PK)
Erkki A. Kauhanen (EKa)
Heikki Kauhanen (HK)
Kullervo Kemppinen (KKe)
Jouni Kitti (JK)
Seppo Koponen (SK)
Jouko Kortesharju (JKo)
Pertti Koskimies (PKo)
Heikki Kotiranta (HKo)
Eero Kubin (EKu)
Kalevi Kuusela (KKu)
Unto Laine (UL)
Esko Lappi (EL)
Matti Leikola (ML)
Martti Linkola (MLi)
Jorma Luhta (JLu)
Arto Marjakangas (AM)
Mauri Melamies (MM)
Kauri Mikkola (KM)
Martti Montonen (MMo)
Eero Naskali (EN)

Rolf Oinonen (RO)
Hannu Ormio (HO)
Pekka Ovaskainen (PO)
Hannu Pietiläinen (HP)
Elias Pohtila (EP)
Erkki Pulliainen (EPu)
Arno Rautavaara (AR)
Tapio Rintanen (TR)
Matti Seppälä (MS)
Jouko Siira (JS)
Risto Sippola (RS)
Martti Soikkeli (MSo)
Inkeri Syrjänen (IS)
Juha Taskinen (JT)
Oili Tuunainen (OT)
Ilmari Valovirta (IV)
Yrjö Vasari (YV)
Heikki Willamo (HW)
Juha Viramo (JV)
Marjatta Virkkunen (MV)
Seppo Vuokko (SV)
Rauno Väisänen (RV)

PHOTOGRAPHERS

Kari Aarnio
Dick Forsman
Ville Hallikainen/LKA
Hannu Hautala
Kari Heliövaara
Aimo Holtari
Pertti Huttunen
Reijo Juurinen
Kari Kaila
Pertti Kalinainen
Eero Kemilä
Seppo Keränen
Heikki Kokkonen
Seppo Koponen
Heikki Kotiranta
Lasse J. Laine
Antti Leinonen
Jorma Luhta
Matti Mela
Kauri Mikkola
Esko Männikkö
Eero Naskali
Pauli Nieminen
Aarni Nummila
Pekka Nurminen

Matti A. Pitkänen
Rauno Pelkonen
Arno Rautavaara
Mauri Rautkari
Martti Rikkonen
Tapani Räsänen
Teuvo Suominen
Juha Taskinen
Pirkka Utrio
Reijo Wallin
Ilmari Valovirta
Tapani Vartiainen
Veikko Vasama
Juha Viista

Cover illustration: Pauli Niemi-
nen (main theme) and Hannu
Hautala plus Kimmo Mäntylä/
Lehtikuva (front gatefoldd)
Title pages: Matti Mela
Contents spread: Veikko Vasa-
ma

TRANSLATION

Gregory Coogan
Leigh Plester
Nick Marsh

MAPS AND DRAWINGS

Teuvo Berggren

PICTURE EDITOR

Dick Forsman

COVER, LAY-OUT AND TYPOGRAPHY

Hannu Laakso

EDITOR-IN-CHIEF

Rainer Palmunen

Original work: Luonnonystävän Suomi,
published by Oy Valitut Palat – Reader's Digest Ab, 1988

First printing

© 1989 Oy Valitut Palat — Reader's Digest Ab, Helsinki

Type-setting: Tammer-Linkki Oy, Tampere
Colour origination: Graafinen Studio Oy, Helsinki
Printed by: Kustannusosakeyhtiö Otavan painolaitokset, Keuruu

ISBN 951-9079-88-2

Printed in Finland

FOREWORD

Finns share a common heritage and a common love for the great outdoors. They are justifiably proud of their "wild" country, where Nature is always close by, closer in fact than some of us seem to realize. Finland would simply not be Finland without its forests, peatlands, fells, lakes and islands and long Baltic coastline.

From north to south, Finland is more than a thousand kilometres long. The south of the country has the luxuriance and rampant greenery of Central Europe; the north includes barren tundra that beckons the hiker, and the boreal coniferous forest, or "taiga", covers most of the country in between. This is also the zone where tens of thousands of water expanses scoured out by the glaciers of the last ice age create one of the world's most magnificent lake districts. Southeastern and eastern species serve to further diversify Finland's flora and fauna. In fact, the country as a whole is regarded as a meeting point of species from the south, north and east.

This book takes the reader to Finland's virtually untouched wilds — some of the last remaining virgin areas in Western Europe — but it also indicates how much is to be seen and experienced close to human settlements, even large ones. It endeavours to show some of the bewildering variety of natural sights that this unique country offers. Clearly, it would be impossible for one person to attempt to portray the whole. Thus it is a pleasure to see that some 70 authors and photographers, the best in the country, have contributed to this work.

As keen as they are on outdoor pursuits, Finns also enjoy nature documentaries on television. Thus it gives me great pleasure that my friend Mr. Veikko M. Neuvonen, who has produced so many excellent programmes of this kind, has also chaired the editorial committee for this book.

I have been studying our country's natural beauty for years — often with a camera in my hand. On behalf of the World Wide Fund for Nature, I have been following efforts to protect some of our most special places and species. It makes me really sad to see, all over the world and sometimes here as well, how Nature is being destroyed and polluted. If things are not going well for Nature, they are not going well for mankind, either. We need fundamentally new attitudes and values on which to form a relationship with our environment. Books can give us a greater appreciation of the beauty of Nature. Thus it gave me great joy when the Finnish chapter of the Fund chose this publication as its Nature Book of the Year 1988. It mirrors a country that has achieved a high level of technological sophistication and yet preserved its natural beauty. This is how we want the world to see us. Let this book be our ambassador.

Pertti Salolainen
Minister for Foreign Trade
Honorary Organizer of WWF Finland.

Contents

A CHUNK OF TAIGA, A PIECE OF TUNDRA

While the term 'taiga' brings to mind the limitless coniferous forests of Siberia, it must not be forgotten that a large proportion of Finland's population of five million people actually lives within the taiga in Western Europe. To gain a good impression of the taiga, you need to go to the top of a high fell. Below, the continuous, undulating sea of conifers, which with distance becomes increasingly blue, is broken only by a gleaming lake or pastel-hued mire. In short, it looks as monotonous as can be. But then so do the rainforests of the tropics!

The monotony of the taiga, or boreal coniferous forest (or even more simply 'northern coniferous forest'), is — thankfully — largely an apparent uniformity. Most of its large mammals are concealed, while even the smaller animals are adept at making use of the thinnest cover. Alternating with the tree stands there are lakes, rivers, streams, peatlands, exposed bedrock, bottom meadows, upland meadows and, further east but still in Finland, steppes.

Man has added further variation to the landscape, in the form of fields, meadows and wasteground, each of which offers a unique habitat to a wide range of species.

The boreal coniferous forest constitutes one of the world's most contiguous ecosystems, as well as one of its most intact. It starts on the Scandinavian peninsula, continues as an unbroken belt through northern Europe and Siberia as far as the Pacific Ocean, and in a very similar form, sweeps on across the continent of North America. Some of the species are common to the whole area, viz. the fox, the elk, the wolf, the glutton or wolverine and among the plants, for example, the Karelian rose and the rosebay willowherb or fireweed. From some of the original species in different parts of this area several new species have already evolved which, however, remain very closely related. The spruce, pine and certain deciduous tree species are dominant species of the taiga in both Europe and North America. Our wild forest reindeer and domesticated reindeer are equivalent to the caribou of the North American continent, while the European beaver is closely related to the Canadian beaver, which has become firmly established in Finland following its introduction.

This is not the whole story, of course. Different regions of the taiga also have their own unique species. For example, the North American chipmunk has no equivalents among the North European fauna.

The River Anterinjoki winds among the rolling fellscape of the Saariselkä region.

Aimo Holttari

KINGDOM OF THE FOUR WINDS

The bare summits of the fells belong to the tundra zone. In Finland the tundra is discontinuous, occupying the higher spots in the terrain, but these tracts of tundra are frequently hundreds of square kilometres in extent.

Owing to the cold and the brevity of the growing period, trees find the limit of their powers at the edges of the tundra and are replaced by willow shrubs, herbs, grasses and lichens. A large proportion of the world's tundra is associated with the permafrost. The subterranean ice may extend down to hundreds of metres. In summer only a thin surface layer melts. The frozen palsa mires may remain unchanged for thousands of years.

In summer the tundra is a hive of activity. While the actual number of species is rather low, the number of individuals seems almost infinite. Swarms of gnats or mosquitoes blotting out the sky are neither fancy nor legend, even if — fortunately for us humans — they do not occur in such proportions every year. Unchecked insect reproduction attracts large flocks of migrant birds to the arctic areas for the duration of the brief summer. Geese, ducks and waders are much in evidence.

The tundra ecosystem is less dissected than that of the taiga. There are species which, in their quest to find food, move from one part of the tundra to another. Such species include the snowy owl and long-tailed skua.

Martti Rikkonen

The arctic fox, which has become adapted to northern conditions, has regretably grown rarer in recent decades, its distribution now being limited to Inari, Enontekiö and Utsjoki.

this far north. This means that the entire Finnish flora and fauna has arrived here during the last ten thousand years. A large proportion of the immigrants, in fact, are far more recent than this.

The first species followed closely on the heels of the retreating glaciers. Wherever the ice left dry land we can imagine the mountain avens and opposite-leaved golden saxifrage taking root and the dwarf birch pushing out its penny-sized leaves to the sunlight. Wherever there were plants there were also animals. The Norwegian lemming, various kinds of deer, and the arctic fox, as well as numerous summer visitors in the form of birds, moved in to occupy the newly exposed ground. However, at least in places in easternmost Finland, the retreating ice drew not only fell-land species, but also plants which we nowadays classify as steppe plants or just plain weeds. Among these were certain goosefoots like Good King Henry, together with mugworts, bistorts, daisies, and plantains. In the arid places along the edges of the glacier a dwarf shrub, Ephedra, also grew. This, despite its superficial resemblance to a horsetail, is a southern relative of our conifers. Even the sea buckthorn, which is now confined to the coast, had a place among the vanguards of the new arrivals.

As the forests spread, many of the steppe plants were figuratively trodden underfoot, but some, like the pasque-flower Pulsatilla vernalis, have managed to cling to eskers, others to rocks, and some, like the sea buckthorn, have found themselves a completely new environment.

Encroaching forest swept the arctic plants progressively more northwards, to the summits of fells where conditions were too cold and windy for tree growth. In the lime-rich district of Oulanka, in eastern Finland just south of the Arctic Circle, brooks originating in coldwater springs, and sheer rock faces, for thousands of years offered a refuge from the shady forests.

As the climate slowly warmed up, the first birch and Scots pine forests began to form. As recently as six thousand years ago the Finnish climate was warmer than it is today. At that time the main tree species in southern Finland were the lime and hazel. Many southern plant and animal species had spread much further north than their present boreal limits. It is from these times that the south European floristic and faunal input dates. This input is seen today in the form of the hedgehog, pine marten, wood warbler and ling.

A cooling climate, peatland formation, and above all the indomitable spruce, which over the last three thousand years has successfully encroached over almost the entire country, caused the extinction of some species. In the most favourable growing places there exist remnants of previously extensive ranges. The large sedge Cladium mariscus at Joroinen, and the rye grass Bromus benekenii at Liperi are classic examples of this kind. These

MIGRANTS FROM ALL POINTS

Despite Finland's northerly location, the country possesses a rich fauna. In places the wildlife is prolific. The main reason for this is the Gulf Stream, which brings warm water over the Atlantic to the coast of Norway, whence some of the benefits of this natural central heating system are passed on to Finland.

The total number of Finnish species, including the lowliest worms, insects, moulds and algae, amounts to about forty thousand. As recently as ten thousand years ago Finland either lay under a kilometre thick continental ice sheet, or formed the bed of a so-called ice lake. Terrestrial plants and animals were literally non-existent

plants are now confined to the region of the Baltic Sea and southern Sweden.

Eastern taiga species adapted to severe winters now constitute the cornerstone of Finland's forest and peatland wildlife. Typical examples are the elk (equivalent to the North American moose), three-toed woodpecker, and crossbills, and among the flora the spruce, bilberry (equivalent to the North American blueberries), and Labrador tea.

NATURE IS STILL CHANGING

In the last few centuries man, in order to improve his own lot, has incidentally created favourable conditions for a lot of species from the south. Many now common species are relative newcomers to Finland. These include the lapwing, blackbird and black-headed gull, all of which were rarities here during the 1800s. The first racoon-dogs spread out from the northeastern border in the 1950s. This species has already crossed the River Tornionjoki that traces out the border between Finland and Sweden.

About half of our approximately 1,500 species of vascular plants have arrived in one way or another with people. A large proportion of them owe their presence to large-scale agricultural practices or to commerce. Among the plants there are examples of rapid conquerers of fresh ground. The mayweed Matricaria matricarioides arrived from America or eastern Asia in the 1800s. Canadian pondweed, which started to expand from a pool in Helsinki at the same time, and the American willowherb, which is currently expanding its range, are other prime examples of this catergory of plant.

THE CHANGING SEASONS

The changing of the seasons serves to vary an already diversified flora and fauna. During the winter our wildlife is at its quietest. Many of the birds are away, the majority of invertebrates are hibernating, and a lot of the mammals are living under the snow. Spring, with its melting snow, floods, bird migrants and general appearance of verdure, is a time of acute change. The landscape alters with each passing warm day. A return to wintry conditions (known in Finland as a 'back-winter') will interrupt the spring only momentarily.

Summer is a time of reproduction and growth. It is also a time of preparation for winter. There is a great deal of rushing about to build nests, feed young, and store up food for colder seasons.

Autumn makes its own changes. The 'ruska' or russet time reflects the preparation of plants for the winter and the anticipation of an eventual new spring. Many birds face the future by migrating out of these northern climes. Elk and deer enter the season of the rut, itself an investment in brighter times to come. The gathering of the harvest of berries and forest mushrooms, or toadstools, constitutes part of the preparation for lean times just around the corner. By putting food by, the bank vole, red squirrel, Canadian beaver, jay and tits take

A forest-bound stream refreshes the hiker.

When they emerge, the flowers of *Pulmonaria obscura are red, but with age they turn bluish. These lovely blooms greet the rambler only in the southern part of Finland.*   Aimo Holtari

out their insurance too. In October and November nature takes on its winter stillness.

PLUNGE INTO THE TAIGA

In the following pages of this book we shall be figuratively diving time and again into the taiga. Each time the landscape will be different, varying from mineral deficient heathlands dotted with Scots pine trees, to lovely birch groves, dark, shady spruce swamps, open aapa mires, and peatbogs with Scots pines. Rocky country and typical coastal or lake shore scenery add their contribution to the variety. Each micro-habitat possesses its own peculiar compliment of species that are adapted to the special conditions therein. Mosses, lichens, algae, insects, spiders, and so on, all tend to exhibit such specialisation.

Nature varies with the season, time of day, and weather. For the rambler no two days will ever be quite the same, no two hikes alike. SV

Aimo Holtari

TRAPLINES AND "EXCESS LANDS"

To our forefathers, the wilderness meant fishing waters and hunting grounds, an important source of livelihood, a place to live and to flee from persecution. The further back in history one looks, the more completely the people of Finland were denizens of the wilderness, dependent on its produce for their survival.

Although its population was thinly spread, the wilderness was never uninhabited. There was no last frontier; wherever fish and game could be found, people came in pursuit.

The Finnish word for wilderness actually means an area without permanent agricultural settlement. Unlike its equivalents in many other languages, it has no connotations of "wildness", "emptiness" or "desolation".

THE LAPPS BELONGED TO THE WILDERNESS

The Lapps (or the "Same" as they prefer to call themselves) needed no word for the wilderness at all, because it was their everyday habitat. And how could it be uninhabited, when they spent their whole lives in it? Of all of Finland's human inhabitants, the forest Lapps, who lived by hunting, fishing and later also from small-scale reindeer herding, were the most perfectly adapted to living in the bosom of nature. They were — in some places until the present century — harmoniously integrated as part of the wilderness. Unlike their Finnish neighbours further south, they made no attempt to clear it, alter it nor subdue it. On the contrary, a prerequisite for their continued survival was stability in natural conditions. There could be no major upheavals, nor could fishing and hunting exceed the regenerative capacity of nature.

The Lapps were the true inhabitants of the Finnish wildernesses, but they were gradually pushed north or absorbed by Tavastian, Savonian and Karelian settlers.

There were still Lapps in Savo and central Ostrobothnia as recently as the 17th century, and evidence that they had once lived throughout the country remained in the form of numerous place names and many references

Hannu Hautala

in orally-transmitted folk tales and legends.

The Lapps lived in communities called "Lapp villages" or "siidas". These were actually extensive districts. In the early 18th century there were 12 in Finnish Lapland, the southernmost of which were the Kitka and Maanselkä communities near what is today Kuusamo.

The siidas finally disappeared in the early half of the 19th century, under the combined onslaught of agricultural settlement and legislation which discriminated against non-settled forms of livelihood. In the forested parts of Lapland on the Russian side of the border, by contrast, the Skolt Lapps' siidas and traditional way of life persevered until the Second World War.

When the Petsamo area was incorporated in Finland in 1920, it brought with it several Lapp villages for Finnish researchers to wonder at. The most interesting of them was Suenjel. Its lifestyle, land use and customs were considered vestiges of ancient times, living models of a social structure that had perhaps once existed everywhere in Finland's forest wildernesses.

FINNISH COLONIES

While the Lapps lived unassumingly and tranquilly in the wilderness, their Finnish neighbours were something else again: to them the wilderness was something to exploit as efficiently as possible, and often even violently.

The Finns had already learnt how to cultivate land by the time their migration brought them to their modern homeland. Although this would long remain merely a supplementary means of livelihood alongside their fishing, hunting and gathering in the wilderness, it held the Finnish tribes in permanent settlements in the southern areas that they had cleared. From those bases they dominated and effectively exploited enormous wildernesses, sometimes ranging hundreds of kilometres from their home villages.

When the Swedish authorities, beginning in the 15th century, began compiling documentary records of their Finnish subjects and their property, they also compiled precise information on the system under which rights to wilderness areas were shared. Already then, however, the wildernesses had seen their best days.

The Tavastians, Karelians and Savonians all "possessed" extensive wilderness areas, but the tribe that best mastered the skills needed to traverse and exploit the wilderness lived in northern Satakunta or Pirkanmaa, the area around what is today Tampere. At the end of the Middle Ages, permanent settlement there was concentrated in a dense network of agricultural villages in a core area along the River Kokemäenjoki and its tributaries. However, the chief source of livelihood remained the wilderness stretching far to the north, to the river sources and even beyond the watersheds.

The wildernesses of Satakunta and Tavastia were private property. The owner was often a private person living in one of the adjacent villages, but could also be a "syndicate", and sometimes the village as a whole.

Wilderness "holdings" could be situated behind a 50 — 300 kilometres river or lake trip from their possessors'

Suenjel Lapp Village

The Skolt Lapps of Suenjel had to be evacuated from their home district when it was lost to the Soviet Union during the Second World War. They were resettled in Sevettijärvi, where only a few vestiges of their former way of life were preserved. Nevertheless, they tried during their years as evacuees to arrange conditions for themselves as close as possible to what they had been in their old home. The best-preserved examples of traditional Skolt habitations still to be found in Finland today are their seasonal dwellings, built during the war and now museumized. They are in the Urho Kekkonen National Park at Kotajärvi, Oskarinjärvi and Luttojoki.

The parts of Lapland that belong to Finland today were incorporated in Sweden in the 16th century. However, the Crown continued to respect the Lapps' village system and the ancient rights that went with it until about the middle of the 18th century. Recent research has shown that beyond the so-called Lapp border, i.e. in the whole of today's province of Lapland and part of what is now the province of Oulu, Lapp villages' ownership of their lands and waters was recognized. The borders between the villages' territories were clearly delineated and physically marked. Old border markings can still be seen in places. A stone cairn on Sinettätunturi Fell has been there since at least the first half of the 18th century.

The Lapp villages paid land tax on their estate. In those days, none of Lapland was owned by the Crown.

As settlement spread northwards, the Lapp villages came under increasing pressure and a variety of regulations diminished their traditional rights. Their siidas were reconstituted as parishes and the authority which landowners had enjoyed was transferred to parish councils, in which Finnish settlers dominated. The method of land registration was changed in a manner that meant the proprietary system in the old Lapp villages was no longer stated. Finally, the records contained no reference to Lapp villages at all. In the 19th century the Lapps' lands began to be redistributed to farm holdings for new settlers and the State assumed ownership of the remaining wilderness areas.

Pointing to the many irregularities involved in the transfer of land ownership from their traditional villages to the Crown/State and settlers, today's Lapps still dispute the State's ownership of its present extensive land holdings in Lapland.

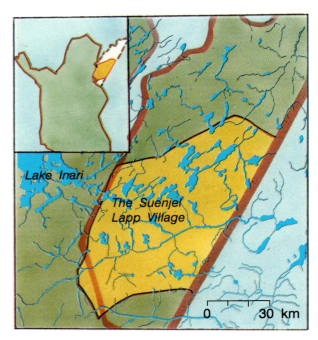

Lake Inari

The Suenjel Lapp Village

0   30 km

Teuvo Berggren

16

home villages. When they were in these remote areas, the backwoodsmen ran traplines and built cabins with storage huts. The Tavastians' "wilderness rights" sometimes also included a few Lapps — or exclusive rights to exact tribute from them.

Researchers have concluded that the earliest stage of the wilderness era was a time of intensive hunting, with the most important prey being seals, wild reindeer, elk and other large and highly mobile animals. Indeed, it may well be that the Finnish tribes' own mobility and capacity to undertake very long trips originated in times when they lived by following migrating herds of reindeer. Pits into which deer were driven and killed can still be seen in some of the few primeval wildernesses that still survive in southern Finland, such as the Salamajärvi national park in Perho and the Torronsuo area in Tammela.

The heyday of the wilderness culture began when the central European fur trade turned to Finland as a source of supply during the period of great popular migrations. The fur trade gave wilderness-based livelihoods an export dimension. Wilderness holdings increased in value, the communities that owned them prospered, and a wealthy merchant class came into being.

The backwoodsmen of Upper Satakunta were not content with the extensive wildernesses in central Finland's lake districts and South Ostrobothnia. Their expeditions took them further and further north, along the river systems of Ostrobothnia all the way to the coast and right up to the head of the Baltic's northern arm. From there, they entered the rivers flowing out of Lapland and followed them to their headwaters and then on to the Arctic coast. People from the Kainuu region are known to have made regular expeditions to the furthest reaches of Lapland as early as the 9th century, to trade, exact tribute and plunder. Even to this day, the Norwegians who live in their country's northernmost province, Finnmark, call the Finns "Kvæns" (Kainuans), and the Lapps "Finnes". Later, from the 12th century onwards, the Kainuu tribe, who by now had — confusingly — begun to be described as the Pirkkalans, continued their trips to the North even more efficiently. In 1328, in fact, they were given Royal permission to conduct exclusive taxing in Lapland. For centuries, they were the colonial masters of Lapland, accumulating great wealth by taxing the Lapps and trading in furs on a large scale.

SETTLING TAXPAYERS

From very early on, some slash-and-burn agriculture had been practised in the wildernesses of Upper Satakunta and Tavastia, but only as a supplement to hunting and fishing. Hops and barley were grown close to wilderness cabins. Far from the watchful eyes of their women folk, the backwoodsmen in their remote cabins used the barley and hops to make a concoction with a clear relationship to today's hunting and fishing culture.

In their own region, the Savonians had developed an

Dick Forsman

Rock paintings describe the hunting culture of ancient generations. Haukkavuori, Kolovesi.

efficient, flexible and shifting form of slash-and-burn agriculture, which did not depend on villages. This enabled them rapidly to move into wildernesses, clear them and establish permanent habitations.

In the 16th century, King Gustavus Vasa needed a lot of money, i.e. taxes, to finance his ambitious reforms. Under his rule Sweden (of which Finland was then a part) was trying to consolidate its grip on its eastern borderlands and to push east beyond the border established in the peace treaty of 1323. Creating permanent agricultural settlements in the northern wildernesses was considered the best means of achieving both aims. Farmers are obviously easier to tax than semi-nomadic backwoodsmen.

And so the Crown took determined measures to promote the north- and northwestward spread of Savonian settlers and their methods of shifting cultivation. To the West, however, the spread of settlement was blocked by the Tavastians' and Satakuntans' hunting reserves, which they were understandably unwilling to yield.

Their resistance was in vain and within a few decades settlement had spread as far north as Lake Oulujärvi. The 17th century saw settlers continue their expansion beyond the border of Lapland.

Crown ownership of wilderness areas had been claimed since 1542, when King Gustavus Vasa of Sweden declared that "uninhabited lands belong to God, Us and the Swedish Crown, and to nobody else."

This proclamation had been made to peasants in Sweden proper, and thus did not actually apply to Finland, but the King assumed the right to distribute lands to settlers anyway, disregarding traditional ownership and usage right. His intention was to promote settlement rather than to acquire lands for the Crown. Indeed, long before Gustavus Vasa took the throne, uninhabited lands had been considered to belong to the Crown in a sense, i.e. others could use them, but the Crown was entitled to tax them.

In Lapland, Gustavus Vasa struck a hard blow at the Pirkkalans by stripping them of the right to tax the Lapps and transferring it to himself. However, the Pirkkalans continued to make trading expeditions to Lapland.

THE BIG SHARE-OUT

The Crown really set about acquiring uninhabited wildernesses in 1683, when it issued its Forest Decree, the main purpose of which was to ensure a supply of wood for the Swedish mining industry. The Decree ordered that all lands which could not be shown to be the property of anybody belonged to the Crown. Gustavus Vasa's declaration in 1542 was presented as the justification for this.

The Decree further stated that the boundaries of privately owned land should first be defined, and any remaining land transferred to the Crown. In cases where private land holdings lacked clear boundaries, each holding was allotted a reasonable area, the rest going to the Crown.

Since, however, there were few mines in Finland and hence little need for pit props, the Decree was implemented only half-heartedly. Nonetheless, the belief that

Hay was gathered from even the most remote river banks to feed livestock in winter. Jouttenaapa, Salla.

Pertti Kalinainen

wilderness lands belonged to the Crown gained gradual acceptance.

The final seal was put on the matter in 1775, during the reign of Gustaf III. A decree was issued with the aim of reparcelling lands to create coherent holdings. Each farm or estate now received 300 — 600 hectares of hitherto undivided forest land per "mantal" (or tax assessment unit) of their holdings. They received even more in Lapland. The remaining backwoods areas (or "excess lands", as they were called) went to the Crown, which had earmarked them for resettlement purposes.

This major land redistribution programme had been carried through almost everywhere in Finland well over a century ago, but in the most awkward northernmost areas it was not completed until the 1960s. The question of water rights in northern Lapland is still a bone of contention.

The backwoods area that went to the Crown back then still form the bulk of the State's present-day forest holdings. They are also the country's largest primeval wildernesses and contain most of its nature reserves.

Most of the State's other land holdings are the result of cancellations of Crown grants. In many cases, Swedish kings made generous land grants to members of the nobility and the church, only to take them back again when the recipients fell from favour. "Gift lands" in what is today south-eastern Finland were distributed by the Russian Czars to their favourites in the 18th century. They were purchased back by the autonomous Finnish grand duchy a century ago and were the last major addition to the State's holdings.

Before the 19th century, there were no special officials to manage Crown lands. Nor were they actually needed, because wildernesses were not yet undisputably Crown-owned, whilst other holdings had been placed at the disposal of various officials, who took care of them anyway. The Crown's interests as an owner were the responsibility of provincial governors, and the only officials responsible for forests in any way were gamekeepers. People made tar, felled trees and practised slash-and-burn agriculture in the wildernesses without any particular supervision on the part of the Crown.

Soon after the middle of the 19th century, the advent of the sawmilling industry boosted the economic value of the State's by now very large forest holdings and the need for a separate official body to administer them became obvious. Not everyone agreed, because the lands in question were supposed to be a reserve for new settlers. However, the argument that won was that of a certain Lars Gabriel von Haartman, who urged the State to become directly involved in silviculture. Rather than parcel out land to settlers, it was decided to keep large coherent forest holdings in government ownership. To take care of them, the National Board of Forestry was created in 1859.

WILDERNESSES STILL BEING SETTLED

The State's land holdings declined sharply after Finland became independent in 1917 and crofters and tenant

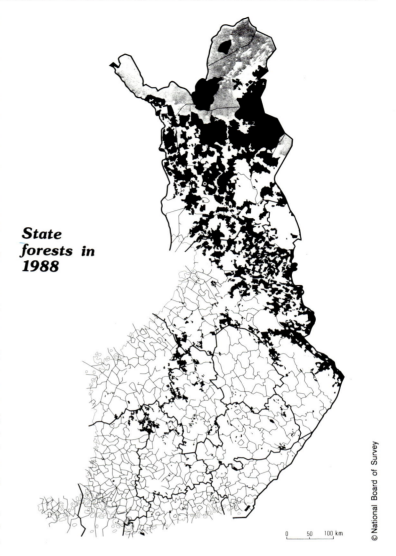

State forests in 1988

© National Board of Survey

0   50   100 km

foresters were given title to the lands they worked. Much more land was parcelled out after the Second World War to resettle evacuees from territories ceded to the Soviet Union. Still more land has been redistributed since then, mainly to improve the viability of smallholdings. Those are the main reasons why most of the State-owned wildernesses in the southern parts of Finland have disappeared.

The creation of new farm holdings in State-owned wilderness areas has now been discontinued, but a new approach to settlement has been introduced in Lapland. In recent years, holdings have been created there under the provisions of the Reindeer Husbandry Act, and to enable non-exploitative livelihoods to be pursued. However, the areas involved are not very large.

The National Board of Forestry had 10.5 million hectares of holdings in 1945. By 1983, the total had declined to 8.4 million. However, the State is constantly buying land for forestry purposes, often smallholdings created after the war but no longer viable. Areas still in a very natural condition are being acquired to create national parks and other nature reserves. HO

Reijo Juurinen

FINLAND'S LAST WILDERNESSES

A definition of what is a wilderness has been formulated in the United States and is gaining acceptance in. Finland as well:
"A wilderness is a trackless area in a relatively natural state and located more than eight kilometres from a road or railway." Often, too, there is a minimum size requirement: 20 sq. kilometres in the western US and 100 sq. kilometres in Sweden. Industrial activity is prohibited or subject to stringent controls, whilst small-scale silviculture is permitted. The primary use is recreational, such as hiking. The products of nature can be used, provided the natural environment itself is not interfered with.

According to that definition, ten wilderness areas remain in Finland. They cover about five per cent of the national territory. There are also five other small fragments of wilderness. All in all, wildernesses cover about seven per cent of the Nordic countries. They are virtually non-existent elsewhere in Western Europe. About two per cent of the territory of the United States can be classed as wilderness. The world's largest wildernesses are in Canada, Brazil, the Antarctic, Australia and in the Asian interior.

BIRTHPLACES OF PROTECTION

The idea of protecting wilderness culture was born and developed in the 1830s, largely through the work of the philosopher Henry David Thoreau and the lawyer-painter George Catlin. As the century drew to a close, a system of national parks was beginning to take shape. Since only areas with unusual natural characteristics were made into national parks, they soon became overpopulated tourist attractions and appreciation of simple "wilderness values" gained ground only slowly. John Muir founded the Sierra Club in 1892 and Robert Marshall the Wilderness Society in 1935.

Respect for wildernesses and official recognition of their existence as a legitimate form of land use was not enshrined in law until 1964, when the Wilderness Act came into force. It obliged states to survey trackless areas and entitled them to create wilderness areas, either within national parks or separately. Only uninhabited areas are recognized as wildernesses, and are required to be in as near as possible to a completely virgin

A view of Naltiotunturi Fell in the Urho Kekkonen National Park.

condition. Few of Finland's wildernesses would meet these requirements, if only because reindeer husbandry has left clear marks on the landscape everywhere in the north.

RECEDING WILDERNESSES

Most of the northern provinces of Lapland and Oulu were classed as wilderness in 1925. There were dozens of wilderness areas elsewhere in Finland except in the extreme south-west. The period between the world wars was, for the most part, one of gradually increasing prosperity for those who lived in those areas. There were logging camps, some of them large, but felling was selective and there are few traces of it left today, because the forests have regenerated themselves. Here and there, the rotting crowns of huge pines show how little wood was actually taken from the forests in those days. The felling sites were very far from roads if there were big

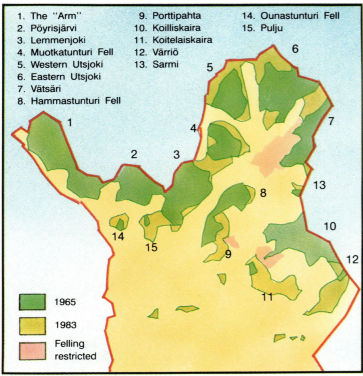

1. The "Arm"
2. Pöyrisjärvi
3. Lemmenjoki
4. Muotkatunturi Fell
5. Western Utsjoki
6. Eastern Utsjoki
7. Vätsäri
8. Hammastunturi Fell
9. Porttipahta
10. Koilliskaira
11. Koitelaiskaira
12. Värriö
13. Sarmi
14. Ounastunturi Fell
15. Pulju

■ 1965
■ 1983
■ Felling restricted

Teuvo Berggren

rivers to loose-float the logs. The entire area east of Lake Inari was thinned in the 1920s and 1930s. More than 100,000 choice logs were floated across the lake and from there down the River Paatsjoki to shipment points on the Arctic Ocean.

The biggest felling project mooted in those days would have involved exploiting the pine forests of the Lutolaakso Valley. The idea was to haul them over the Saariselkä ridge in lorries, to be floated via Lake Luirojärvi to the seaport of Kemi. The trees had already been marked and the road was nearing completion when the Winter War broke out in November 1939 and forced the project to be abandoned. But this was only a temporary

respite. The war taxed the nation's resources and reconstruction after it added to the strain.

The road network in northern and eastern Finland developed rapidly after the war, but was still tenuous enough to leave extensive low-lying forest tracts in between. Soon, however, rapidly developing mechanical harvesting methods, road haulage, the building of forest roads good enough to take motor vehicles and the opening of a large pulp mill in Kemijärvi made sharp inroads into the forest areas that had remained relatively untouched. Exploitation reached deeper and deeper into the backwoods and higher up the hill slopes. The assault on the wildernesses intensified.

Profitability became the key word and the last outposts of the forest wilderness fell in 1982, when it was decided to build a bridge across the River Paatsjoki to facilitate access to the wood resources east of Lake Inarijärvi.

THE WILDERNESSES TODAY

Finland's wilderness areas covered nearly 25,000 sq. kilometres (roughly the size of Belgium) in 1966. They had completely disappeared in eastern Finland, but some fragments remained in the province of Oulu, which lies to the south of Lapland. In fifteen years, four highway projects and thousands of kilometres of forest roads reduced the total wilderness area by a third. The Tenonvaara and Näätämö roads limited the wilderness in the northernmost part of Lapland to its present size, commercial exploitation began in the Sompio-Savukoski forests, whilst further south the Jonkerinsalo lowland forests and Lapiosuo bog were destroyed. By the end of the 1970s, only a couple of areas more than two kilometres from a road remained untouched. Young conservationists tried to arrest this regrettable development by collecting hundreds of thousands of signatures in support of an appeal to preserve the Koilliskaira forests in the extreme northeast of Lapland. The National Board of Forests tried to soften the impact of forest roads by closing those leading to the most sensitive areas with booms, but this decision had to be reversed when the Ombudsman ruled that all citizens had equal rights of access to these roads. When the Urho Kekkonen National Park was established in the Koilliskaira area in 1983 and the Lemmenjoki National Park was extended, it meant that both a dream and a nightmare came true for environmentalists. Two splendid primeval forests had been preserved for posterity. At the same time, however, a prediction made by silviculturalists as far back as the 1960s had been proved sadly true: forest preservation combined with recreational use and wood production, no matter how well intentioned such an arrangement may be, simply does not work.

As things stand at present, it seems that the Lemmenjoki and Koilliskaira wildernesses will be preserved, as well as, probably, those in the "Arm" (the western protuberance of Finland between Norway and Sweden) and the area north of Vätsäri. All other areas are threatened. Is that a prospect that the nation can contemplate with equanimity? RO

Aarni Nummila

COASTAL
FINLAND

THE ARCHIPELAGO SEA

A mosaic of sea and land

Since the last Ice Age in the area between Finland's southwestern coast and Åland tens of thousands of small islands and islets have sprung up. This extensive, dense archipelago has no equal anywhere in the world. Elsewhere archipelagoes tend to be situated in salty seas, in a completely different climate, or to form part of a mountain chain or fjorded coastline. When elsewhere the ceaseless movement of the tides and strong currents have eroded island shores, our own islands are slowly being uplifted from the sea: every century there is a rise in elevation and a subsequent shallowing of the sounds by as much as 50 cm.

So extensive and diversified an archipelago contains a wealth of sights and tales of Man's eternal struggle against the elements hidden in its labyrinths. The Archipelago National Park is currently being formed out of the area lying to the west of Kemiönsaari and south of

Seppo Keränen

Grey seals differ from marbled seals in the shape of the head. The former has a long muzzle and lower forehead. Grey seals give birth to pups on the ice in February-March. A pup stays with its mother for about a month.

Korppoo and Nauvo. The national park will make it easier for hikers coming from the mainland to become acquainted with archipelago wildlife and cultures. This area is otherwise bereft of accommodation, eating facilities, and boats.

The national park is best viewed from a seaworthy boat capable of standing up to rough seas. Even so, the visitor may well find himself stranded for two or three days while a high wind blows! Rocks just beneath the surface create a further hazard, as many of the sounds are still uncharted and even islands may be omitted from charts.

SPLENDID VIEW FROM HÖGLAND

One of the most lovely water routes through the islands and across the open waters of Gulkrona runs through "Paraisten portti", a narrow sound bounded by steep cliffs. Soon after the narrowest point, the vista opens out on to scattered skerries and distant forested islands.

The eye is drawn irresistibly to a large rocky island,

Högland, with its cone-shaped profile. Its deepwater shores make landing easy, but one's boat remains at the mercy of the sea, for there is no sheltered natural harbour whatsoever.

In the past a lighthouse keeper lived on Höglund who was later replaced by automation. On the other side of the island old pastures are covered with alder. The loss of people and encroachment by vegetation are signs of the times in the Archipelago.

From the 45-metre high peak of Högland a splendid view unfurls. Hundreds of thousands of years of geological history can be appreciated as one looks out over the seascape. An originally square expanse of rock several score kilometres in length dropped to tens of metres below its surroundings to form the Gullkrona depression, the straight edges of which can clearly be seen to the north and east.

Högland belongs to the Outer Archipelago. Open vistas, barren rocky slopes and pines permanently crippled by wind stir the same emotions as Lapland. Here, too, distances are vast and inhabitation minimal.

Many shy, now endangered animal species have made their homes here. From Högland's heights one may sometimes still glimpse the white-tailed eagle. In the Gullkrona open sea area a grey seal or two may lie basking on some exposed rock, as though blissfully unaware that the Archipelago is really the home of the marbled seal, while grey seals ought to be living far out to sea. Sadly, even the marbled seal is a rarity today.

ISLANDS CONSTRUCTED DURING THE ICE AGE

In clear weather from the top of Höglund one can see seven or eight kilometres to the south a pair of elongated sandy islands, named appropriately enough Sandskär and Sandön. These pine-covered islands constitute a part of the Salpausselkä ridges that formed in Finland towards the close of the last ice age and, as it were, spilled out into the sea from Kemiönsaari. The ten thousand year-old edge moraine deposits of this ridge (known as Salpausselkä III) form, if you like, a vertebral column to the southern part of the Archipelago. Some 300 metres of open water lie between the higher island of Kemiönsaari and the narrow, reef-like Sandskär. This pattern is repeated continually in a west-southwesterly direction. Finally, sixty kilometres away at Utö, the Salpausselkä ridge disappears beneath the sea. Myriads of islands form the Archipelago between Kemiönsaari and Utö, providing an every-changing variety of scenery which includes reefs, sandy beaches, heaps of cobblestones, and heathlands dominated by ling. Sandön is a famous Finnish beauty spot.

TOWARDS THE OUTLYING ISLANDS

One of the most thriving southern Archipelago fishing villages in an age when the latter are rapidly disappearing is Högsåra. On its north shore, where Russian ships used to anchor, there is now a tiny harbour for visiting boats which provides a range of basic tourist services. If an overnight stay in such a safe retreat is not to the intrepid visitor's liking, he can always tie up at the natural harbour of Benskär, some three kilometres further west.

South of Tunnham one suddenly finds oneself at the very edge of the Archipelago. The outlying villages are famous for their long and colourful history, facets of which include an eternal unrelenting struggle against a harsh environment, pirate legends, plundered ships run aground, and smuggling. In autumn constant gales make the area's most important industry, open sea fishing, literally impossible. 'Roads' across the frozen sea in midwinter are treacherous, frequently breaking up as the sea moves restlessly beneath them. Yet all four remote villages continue to function, life going on in them as it has for hundreds of years. Modern boats equipped to withstand the ice, and other contemporary technological

achievements, serve to make things just that little bit easier.

WRECKS AND SEALS

Countless ships lie at the bottom of the sea in the Outer Archipelago. Shipwrecks provided the local populace with useful materials as an adjunct to the excitement of rescue operations. Even today the waves bring in driftwood that comes in handy on those remote skerries.

The famous wreck of the three-master St Mikael, which went down in October 1747, lies on the sea bed at Borstö, Nauvo. This ship was on a voyage from Amsterdam to St Petersburg, where it was to have delivered luxury goods to the Russian Court. Even closer to Bortsö, the barque Nordenstjerna, loaded with candle fat from Riga destined for New York, was claimed by the sea in December 1809, the account of its fateful last brush with nature written in lurid detail in the ship's log. Items saved from these wrecks now reside in Borstö museum, from which the visitor gains a first class impression of seafaring and life in bygone times. The museum is located in two old buildings right in the centre of one of the Archipelago's most delightful villages. Other fascinating sights include a windmill and a ship's figurehead that drifted in on the pack ice at the turn of the century and which now gazes out from a high promontory over the briny whence it came.

Seal hunting implements, gear and firearms are also on display at the museum. In the dim past grey seals roamed the shallows in colonies of up to a hundred.

Seppo Keränen

The heartsease or wild pansy grows both among the rocks on Archipelago skerries and in fields further inland.

Grossly affected by pollutants, grey seal populations have dwindled to around a couple of thousand individuals in all.

LONG BANKS OF COBBLESTONES

Jurmo, lying west of Borstö, on the Korppoo side, must surely be one of the Archipelago's strangest landforms: it is a ridge composed of sand and cobblestones supporting a unique heathland community. It rises from the sea, runs for five and a half kilometres, and is punctuated at either end by cobblestone 'reefs'. Jurmo is Salpausselkä III's most spectacular section.

No forest worthy of the title has grown on Jurmo since Gustav Vasa's troops in the 1500s burned the island's vegetation to discourge 'wreckers' from using the site as a lure for enticing unsuspecting victims on to the rocks. Whenever there was a gale blowing, these brigands would light a beacon atop the island, thus duping approaching ships into thinking they had located the light on Utö island. When the unfortunate ship ran aground, the pirates quickly dispatched the crew and plundered the wreck.

Jurmo is also famous for its wildlife. Ice floes gather in the spring in the shallows separating Jurmo from Utö, attracting thousands of migrating seabirds. Eider are present in the largest numbers, but in May the cries of sizeable flocks of long-tailed ducks ring out over the water.

Shelducks nest in fair numbers on the sandy beaches, and arctic skuas loop and dive with breathtaking speed over the skerries. There are a few razorbill colonies in the vicinity, but the razorbill, like its relative the black guillemot, is endangered. Feral mink attack the nestlings, and sometimes even incubating adults, of these birds in their exposed breeding sites, thereby depleting their numbers.

UTÖ — GATEWAY TO THE OUTER ARCHIPELAGO

The island of Utö, with its lighthouse, is located some thirteen kilometres southwest of Jurmo. Utö has traditionally differed from the other Outer Archipelago villages in being populated by a community of officials, whose male children have habitually become pilots and lighthouse keepers. Utö's lighthouse and pilots have guided trade ships safely through to the Inner Archipelago since at least the 1500s.

The Utö lighthouse is a spectacular edifice. Built of reddish-grey stone, it was erected in 1814 to replace the lighthouse destroyed during the wars. The lighthouse keeper or one of the older pilots are usually glad to show people around. Halfway up the tower there is an intriguing church.

Many of the boats which put in at Utö after provisioning go on to places even further afield. An ancient route runs from Utö to Åland, via Kökar and Föglö, to the capital, Mariehamn. So difficult is the labyrinth on the southern side of Kökar that the first part of the route is now omitted from charts, and boats follow a route leading north.

ÅLAND — A WORLD APART

The Åland Islands, or Åland as they are often simply called, cover half of the Archipelago Sea. This western side of the sea differs sharply from the Kihti region occupying the eastern side, mainly for geological reasons. The red granite is sure to be noticed. The ice age mixed limestone boulders from the seabed with the soil on the islands, with the consequence that there are now lush copses and meadows supporting a rich variety of plantlife. Ash, oak and wych elm grow in abundance, together with many herbs that are rare, or not found at all, on the Finnish mainland. On the island of Kökar, beyond the provincial border, rare orchids, viz. Dactylorhiza sambucina, Orchis mascula and Cephalanthera longifolia, flower in the meadows.

Villages lying on the west side of the provincial border are noteworthy in being still inhabited, with newly-erected commercial greenhouses and tourist enterprises testifying once again that these stalwart Åland islanders never give up. Despite the activity, there are few summer houses here, these being concentrated mainly on the islands close to the mainland. This is due in large measure to the law, which stipulates that anybody buying land in Åland must live on it. The islands are so extensive that the twenty thousand or so fishermen's huts and summer houses, with their blue, red and white Åland pennants, blend in perfectly with the landscape. JH

Archipelago Sea National Park

Dragsfjärd, Houtskär, Korppoo, Nauvo,
Intended surface area 30 sq.km.
Established: 1983
Under National Board of Forestry management.

Connections: No proper facilities as yet exist in the national park, so that visitors are expected to be self-sufficient. The park can be reached either by private boat or by one of the regular service vessels, e.g. ms "Utö" from Turku, ms "Rosala" from Käsnäs, ms "Kristina" from Prostvik (Nauvo), or by the waterbus plying the Turku—Nötö route.

Services: The central service point of the Archipelago Sea area is Nötö, where there is a shop, fuel station, telephone, and the Turku outdoor recreation area. Private accommodation is available at Vänö and Hittinen. There is an unlocked cabin at Konungskär, a natural harbour and public convenience at Hästö. There is a well-maintained wooded meadow of the traditional kind at Boskär.

Further information: National Board of Forestry, Hämeenlinna District Office, tel. 917-25 663

Pertti Kalinainen

The Disappearing Wooded Meadows

Wooded meadows are lush meadows dotted with groups of deciduous trees and shrubs. They were originally created by the clearance of glades in deciduous woods or the use of shore meadows for hay. Scattered deciduous trees and shrubs were left growing in these meadows, especially fruit-bearing species and species that could be used for building and carpentry, or for leaf fodder. In the course of time hay making, grazing and other forms of human management created typical wooded meadows. Similar meadows might also arise on abandoned fields, often established through slash-and-burn cultivation.

A mosaic of plant communities

A wooded meadow consists of two distinct kinds of plant communities: small copses of deciduous trees and shrubs, and patches of open meadow, which together form a park-like mosaic. The trees and shrubs provide adequate — and necessary — shade for the sward.

The transition zone between the copses and the glades, the

Cowslips grow wild on wooded meadowland. They are very abundant in some parts of Åland.

ecotone, is very significant and the wooded meadow often consists of one single ecotone. It is a well known fact that the number of species in an ecotone is considerably higher than in either of the two adjoining communities, or even in both combined. Thus the wooded meadow has the highest number of plant species of any vegetation in Finland. More than 40 different vascular plant species can be found in one square metre of wooded meadow.

About 30 species of trees and shrubs form the copses of the wooded meadows. Common species are the silver and downy (or common, or brown) birch, common alder, (great) sallow, aspen, rowan (or mountain ash), and bird cherry. Species the like wych elm, oak, maple and ash, with exacting ecological requirements, are abundant in places. Wooded meadows often also support the

Seppo Keränen

crab apple, Finnish and Swedish whitebeams, common hawthorn and buckthorn. The most common shrub is the hazel, but the wealth of species in these wooded meadows also includes the juniper, mountain currant, cinnamon rose, short-pedicelled rose, soft-leaved rose, common cotoneaster, blackthorn, guelder rose and fly honeysuckle.

The sward

The field layer is very rich in species. The wooded meadows are at the peak of their splendour in spring, when they are adorned with the flowers of the wood anemone, yellow anemone, hepatica, bulbous buttercup, lesser celandine, purple corydalis, meadow (or bulbous) saxifrage, spring vetch, cowslip, yellow star of Bethlehem, elderflowered orchid and early purple orchid. At midsummer the most conspicuous species is perhaps the wood cranesbill. In July several tall herbs and grasses are in flower, such as dropwort, meadowsweet, bloody cranesbill, wild angelica, cow parsnip (or hogweed), northern bedstraw, lady's bedstraw, nettle-leaved bell flower (or bats-in-the-belfry), brown-rayed knapweed, twayblade, spotted orchid, woodland meadow grass, cocksfoot and wood millet.

A similar rich diversity of species is found in the ground layer of mosses, as well as among the fungi and insects, supported by the wooded meadow.

A product of human management

The structure of the wooded meadows, i.e. the mosaic of copses and meadow glades, is the outcome of human activity. Once the influence of man ceases, the wooded meadows always change back into forest. In other countries wooded meadows are found in central and southern Sweden, on the islands of Öland and Gotland, and in the coastal areas of Estonia, including the islands. Further south, vegetation complexes similar to the Finnish wooded meadows are chiefly found in mountainous areas, such as the Caucasus, the Balkans, northern Italy, and the Pyrenees.

Very few wooded meadows remain in Finland toady. Only a few small areas are managed in the traditional way in the Åland islands, and there are a few nature reserves in which wooded meadows are maintained. There are also some similarly managed wooded meadows in the Turku archipelago, just east of Åland.

Wooded meadows probably date back to the Neolithic Age, when deciduous stands served as sources of leaf fodder. However, the wooded meadow with which we are familiar today did not emerge until somewhat later, when hay making began. The management of wooded meadows was remarkably similar in its features from place to place, at least in the Baltic region.

Wooded meadow cultivation comprised four phases:
1. Raking. During this spring cleaning operation dry twigs and leaves were raked into heaps which were either burned or left to decay in a suitable place, for instance in a hazel thicket. This was done when the wood anemone was coming into bloom.
2. Hay making. The meadow glades were mown in July when the timothy grass started to bloom and the seeds of the hayrattle were ripe.
3. Grazing. A few weeks after the hay had been cut, horses and cows were allowed to graze in the wooded meadows.
4. Lopping. In many wooded meadows certain deciduous trees, such as wych elm, silver and common birch, common alder, aspen, rowan, maple and ash, were pollarded at intervals of 3 – 5 years.
5. In addition, the copses in the wooded meadows were trimmed back every few years to prevent them encroaching on the meadow glades.

In some wooded meadows the trees were never pollarded. Such was the case, for instance, on the islands of Idö and Brüskär in the Åland Islands, and in Estonia. Instead the trees were felled and the shoots sprouting from their stumps were cut from time to time. These wooded meadows can be regarded as a kind of coppice. C-AH

The Protected Apollos

Many things in Finland are not as they used to be. As recently as the 1950s the apollo used to fly commonly in southern Finland. Up until the 1940s the clouded apollo inhabited most parts of the southern coast from Pellinki to Hankoniemi. Since then both species have declined alarmingly, their distribution now being limited, with a few exceptions, to the southwestern region. Why is this? Have the apollos' habitats elsewhere in the country changed so radically?

As their populations began to dwindle, Finland's apollo species came under official protection in 1976.

The apollo *Parnassius apollo*

The apollo is difficult to confuse with any other butterfly species. One of Finland's largest lepidoptera, it bears distinctive red spots on its hindwings. Its soaring flight is most characteristic: it may be on the wing even in a high wind so long as the sun is shining. Only the forewings beat strongly, the hindwings acting as stabilisers. This gives the flying insect the appearance of a triangle tapering towards the rear.

Apollos tend to fly over dry, open rocky terrain, their caterpillars feeding exclusively on a species of stonecrop, *Sedum telephium*. The eggs overwinter, the larvae feeding in the spring and summer only when the sun shines. Adults are generally on the wing in July and early August. Although the species has declined considerably, a single small population of the apollo has survived to this day (1988) in Uusimaa Province. A similar extant population thrives in the Lake Saimaa area. In contrast to the clouded apollo, the apollo has also disappeared from the mainland of Åland, although it occurs commonly on the island of Föglö.

When research into the causes of the decline of this insect had been carried out, it was discovered that there had been no particularly catastrophic year weather-wise, the species have vanished from different localities in different years. For this reason, an increasingly maritime climate, and shared microbes, have been put forward as reasons for the decline of Finland's *Parnassius* species.

Could human impact on the butterflies' environment, however, be responsible? Cattle are no longer put out to graze in woodlands, so that other vegetation is permitted to choke the stonecrops, while flowery meadows are now much less common. Or could acid rain have had an adverse effect on the foodplants?

The decline of the apollos certainly seems to have gone hand in glove with the decline in grazing and in flowery meadows. The acid rain theory is lent support by the situation in Sweden where, according to L.-Å. Janzon, the last surviving apollo populations all inhabit lime-rich areas. Paradoxically, however, the reddish *Trentepohlia iolithus* green alga which occurs in the same rocky terrain as the apollo is a calciphobe species. Besides, there is no mechanism known by means of which acid rain could conceivably affect either apollos or their foodplant.

With the permission of the Ministry of the Environment, apollo eggs have recently been removed from the species' last stronghold in Uusimaa Province in an attempt to re-establish populations in the western sector of the Province. The failure of this experiment leads one once again to suspect changes in the environment as the cause. This does not explain why the southwest is such an ideal region for the species! If the environment on the mainland of Finland has largely become hostile, there is no reason to anticipate recolonisation by the species. It is thus necessary to concentrate on the management and monitoring of surviving populations.

The future of the apollo is

Dick Forsman

Seppo Keränen

A larger size and red spots enable the apollo to be immediately distinguished from the clouded apollo, which has no red colouration at all.

bleak, especially in inland districts. With the assistance of the WWF and other bodies an endeavour has been made to inventory inland populations with a view to saving them from extinction. The results give cause for extreme anxiety.

The clouded apollo
Parnassius mnemosyne

The clouded apollo can be distinguished from the 'whites' by its transparent forewings edges and the concave inner edge to its hindwings.

It flies early in woodland meadows where its larval food-plant, Corydalis, grows. This type of habitat is very sensitive to changes, the spruce encroaching as soon as grazing by cattle ceases.

Capture-recapture experiments in Åland have revealed populations consisting of several hundred individuals. These tend to fly, however, only within a very restricted area. The Archipelago Sea area also has extant populations of the butterfly. Our only inland population, located in a river valley at Somero, will continue to survive for as long as cattle are allowed to graze there.

Additional inland populations almost certainly once existed in Finland, as Linnaeus gave the insect its scientific name on the basis of a specimen captured by Pietari Adrian Gadd "ad montes Tavastiae" — literally "from mountains of Häme". This specimen is housed in the Linnaeus collection in London. KM.

31

EASTERN GULF OF FINLAND
Breakers and rocky islets

Our island string of pearls winding towards the coastline narrows at the eastern end, and their frequency is less than in the west. Nevertheless the eastern Gulf of Finland does possess its own unique attraction. It is a landscape of open waters, Scots pine covered islands and treeless, weathered, rocky islets inhabited by birds. For the bird watching enthusiast it is the enchantment of the springtime masses of migratory birds, the morning-suited columns of feathered feeders, or the breeding pairs of increasingly scarce lesser black backed gulls. For the fisherman it means the silver-sided migratory sea trout chasing after a lure. For the historian and anthropologist, the independent folk culture of the islands — a lot of which has already disappeared. The eastern Gulf of Finland conjures up childhood memories and a lost birthland. For the residents of Porvoo, Loviisa, Kotka and Hamina, as well as for many village dwellers, it is their very own archipelago, their home.

Idyllic, slumbering Haapasaari. Once the smallest parish in Finland, nowadays belonging to the City of Kotka.

Arno Rautavaara

32

Reijo Juurinen
Small-scale fishing means extra income for the coastal and archipelago folk. Rarely a sole means of living nowadays.

The eastern Gulf of Finland is not merely open sea and rocky islets, it is also a long and winding coastline which shore-based nature lovers reach by road. In many places the sea pushes its way through long bays deep into the heart of the agricultural land and conversely,' roads stretch to the ends of the peninsulas and to the islands themselves.

BY SEA TO THE EAST
For the boating enthusiast the eastern Gulf of Finland is easy water. Here you do not encounter the hosts of seemingly identical islands to be found in the southwestern archipelago, nor a single treacherous shoal as in the Vaasa waters. Here the islands are comfortably spaced out and the channels clear.

The nearest significant nature conservation area east of Helsinki is the Söderskär island group in the Porvoo district. The disused old lighthouse greets visitors from afar. In earlier days these red buildings were used by the pilots department, nowadays they are used as a game research station. Söderskär is a favourite haunt of boat-

ing enthusiasts but it should be remembered that during the nesting season you can only travel around the inhabited islands. The other islands are protected for the nesting of the thousands of eiders and other birds, as well as for research purposes.

Seven kilometres north of Söderskär is Pirttisaari island which can be reached by water bus from Helsinki. From Pirttisaari the journey continues over open waters with only a few bird-inhabited islets rising from the sea. The open sea gives way to a quite different type of landscape. Southeast of Porvoo is the Pelling region — the densest and most extensive separate island group in the eastern region of the Province of Uudenmaa. If the saltiness of the water didn't give away the fact that you were at sea, you could easily believe you were having a boat trip on Lake Saimaa. Here too you find narrow but clear boat routes interspersed with wider stretches of open water. Many of the islands are steep and rocky, studded with Scots pine and, as on Lake Saimaa, there is the magnificent sight of ospreys flying through the blue sky. The Pelling region is conveniently situated halfway

34

between Helsinki and Kotka.

The most usual way to travel eastwards from Pelling is along the southern side of the most continuous island belt, along the archipelago route used by the merchant vessels in wintertime. In actual fact it is only beyond Pelling that the area usually referred to as the eastern Gulf of Finland starts. On the southern side of the route are just a few islands of different sizes, including large forested islands. The largest of these can be seen far away on the horizon, Suursaari with its many peaks nowadays belonging to the Soviet Union.

Here the wide open space you seek reigns supreme. Sailors can select their route as they please; no real need to choose one of the marked routes unless you are making the trip in a really large vessel. The greatest problem you'll have to contend with on your trip is the growing number of salmon traps and nets. Extensive restocking of these waters with salmon and trout smelt has swelled their numbers — there's good fishing to be had in the waters of the Gulf of Finland.

At the border of the districts of Ruotsinpyhtää and Pyhtää we move from the Province of Uudenmaa into the Province of Kymi. At Pyhtää the language changes too; behind us we leave the Swedish language with its broad archipelago accent — Finnish with a Kymenlaakso accent is spoken in the eastern archipelago. The names of the islands are mostly Finnish, strange sounding names like Jähi, Pekko and Kolseli, but there are some Swedish names too, as during the Middle Ages the eastern Gulf of Finland was mostly populated by Swedes.

Approaching Kotka and Hamina we again see more seagoing traffic, not enough however to cause a jam. In Kotka it is traditional to spend summer weekends at sea. You immediately notice the great number of wooden fishing boats in the traditional design. Age old boat building traditions are fostered in the villages of the Kymenlaakso coast and archipelago — more so perhaps than in any of our other coastal areas. The great demand for new boats of this design, as well as the number of ancient postwar models still going strong, testify to the excellence of this particular design.

Among the most popular places to visit are the old outer archipelago villages of Kaunissaari and Haapasaari. Not only can you get there by your own boat, but in summer by passenger boat too. Many other islands as well and also, unfortunately, the small islets occupied by nesting birds receive summer visitors. The professional salmon fishermen take their lines far out to the open waters — up as far as the leased waters of Suursaari island.

THE DESCENDANTS OF SUURSAARI

Right up to the last war the huge island of Suursaari was the focal point of inhabitation and the archipelago way of life for the whole of the eastern Gulf of Finland. It was an important centre for seafaring, fishing, boatbuilding and trade. Some smaller inhabited islands remained on the Finnish side and their populations increased to a certain extent with the evacuation of the lost island. Kaunissaari

and Haapasaari are often referred to as the descendants of Suursaari. The permanent archipelago folk have practically disappeared from these islands; only a few elderly folk live on the islands all year round. There is somewhat more life on Haapasaari as the coastguard operates there as well as a naval station and so there is a shop open all year round. Both Kaunissaari and Haapasaari liven up in summer when the former islanders and their offspring arrive to spend their holidays.

Both islands possess an excellent harbour. Haapasaari has no accommodation, no camping site, nor does it have a restaurant, but those wishing to sleep on their own boats can drop anchor at the visitors' berth. Kaunissaari on the other hand boasts a camping area, a restaurant as well as accommodation and is better suited than Haapasaari for visits longer than a day. In addition to this the finest sandy beaches in the eastern Gulf of Finland can be found on Kaunissaari.

The villages of Haapasaari, Kaunissaari and Tammio are amongst the most beautiful in the whole area. The houses are tightly grouped around an excellent natural harbour, their colours and architectural style in harmony with the countryside. Kaunissaari has a small museum and in summer the traditional way of life can be seen through plays performed in the old school of Haapasaari. An information centre for the nearby national park will be established on these islands.

EASTERN GULF OF FINLAND NATIONAL PARK

The Eastern Gulf of Finland National Park, established in 1982, encompasses the outermost islands of the Kymenlaakso region. It extends for 60 kilometres from the eastern border to the borders of the Province of Uudenmaa. The total land area of the islands in this extensive area is a mere 5 square kilometres. The waters do not belong to the national park, neither do the inhabited and privately-owned islands.

Despite the meagreness of the land area this national park is one of the most representative examples of archipelago nature in the eastern Gulf of Finland and is a major conservation area for seals and nesting birds. Mostly the islets are treeless, or with very few trees, although there are a few larger, wooded islands. Kilpisaari and Ulko-Tammio for example, not only have Scots pine-covered heathland, but also verdant deciduous woods. The island of Pitkäviira in the western part of the park is unique, a two kilometre long, narrow, wooded sandy esker.

The eastern Gulf of Finland has several razorbill colonies and is possibly the most important area in Finland for the increasingly rare lesser black-backed gull. A number of other typical archipelago birds make their nests in this area, including the greylag goose which is quite rare so far east.

These rocky islets are gently sloping and weathered. The land uplift in this area is a mere 30 centimetres every century and so the flora has become firmly established. Here the rocky islets exposed from the sea do not experience the same floral onslaught as in the Gulf of

The beautiful purple loosestrife is a typical archipelago species. It is still flowering in autumn when most of the other plants have already finished flowering.

Bothnia where the land uplift is rapid. Instead the rocks may be exposed for half a century before they get their first permanent vascular plants. One after the other the different flowering plants, grasses, bushes and trees become established on an island. In the heart of summer these islands, particularly those with large bird populations, resemble beautiful flower gardens.

The national park area is a highly significant seal conservation region. In many years a great proportion of the Baltic sea grey seal population give birth on the ice of the eastern Gulf of Finland. Seal catching has played an important role in the livelihood of the inhabitants of this area, but nowadays there is neither need nor reason for seal catching.

You can explore the Eastern Gulf of Finland National Park in every season, though in summer you should remember to leave the nesting birds in peace. Every spring numerous bird watchers make their way to the area, to the nearby islands of Virolahti and to the coastal rocks to observe the mass migration of the arctic birds. In autumn the fishermen are drawn to these waters. One part of the park is located in the border zone where travelling is not permitted without special permission. In the border zone region, though not actually in the park itself, is the well-known, shallow gulf of Vilkkiläntura which attracts birdwatchers at the beginning of May to observe the huge feeding flocks of whooper swans and Bewick's swans.

ASPSKÄR — EASTERN GULF OF FINLAND'S BIRD PARADISE

Fifteen kilometres west of the national park, in the Pernaja district, are the six islands of the Aspskär nature reserve. Conservation and research work has been carried out on Aspskär since the 1920s.

The area is under guard throughout the nesting season and no one is permitted to land on the islands between April 15th and August 15th. Aspskär has been a conservation area for so long that its importance is well known and so seafarers know well enough to leave the area in peace. Haverör is the home of the largest razorbill colony in Finland — over 500 pairs. In addition to the razorbills, over 300 pairs of herring gulls inhabit the small rocky island, as well as Finland's only colony of guillemots (55 pairs) and many other species. As elsewhere on the coast the number of herring gulls has increased while conversely there has been a decrease in the number of lesser black-backed gulls. Over the last few decades Finland's black guillemot population has decreased catastrophically.

The Aspskär area is a good example of how essential it is that our finest bird islands are controlled by prohibiting landing during the nesting season and by guarding the area. The growth in pleasure cruising has increased the disturbance throughout the archipelago.

Sailing is a splendid hobby and an excellent way to spend a holiday but it must be remembered that in the bird-inhabited archipelago the holidaymaker is the visitor and not the landlord. AR

The Eastern Gulf of Finland National Park

Virolahti, Vehkalahti, Kotka and Pyhtää, land area 5 km^2
Established: 1982
Under National Board of Forestry management

Connections: Regular boats ply between Kotka and the inhabited islands of Haapasaari and Kaunissaari. The excursion boat from Kotka calls at Ulko-Tammio.

Services: The only sheltered harbour in the national park is on Ulko-Tammio. There is a jetty and an empty cottage. On Kaunissaari there is a camping area, private accommodation and a restaurant. Haapasaari has a shop.

Maps: Miniature sea chart series 1:50 000 series A
Further information: National Board of Forestry, District office of Hämeenlinna, tel.917-25663 (Hämeenlinna).

Do Butterflies and Moths Migrate?

The study of insect migration in Finland is comparatively new, not having emerged as a science in its own right until the 1960s. An entomologist, upon discovering a painted lady butterfly at Utsjoki, in furthermost Lapland, in the 1940s imagined it to have come over from Norway. Later

The red admiral often migrates up into Finland from southern Europe. It may survive until October, but cannot withstand the winter.

it has become common to refer to some exotic butterfly or moth captured here as having "come across the Gulf of Finland".

Nowadays we are aware that the extent of butterfly and moth migrations is of quite another order of magnitude. According to weather charts, the painted lady mentioned had arrived in Lapland from North Russia, to which warm air currents had pushed it from much further south. Migrations to Finland from the south and southeast, on the other hand, frequently start at the latitude of South

Russia and Hungary. Naturally, shorter migrations also take place.

In annual reviews of migration, information received by the Finnish Lepidopterological Society is compared with weather charts. Indeed butterfly and moth enthusiasts are able these days to anticipate migrations merely by studying weather charts.

Butterfly and moth migrants carried by air currents

In analyses of migrations and the weather carried out in 1946-

66, it was discovered that migrations are linked in general with certain kinds of weather conditions, viz. warm southerly to southeasterly winds. Material collected in 1972-81 has served to reinforce the concept. Favourable air currents that are sufficently warm and strong occur mainly in May and again in September-October, but the maximum number of migrants become involved with these in the summer months. At that time every "favourable" air current flowing into Finland brings with it several migrant species. "Moderate" currents

Dick Forsman

carry an average of 0.5 species each, or in other words one species for every two weather situations.

The fact that winds have been shown to be the main factor involved in insect migration naturally begs the question as to whether migration is in fact involved at all: are the insects not simply drifting up into Finland? The answer is no, since in every case studied it has been observed that the insects (be they aphids, locusts, butterflies or whatever) have been migrating irrespective of the presence of an air current. Sustained flight on moving air masses constitutes migratory behaviour that is characteristic of only certain species, including the 50 kinds of Lepidoptera that journey to Finland.

Migrations from far in the southeast

For explaining migration so-called trajectories have been used which reflect the course of air molecules over a certain period of time. Such explanations always remain hypothetical to some degree. Much more concrete conclusions can be drawn if facts are to hand concerning migration routes, or if the actual distances covered can be determined in some other way. Such data is available on two migrations that have been observed in Finland.

The gipsy moth, Lymantria dispar

The elucidation of the facts of the 1958 migration has all the features of a detective novel! The appearance of nine individuals at the end of July was regarded at first, on the basis of meteorological charts, as constituting a migration. Only later was it appreciated that far from being the brownish moths found in Central Europe, these specimens were milky white in colour and hence representative of the southeast Russian subspecies.

The same mass movement had been observed on the southeastern edge of Moscow just three days prior to the event. In the course of an hour 592 individuals had flown into a mercury vapour lamp. Subsequently the entire porch be-

came covered with the moths and counting them became impossible. While the gipsy moth does fly by day, a trajectory study showed that migration had occurred at night. The Moscow mass flight and the first arrival in Finland were both observed on the warm front coming from the southeast.

The origin of the migration was worked out using the Soviets' long-term monitoring study. Early in the spring of 1958 caterpillars had caused damage to some 280,000 hectares of forest in the Province of Ryazan some 300 kilometres southeast of Moscow. They had completely stripped the leaves of oak and Scots pine trees in an area of 74,000 hectares. The ground under the trees was sometimes covered with a layer of dead caterpillars 15 centimetres thick. It is not surprising that such conditions led to a major migration taking place.

Small mottled willow Spodoptera exigua

A subtropical noctuid moth suddenly began to appear among Finnish light trap catches in August 1964. The species was first detected in Finland in 1958, in conjunction with the gipsy moth migration alluded to above. When records were compared, it was found that 1500 specimens of the small mottled willow had been collected in 1964. Data on light trap locations and the movement of the moths was then fed into a computer, which concluded that tens, or even hundreds, of millions of small mottled willows had crossed Finland's southeastern border.

Trajectory analysis showed that the moth swarm had arrived from the direction of the

Caspian Sea, originating possibly in West Kazakhstan. Reports were sent to Soviet experts and eventually the same answer was received from Moscow and Leningrad: "In 1964 this pest has not been recorded from the territory of the Soviet Union outside certain Central Asian republics (of which Kazakhstan is one), in which mass migrations have been noted." Thus, two different methods of approach indicated the same place of origin of the migration.

Crossing Finland in three days, the vanguard of the migrating swarm proceeded to curve westwards into Estonia, Latvia, Sweden, Norway and Denmark. With the proviso that the insects only flew at night, their progress precisely matched the speed of the air current. In the course of a fortnight the moths covered something like 3500 km, placing the event among the longest Lepidoptera migrations known.

Are there really migrant species?

Butterfly and moth migrations are frequently compared to bird migrations. It appears that only the North American monarch butterflies are individually subject to seasonal to and fro migrations, travelling from southern Canada to Mexico and California for the winter and then returning in the spring. In the case of the monarch there may be several summer generations between two generations of migrating individuals.

Those Finnish butterflies and moths exhibiting seasonal migration tend to spread the task over two or more generations. Such species include the painted lady, red admiral and large white butterflies, of which only

the last mentioned has, however, been observed making southerly migrations.

Large whites in most years fly in over the Gulf of Finland in the late May to early June period. They fly with the wind, making use of warm southeasterly air currents, possibly under the influence of the lengthening day. The butterflies oviposit on crucifers, the new generation hatching from mid-July on.

During the shortening days of late summer the direction of flight in relation to the wind direction is different: the insects now endeavour to fly against the wind. Nobody knows how much effect the compass direction, more specifically the direction of the sun, has on their behaviour. Once when a strong but warm north wind was blowing, large whites were observed 'migrating' back to the south, though they were in fact facing, and attempting to fly against, the wind coming from the north! The strong air current was forcing them south.

Only a few dozen, or at most a few hundred, individuals are observed in a day when the spring migration is taking place. For instance, at Rönnskär, Porkkala, on 19.5.1966 an average of 77 individuals an hour were counted. The autumn migration may be greater: on the southeastern edge of Hankoniemi peninsula a seven-mile transect showed that something like 7000 butterflies an hour were on the move.

Upwind migrants

Migrations of bumblebees and wasps differ from those of butterflies and moths in that the migrating individuals (which are all queens) invariably fly against the wind. Arriving on the coast, they change direction and start to fly along it. Warm southeasterly winds cause migrating wasps and bumblebees to fly due east or north-east along Finland's south coast.

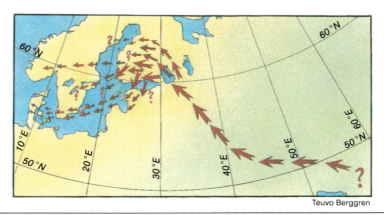

The migration route of the small mottled willow moth from north of the Caspian Sea through Finland to other parts of northern Europe in 1964.

Teuvo Berggren

Lepidoptera migrants: 1. Large white 2. Small white 3. Green-veined white (a = underside) 4. Bath white 5. Pale clouded yellow 6. Clouded yellow 7. Peacock 8. Yellow-Legged tortoiseshell 9. Red admiral 10. Painted lady 11. Death's-head hawk-moth 12. Convolvulus hawk-moth 13. Dark sword grass 14. Silver Y 15. Rush veneer 16. Diamond-back moth 17. Small earth bumblebee 18. Large red-tailed bumblebee 19. Red wasp 20. Norwegian wasp 21. Syrphid 22. Libellula quadrimaculata 23. 7-spot lady-bird

In 1975 the largest number of bumblebees observed amounted to 800 individuals an hour over a 100-metre transect, while wasps numbered 20,000 on a transect 800 metres in length. Bumblebees have also been observed crossing the Gulf of Finland, and it is almost certain that wasps do the same under favourable conditions. Furthermore, dragonflies and hoverflies have also been noted flying against the wind on the coast of the Gulf of Finland.

An unsettled environment leads to migration

According to Southwood's theory of 1962, migrations take place when a population is obliged to forsake an environment that is only hospitable for a limited period. On a small scale such environments include pools and puddles that dry up in summer, and carrion or dung heaps that are in a suitable condition only for a certain time. Many migratory Lepidoptera species inhabit continental areas, especially steppes or prairies, where plants flower only for a brief period in the spring.

The gipsy moth is famous for two chief reasons: it is a favourite guinea-pig of geneticists, and it has created havoc in North America, where it was released. In 1958, vast numbers of gipsy moths migrated from southeastern Russia over the Moscow area to Finland, from where nine males were reported. The European gipsy moth male is a local animal, while the female is practically flightless. In the United States people have even published record flights for the female: in a few cases 5-10 metres, and in one case an impressive 20 metres plus! In the neighbourhood of Moscow, however, even the females migrated, and the writer himself has observed thousands of the female moths flying with the wind against a darkening evening sky in the Altai mountains.

Previously it was considered that the only migratory phase of the gipsy moth was the small, hairy larva which can be carried even scores of kilometres on the wind. Why should the continental gipsy moth, therefore, need to migrate as an adult?

The exact reason seems to be linked with an unstable environment. If the caterpillars completely strip the trees of leaves or needles in consecutive years in steppe forests, where summer dryness is a constant threat, the forests will easily be killed. As these forests are mere strips, the moth needs to "get away" from them when necessary.

Although different factors underlie bumblebee and wasp migrations, the general principle is just the same as with gipsy moths. The denser the population, the better chance nest and other parasites have of causing a serious threat to their colonies. Food may also become short if the queens remain in one locality. Hence, it pays them to move elsewhere. The wind provides a natural aid to orientation without which it would be easy for the queens to come back to the place they were born in, so they fly upwind.

Migration is one means by which insects have adapted to the special features of their environments. Making use of such strategy, many insect species have acquired extensive summer breeding grounds in the north. Others avoid temporarily inhospitable environments. KM

The Bird Skerries of the Gulf of Finland

Gulls, terns, waders, ducks and razorbills are the main components of the avian population which most abundantly and conspicuously inhabits the outermost islands and skerries in the archipelago fringing the south and south-western coasts of Finland. Most of them nest in colonies. The colonies are not very large, the islands being small, but they are crowded and there are many of them.

Our national epic, the Kalevala, relates how the bird skerries came into being: when the Water-Mother's knee rose up from the sea, the first bird to nest on it was "a beauteous teal". Present-day ornithologists would not agree. They would argue that it was probably an eider duck. This is a pioneering species, which can establish a nest in the most insignificant depression in a rock, using only its own down as building material. Today, the eider duck is by far the most common species among the birds of the Finnish archipelago. The herring gull comes second.

However, eider ducks and herring gulls did not always dominate the bird communities in the Gulf of Finland. Although there were fewer individual representatives of various species, the range of species was wider than it is today. The populations were better balanced, with no species represented substantially more heavily than others. Even today, all of the species are still represented, although some populations have dwindled alarmingly.

Nesting zones

The structure of the archipelago's avian population can be presented rather naturally along the same lines as the different zones into which the archipelago itself is divided. Furthest out, where the skerries are small and treeless, arctic terns, great black-backed gulls and razorbills, are dominant. The arctic tern colonies are nowadays declining, although their noisy, high-pitched chatter is still a characteristic feature of their maritime habitat. Not far from tern colonies one always finds the turnstone, the archipelago's most common wader. Great black-backed gulls have become more numerous and are pushing further into the archipelago. Whereas they used to build their solitary nests on the outermost islets, they are now gradually beginning to nest in colonies. Razorbill colonies have always been few and far between on the rocky outer skerries, but its relative the black guillemot is one of the species that is declining in number. In former days it was one of the most common birds nesting in the Gulf of Finland.

As one moves inwards through the archipelago and towards the mainland, the islands become somewhat larger and have more vegetation cover and more sheltered shorelines. The variety of bird species is also greatest. Especially in protected areas, the skerries are true bird paradises. Where grasses and junipers grow in profusion, many different species nest right beside each other. Eider nests can cover a continuous area as large as a couple of hundred hectares.

Herring gulls dominate the bare, smooth rocky parts of the skerries. The various species of ducks, mallards, widgeons, tufted ducks, velvet scoters and goosanders, nest where vegetation gives them cover. Populations of redshanks, oystercatchers and, in places, ringed plovers are increasing. The species that formerly dominated the skerries, the common gull and the lesser black-backed gull, are declining alarmingly in numbers. On the outermost islands, the former's colonies, once hundreds strong, have shrunk to small groupings. Colonies of the latter are nowadays found only rarely. The species that has suffered the most catastrophic decline is the Caspian tern. This bird, now nests in no more than half a dozen colonies in the Gulf of Finland.

Human influence

People have clearly influenced the development of most populations, for better or worse. The reason for the sharp decline in the Caspian tern population is not exactly known, but the misguided destruction of nests in the name of gamekeeping has certainly contributed. In attempts to reduce the herring gull population, people, either through ignorance or indifference, have destroyed Caspian tern nests as well. Adult birds have been shot in and near fish farms. On the other hand, human activity has indirectly contributed to the increase in the herring gull population through dumping and fish processing. This highly adaptable species quickly learnt to exploit the new food resources created by these activities, and thanks to its improved reproduction rate multiplied explosively. Measures are now being taken to curb this growth, often with disastrous side-effects on other species.

Eider ducks have benefited from a sharp decline in the human population of the archipelago (resulting in fewer eggs being collected), restrictions on hunting and the establishment of large sanctuaries. These birds have been in the Baltic for a very long time — the oldest bone finds date from the Bronze Age. Populations are again in decline due to a variety of reasons which include over-hunting in places and frequent oil spills. While things were going well for the eider, however, the herring gull also benefited, because eider chicks are among its favourite foods.

The velvet scoter, lesser black-backed gull and black guillemot, which nest late (in June and July), suffer from the disturbances caused by boating. The black guillemot population also suffers from the loss of adult birds in salmon nets and the severe damage that wild mink are doing to nests in the few remaining colonies.

Naturally, the bird islets in the Gulf of Finland have always been in a state of change. However, it appears that human action is affecting the pattern of avian populations more than ever in the past. This is not necessarily reflected in a declining overall population, which may remain as great as ever but with a diminished variety of species. MH

Arno Rautavaara

The Caspian tern, which is nearly the size of the herring gull, is becoming rare due to the influence of humans in the archipelago. It should be left undisturbed on the islets where it nests.

The razorbill colony on the islet of Aspskär in Pernaja is one of the largest in Finland.

Arno Rautavaara

The Migratory Rush of Arctic Water Fowl

Birds which nest in northern areas arrive relatively earlier in spring than those which nest further south. They have to if they are to breed successfully; in the brief northern summer, those that start their nests early have time to get their young flying before the cold of autumn descends. The further north one goes, the more essential it is to nest early — and the more intense and concentrated the rush of migration to those places is. Whole populations make the move in one concerted rush from their southern wintering areas to their summer nesting places — and back again.

The best place in Finland to observe this phenomenon is on the outer islands of the archipelago, where waves of birds on their way to the wetlands and seashores of the Arctic sweep across our coast. This

Brent geese can be seen on their annual migration also during the day, whereas most long-tailed ducks pass over as dusk falls.

migration involves hundreds of thousands, perhaps millions of birds.

In the ecological sense, these species are community nesters and remain in flocks all year round. The overwhelming majority of arctic birds which migrate across the Gulf of Finland are long-tailed ducks and common scoters. From one observation point on one of the outermost islets in the archipelago, between two hundred thousand and five hundred thousand migrating birds can be observed on some of the best days in late May and early October. Dividing them into flocks is difficult as wave after wave of birds fly past in long fronts. The omnipresent ringing voice of long-tailed ducks, formations flying at dizzying heights and unbroken processions sweeping just above the shallows and waves of the open sea are a spectacle guaranteed to impress anybody.

This great movement forms the bulk of the annual migration, but within it the fly-past of brent and barnacle geese, although smaller in volume, is its most chronologically intense and often most spectacular part. In the space of only two or three days, fifty thousand or

Dick Forsman

Tapani Räsänen

42

so barnacle geese sweep across the Gulf of Finland and the south-eastern part of our country in a great barking flock. They have overwintered on the coasts of Britain and the Netherlands, gradually transferred to Gotland and the islands off Estonia to fatten themselves up, and then, around 20 May, set off en masse for their nesting grounds on islands in the Barents Sea. They fly over Finland without stopping.

Brent geese, in turn, migrate more concentratedly. There are several days of main migration and the birds arrive from further afield and, apparently, without regular rests in traditional places as is the pattern with barnacle geese. The brent geese fly over the Gulf of Finland in dense flocks, following the belt of outer islets and generally close to the water. They do not take a short cut overland towards the north-east as barnacle geese do. Flocks can contain as many as several thousand birds, usually a few hundred, and form dense clusters and long lines. The flock keeps up an incessant growling noise as it flies. More than a hundred thousand brent geese can be seen in the Gulf of Finland in a good spring, although the numbers migrating vary sharply from year to year. That is because unpredictable conditions in the arctic nesting areas markedly affect the success of breeding. In recent decades, however, the general trend in numbers of both brent and barnacle geese has been slowly upwards. The autumnal return migration is less concentrated and, depending on the winds, can be overland or even along the southern shore of the Gulf of Finland.

In addition to geese and water fowl, a massive migratory flood of divers also travels along the Gulf of Finland. Flocks of divers and red-throated divers, twenty thousand or so birds altogether, can be seen forging ahead at a steady pace every day from April to July. When they fly back in autumn, they choose another route and are much fewer than in spring.

A rich diversity of waders is also part of the overall pattern of migrating arctic birds. How easy or difficult it is to observe them depends even more on weather conditions than in the cases of ducks and geese. Some years, oystercatchers, whimbrels, bar-tailed godwits, grey plovers, dunlins and sanderlings fly low and can be seen in flocks of hundreds. In other years, when they apparently fly over at high altitude, they are almost completely missing from the skyscape of the archipelago.

When one studies a globe of the world, it is obvious that the birds flying along the Gulf of Finland make a longish detour by deviating from their north-eastwards migratory course. With all their stamina and speed, why do not not just fly straight across the interior of Finland in their haste to reach their nesting places? After all, the Gulf of Finland does not contain extensive marshlands where tens of thousands of waders could feed and rest, nor reedy shallows for geese, nor large herring shoaling grounds where divers could eat their fill.

Perhaps the temperature over the cool water is optimal for arctic birds. It could also be that subsequent connections determine the birds' choice of route. They hardly stop at all in the Gulf of Finland. Perhaps they do pause in the White Sea. The route via the two huge lakes Ladoga and Onega is a better alternative than via the much smaller Lake Oulu and the rivers of Lapland. Their passage over Finland remains but a brief interlude in the arctic birds' flight northwards. They spend at most two or three hours in our air space. MH

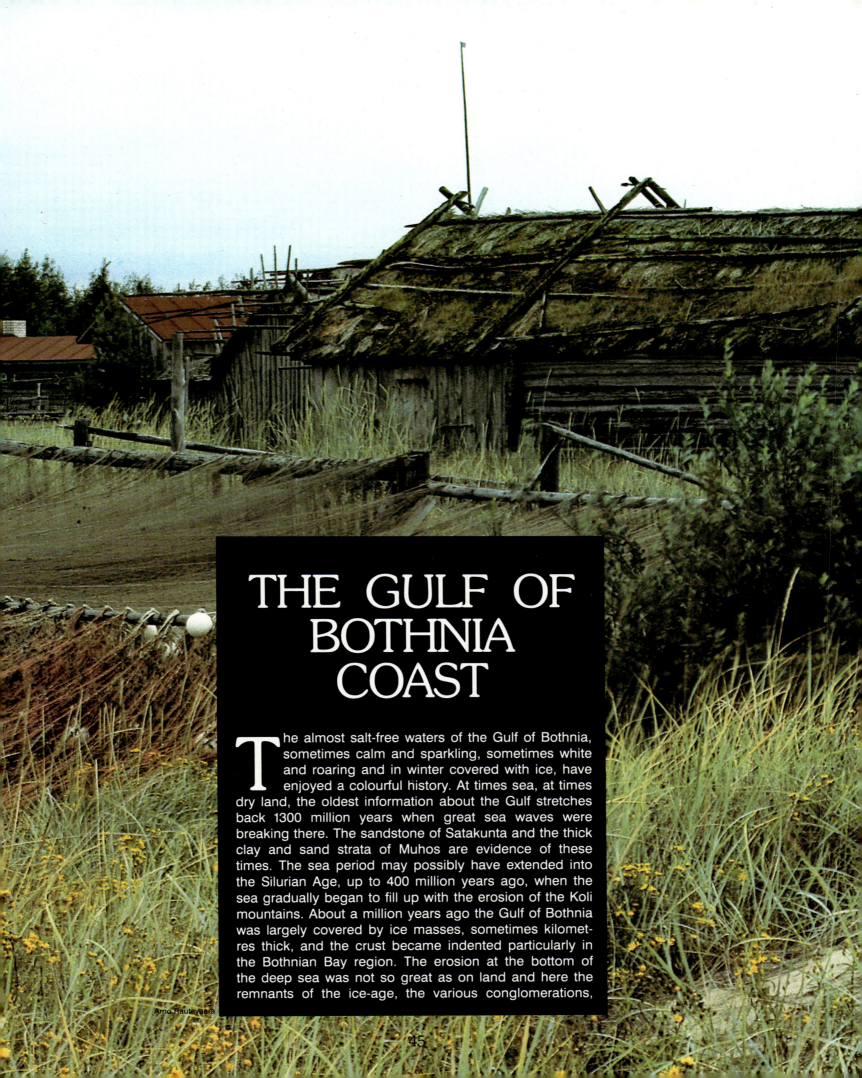

Arno Rautavaara

THE GULF OF BOTHNIA COAST

The almost salt-free waters of the Gulf of Bothnia, sometimes calm and sparkling, sometimes white and roaring and in winter covered with ice, have enjoyed a colourful history. At times sea, at times dry land, the oldest information about the Gulf stretches back 1300 million years when great sea waves were breaking there. The sandstone of Satakunta and the thick clay and sand strata of Muhos are evidence of these times. The sea period may possibly have extended into the Silurian Age, up to 400 million years ago, when the sea gradually began to fill up with the erosion of the Koli mountains. About a million years ago the Gulf of Bothnia was largely covered by ice masses, sometimes kilometres thick, and the crust became indented particularly in the Bothnian Bay region. The erosion at the bottom of the deep sea was not so great as on land and here the remnants of the ice-age, the various conglomerations,

Aarni Nummila

Black guillemots nest on the stones and rocks of the outer archipelago of the Gulf of Bothnia individually or in small colonies.

SOUTHERN AND NORTHERN SPECIES

The Gulf of Bothnia is a cool sea and the birds nesting in the Gulf are generally northern species. In the Bothnian Bay, which is considerably cooler than the Bothnian Sea, you find, for example, common scoters, red-necked phalaropes, Temminck's stints and jack snipe. Surprisingly, southern species can be found even in the north of the Bothnian Bay.

Mute swans, rock pipits, reed warblers, marsh warblers and even Canada geese and eiders nest in the Bothnian Sea, although not in the Bothnian Bay. One of the distinctive species found in the Bothnian Bay is the little tern which makes its nest in the sparse vegetation of the open shores and which perhaps can't find a suitable nesting habitat in the Bothnian Sea. The yellow-breasted bunting, which has spread from the east, and the even rarer Terek sandpiper are also encountered here.

ridges, endmoraines and drumlins are better preserved than on the land. Gradually they uplift from the seabed, forming new island groups and chains.

THE GULF OF BOTHNIA TODAY

The Gulf of Bothnia is the Baltic Sea's northernmost arm with a north-south distance of over 600 kilometres. The North Quarken threshold divides it into the Bothnian Sea in the south and the Bothnian Bay in the north. The scenery of the Gulf of Bothnia has been fashioned by the steady, calm uplift of the seabed and by the play of sea forces on the coast – waves, currents, ice and wind.

The temperature and amount of sunlight, the salinity and nutrient in the water, the length and productivity of the growing season all decrease towards the north, while the tidal variance increases. There are differences too in the make-up of the sea bed and shoreline, differences which are consequently reflected in the flora and fauna.

Saltwater and freshwater species, as well as northern and southern species, are found here. Southern species and saltwater dependent species disappear one after the other as you travel northwards, as indeed do the northern and freshwater species in the opposite direction. There are species unique to the Baltic region which exist nowhere else on earth.

LOW SALINITY WATER AND SALTLANDS

The actual salinity of the land is greatest near the water's edge to where the halophytic vegetation is largely confined. The saltiest areas in the Gulf of Bothnia are generally those coastal lands which uplifted from the sea around 30 – 50 years ago. The weather has also had an influence.

The salts of the saltlands gradually leach out as the land rises and the water level recedes, after which the ordinary vegetation develops. The alum lands are however very difficult to cultivate because of their acidity.

UPLIFTING LANDS

Nature in the Gulf of Bothnia is in a continuous state of flux. The land uplifts and the sea gives way. New rocks appear, become connected to the mainland as peninsula, the bay becomes land, the shoreline moves.

The Bothnian Bay is the centre of this uplift which is currently around nine millimetres per year. The corresponding rate for the southern Bothnian Sea is around a third of this. The uplift immediately following the melting of the glacial ice was much faster than nowadays. On the lowest lying shores the coastline shift can be seen in just a few years. In the remotest corners of the sheltered bays the coastline can extend seawards tens of metres every year due to the material carried by the rivers. As a result of this uplift Finland gains nearly a thousand square kilometres of land every century.

IN NEED OF CONSERVATION

The coastal areas of the Gulf of Bothnia have long been inhabited. The dwelling places of the Comb Ceramic folk (3000 – 1800 BC) extended from the south as far up as the Oulu river. With the increase in inhabitation, peoples' mark on nature became greater, slowly at first, later accelerating. Nowadays these marks have reached worrying proportions.

Habitation and industry often dominate the finest areas in terms of original nature. Sea traffic is a permanent threat to the aquatic ecosystem. The coastal waters are dammed, banked up, disturbed. Ditching and tillage have destroyed many bogs. The use of environmental poisons has disturbed seal reproduction and in places the coastal waters are polluted. The uplift encourages the preservation of the coastal nature but also presents new challenges, as the uplift and its consequent phenomena should be monitored under natural conditions.

Sea buckthorn berries stay fresh a long time — a boon for the large flocks of overwintering birds.

THE KOKEMÄENJOKI RIVER DELTA

The delta of the Kokemäenjoki river is the most representative delta area in Finland. It is our counterpart to the enormous deltas of the Danube, Volga and Guadalquivir, somewhat more modest of course, as befitting these barren conditions. The delta expands seawards as a result of the material washed down with the river and the uplift. A good thing too, as otherwise people would have made it smaller. It's been dammed and banked up, dried and dug out, changed and utilized. On the land side the characteristics of the delta have disappeared, but on the sea side there is still a 1500 hectare area of delta from where the actual bottom meadows have disappeared.

The flora of the Kokemäenjoki river delta is a mere puff of wind compared with the lush south. The view is dominated by aerial shoot vegetation. The ground is carpeted with water moss and plants whose leaves hug the ground. A meadow of submerged leaves sways in the water, while the surface is a mass of water lilies and pondweed.

The delta is a paradise both for ornithologists and hunters. Many quite rare species have been seen here and in autumn hundreds of waterfowl fatten the hunters' rucksacks. The waterfowl population is plentiful — around fifteen different species and nearly 800 pairs. The species found here have a distinct southern stamp.

The Kokemäenjoki river basin area has been inhabited and cultivated for such a long time that even the burden the river must bear is traditional. Flora requiring clean water is missing from the delta area.

LIMINGANLAHTI AND HAILUOTO

The finest examples of the low lying Bothnian Bay meadow shores are at the upper end of the Liminka Bay, in the region of the Siikajoki river and Hailuoto. The flatness of the area stems from the clay and sandstone strata which are younger than the primary rocks. The coastal nature has its own magnificence. Here the land uplifts almost a metre every century.

Humans are also changing the face of nature. In time, the reaper and cattle have created a landscape of open meadows. The economic utilization of the shore meadows has stopped. Reeds now dominate on the water side and willow on the land, resulting in a monotonous entanglement supporting only a few plant and bird species. Nature is becoming impoverished.

The best way to study the coastal nature is from the purpose-built observation towers at Sannanlahti and at the mouth of the Temmesjoki river in the Liminka Bay area. There is also an information centre with towers for birdwatching at Virkkula.

At Luodonselkä the aquatic flora is relatively sparse whereas at the upper end of Liminka Bay, where a great deal of fine particle matter and nutrient has been washed down with the river, the vegetation is lush. Many of the species to be found throughout the area are at their strongest here and form a dense mat of vegetation. Reed patches are plentiful and the flora is at its lushest at the mouths of the rivers and ditches.

The most exotic species of the watershore is Alisma gramineum which grows in many parts of the area, in some places abundantly. It occurs nowhere outside the Baltic region, making it one of the rarest aquatic plants on earth.

BIRDLIFE VARIETY

The eastern shores of Liminka Bay and Hailuoto form a unique ornithological area. Great numbers of birds nest here and it's an important resting area for migratory birds. Great numbers of swans, geese and other water-fowl and waders break their journeys here to rest and feed in spring and autumn. The area is especially well known as a resting point for thousands of geese, particularly the bean goose, but also the lesser white-fronted goose, white-fronted goose and other species. It is, in fact, the most important resting place between south Sweden and the White Sea for the bean goose. Flocks of swans linger here both before and after midsummer. Nowhere else in Finland do as many grey-lag goose nest as here.

Around twenty species of waterbirds nest in the area and tufted duck abound. The end of summer sees many birds gathering here. Here you find different species, young and old, those which can fly and those which cannot, there are those which were born here and those which have come from elsewhere to spend summer here. There is room for all and peace — at least until the shooting season starts on the 20 August when hundreds of guns spew out pellets and death. It is the end of the journey for many birds.

A great number of seagulls, terns, sandpipers, ruffs, curlews, lapwings and others, nest on the shore meadows and rocks. It's the home of northern Finland's largest colonies of black-headed gull and little gull as well as 18 species of wader.

BOTHNIAN BAY NATIONAL PARK

The northern Bothnian Bay contains a national park planned by Sweden and Finland over many years in order to preserve the character of the outer archipelago. In this plan the largest and most valuable area is situated on the Swedish side. 13000 hectares of water and 240 hectares of island are on the Finnish side and this area is entirely the property of the State.

The area consists of extensive open seas and far flung island groups. The islands are primarily in the open sea area where the marine influence is strongly felt. The islands are low — only a few metres in height. The youngest have only just peeped above the surface while the oldest are not more than a thousand years old.

The bedrock is nowhere to be seen. The islands are of washed moraine and the shores are generally rock-bound. The continental glacier had a decisive influence on the scenery and the path of the ice flow can be seen from the way the island and underwater scenery runs from northwest to southeast and from north to south. Above the waterline there is generally a narrow strip of meadow, though not in places where the shore is rock-bound or steep. Here and there on the upper part of the field you find thickets of sea buckthorn, confined as they rise by narrow groves of grey alder. Meadow-sweet is one of the typical species growing in the groves.

The alder groves gradually give way to birch and rowan woods. The higher ground is drier and sporadic junipers appear between the birches and the birchwoods gradually change to juniper heaths, but not even juniper grows on the driest heath. Many of the island tops are rocky and completely devoid of any taller vegetation.

The flora specialities include species indigenous to the Gulf of Bothnia. On the rocky outcrops and treeless islets, and also to a certain extent on the larger islands, the terns and waders control the airspace while the scaup ducks and mergansers hold dominion over the water. The birds here bear the stamp of the north.

The fishing culture is represented by the fishing village of Selkäsarvi and by nine other fishing fleet bases. Professional fishing has strong traditions going back to the 1700's. Even at the beginning of this century Selka-särvi had a population of around three hundred during the baltic herring fishing season. The buildings of the village and the fishing bases were constructed in the traditional style and are regarded as having cultural and historical value. JS

Lauhanvuori National Park

Isojoki, Kauhajoki, 26 km²
Established 1982
Under National Board of Forestry management

Connections: Buses from the direction of Kauhajoki and Honkajoki stop by request in Perä-Hyyppä, from where a 5 km forest road goes through the park. A road runs from Isojoki to Perä-Hyyppä via the Lauhavuori peak.

Services: Many paths and tracks run through the forest. There is an outdoor cooking place and two areas for tents. A central information point is located on the peak of Lauhavuori.

Maps: Basic map 1:20 000 nos. 1233 06, 1233 09, 1234 04, 1234 07. Smaller scale version of basic map 1:50 000 nos. 1234 1, 1234 2.

Further information: The National Board of Forestry, Parkano district office, tel. 933-81821 (Parkano).

Migrants from Near and Far

Migratory birds are an artificial and very heterogeneous group. They include species of widely differing appearances and lifestyles. The only feature that they have in common is that they periodically congregate and migrate. Sometimes, too, species which are considered unquestionably local, such as sparrows, black woodpeckers and grey-headed woodpeckers, can behave in much the same way as migratory birds.

What is a migratory bird?

An important common denominator for most species of migratory birds is their dependence on nourishment that varies strongly in quantity and availability from year to year. Many are highly specialized in their eating habits, living on the seeds of only one species of plant.

The Siberian nutcatcher is dependent on the seeds of the Siberian pine, and the two-barred crossbill specializes in larch seeds. When their respective sources of food fail to produce an adequate seed crop, hunger forces the birds to migrate in search of food. Rather than face certain death at home, they set off and, if they are lucky, come across an area with sufficient nourishment to

keep them alive.

Massive invasions are caused by the combined effects of several different factors and are therefore fairly rare. If the spring and early summer have been favourable, nourishment has been in abundant supply and nesting has succeeded well. This creates "overpopulation", which can trigger a wave of migration.

Where do the migrants come from?

A considerable share of the migratory birds that we see in Finland come from beyond our borders, most from the heart of the vast taiga regions far to the east. Alone the modest numbers involved indicate this. In addition to that, some of the migratory birds seen here, such as the Siberian nutcracker, the nuthatch and the two-barred crossbill, do not regularly nest in Finland. If conditions are favourable here, they may stay on and nest after their migration, but usually depart again after one season.

Ringing has greatly added to our understanding of birds' migratory habits. During large-scale migrations, blue, great and long-tailed tits which have been ringed in the Soviet Union are regularly found in Finland. Likewise, migratory birds ringed in Finland, espe-

In autumns when migrations take place, nutcrackers are found virtually anywhere in Finland, but they nest only in the south.

cially great spotted woodpeckers, have later been found far to the east.

It used to be generally believed that migrations led to the mass demise of the birds taking part in them; ornithologists spoke of "death migrations". There is no doubt that a considerable number of the birds die of exhaustion or hunger along the way, but the strongest and most adaptable survive the ordeal of their journey and may remain at their destination to nest. Thus migrations also serve as a kind of experiment in expanding breeding ranges, and there are numerous happy examples of new permanent residents that this has led to.

Many bird migrations are observed in Finland for geographical reasons. Since most migratory birds are genuine boreal species, they hardly ever cross seas or even large open lakes. That is why they hug coastlines while keeping as closely as possible to their original courses. When they come from the east across Finland and reach the Gulf of Bothnia, they swing south and continue to Sweden when they reach the islands in

At the end of their migration, nuthatches often move in as guests at feeding places and stay all winter. Some even stay on and nest nearby, but no permanent population has established itself in Finland.

the narrowest part of the gulf or the chain stretching from the Finnish mainland via Åland to the Stockholm archipelago. That is what gives these districts their special interest for ornithologists.

Seed-eaters

Some years, the high-pitched "blit-blit" call of crossbills is one of the most characteristic sounds of our forests, but in other years can be hardly heard at all. It all depends on the

Antti Leinonen

crop of fir and pine cones. With its powerful beak, the parrot crossbill specializes in forcing open pine cones, whereas the less well endowed crossbill prefers easier fir cones. Thus our crossbill species' fortunes depend on the crops yielded by their respective favourite softwood trees. Pines and firs do not always have good cone crops the same year. Thus crossbill migrations can consist entirely of either the small or the large species some years, whilst other years both species can be seen in mixed flocks.

As the weather grows warmer in spring, the cone scales open and the seeds drop onto the snowdrifts, where the crossbills can eat them. That is why these birds nest already in winter. They mostly set off again immediately after nesting, and in some years large numbers of them can be seen migrating already in early summer. Other years, by contrast, they do not arrive until March — when they seem to appear out of nowhere — and immediately set about their nesting chores.

The great spotted woodpecker also depends on the softwood seed crop to keep it alive during the winter. In years when seeds are abundant, it needs only a very small area to supply it with its food needs and then one can see these birds in the forest at intervals of only a few hundred metres, busily picking away at cones.

The parrot crossbill mainly feeds its young on pine seeds. It has to begin nesting during the winter, when the seeds are still inside the cones.

Great spotted woodpeckers usually get under way in August, but in years of major migrations the birds can be observed on the move even earlier. As is generally the case with migratory birds, movement over land generally attracts little attention and it is only when the migratory wave reaches the coast that its true scale becomes apparent. Tens of thousands of great spotted woodpeckers take part in the biggest autumn migrations. Indeed, the record number observed at one point on a single day is over ten thousand!

Populations of coal tits and siskins also depend on the pine seed crop. Whenever pines in the taiga to the east, have failed to produce seeds, coal tits have migrated to Finland in large numbers. The siskin is less dependent on pine seeds than the coal tit, but in years when these seeds are abundant in early spring many of these birds arrive here to nest.

The vole hunter

Just like softwood trees, voles, too, reveal a certain rhythm to which their numbers increase and fall, flourish and collapse. In northern areas, this rhythm quite clearly follows a 3 — 4-year cycle. In years when the vole population is at its peak, owls gather in extensive areas in the best districts to feast on the abundant supply of easily catchable food. The owl population is dense at such times and some species can rear as many as ten young at a time. It is obvious that by the end of a breeding season there are many times more owls in an area than on the threshold to spring. Often, too, vole populations go into decline during the autumn after the year in which they have peaked, which means hard times for the owls as well. The owls, which specialize in voles, have no choice but to "set off with their begging bowls".

There have been several spectacular owl migrations in recent years. An unprecedented number of hawk owls were observed in the southern parts of Finland in 1976. The birds began appearing in the beginning of September and their numbers had peaked by the middle of October. Most of them spent the whole of the following winter near the farmlands along the southern coast, foraging for short-tailed voles. Only when the nesting season was approaching did the birds leave their winter homes for parts unknown.

Owls were on the move again in the early winter of 1981, this time great grey owls. These large birds were observed all over southern and central Finland, where they had formerly been considered an extreme rarity. A similar migration of great grey owls followed already in early 1984, when these denizens of the backwoods appeared in dozens on the outskirts of Helsinki. On both occasions, the owls appeared to be quite without fear and curiously landed very close to people. The great grey owls had to pay a heavy price for both migrations. There was not enough food. Many died and others were found numbed and wretched. Numerous attacks on dogs, hares and pheasants testified to the dire straits in which these birds found themselves. In their case, there is every justification for seeing migration as a journey of no return.

The most commonly migrating member of the owl family is Tengmalm's owl. However, because it happens to be nocturnal, unlike the great grey and hawk owl, its movements are considerably more difficult to follow. Without our coastal birdwatching posts, it would be difficult to know much about the autumnal wanderings of this small bird. With the aid of ringing, ornithologists have established that it leads quite a vagrant life. It can nest in eastern Finland one year, Norway the next and in, say, western Finland after that. Migrations begin when the vole population declines catastrophically and end when an adequate supply of nourishment is found. Indeed, the life of a Tengmalm's owl resembles that of a nomadic tribe wandering in search of sustenance.

The handsome snowy owl also migrates on occasion. Some individuals are found in southern Finland every year, mainly on the west coast and the Åland archipelago, but there has not been a large-scale migration since the 1960s. This bird is not as one-sidedly dependent on voles as the great grey owl and can get by with other food when they are not available. Some migratory birds could be better described as "partial movers". A good example is the treecreeper. Some years they are on the move, even in flocks, whereas in ordinary years they are found individually as members of tit and goldcrest flocks in forests. It is possible that treecreepers are prompted to migrate when populations become too dense. The same may well apply to tit migrations.

Other migratory species are the waxwing, the pine grosbeak, the mealy redpoll, the jay and the bullfinch as well as all of our tit varieties except crested tits, which are local and live in softwood forests. The migratory habits of various species and the ecological adjustments that cause them vary in detail, but are in broad outline the same as with the species already mentioned. DF

Aimo Holtari

FINNISH LAKELAND

FROM HAUKIVESI TO KOLOVESI

- picturesque Saimaa

Saimaa is not just one lake but rather a maze of dozens of open, ragged, endless large and small waters covering an area of 4460 km². It's difficult to say with absolute accuracy where Saimaa begins and where it ends, since the folds of the small bays obscure the whole picture. If however you look at the map, you can see that Saimaa begins in the north, outside the town of Joensuu into which the Pielisjoki river flows, and ends in the Saimaa channel and Vuoksi.

Only by travelling through Saimaa by boat can you appreciate the role played by the Ice Age in fashioning the diverse nature of this waterway. Saimaa has manag-

ed to preserve its wilderness nature, although the human influence on its nature grows with the years. Saimaa has just one national park, Linnansaari, which is situated at Haukivesi. Because of this we commence our journey from historical Olavinlinna on the middle course of Saimaa and wend our way towards northern Saimaa.

TO THE LAKE WILDERNESS

When the stony towers of Olavinlinna are concealed by the island of Hirsipuu, the waters of Haapavesi open out before us. Rowing briskly we soon reach the rugged, rocky Matarinsalmi straits. Only then can we bid farewell to the hillock upon which the town stands, the Matarinsalmi straits being the only channel leading northwards. The best way to navigate these labyrinthine straits is to follow the shipping channel. The rocks rising from the western bank protect the countryside and animal life of the area. Just such is the domain of the great horned owl, the lynx and the elk. We arrive at the southern tip of Haukivesi.

Pikku-Haukivesi begins here and ends seven kilometres away at Seurasaari with not a single island in between. The western shore affords protection from the wind. The long, crosswise island of Seurasaari is like a stopper in the water, with all the waters of northern Saimaa flowing round it. It's an interesting island of sand and gravel, created in a fold of the receding continental glacier. In the island pools you can find beavers which have learned to survive on the island of open waters all year round. These islands make an excellent place for the rower to take a rest from his labours. The traveller can spend a peaceful night on the island of Hietasaari which is situated on the eastern side of Seurasaari island.

THROUGH THE LINNANSAARI NATIONAL PARK

Onwards from Seurasaari, travelling northeast we continue through the only national park in this part of Finland, Linnansaari, 40 kilometres long and practically the whole width of Haukivesi. It's the only national park in the whole of the Saimaa area and provides the best possible living conditions for many species of plant and animal life. Rowing through the park you may well chance to see a genuine, gentle-natured Saimaa marbled seal. Ahead of us is first Tuunaanselkä, which is about 10 kilometres long and 7 wide.

In autumn, this deep water attracts keen fishermen eager to hook the red-fleshed Saimaa lake salmon and trout. In summer many seining crews can be seen following the shoals of vendace. The traveller will find it well worth his while to row ashore and buy the cheap fresh fish.

Before too long has passed the rower will have become well acquainted with the park's large osprey population. Fourteen nesting pairs within a stretch of twenty kilometres form the densest osprey population in Finland. These handsome birds have built their twig castles on the crowns of the stunted Scots pines and, in

The poplar admiral, the largest butterfly to be found in Finland, can be seen on the wing during sunny July days in eastern Finland.

some cases, have underestimated the strength of the wind. The rower too should keep a weather eye on the horizon and pull for shore in good time to escape the sudden thunderstorms. In the northwest rises the large, undulating, forested island of Linnansaari from which the national park takes its name. Rowing towards the island's western shore we pass small rocks where graceful terns spring twittering onto the crests of the waves. A colony of herring gulls can be heard screeching on a neighbouring island. In this area too, the herring gulls have seized the islands from the lesser black-backed gulls.

Linnansaari used to be the only arable island in Haukivesi. On the northern tip of the island of Laattaansaari (whose name is derived from the Finnish word for flagstone), in a cove of Linnansaari, is a farmhouse. Deserted in the mid 1950s this farmhouse with its surrounding buildings and flowering meadows gives some idea of what life was like for the land-clearing farmer. There is a camping area near the farmhouse from which a network of paths traverse the northern tip of this four kilometre long island. Behind these seemingly barren, shoreline woods we come to some lush groves. About a quarter of the land area of the park consists of deciduous woods: linden, speckled alder, great sallow and common alder seek room to grow in the fertile soil from the onslaught of the spruce thickets. Within a distance of a few dozen metres you can find practically all the different types of forest nature; rocks and heathland, coppices, swampy woods, sedgy meadows and shores. The traveller's attention will be drawn to the red berried mezereum, tall rushes, Solomon's Seal and stonecrop. Many interesting plant species grow here, making these islands a paradise for the plant biologist. Pleasant birdsong can be heard from the edges of these untouched woods. Wood warblers, greenish warblers, red-breasted flycatchers and white-backed woodpeckers give just a hint of the richness concealed in the islands of this park.

You find a large number of elks on these islands. They calve in peace in these woods, sometimes on quite small islands. In the first weeks of summer the elks with their calves swim to better pastures during the quietest hours of the night. The enormous, centuries old badger sets and paths can be found in the nooks and crannies

Juha Taskinen

54

There is a clear division of labour in the osprey family. Mother guards the nest while father goes fishing for the family food. Juha Taskinen
The back markings of the nearly full-grown chicks differ from that of the parents.

of the spruce thickets. In some places the foxes, raccoon dogs, wild mink and pine marten terrorise the other animals of the islands, neither is it unknown for lynx and bear to pay a visit.

A rock reaches up at the northern end of Linnansaari from where you can see the most beautiful scenery of the park. In the west, Peonselkä shimmers in the sunlight and in the north the maze of green islands. On the lower part, the narrow Surmaluoto splendidly displays the work done by the Ice Age. Nobody remains to tell the story of this hill, although one can imagine the place having been a fortress, the last place of refuge. Beacons could be seen from a great distance from here. On scorching July afternoons, in the aspen groves of the northern tip, you can find the beautiful, dark poplar admiral butterflies fluttering about the poplar crowns and occasionally flying down to quench their thirst.

We continue through the island maze to the northern parts of the park. Barren, open waters are suddenly revealed behind the rich straits. The cry of the black-throated diver and the shriek of the lesser black-backed gull can be heard from afar in the peaceful evening. In

places, on the low, reedy skerries, black-headed gulls and little gulls nest side by side. Our journey pauses at the rugged island of Vuorisaari before crossing Kuivaselkä. It's just another ten kilometres to the northern end of the park. Vuorisaari has deciduous woods and at the beginning of summer you can here the clear piping of the national bird of South Savo, the golden oriole, in the woods near the shore.

We have now reached the northern border of the national park; you can tell by the number of sauna buildings which dominate the shoreline more and more. Returning to the southern end of Linnansaari we steer our boat towards the beautiful Oravi canal. There's a delightful waterside village here whose spirited history began with the excavation of the canal and continued with the manufacture of mortar for the banks. The factory is no longer here, but remains of the lake ore smeltery can still be found under the water.

THROUGH THE ISLAND MAZE TO KOLOVESI
The shipping channel northwards twists and turns between the islands and is easy to follow. The traveller will,

The wide-eyed flying squirrel is primarily a nocturnal species found in the northern coniferous regions.

Esko Männikkö

in the hollows of the swampy thickets. Cranes inhabit the sedgy meadows, but in midsummer the traveller will neither see nor hear them.

The special feature of the Kolovesi landscape is its narrow straits. Rugged rocks rise from the sides, whereas the nearby bay is low and fertile. Everywhere the waters are clear and in places up to 40 metres deep. You can imagine what a tremendous difference in height there would be in the straits if the waters were to disappear — the peaks would be 100 metres high in places. One special feature of this sterile water is the high bream population due to the excellent breeding grounds in the fertile bay.

The shallow Käkövesi (in Finnish "Cuckoo Water") stretches for four kilometres, and on summer evenings it is easy to understand how it got its name, as nowhere else can you hear the cuckoo calling as loudly and clearly as here. The narrow straits and rugged rocks create perfect acoustics for the cuckoo song. Here you can find a place for the night much more easily than elsewhere on Kolovesi. At the mouth of Käkövesi, in the direction of the morning sun, is one of the largest rocks, Haukkalahden-vuori. The arms of this watercourse are so narrow that looking northwest from the peak, the landscape resembles a winding riverbed. Before long the determined climber will come across the finger paintings on the rocks made by the original inhabitants millenia ago. Do the drawings of animals and people signify a good hunting place? Would the fallen deer depicted on these rocks have met their fate being driven by our forefathers to the tips of these promontories? Or did the artist relax in the charm of this beautiful area to listen to the evening sun and make his mark; trying to appease the great powers that be? JT

however, miss a great deal unless he ventures into the countless mazes in this watercourse. Nowhere else on Saimaa can be found such a broken chain of islands. This is the dream of all oarsmen. The watercourse begins in the southwest at Enovesi and ends in the northwest at Tappuvirta. Its islands are rugged and covered in conifers. Thanks to the narrow straits these islands are full of game. The vendace population in these waters is different to Haukivesi. Here they grow larger and are naturally much sought after.

From the northwest corner of Joutenvesi the channel leads further upwards. Passing the Vaaluvirta ferry we are already at the gateway to Kolovesi. The narrow shipping channel winds courageously onwards, pushed by the strengthening current. Rowing against the current we get to Kinkonselkä where we leave the shipping channel and steer southeast.

KOLOVESI — LAKE NATURE SANCTUARY

You know instantly when you get to Kolovesi. The water becomes crystal clear and the narrow, stony-banked straits lead ever deeper. At Kotaselkä, by the Murtosaari island, Kolovesi splits into two channels divided by the large Vaajasalo island. Vaajasalo itself is so small that you can go round it by land in a day. You may even encounter a Siberian jay, or certainly a three-toed woodpecker rustling in the age-worn spruce bark, somewhere

---

Linnansaari National Park

Rantasalmi, Savonlinna, Kangaslampi, 25 km²
Established: 1956, extended 1982
Under National Board of Forestry management

Connections: Only by water, in summer by regular boats from Rantasalmi, Oravi and Savonlinna. Details about water taxis and hire of rowing boats from Rantasalmen Matkailu (tel. 957-81478). Rowing boats can also be hired from Porosalmi holiday village or Oravi.

Services: A signposted trail network on the main island (2 km and 5 km), nature trail (2 km), two camping areas and cooking place. Elsewhere in the park are a few maintained camping areas.

Maps: Basic map 1:20 000 nos. 3233 12, 3234 05, 3234 07, 3234 08, 3234 10, 3234 11, 4211 02, 4211 03, 4211 05, 4211 06, 4212 01.

Further information: National Board of Forestry, Savonlinna district office, tel. 957-21604 (Savonlinna) or from the park warden, tel. 957-387132 (Oravi)

Juha Taskinen

The Arctic Ocean is the home of the ringed seal family and the overwhelming majority of the millions of these animals that inhabit our world live there. The Arctic ringed seal is a creature of the open spaces. It spends its winters on the unbounded ice plains, and when the seas are open it is generally at home dozens or even hundreds of kilometres from land.

The Saimaa ringed seal's habitat is just about a different as it is possible to be. Above water, the greatest difference relates to the view that the animal commands. A Saimaa seal lolling on a shoreline rock is often so well concealed by reeds or bushes that it is unlikely to be able to see for any more than a few metres.

Whereas the Arctic ringed seal, a favourite prey of polar bears, is an extremely wary animal, its cousin in Lake Saimaa lacks natural enemies and has developed into a denizen of shorelines with dense vegetation cover.

Hundreds of generations of development

The history of the Saimaa ringed seal began away back in the late stages of the last ice age, when some of the seals that had lived in the sea fringing the continental ice shelf were cut off in the inland sea that later evolved into the Baltic. When the last of the continental ice had melted, the world's northernmost seal species withdrew into the waters surrounding the polar ice cap, where it thrives to this day. The seals isolated in the Baltic region about 12,000 years ago later evolved into the Baltic, Saimaa and Ladoga sub-species.

Cut off from the wide ocean, the seals had to adapt to many kinds of new conditions as the Baltic went through its various stages of development. Salinity levels varied widely. In some places the water was as saline as that of the oceans, in others brackish or almost fresh. As the land was uplifted, some parts of the sea were transformed into lakes, which retained their seal populations.

The ancestral form of today's Saimaa seals evolved into a separate sub-species nearly 9,000 years ago. In the early stages of uplifting, seals appear to have been isolated in several Finnish lakes. The fact that they are today found only in Saimaa, the country's biggest, indicates that this lake is close to the minimum size required to sustain a population of these animals.

Good sight and a nest on the shore

As in our other lakes, visibility in the waters of Saimaa is much less than in the sea. As a result of this turbidity, the seals have been constantly developing better sight, which is today evidenced by the size and shape that their skulls have acquired to allow for the increased importance of their eyes.

Saimaa ringed seals eat more or less the same fare as their Baltic cousins. Small fish that swim in shoals are the main source of nourishment. The most significant difference is that Saimaa seals eat very few crustaceans, which are important in the Baltic, not to speak of the Arctic Ocean. In Saimaa, these easily-caught bottom-living creatures are compensated for by slow-moving fish that swim near the lakebed and shore.

The most striking way in which the Saimaa seal has had to adapt to its environment concerns its winter nest. Ringed seals that live in the ocean spend their winters and give birth in nests burrowed into snowdrifts, with the only exit a hole in the ice leading directly into the water. Out at sea, they nest on jagged ice floes, on which the wind has formed snowdrifts. Lake Saimaa boasts no ice floes, nor do large snowdrifts build up on the surface of the ice there. The only place where snow piles up is on the lakeshore, which is also where the seals nest. They enter their snow cave, which is a couple of metres long, from the water, but the other end of the cave is often on firm ground. This makes them very vulnerable to fluctuations in the water level during the winter.

Will it survive?

The original population of Saimaa ringed seals was probably very small. At least, it is very difficult to imagine that it was ever large. Thus it is unlikely that its genetic pool has been dangerously impoverished even at times when the population was tiny, as it is today. There is usually a danger of genetic impoverishment when a species has rapidly declined in number below a certain "bottleneck".

There are now only about 150 Saimaa ringed seals alive. That is an extremely small number for a distinct sub-species of mammal, and indeed the Saimaa animal is one of the three rarest seals in the world. The population has been increasing gratifyingly, if slowly, since the beginning of the 1980s thanks to intensified preservation measures. Prohibition of net fishing in breeding areas for periods of several months has proved the most effective measure; as recently as the late 1970s, as many as half the cubs born each year perished when they became entangled in nets during their first two months of life.

The Saimaa ringed seal is one of the animals on the Worldwide Fund for Nature's (formerly WWF)'s international list of endangered species. A working group appointed by the WWF in 1979 has made a significant contribution to protecting the animal.

Ensuring the continued survival of the Saimaa ringed seal will also require long-term measures: some of the seals' favourite shoreline areas will have to be reserved for them and pollution in the lake will have to be prevented. In these respects, the interests of the Saimaa ringed seal run parallel to those of people who appreciate recreational amenities. EH

The Two Divers: Setting the Mood on a Summer Night

The black-throated diver's primeval barking call and its shrill wail rising as dusk falls late on the summery lakeland is one of the most electrifying sounds of nature. This bird is an impressive sight as well. Its colours are restrainedly stylish and its shape a study in elegance. Those who study its behaviour can also have the privilege of observing mysterious rituals with many participants.

It is hardly surprising that many beliefs and legends have been associated with this bird. Some have ascribed its shape to the Devil. Believing that creation was a simple skill, Old Nick brought a handsome bird into being and boasted of its skill in flying. But he forgot to give it legs. Its webbed feet protruding behind its rudimentary tail reveal that it is a creation of the Devil.

There may be something to these popular beliefs, because diver-like birds swam on and beneath the waters of our planet as early as the Carbonaceous age 100 million years ago.

Long-lived, but a slow breeder

The black-throated diver's favourite habitat is a bleak open expanse of clear water, the kind of place that is easily overlooked when bird habitats are being protected, but which are such a common feature of the Finnish landscape. It prefers large island-dotted inland water bodies and remote forest lakes, but not very small ponds, which cannot provide a long enough ''runway'' for the bird's ponderous take-off.

The black-throated diver has an unusually long lifespan for a bird. Many live longer than 20 years, and some even reach the venerable age of 30. It is no longer persecuted as a plunderer of fish stocks, but many still die in fish traps and nets.

Associated with the bird's longevity is its low reproduction rate. The female lays two dark-brown eggs with black spots in a nest by the edge of the water in mid-May at the earliest.

Because she leaves her nest long before approaching people or boats are even in sight, predators like crows can easily attack the eggs or chicks. Since, however, the bird lives so long, populations can appear stable even if nesting fails completely several years in a row. Its poor reproduction rate is nowadays causing concern. The main reasons appear to be regulation of water levels and, above all, a lack of tranquility on large open expanses of water. The birds

water as it flies between the pond where it builds its nest and the waters where it catches its food. It nests throughout Finland, usually on the boggy banks of backwoods ponds and in salt marshes, but is much rarer than the black-throated diver. Groups of these birds assemble for atmosphere-laden rituals on lakes in Lapland in summer, and their shrieking calls can make a chill run down one's spine.

The red-throated diver, too, is vulnerable if its nest is disturbed during the hatching period. The national network of forest roads has brought nesting places within range of more and more people and the number of holiday residences has increased everywhere. If it is disturbed, a red-throated diver abandons its nest, leaving an easy meal for crows and other predators. Those which nest on the banks of ponds seem to produce fewer young than those who build their nests on small islands. This is probably ascribable to wild mink and other predatory mammals prowling the banks.

The general consensus is that the red-throated diver population has been in recession for the past few decades. By contrast, reproduction rates have been moderately good in recent years. Since environmental toxins generally reduce reproduction rates by a noticeable margin, the red-throated diver does not appear to be in danger in this respect and its future will be assured if only it is allowed to nest in peace and the remaining ponds where it builds its nests are preserved.

A report published in summer 1986 by a working party established to study means of protecting endangered flora and fauna species lists both the black-throated and the red-throated diver as species to be kept under observation because they are declining in numbers. With the assistance of the World Wildlife Fund, an attempt to give the red-throated diver population a boost by building artificial islands for them to nest on has been carried out. The results have been promising and many pairs are already using the islands. OJ

An enchanting atmosphere on a forest pond on a summer night as a red-throated diver alertly keeps watch on events from her nest on a tiny islet.

The black-throated diver's back has distinct white bars, whereas the red-throated's is a uniformly dark colour.

are more successful at raising their young in smaller lakes.

The denizen of forest ponds and salt marshes

The red-throated diver often fishes in large open expanses of water. Its gutteral quacking and cackling sounds ring across the

The Feline Predator

Juha Taskinen

Eero Kemilä

The lynx is an unsociable animal. All alone, the male prowls his territory, the size of which can range from a few dozen to hundreds of square kilometres. The female and her kittens wander either within the male's territory or outside. The kittens (born in May) develop slowly and stay with their mother until the following February.

The heartland of the lynx's distribution range lies south of Finland. Both the species' size and its hunting technique lend themselves to preying on deer. However, it is also good at catching hares, and thus can thrive in areas where these animals are plentiful.

One reason why we consider the lynx "Central European" is that it has never spread to Lapland in any numbers. Some "vagrants" have strayed there in search of hares, ptarmigan and reindeer, but have rarely stayed for a longer time; they have been nomads in the real meaning of the word.

A prized prey

The lynx is quite valuable to hunt. Its meat is edible, and indeed tasty, nourished as it is with game. Its fur commands a good price.

By the 1950s, the lynx had been virtually eliminated from the pattern of Finnish fauna. Already towards the end of that decade and in the beginning of the following, however, it began to appear here once again. Some came from Sweden, skirting the head of the Gulf of Bothnia, but most came along the isthmus between the Gulf of Finland and Lake Ladoga.

Some took up permanent "residence" in the south-east-

ern border region. This region has had Finland's densest lynx population for the past twenty years, although reasonably large populations have since established themselves also in North Karelia and the interior of southern Finland, where deer and hare provide a good supply of food.

In winters when there has been heavy snowfall, hungry deer have provided lynxes with an easy prey. The predators have only needed to lurk near the places where fodder has been laid out for the deer. The lynx population of Finland is now nearly five hundred.

The protected predator

The lynx's hunting tactics are based on keen hearing, which enables it to locate its prey, a creeping approach and a fast final spurt to make the kill. This

requires both patience and a sprinter's skills. When it makes its final effort, the surface underneath must not give way. If it does, the animal loses speed. That happens when the surface is soft deep snow. The very snowy winters of the early 1980s proved disastrous for the lynxes of central and southern Finland; hares went their way and the lynx, especially young ones, suffered badly. Some starved to death, others ventured into haybarns and farmyards in search of nourishment.

The lynxes' most important prey, hares, are well adapted to living in an urban environment. 19 of them were once counted in a smallish section of pasture at an agricultural research station in Viiki on the eastern fringe of Helsinki. Lynxes, too, have followed hares to cities and have been seen right on the outskirts of large centres like Helsinki and Turku. Adaptation to a cultured environment offers the prospect of expanding the range of their habitat, but it also poses the dangers of culture.

The feline predator's nesting places seem to be in the wildest parts of the areas where they live. The few that have been found were in the least accessible and hilly terrain available, ensuring that the mothers have been able to rear their kittens undisturbed by curious intruders. Only when mother and kittens have left their nesting place and gone elsewhere in search of prey have people become aware of the kittens' existence.

The lynx was declared a protected species in Finland in 1968 and the population has been "managed" in an exemplary fashion ever since. Permits to shoot lynxes are occasionally granted by the Ministry of Agriculture and Forestry. Before a permit can be granted, the population of the area in question must be carefully studied. The average number of permits issued each year was between 10 and 20, but in 1984 — perhaps somewhat surprisingly — the number was raised to about 60.

EPu

ON KARELIAN BIRD LAKES

Some forty years ago a young ornithologist, Bernhard Lindeberg "discovered" Siikalahti at Parikkala. After the war he began an relenting struggle against plans to dry out the bay, a campaign which ended in 1968, with the government finally deciding to make Siikalahti — unquestionably Finland's best habitat for waterbirds — into a nature preserve.

Siikalahti is reached through groves of grey alders and idyllic rustic communities along the sandy road between Kangaskylä and Kaukola.

NIGHT TIME CONCERT

The song of the sedge warbler provides an unceasing background chorus all over the vicinity. The whip-lash cries of the spotted crake reveal the whereabouts of

Tapani Räsänen

Black-headed gulls nest in colonies which may number thousands of individuals.

dozens of furtive shapes among the reeds. Hour after hour they call in unison. With daybreak, the spotted crake's relative, the water rail, ceases giving vent to cries resembling, regrettably, the protestations of a stuck pig, as the parent birds' entire attention is devoted to the nest.

A solitary screech echoes in the darkness as a larger than life black-headed gull glides over the open pools towards its nest. The metallic honking of the coot sounds constantly from the smaller pools. The long drawn-out whistle of the wigeon, the clear "prip-prip" of the teal, the shoveller's snuffling utterances, and the grating of the garganey — voices, birds, life. Suddenly a strange, almost unbelievably low booming sound reverberates through the generally higher pitched trills and squeaks. Seven times the deep note is repeated, for all the world as though somebody were blowing across the top of an empty bottle. The hidden fog-horn is first answered from closer by, and then a third joins in. The owner of this bass voice is the bittern, indisputed lord of the lake.

Something like a couple of centuries ago the weird booming call of the bittern put fear into the superstitious people of the Karelian isthmus. Later, when the most fearless of the menfolk had crept into the high sedges prepared to face whatever demon lurked there, they found there no deranged bull, devil, or other extra-terrestrial, but a bird that resembled a large brown owl stretched out of shape.

The bird concert of the wetlands is a medley of the melodious trilling and ditties of dozens of thrush nightingales ensconced in thickets and woodland meadows, the croak of corncrakes, the incessant zithering of grasshopper warblers, and the penetrating, sharp whistles of marsh and blyth's reed warblers.

DAWN LIGHTENS THE SKY

At around three or four in the morning the short night ends as the thick mist shrinks back before the onslaught of the rising sun and the stirring breeze. With its blanket thus removed, the habitat comes into view. Compared to the nocturnal concert the view may not be quite as awe-inspiring, but it has a richness and diversity that are

Distinguished by the dark undersides to its wings, the lithe little gull, unusually for gulls, is insectivorous. It is seen here hunting for insects over a reed bed.

Heikki Kokkonen

unequalled elsewhere. This wetland simply teems with life.

Sedge warblers call happily as they hop busily among the bushes and reeds throughout the morning, but one after another the crakes and rails fall silent. The spasmodic booming of the bittern remains as a travesty of the night's concert. Pure white black-headed gulls glide slowly over their colony as their spouses conscien-sciously incubate the eggs. Warned off by the threat-ening behaviour of the gulls, a male marsh harrier sheers away from its course over the yellow-green reed beds, its mate waiting patiently at the nest on an island shore.

Dozens of pochards and tufted ducks, teals and wigeons glide over the open water. Pairs of scaups strain out food with their flattened bills among the rapidly growing horsetails. At the very edge of the vegetation a jet black coot with a white splash on its forehead splash-es about in the company of a horned grebe, whose soft cries are lost among the general cacophony from the gulls. Ospreys attracted by fish splashing near the sur-face constantly panic the teals, while the other birds carry on unperturbed.

SIIKALAHTI'S FUTURE SAFEGUARDED
With the lowering of the water level of Lake Simpelejärvi, the Siikalahti bay has become a roughly four square kilometre paradise of water plants and birdlife. Waste-waters from Parikkala have accelerated the rate of en-croachment so much that in recent years duck species favouring low meadows and open pools have begun to decline.

Owing both to lime-rich bedrock and eutrophication as a result of human activities, the vegetation at Siikalahti is exceptionally luxuriant for so northerly a climate. The flora contains a large number of species that are rare in Finland, and some which are not found anywhere else in the world. The butterfly and general insect fauna, which has distinct southeastern affinities, is rather less well known than the flora. Among the mammals it is the musk rat that arrests the attention most frequently.

The richness and diversity of the avian fauna have made Siikalahti Finland's best habitat for wetland birds. Outstanding members of its fauna are 5-6 bitterns, 2-4 pairs of marsh harriers, 5-6 great reed warblers, 30 spotted crakes, 30 water rails, 1-7 little crakes, 2-3 moor-hens and 1-3 yellow-breasted buntings. All of Finland's duck and grebe species nest within this bay, amounting to a total of some two hundred birds, as well as a corresponding number of coots. Almost one thousand sedge warblers and their young occupy the reed beds, while one and a half thousand pairs of black-headed gulls regularly nest on its pools. The grand total of nesting wetland birds at Siikalahti is approximately three thousand pairs, i.e. almost eight hundred pairs per square kilometre. Among the water meadows, thickets and copses the density of birds increases by around a hundred per cent, when one adds the large numbers of thrush nightingales, warblers, whitethroats and other mi-grants.

Siikalahti is a habitat that has been formed partly as

Characteristics of the sedge warbler, seen here singing its heart out among the waterside vegetation at Lake Sääperinjär-vi, are a generally striped appearance and a white streak just above the eye.

a result of human impact and whose value can only be maintained by natural management. In order to reduce the rate of encroachment by unwelcome water plants, the water level in summer is kept artificially high by means of embankments and pumping stations. The effect of these measures on the flora and birdlife is being monitored very carefully indeed, in the hope that results may be forthcoming which will enable general management methods to be developed for other important wetland sites. Such practical conservation activities have been participated in by such bodies as the WWF, which has constructed an information centre here, complete with nature trails and bird observation towers.

LAKE SÄÄPERINJÄRVI
The scenery at Värtsilä and Sääpärinjärvi is very exotic. Enclosed by foot-hills there is a several kilometre long verdent valley with a patchwork of fields, wild cherry copses and silver birch woods. Early on summer morn-ings the valley resounds to the sweet songs of thrush nightingales and blyth's reed warblers, as well as to the happy chattering of tree sparrows. The valley's most significant entity is Sääperi, a shallow lake surrounded by groves of willows and sedge and reed beds, which attracts many rare bird migrants from the southeast. Here, for example, gather the yellow-breasted buntings of north Karelia which outside the USSR nest only in Fin-land. From the observation tower vast numbers of black-headed gulls, ducks and waders are visible — they have all gathered here at this convenient little lake to nest. PKo

63

Heikki Kokkonen

FROM THE RIVER KOITAJOKI TO RUUNAA

The boundary between Finland and the Soviet Union runs from the northeast to the southwest via Lake Mekrijärvi to Selkäkangas through a large valley. On the southern side of this valley lies the small but representative Petkeljärvi National Park. It offers neither spectacular fells nor vast bluish expanses of forest, but exempli-

The Karelian rose, the provincial flower of North Karelia, grows in damp situations.

Pertti Huttunen

fies a landscape composed to a large extent of ridge-like eskers laid down during the melting of the continental ice sheets some 10,000 years ago. These eskers are now clothed in Scots pine forests and separated by clearwater pools and minor lakes.

PETKELJÄRVI NATIONAL PARK AND 'TAITAJA TRAIL'

Arrival at the national park for the first time never fails to impress. Clearcuts and young plantations alternate on the national park boundary with mature stands of Scots pines. These pine trees, whose age ranges from 100 to 150 years, withstood a major forest fire that occurred 90 years ago and signs of which are in evidence today in the form of scars on the butts of trees and charred stumps. The park's wild appearance is emphasised by large numbers of decaying standing trees and fallen, rotting logs.

Damp hollows in brook courses and eskers add their own individual splash of colour to an otherwise rather monotonous landscape of heaths. There are many old silver birches and bow-shaped wild cherry trees. An abundance of crowberry in the shrub layer of Scots pine forests is a primary feature of the north which is admirably demonstrated here. This feeling of being in the northern forests is in-

tensified by the echoing, sawlike buzz used by bramblings to advertise their presence in the early summer, as well as by the short, tinkling utterances of rustic buntings. Otherwise the forest birdlife differs little from that normally associated in Finland with forests growing on poor mineral soils. There is one main exception: the wealth of old trees provides tits, redstarts, tree creepers and pied flycatchers with far more nesting sites than average, enabling larger populations to exist in the national park.

Lakes within the park are of the clearwater, so-called oligotrophic type where nutrients are present in low concentrations. Their barren shores are almost completely exposed, providing an ideal habitat for the common sandpiper, which is the park's most abundant wader. Its plaintive cry as it runs and bobs wagtail-fashion along an open shore will soon become as familiar to the rambler as the wheezing of the brambling. Petkeljärvi National Park's mascot, however, is the black-throated diver, whose wild cry in summer echoes over the labyrinthine waters of Lake Valkeajärvi.

Peatlands in this particular national park tend to be on the small side and fringe the pools lying on the eskers. In these low-lying sphagnum pine bogs labrador tea grows in competition with Chamaedaphne caylculata and arctic cloudberry.

For the hiker with time on his hands, one can recommend the park's relatively new nature trail. This more than six kilometre long trail passes through some of the loveliest esker scenery. The Pitkäjärvi area also has an interesting military history. During the time of the Winter War an important front ran between lakes Petkeljärvi and Nuorajärvi. Ounassalmi, a few kilometres north of the national park, saw heavy fighting. Monuments of such troubled times include entrenchments, now much collapsed, on the eskers lining the beach of Lake Petkeljärvi. A few of the trenches at the present-day Petraniemi camping site have been restored. The Petkeljärvi National Park is an excellent place from which to start off along the so-called 'Taitaja Trail', which is a major local hiking route. Covering over a score of kilometres, the route winds through terrain largely made up of eskers. It is an easy trail to follow and would be worth double the effort, as the scenery is breathtaking. From the backs of narrow eskers rising dozens of metres above their surroundings a good view is to be had over small clearwater, labyrinthine pools towards a patchwork quilt of light green and brown peatlands. The lake scenery remains with the hiker along the whole 20-kilometre route, sometimes appearing on the right, at others on the left.

After Isso one can take a well-earned rest at the Ruhkaranta holiday village. The best part of the Taitaja Trail is still to be covered, however. This is the terrain lying between lakes Isojärvi and Putkela. On this section of the path almost the entire journey takes place along a narrow esker, which is later bordered on both sides by water. The length of this section is about ten kilometres and the route ends at Putkela, alongside the road leading from Ilomantsi to Hattuvaara.

THE 'TAPIO TRAIL'

Hattuvaara fell is just about as far east as you can now go in

Finland, as it stands right up against the Soviet border. The fell is surrounded on almost every quarter by extensive peatlands. Thickets of grey-green alder and birch adorning the fell's slopes testify to a long and bitter confrontation with mankind. This area has been burned off hundreds of times during its 400 years of human settlement. Their proximity to the border has profoundly influenced the lives of local inhabitants. Sometimes they have flown east to escape Swedish forces, and at other times, under pressure from the east, they have sought sanctuary further west. A small orthodox village church (or 'sasouna') still stands proudly on the summit of Hattuvaara fell, having weathered innumerable storms.

The route begins at Tapionaho and the trail follows the limit of the border zone for about a kilometre, the actual (though prohibited) trip to the border itself being only a kilometre or two. However, soon the trail curves away from the border zone and continues over planks laid down on Tapiosuo bog. There is then a river crossing over the Koitajoki, the sturdy shapes of old, thick-limbed spruces being reflected in the water. Numerous old ox-bow lakes serve to supplement the luxuriance of plant growth along the river's course. Alongside the route one can see the work of beavers in the form of old trees cut in two, and substantial dams. While these are not the work of Finland's endemic beaver, but of one of its foreign relatives, the Canadian beaver, they now form an integral component of the Finnish wilds.

You may find the sharp-clawed prints of a wolf in sandy places lining the Koitajoki river. Wolves tend to move about most commonly here, on Finland's eastern border, where they can slip very easily, close on the heels of their prey, into the USSR.

At approximately the halfway point along the Tapio Trail a cooking and sleeping 'lean-to' has been constructed in the old log-rafters' style. Here it is a pleasure to brew up coffee or tea and stretch out tired limbs. The marked trail ends at Polvikoski.

KOIVUSUO STRICT NATURE RESERVE

Koivusuo and its environs used to contain Finland's largest assembly of eccentric 'string bogs', a type of peatland with an elevated surface covered by ridges and pools. Half of these bogs have recently been ruined by the setting up of peat production centres, however. Fortunately peatland wildlife and habitats as a whole are exceedingly well represented in Koivusuo Strict Nature Reserve, which has the disadvantage from the casual hiker's point of view of not being open to the general public. These intact peatlands, together with small tracts of forest standing on elevated parts of the bogs continue to form a valuable wilderness complexity.

The cart track running from the south changes at the edge of Pirhunsuo bog into a path lined with wooden planks and logs to make the crossing easier for the hiker. On the western side wettish Pirhonsuo opens out. In keeping with a

---

Petkeljärvi National Park

Ilomantsi 6.3 sq.km., land area 3.6 sq.km.
Established 1956
Under National Board of Forestry management.

Connections: A 6 km long road from the Möhkö highway connects with the park and there is a coach service along the highway.

Services: Marked trails 3.5 km and 5.5 km, as well as the major hiking route, the 'Taitaja Trail' (22 km), ending at the village of Putkela. Nature trail 6.4 km long. Camping site.

Maps: Basic map 1: 20 000 nos. 4243 06, 4243 09 + 4243 12.

Further information: National Board of Forestry, District Office of Ilomantsi, tel. 974-22 444 (Ilomantsi).

Pekka Nurminen

The Canadian beaver has settled down well in Finland's north Karelia region.

Patvinsuo National Park consists mainly of oligotrophic treeless raised bogs. With their remote location and abundance of wettish areas, these provide a refuge for many rare species of animals.

bygone Finnish agricultural practice, this treeless sphagnum bog has at one time been used for hay making. On the other side of the bog the trail ascends via a gently-sloping moraine deposit towards Pirhuvaara fell. The branches of 100 year-old spruce trees on the lower flank of the fell are hung with wispy beard mosses. Once common all over southern Finland, the latter are becoming an increasingly rare sight.

After about a kilometre, one meets the waters of the River Alajoki flowing between pale green forests. The sedgy meadows lining the river, like the lush areas of Pirhonsuo bog, were once made use of by the inhabitants of Hattuvaara as a source of naturally growing hay. It is from these times that the small bark-roofed hay makers' cabin standing on the Koivulampi pool bog dates. If the figures carved into the logs forming its walls are reliable, this cabin is now 120 years old. There are one or two pubescent birches growing near to the cabin: Koivusuo bog was named after these trees, 'koivu' being Finnish for birch.

Sweeping across the western slope of Pirhuvaara fell there is a whole grove of lovely birches. These have replaced the original vegetation on land originally subject to slashing and burning. This type of forest resulting from human impact provides an excellent reference point later when one enters the virgin forests of Pieni Pirhuvaara fell, with their ancient spruces and aspens, some of which are so old that they now lie rotting on the ground. There the boreal forest 'atmosphere' is reinforced by the profusion of fallen, moss-festooned spruces and in spring by the tinkling song of the red-breasted flycatcher. The copse on the fell slope lower down merges into a so-called transitional forest sphagnum mire.

Behind Pieni Pirhuvaara fell, Kelokkoaho thrusts up above a plateau of bogs. Its name refers to the custom of slashing and burning and the lower slope of the fell still bristles with tree stumps bearing very obvious signs of fire. The discovery of signs of this ancient style of land use here in the remotest part of Ilomantsi is indicative of the scale on which such forms of agriculture were practiced. Forests now considered virgin, on the basis of tree growth and other aspects of the vegetation, may well several hundred years ago have constituted rye fields.

One of the outstanding features of Koivusuo Strict Nature Reserve (to which ordinary members of the public are denied access) is the northern birch mouse, a brown rodent with a distinct median black stripe running along its back from its forehead to the base of its tail. The species has a very patchy distribution in Finland and Ilomantsi appears to represent the extreme northern limit of its range.

Owing to the Continental climate and snowy winters, the region's forests and bogs exhibit a good deal of northern features which are also reflected in the birdlife. The northern Siberian jay and waxwing nest in the park's forests, while the brambling's buzz-saw-like call can be heard from a great distance away. In recent years the whooper swan has

Heikki Kokkonen

tended to nest along the River Alajoki, and this bird can frequently be observed feeding on the Koivulampi pool. While the most famous of the peatland birds is the wimbrel, the golden plover's plaintive cry is also frequently heard ringing over the peatlands. The cries of cranes on early summer mornings penetrate even the noise from the local peat production centres.

RIVER KOITAJOKI

The River Koitajoki, which has its origins on the Finno-Soviet border, flows along the eastern boundary of Koivosuo Strict Nature Reserve, then has a mad fling at the Polvikoski rapids before calming down to become a serene wilderness river. Its dark waters disappear behind the border, only to return to Finland twenty kilometres or so further south. Harnessed in the early 1800s, the waters of the Möhkönkoski rapids led to the establishment of Ilomantsi's first industrialised village. Lake ore was crushed to form pig iron and then, as iron manufacturing became unprofitable, the mill continued its industry for a few decades more, but finally closed down in 1907.

After the Möhkönkoski rapids the Koitajoki expands into a large lake, called Nuorajärvi, which is rather straight-sided,

before continuing its journey north and skirting Lake Mekri-järvi's esker bay to the northwest. The main direction of flow of the river has always been opposite to the main direction of post-glacial uplift. This to some extent accounts for the boggy nature of the river's banks. Impetus was given to bog formation, however, by the Ilomäntsi ice lake 10,000 years ago. Dammed by a mass of ice, this lake ebbed across the southern side of Selkäkangas, burying under it all of central Ilomantsi. When the continental ice sheet finally withdrew, the waters of the ice lake flowed out down the channel of the River Pielisjoki and in this way reached Lake Saimaa. The areas now exposed very quickly developed into peatlands. Lake Mekrijärvi is more of a broad sound along the Koitajoki than a lake. On the eastern shore of this extremely darkwater lake there stands an old village which is also called Mekrijär-vi. This used to be the home of famous minstrels or rune singers. On the shores of the lake the cottage of minstrel Simona Sissonen has remained intact to the present day.

Beyond Lake Mekrijärvi the river begins to meander. Its fringing sedgy meadows are very popular feeding and nesting grounds for waterbirds. Previously the sedgy mead-ows constituted a natural meadowland habitat to which the local populace would journey from astonishingly great dis-tances in order to cut and gather hay. With the abandoning of this kind of haymaking activity several decades ago, the original sedgy meadows very soon became encroached upon by trees and shrubs, especially willows. Skirting Keson-suo bog, the Koitajoki debouches via the Lylynkoski rapids into Lake Tekojärvi, where it joins the waters of the River Koitere. The original Koitajoki channel is now closed off at Hiiskoski, and flowing at breakneck speed through the stones and boulders of the old rapids, the waters pass through the turbines of the Pamilo tunnel power station into the River Pielisjoki.

IN SUOMUNJÄRVI – PATVINSUO NATIONAL PARK

Lake Suomunjärvi has a surface area of slightly less than 6.5 square kilometres and more than 20 kilometres of sandy shores. Islands and promontories, underwater shoals and shallows split the lake into three sections. Skirting the lake, one may possibly glimpse an osprey. The lake does not provide these birds with a well-stocked larder, so that they are forced to hunt over a wider area. Within binocular range one is almost sure to spot a black-throated diver, which nests on the lake. On early summer evenings the cries of the divers echo out over the water, creating a true wilderness feeling. Towards summer's end the divers can often be seen in scattered groups. On the lake's western shore the hiker may direct his steps northwest to Hietavaara and Lake Iso Hietajärvi, both of which lie within the national park. The trail winds through mature Scots pine forest in which the oldest trees are round about two hundred years old. Here and there stand bleached dead trees, or 'snags', with a characteristic twisting type of growth evident on their trunks. The last forest fire, signs of which are still visible on the oldest trees, swept through the area 120-130 years ago.

PATVINSUO BOG

Thrusting up at the edge of the Lieksa road, Surkanvaara fell beckons the hiker to its summit. In fact, there is no especially spectacular view to be had from its crown, the near landscape being dominated by tree-dotted Patvinsuo bog. Peatlands stretch right up to Lake Koitere, lying a league or so to the south. The open 'aapa' bog is pimpled with hills that through heavily-lidded eyes are perceived as islands rising to an appreciable height above the flat surface. Smaller 'islands' and tracts of forest pepper the remainder of the landscape. In places rocky 'shores' serve only to enhance the impression.

Between these peatland hills nestle treeless Sphagnum bogs which are at their most spectacular on each side of the trail leading south from Lake Suomunjärvi. These bogs are waterlogged and poor in nutrients. The hiker should avoid them if possible as they are treacherous in places and at the very least make the going extremely difficult.

A diversity of pine bog flora can be found along the fringes of the patches of forest. An eastern bog plant, Chamaedaphne calyculata, blooms there in May-June, The dwarf shrub, Labrador tea, attempts at many points to creep up on to the drier heathland. Peatlands within the national park are all of the oligotrophic type and contain no plant rarities.

Several pairs of whooper swans and bean geese nest regularly in Patvinsuo National Park. The whooper swans tend to choose hummocks in the wettest places as sites for their nests, the incubating hen thus having an uninterrupted view over a large area of the bog. Bean goose nests will only be found by accident; with luck, too, one may see the parents leading a straggling line of goslings through the low vegetation. Waders, like the whimbrel and golden plover, having a northerly distribution, are among the standard components of the local peatland fauna. The whimbrel's piping cry is heard here even more frequently than that of the common curlew, which is a bird of the south. Tumbling, cavorting lapwings take up residence on the bog in spring, to the accompaniment of wood sandpipers and green-shanks.

In 1940 a few Canadian beavers were introduced in the area. Owing to a scarcity of food, the beaver population has already to some extent declined. Following the course of the brook is not easy owing to the underbrush, but the beavers in this respect have assisted the rambler by building dams at regular intervals, enabling the hiker to cross over the stream when the going gets too tough on one side.

THE RUUNAANKOSKET RAPIDS

The hiker wishing to become acquainted with the Ruunaankosket rapids would do best to start either from the border guard post at the end of the Ruunaan road, or from Neitikoski, as both these places can easily be reached by motorised transport. Organised rapids boats leave from near the border guard post. It is possible to use one's own boat or canoe, but one should possess the necessary experience and skill before venturing downstream.

About five kilometres from the point of departure one meets the first, and rather gentle, rapids, known as Paasivirta. The otter has taken up residence here. It is thrilling to watch an entire family of these lithe, sleek animals playing or hunting for food, as one squats immobile by the rapids. Before Haapavitja there is a small expanse of quiet water, after which the waters swirl and foam for a distance of a couple of kilometres. On the western side of the Haapvitja rapids stands a small patch of virgin, or primaeval, forest containing old, mature Scots pines and extremely large wood ants' nests. A few magnificent 'snags' curve dramatically out over the broiling waters. Every year the National Board of Forestry stocks the waters with take-sized rainbow trout and migratory sea trout. A vestige of the original trout population probably remains. Grayling populations are on the increase.

During its Neitiniemi stages, after Haapavitja, the water turns sharply to the west. At Neitikoski the back-packer will find it easiest to arrange for a boat to take him to the other side, otherwise he will be obliged to circumnavigate several large bays. The Neitikoski rapids are short but violent. They will appeal, however, to those experienced with shooting rapids. Above the rapids, at Kattilanniemi, beaver lodges and other signs of these animals are in evidence. Alongside the watercourse the forests have hardly been touched by the logging industry. While awaiting legislation on protection, the forests lining the shore have been managed very carefully. The observant eye will, however, discern signs of ancient fellings. At one time it was unprofitable to log from any place not close to the waterways.

After the Kattilakoski rapids one comes to the most turbulent descent, the Murroonkoski rapids, where the water literally broils and foams as it rushes along at breakneck speed. Following a section of placid water, one reaches the last of the main Ruunaa rapids, the temperamental Siikakoski rapids. If the rambler has elected to hike along the shore, as distinct from resorting to a boat, he will find it judicious at this point to change over to the river's east bank. The trip by rapids vessel ends at the Naarajoki river bridge.

FROM THE NAARAJOKI TO THE JONGUNJOKI

North of the Naarajoki bridge one finds a pleasant change in the terrain in the form of dryish heaths dotted with Scots pine trees. By this stage the Lieksajoki has become the Naarajoki, which now proceeds to transcribe a long curve to the northwest, before debouching into Lake Hämeenjärvi. The River Jongunjoki spills out into the northern end of this same lake. Five kilometres downstream from the bridge lie the Naarakoski rapids, slightly below which one meets the twisting ribbon that is the Käpykoski rapids, on which a stone-built dam channels the waters to one side.

Northeast of the Naarajoki river rapids lie the Piilosensärkät eskers, which these days are incorporated in the national esker protection programme. This chain of northwest-southeasterly eskers is punctuated by a clutch of small water bodies, the Piiloslampi pools.

After the Piilosensärkät formation, eskers continue on almost as far as the River Jongunjoki. Close to the Nurmijärvi-Kivivaara road there is a cave which was hewn out during the Winter War, as well as other signs of the land having been used for military purposes. It is possible to ramble for several hundred metres along the entrenchments here and to study the long line of upright stones that were placed as an obstacle to tanks. Paths along the esker lead one to the Jongunjoki watercourse.

BY CANOE DOWN THE JONGUNJOKI

As the river trip from Jonkeri to Nurmijärvi covers some sixty-eight kilometres, the journey can be expected to occupy more than a single day. At the top end, if one so wishes, one can shorten the route by leaving from either the Teljo bridge or the Valama road at Aittokoski, but in this case one misses a lot of the more interesting rapids. Similarly, at the bottom end one can abort the trip at Viitakoski, immediately after coursing down the final set of rapids. The rapids total 38 and the overall drop in altitude amounts to around 80 metres. These rapids are classified by Finns as either 'easy' or 'very easy' — which means that it is still possible to get a severe drenching!

The River Jongunjoki used to be an important log-floating route. The dams along the lower sections of lakes Alanteenjärvi and Kangasjärvi were in fact constructed to this end. These stone-built dams served to back the waters up to a useful depth. Timber is no longer floated down the river and the loggers' cabins have long since fallen into a state of disrepair. The trails used by these people have become overgrown by moss and scrub. Indeed, progress along the river banks today is anything but easy, so dense is the undergrowth.

The upper reaches of the route are supplied with two official camping sites, one at Lake Kangasjärvi and the other at Hiidenportti. At the latter location the river becomes compressed by steeply rising cliffs, while at the same time making a turn. Shooting the rapids calls for skill. As the gap between the adjacent walls is conveniently narrow, it has been possible to construct a bridge across the gorge from thick tree trunks. Apart from this means of crossing the torrent, the hiker has only the old log-floaters' dams to bring him from one side to the other at the top end of the river course.

In the vicinity — just to confuse you — there is a second place which is also called Hiidenportti, and this too is well worth taking a look at. To reach it, you run the canoe aground on the west shore of Lake Kangasjärvi, take a compass bearing and strike out due west towards the small pools on Kaakkurisuo bog. Steps have already been taken

to turn this area into a nature reserve and some of its forests to this end have been deliberately left untouched by the National Board of Forestry. The small pools on the Kaakkurisuo bog used to be inhabited by the red-throated diver ('kaakkuri' being the Finnish name for this bird), but while the name remains, the birds have gone.

Hiidenportti proper lies along the Louhipuro stream, taking the form of a few hundred metre-long canyon pointing north and south. Vertical walls 20 to 30 metres in height enclose the brook, which at this point is only a few metres wide. On the surface the water does not appear to be flowing at all, as the wind does not reach this spot. The waters are deep and even with a long pole one finds the bottom still out of reach. Legend has it that the dark depths are inhabited by very large pike, but that is as far as the story goes, for nobody has ever actually seen them. It is easy to cross over this stream at either end, if one is brave enough, since the waters in places disappear under a floating bog. Although the foundations may tremble alarmingly as one steps across, if one chooses a sensible place, one is soon across. On the southern side of Hiidenportti the stream runs for almost a kilometre under the bog, before emerging as a normal stream to drain into the River Suolajoki. Its waters pass on down the latter into the River Jongunjoki. Fragments of spruce forests and stoney heaths covered with Scots pines here constitute a wilderness that has been spared the axe. Should the hiker stray into the southern part of these natural forests, he will come suddenly upon modern clear-cuts and fresh drainage ditches.

After the fast-flowing upper reaches of the river it is a delight to drift quietly along in a canoe or boat and admire the river banks at leisure. On a sunny day blue-winged Agrion damselflies flit in large numbers among the vegetation. The observant naturalist will also be able to spot the demure, brown-winged females perched on willows or reeds. Above the Viidakoski rapids the first houses and hayfields hove into view, bringing the intrepid explorer gently back to civilisation. PHu & EL

Patvinsuo National Park

Lieksa and Ilomantsi, 100 sq.km
Established: 1982
Under National Board of Forestry management.

Connections and services: There are no services at present available in the national park; neither is it possible to reach the park by public transport. The closest coach route is the Lieksa-Kitsi highway, from which there is a 15 kilometre hike to the national park. Another road leads up to the park from Kivilahti towards the south, and a third from Pallosenvaara to the east.

Maps: 1:20 000 nos. 4331 08, 4331 09, 43331 11, 4331 12, 4333 03.

Further information: National Board of Forestry, Lieksa District Office, tel. 975-23 311 (Lieksa).

New Arrivals from the South-East

As the first rays of the orange-red morning sun strike the bright green groves on the shores of Lake Simpelejärvi, a loud, fluty whistle "weela-weeo" and a deeper "chuck-chuck-weeo" resounds from the foliant upper branches of a tall birch. Those sounds are so characteristic of the south-eastern Finnish lakeland that everybody recognizes them as belonging to the golden oriole. The decorative yellow-and-black summer visitor is a welcome arrival in the Saimaa and Päijänne lake districts, but only rarely seen (or heard) anywhere else in Finland.

The golden oriole is a good example of more than a dozen species of birds found mainly in the south-eastern corner of Finland and in few other places, although a few species have spread further north and west.

Many of them did not make an appearance in Finland until the 19th or the present century. They nowadays live mainly in the south-eastern and southern parts of the country, which represent the northernmost and north-westernmost limits of their overall range of distribution.

Their presence in the south-eastern region often reflects the way in which the species spread to Finland: the Karelian isthmus between the open water bodies of the Gulf of Finland and Lake Ladoga is a natural route along which to advance. For more eastern species, the isthmus between Ladoga and Lake Onega is a similar gateway to new living space.

South-eastern plants and mammals

Plants, mammals and insects are usually slower to colonize new areas than birds, which can easily overfly large unfavourable tracts of country. That makes the isthmuses north and south of Lake Ladoga even more important for plants and mammals than for birds.

South-eastern plant rarities include northern wolfsbane and greater meadow rue, both of which flourish in the verdant groves near the Soviet frontier, and golden dock, which grows in the meadows fringing Lake Simpele. That hairy-stemmed denizen of ridge forests in

Tapani Räsänen

The dotted-cheeked tree sparrow is a common sight in some places in villages near the south-eastern border. The species is almost totally absent elsewhere in Finland.

The yellow-breasted bunting's habitat in Finland is a narrow zone from the south-east to the shore of the Gulf of Bothnia.

Heikki Kokkonen

spring, the pale pasque flower, has spread further west. A good example of south-eastern insects is a species of bumble bee completely dependent on wolfsbane and a decoratively dark large butterfly, Limenitis populi, whose numbers declined sharply in the 1960s, but have since been on the rise again.

Our south-eastern mammal fauna include the forest shrew, which inhabits the banks of wilderness streams, the striped field mouse with the distinctive black stripe that gives it its name, the now extremely rare wild boar and the rapidly spreading raccoon dog.

The south-eastern bird choir

Birds are the most visible and audible element in our south-eastern flora and fauna, besides which many species are outstandingly "good" singers. Nightly concerts performed by nightingales and warblers in early summer are an incomparable artistic performance.

The nightingale has spread as far as the west coast in recent decades, but is still most numerous in the south-east. There, its captivating clacking of castanettes, its flowing roulades and clattering are an omnipresent part of the background sounds.

There is much for the experienced ornithologist to hear in the south east at night. From one and the same bush, come

in rapid succession the songs of swallows, redstarts, wagtails, yellow wagtails, wheatears ... Clear whistles and resounding clicking are subduedly repeated — a Blyth's reed warbler! In the course of half a century, this master of mimicry and the best singer among our avian wildlife, has become more and more numerous. Once a rarity among rarities, it is now the most common night performer after the nightingale. Ornithologists from western Europe are more than willing to come to Finland if only to hear this bird, because Finland is the only place outside the Soviet Union that it is known to nest. Its close relation, the marsh warbler, which also mimics other birds, but in furiously hurried bursts, is rarer in south-east Finland.

The cirl bunting and the river warbler sing trilling songs rather like the chirping of grasshoppers. Not even when they stop does silence blanket an autumn night, because the long-horned grasshopper — another immigrant from the east — contributes its clicking to the characteristic atmosphere of the region.

The golden oriole is by no means the only striking daytime singer among the birds of the south east. The ostentatiously coloured yellow-breasted bunting thrives in waterlogged abandoned meadows in the Parikkala, Tohmajärvi and Värtsilä

districts. The cheery voice of the willow warbler is more common than usual in the splendid hillside fir stands after warm air streams in from the south east in May. Another relatively recent new arrival that has consolidated its presence well is the handsome scarlet grosbeak.

South-eastern Finland's characteristic birds also include the pretty little tree sparrow, which thrives in a narrow strip along the border between Lappeenranta and Tohmajärvi.
PKo

An Unwelcome Visitor

Lipoptena cervi, an unpleasant member of the Hippoboscidae family of louse flies, has been spreading through Finland since it first came in through the south east in 1960 and has now reached a line stretching roughly from Pori to Sotkamo. The elk is its natural host, but it has also afflicted people out and about in the forest. One hunter was attacked by as many as 250 of them in an hour. The flies mature in August and September, immediately light on the first elk they can find, drop their wings and begin gorging themselves on blood. They are disgusting when they get into one's hair or under one's clothes, although not all of them bite. Oddly, only Finns — about one in three — suffer allergic reactions from this insect's bite.

Teuvo Berggren

73

Slash-and-Burn

The Finns used to practise a form of shifting cultivation called slash-and-burn or swidden, which has been altering the form of their country's forest landscapes for centuries. Its effects are still clearly visible.

Origins

Slash-and-burn was the earliest form of agriculture in many parts of the world. As its name indicates, it involved cutting down trees and bushes in forests and on scrubland, burning the vegetation and strewing seeds on the soil, now enriched by the nutrient-bearing ashes.

At first the soil was neither ploughed nor dug. The crop plants grew on the undrained land amid stones, tree stumps and unburnt trunks and roots. But the land yielded crops for only one to three seasons. The nutrients in the thin layer of ash were completely absorbed by the plants during that period or washed off by rain; after that, the farmers abandoned the land, which could not be cultivated again until new trees and bushes had grown there. If one attempts to cultivate burnt-over land for longer, its ability to nourish crops is exhausted. Then it must either be abandoned or a changeover made to field cultivation.

This form of shifting cultivation was formerly practised everywhere in Finland, with the exception of south-east, central and northern Lapland, the islands in the Gulf of Bothnia and many areas along the coast. However, the region with which slash-and-burn is most closely associated in the minds of today's Finns is the eastern part of their country: Savonia (or Savo) and Karelia.

In the Middle Ages, the only areas with fixed agricultural settlement on any larger scale were in Eastern Finland in the South Savo area. However, there was a considerable concentration of settlement in the area that now lies east of the Finnish border, especially in the part of Karelia fringing Lake Ladoga.

Pertti Huttunen

Big clearances

The pioneers who had settled the Savo heartland adopted a new eastern slash-and-burn agricultural method in the Middle Ages. The method differed from anything used earlier in Finland and apparently came from Russia, via the Karelian areas. It was now possible to burn forests containing large coniferous trees to produce land capable of yielding, albeit for only a few seasons, large quantities of rye per hectare. Farmland burned out of forests that had never been touched by the axe gave the Savonians an abundant supply of food and enabled them to spread rapidly into new areas to the north, east and west of their heartland. These migrations were stimulated not only by population growth, but also by the policies of Finland's then Swedish rulers. In the course of the 16th and 17th centuries, Savonian pioneers settled the regions that are today North Savo, Central Finland, North Karelia, the environs of Lake Oulujärvi, Kainuu, and even parts of the zone of southern Lapland.

Before the Swedish rulers distributed the forest to private peasant households from the years 1757 and 1777 onwards, anybody who wanted to could move onto and work it. A claim could be staked by cutting marks in tree trunks. The area in question was then reserved for the next ten years. The first step was to chop deep notches into the largest trees, after which they began drying out. The following spring, or perhaps even a year later, the settlers skied to the notched trees and felled them so that they lay side-by-side. The stoutest pines

Burnt over for cultivation as recently as the 19th century, this woodland now grows birch. The pile of stones picked from the fields is a hint of the toil that those farmers of the past performed.

were left standing among the felled ones intended for burning. The wood on the ground dried out during the spring and summer and one year later, when the weather presented the opportunity, the pioneers returned and set the lot alight. Once the fire had burned itself out, the unburnt remnants were gathered up into piles. The land was now left for a year to absorb the lye salt that the fire had produced. The piled-up remnants were then burnt. Nourished by the ashes, the grain crop grew in a landscape where some big trees still stood, having survived the fire. Thus the creation of farmland from forest was a complex task that arable cultivation, and the wood material produced by the forests began to be used for tar burning. In south-western Finland, it was restricted to small deciduous forests near villages. It continued to be practised in Savo until the early years of the present century, also in deciduous woodland. In the final stage, the method was used to produce land for turnips or in some cases barley, and to create pastures. This practice was abandoned in western Finland in the late 19th century, in East Häme in the 1910s and 1920s and in some East Savo districts only after the Second World War. In the 19th century, however, large-scale clearances, intended for several years of cultivation, were still conducted in Savo and North Karelia. "Rolling" was a relatively late innovation in slash-and-burn; when large areas were burnt over in the old days, the heat of the fire was enough to scorch the earth thoroughly, but "rolling" had to be done when smaller areas with less wood material were cleared. This meant that, using long poles as levers, burning logs were moved onto parts of the ground that had not yet been charred.

A waste of forest

In the period when slash-and-burn was at a peak, the regions where it was practised were quite prosperous in places, because this was a method that yielded well. However, a crisis developed in eastern Finland in the second quarter of the 19th century. Large-scale clearances, a too-short cycle of burning and cultivation and the limited number of crop varieties sown had consumed too much forest and impoverished the soil. The distributions of land had created private holdings, which could be inherited, and there was little "free" land left to claim. The Crown, too, was anxious to eradicate slash-and-burn in favour of fixed agricultural settlement. The authorities considered slash-and-burn a waste of forest, as it indeed eventually proved to be. As the last virgin forests disappeared, the same land was burned over, used for crops for a time and then left for the forest to re-

claim, before being cleared again. This was repeated too frequently. Slash-and-burn was a squandering of forest resources, and as pressure of population mounted, these resources were no longer adequate to bear the strain.

By the end of the 18th century, a considerable part of eastern Finland had been slashed-and-burned to the extent that travel writers of the period described it as more a land of scrub and stony wastes than of forests.

The signs today

As the 19th century advanced, slash-and-burn changed in character even in eastern Finland. Slowly but surely, large-scale clearances gave way to much smaller operations, usually intended to transform deciduous woods into good pastureland for the growing cattle population. By now, however, the main food crops were grown on land that had been cleared of tree stumps and stones, drained and fertilized with animal manure. In the final stage slash-and-burn was practised only by the lowest socioeconomic groups; the more prosperous farms had gone over entirely to field cultivation and intensive animal husbandry. The wood-processing industry, which grew strongly from the 1870s onwards, also helped reduce the popularity of slash-and-burn agriculture.

Today, there are still many areas of eastern Finland in which the forests are in a very early succession stage following slash-and-burn. The features which reveal this are open patches of grazing land, extensive stands of speckled alder and places in which birch is virtually the only tree species. Close to those areas one can also find dense stands of fairly young spruces, in which shallow ruts that were once drains and ruins close to piles of stones collected from the fields reveal how recently slash-and-burn agriculture was practised. With good luck, one may still find the remains of a wooden harrow in the forest — or with bad luck fall into a hole that obviously was once a turnip pit. MLi

Rotting the Forests

One of the "Seven Brothers" in Aleksis Kivi's famous novel was nicknamed "Tinder Matti", because he used the soft material inside tinder fungus as dry kindling. This shelflike growth specializes in decaying birch.

Wood decay is a familiar — and often bothersome — phenomenon everywhere. Although much is known about the processes that cause it, the full picture is still not clear.

One notices its effects most clearly when one walks in a forest that has never felt an axe. At the feet of stately spruces lie rotting trunks with fungi, often of the polypore family, growing on their flanks.

When a tree is wounded

Fungi produce tremendous numbers of reproductive cells, called spores, which are scattered into the environment with

Aimo Holtari

Heikki Kotiranta

wind currents. Mycelia, clusters of new fungi, sprout anywhere that the spores find a suitably moist resting place, but soon perish if they fail to find a growth substrate containing the nutrients they need. They cannot penetrate healthy bark, so they need places where branches have been broken off, where frost has cracked the bark or where birds or insects have caused scars. Trees often bear numerous scars of various kinds, but that does not necessarily mean that they are infected by fungi. The place where a small branch has been broken off is occluded by a layer of scar tissue, which prevents mycelia from penetrating to the nutrients below it. If the wound is larger, several structural changes intended to prevent microorganisms from penetrating the trunk take place in the tree. Other defensive mechanisms include chemical processes, such as the secretion of resin. Sometimes, however, these methods fail and microbes (bacteria, yeastlike fungi, moulds and basidiomycetes) get through and set about their destructive work.

It was long believed that only basidiomycetes, such as red-belt fungus and honey fungus, were the culprits behind tree decay. However, it is now known that bacteria, yeasts and moulds are often the first microbes to colonize wounds. Although they do not actually rot the wood themselves, they break down structures that the real decay-causing fungi cannot master. Mycelia of decay-causing fungi can be in a tree at the same time as bacteria and moulds. There they await their opportunity.

The progress of decay

Some rotting trunks are fibrous and light coloured inside, others fairly hard, but brittle, and brownish. Wood consists of fibrous cellulose, gummy hemicellulose and the brown material lignin. The fungi that cause decay in trees consume these in varying proportions. Those that eat mainly lignin and some cellulose leave light-coloured fibrous wood. Others, which prefer cellulose and hemicellulose, leave brownish brittle wood that breaks off in cube-like pieces.

A fungus can often grow inside a living tree, invisible but rotting it away all the time. Sporangia, which reveal the presence of fungi that have weakened it, often appear on the stump and trunk of a tree blown down by a storm.

Red-belt fungus, which is common in primeval forests, is one of the most attractive of the polypore family of fungi. It consumes cellulose, leaving almost pure lignin. A tree killed by red-belt fungus is not completely permeated by its mycelia; other fungi, too, can live there. In fact, most polypores are harmless to living trees, consuming only those that other fungi have killed. Many of them, such as red-belt fungi and a related species that lives on spruces, do not cause the final disappearance of fallen trees, but are eventually succeeded by other species, which in turn yield to others, and so on until all that remains is a moss-covered mound of wood in an advanced state of decomposition and barely recognizable as having once been a tree at all.

As bothersome as they often are, decay-causing fungi play an important role in the cycle

The range of polypore species is richest in old primaeval forests: red-belt fungi in the Pyhä-Häkki National Park. Unfortunately, this species thrives all too well in commercial forests, where it rots both pine and spruces.

of nature. Without them, wood material would lie unused once it has died. Thanks to them, it is converted into nutrients that new life can use. Fungi also play a key role in creating humus.

When harvesting methods are so efficient that trees are removed from forests, branches roots and all, there is nothing left for these agents of decomposition to feed on. The next generation of planted trees can grow only with the aid of artificial fertilization — if at all. A rotting tree in a forest does not signify so much the end of one life as the continuity of living nature. HKo

Hannu Hautala

KAINUU
REGION

VUOKATTI AND HIIDENPORTTI

Vuokatti fell rises sheer on the southwestern side of the village of Sotkamo above the surrounding forest and lakeland terrain. A road was constructed many years ago on Iso Pöllyvaara fell, so that nowadays visitors to the fell can practically reach the summit without even stepping out of their vehicles. Previously it was necessary to climb up on foot, and then the 200 metre ascent to the quartzitic rock forming the summit required one to be sound in wind and limb. The views from the top of Vuokatti are nothing short of breathtaking.

VUOKATTI FELL

Despite the convenience of a motorcar, a true picture of Sotkamo can only be obtained by shouldering a rucksack or haversack and disappearing for a few days into the craggy terrain and forests of the region. The forests here and there have been passed over by the sophisticated logging equipment that has replaced the axe.

Pekka Nurminen

Hiidenvaara, at the extreme southern tip of Sotkamo, is an ideal place from which to set out.

Hiidenvaara fell rises to over 340 metres. Up until very recently it remained an unexploited wilderness of primaeval forests. Its slopes now bear the large scars that are clearfellings. After logging, these have been ploughed and the deep furrows are visible from a long distance away. Some of the forests have mercifully been reprieved for the time being at least and the visitor can still back-pack among intact forests clothing the slopes. You may find signs of the enormous eagle owl, which is rare in the Kainuu region. Up until the 1950s there was always a pair of golden eagles living in a wilderness bearing no signs of the work of logging equipment. Occasionally perhaps someone would destroy the nest or even shoot one of the adult birds.

Thirty years ago everything suddenly changed. A logging road was built into the heart of the region and large-scale felling began. With logging taking place right next door to their nest, the eagles disappeared, only to return in the mid 1960s. Their nest site had now become a wide open expanse dotted with trees left for seeding purposes.

Nesting continued uninterruptedly season after season, until in 1983 it abruptly stopped — possibly owing to the attentions of foreign egg-thieves or bird of prey hunters. By the spring of 1984 there was no sign of the nest, as the large branch that had supported it had snapped under the weight of snow.

All this notwithstanding, on the approach to Ruostevaara fell, if you are carrying binoculars, carefully scan the clearfellings on the western slope. The pair of golden eagles are known to inhabit this area still and the naturalist may be lucky enough to catch a glimpse of these magnificent creatures which, with unhurriedly flapping wings, rise gracefully into the air.

DEATH OF A WILDERNESS HOUSE

At the foot of Ruostevaara fell in the centre of a small field at an altitude of over 300 metres proudly stands an old grey house and its outbuildings. For decades the Ruma house stood alone in the wilds well away from its nearest neighbour, at the end of little-used paths. Despite the eventual construction of a road up to the house, the small-holding was doomed. The house, around which the fell summit forests during the winter are clothed in such a heavy blanket of snow that the scene comes straight out of a fairy tale, has been deserted since the late 1960s. Nowadays it is still used during summer and the people living there look out on one of Finland's loveliest landscapes.

Alongside the road running northwest from the Ruma house there is a shallow dip at the bottom of which there are innumerable glasslike small fragments. These in fact are quartz crystals. Some of them are malformed, some are smooth, but the hiker who cares to take the trouble to examine them may find a clear, regularly formed crystal that flashes in the sun like a cut diamond. Smokey kaolin deposits occur in the same area which have been surveyed by interested mining companies. The Ruma house road joins the logging road going from Siirviönlehto to Maanselkä. The person who walks across the top of the Vuokatti chain is forced, however, to cross the road and continue north.

Among ancient spruces hung with beard-moss magnificent thick aspens grow whose canopies have been shaped by snow. The trunks of these aspens — not unusually for Finland — are full of woodpecker holes. The rarer three-toed woodpecker may with luck still be met hacking away at the bark of a dead spruce, while the more generally distributed greater-spotted woodpecker is common in years when conifer seeds are plentiful. Then too in this area it is possible to see birds of the crossbill tribe, of which the crossbill and parrot crossbill may be extremely abundant. In the low and stunted and twisted fell-summit spruce forests the two-barred crossbill also nests, but this species is not common even in the best 'seed years'.

Continuing the journey via the Aitolampi pools towards the more than 340 metre high Viiltovaara fell, the rambler may find many waders around the pools and on the peatlands. Among the tangle of vegetation at the edge of a bog or mire he may come across a Siberian jay family, while the black woodpecker's piercing cry echoes from the neighbourhood of the old aspen stand. In good vole years the Tengmalm's owl is common here in the gracefully undulating and peaty areas of the fell chains. The same region is also the standard place for the hawk-owl and on the peatlands the hen harrier can be seen gliding.

From Kalettomanvaara one descends to a wide and fairly deep, as well as very heavily logged, ravine. From there the ascent to Naulavaara fell begins. Right away during the first stages of the ascent one finds hidden among a patch of spruces the Havukka-aho cabin. Around this there are old clearfellings dating from several decades ago. These have partly become overgrown with underbrush and have partially been replanted with conifers.

Naulavaara fell is broad and fairly flat. Since there is no clear sheer ascent it is difficult to decide when one has actually attained the summit. At one point, however, one reaches an altitude of 368 metres. No single fell in the entire chain exceeds this height.

VILLAGES AND HIGH FELLS

The journey continues north towards Ylä-Mustinjärvi lake. Starting at Naulavaara fell, clearcuts have appeared here and there and a regrettably large number of them bear signs of artificial drainage in the form of deeply ploughed furrows, making them extremely difficult to cross.

The River Mustinjoki flows along a rift valley. Alongside the river there are large numbers of soapstone boulders. Soapstone is used in Finland for making fireplaces and stoves. Soapstone contains an abundance of talc which is perceived as a slipperiness when one rubs one's finger across the surface of the stone.

Slightly less than two kilometres away to the northwest there is a rift in the rocks running for several hundred metres. This is called Vuorirotko and along its bed runs the Vuoripuro stream. The 20-metre high walls

Antti Leinonen

Common throughout Finland, the kingcup is one of the first flowers of spring. In Kainuu it thus flowers in June.

of the gully have almost certainly once been the nesting places of the peregrine and golden eagle.

The kingcup is a common plant of the shores and fringes of lakes and one of the first flowers of the year over the whole country. Alongside the wilderness brooks of Kainuu it does not come into flower until June.

In the Teerivaara fell region the hiker walks towards the Urho Kekkonen National Park hiking trail (named after a previous president of Finland, Urho Kekkonen, this is marked with the statesman's initials 'UKK'). It offers fairly easy walking and avoids the worst and sheerest places, so that hikers who are beginning to feel fatigued would do well to make use of it. The trail also provides a good view of the most picturesque places, even though making one's own way across country with a map may enable one to see perhaps a bit more of these. After Teerivaara and Mustinlehto the terrain becomes very craggy.

At the bottom of many of the valleys one comes across a brook, in the neighbourhood of which there will be a lush growth of ferns. In these gullies the knowledgeable botanist will find a lot of old and in-teresting acquaintances. Lime occurs here and there in the bedrock, increasing the luxuriance of gullies and giving rise to a number of fens rich in plantlife. At this stage in the hike the fells no longer top 300 metres. On the steep slopes the going is difficult and calls for extreme caution. The south and southwestern slope of Martinvaara fell are so sheer that there is no question of going over them. At the foot of the sheer slopes there are dense knots of spruces. In these, in contrast to other parts of Kainuu, where they are rare, large numbers of wood warblers and chiffchaffs sing in the early summer.

The northern slope of Tolhovaara fell is both steep and rocky. There the spruce comes to an end and the dominant tree becomes a gnarled and twisted, low-growing Scots pine. The entire northern part of the fell consists of forests which on a summer night ring to the sweet song of the bluethroat and are worth visiting at this time of year for the sheer joy of listening to the liquid notes pouring out into the glades.

The quiet three-toed woodpecker prefers to live in old forests untouched by loggers. It carves out its nest

The quiet three-toed woodpecker prefers virgin forest.
In contrast to other woodpeckers, is usually nests in
coniferous tree trunks.

summer, the owlets are ready to leave their nest, if they have not yet done so. They are unable to fly for a week or two yet and walk about in the forest near the nest. If a human being approaches too close to a sitting parent or young brood, the mother may click her beak and growl like a dog in an attempt to warn the intruder off. This warning should be taken seriously, as the grey great owl under such circumstances will readily attack even a large man, inflicting painful scratches with its sharp talons. Since prey is also killed with the claws, these become a breeding ground for bacteria, some of which may be inserted into the wound. It is wise, therefore, to keep your distance if you chance on a nesting owl.

STEEP CANYON

Many of the visitors to Hiidenportti National Park are eager to see the steep-sided canyon running through the reserve from which the park has acquired its name ('Hiidenportti' literally means 'The Devil's gate'). In the vicinity of the first now-forested fields on Kovasinvaara fell, the track forks. When going towards the valley, one takes the left fork. After 500 metres the terrain becomes very stoney and most of the canyon, with its dozens of metres high rock faces, is suddenly revealed. The steepest rocky sides come to an end in the Hiidenportti area after a distance of only a few hundred metres, but the smaller cliffs go on in a southeasterly direction along the rift. There the hiker is offered further glimpses of primaeval Kainuu-type forested wilderness, in which peatlands of relatively small extent alternate with low-lying heaths. On the heaths hundreds of years old Scots pines decorated with the scaly bark typical to mature specimens of this tree thrust their flat canopies, like 'emergents' in a tropical rainforest, way above the surrounding trees. In the spruce forests clothing the damper soils the beard mosses hang down, like the wispy beards of old Chinamen, at roughly head height. PH

hole more frequently in coniferous trees than do the other woodpeckers. Although there are now only a few kilometres left of the Vuokatti hiking route, during the final three kilometres one is forced to climb no less than three fells, as well as to cross the deep valleys between them. If the hiker has not arranged to be picked up by motorised transport, he or she must now descend the Vuokatti downhill skiing slope before getting a lift to enable the trip to continue.

HIKING IN THE WILDERNESS

The great grey owl is one of the bird species nesting in ancient coniferous forest stands. This large and handsome bird is a vagrant (as distinct from a migrant), going from one high vole population area to another. In the Hiidenportti area the great grey owl generally appears at intervals of 3-4 years, when local vole populations reach their peak. Generally this owl chooses an old goshawk or buzzard nest as its nesting place, but it may also make use of a deep hollow on top of an old tree stump.

The owl lays in April, which is rather early in the year, and then proceeds to incubate the eggs for a month. When hikers arrive in the park at the beginning of

---

Hiidenportti National Park

Sotkamo, 40 sq.km
Established 1982
Under National Board of Forestry management

Connections: It is not possible to reach the park by public transport. The road from Sotkamo to Hiidenportti runs via Tipasoja. At its nearest point, the road comes to within a kilometre of Hiidenportti.

Services: The area is supplied with marked hiking trails. Alongside the trail from Lake Peurajärvi to Hiidenportti there are several cooking and camping spots with 'lean-to' sleeping places. Outside the park, on the southeastern side, lies the Peurajärvi recreation fishing area belonging to the National Board of Forestry.

Map: Basic map 1:20 000 nos. 432 08, 4322 11, 4322 12.

Further information: National Board of Forestry, Vaala District Office, tel. 986-26 571 (Kajaani).

Tar Burning, A Bygone Use of Forests

The roots of the Finnish word for "tar" (terva) show that the Finns have been familiar with this substance for at least a couple of thousand years. An old saying has it: "Whatever you do, do it with tar."

Background to tar burning

Voyages of exploration launched from countries far from Finland as the Middle Ages ended and the modern era was being ushered in were to have an indirect, but significant impact on conditions in Finland. Inspired by what the explorers had discovered, many European nations began vying for colonial possessions across the seas, and demand for ships grew to unprecedented proportions. Enormous quantities of tar and pitch were needed to build and maintain these vessels and their hemp ropes. Throughout the era of wooden ships and even for some time thereafter, Finland was the world's most important tar producer.

Exports began as early as the middle of the 16th century, initially at a level of a few hundred barrels a year. The volume grew steadily and by the end of that century thousands of barrels were being shipped from the ports of Viipuri and Turku. The tar trade entered a period of even more intensive growth in the early part of the following century. Viipuri handled 54,000 barrels in 1647. That represented a little over half of Finland's total tar exports.

Exports reached their peak in the 1860s. 227,000 barrels, i.e. over 28 million litres, was produced for export in 1863. A steady decline began before the end of the same decade and the annual volume had fallen below 100,000 barrels by the end of the century. Tar burning remained an important means of livelihood in the Kainuu region until the second decade of our century. It enjoyed a brief revival during the depression years of the early 1930s.

Our Tar Region

Tar was a cheap bulk product and producing it was economic only within a relatively short overland distance of an export harbour. However, if there were good water routes along which it could be brought to the coast, it could be profitably made deep in the interior. Large-scale production was initially concentrated in two regions: in the Saimaa and Päijänne lake systems and in Ostrobothnia on the west coast. There was also some production in Uusimaa (the province in which Helsinki is situated) and in another area in the south-western corner of the country.

When Viipuri, the seaport through which eastern Finland's exports flowed, was lost to Russia under the terms of the Treaty of Uusikaupunki in 1721, tar production in the Finnish interior went into a catastrophic decline. Production now shifted increasingly to Ostrobothnia. When the coastal forests that fuelled the industry were exhausted, production gradually shifted further inland. West and South Ostrobothnia were the main production areas in the 18th century, but North Ostrobothnia's role began growing towards the end of the century and Oulu became the main export gateway. Tar was brought to the city in large rowing boats from as far east as the Kainuu region. After Finland was wrested from Swedish rule in 1809 and became an autonomous grand duchy within the Russian Empire, Kainuu became Finland's and the world's last stronghold of tar burning.

Debarked forests

Tar was always made from pine. In spring, when the trees were bursting with sap, their bark was stripped away up to a height of over a fathom (or about two metres). A strip about the width of a hand was

1. Tar trees are stripped of bark up to about the height that a man could reach standing.
2. The trees were felled 3-4 years after they had been stripped and then taken on horse-drawn sleds to the pit. Splitting them into strips was best done in winter, when the wood was brittle.

Pictures on this and the following two pages by Eero Naskali.

left on a tree's north side to keep it alive. A couple of summers later, the bark stripping was continued using a stepped frame. Stripping away the bark accelerated resin formation in the debarked section of the tree. Each tree yielded a trunk section four metres or so in length for tarmaking. The best result was obtained when the stripping was done in three stages, enabling the maximum amount of resin to form. The trees stripped were in a stand taken over in a common forest, i.e. one which anybody was entitled to use.

Three or four years after they had been stripped of bark, the trees were felled. It was customary to do this after Michaelmas, when the harvest was home and the bogs and lakes had frozen enough to bear the weight of a man. The trees were felled and split up using axes. Before the snow became too deep, the trunks were drawn by sled to the edge of the tar pit and laid out in rows. When heavy frosts descended and the wood became brittle, the work of splitting it into thin strips began. This was done by two men, striking in turn with their axes. The wood was split into strips thinner than a fencing board and wedge-shaped in that one end was thicker than the other. These were then stacked around the pit.

Trenches and funnels

There were two kinds of tar pits: long trenches and deep funnel-shaped pits. Tar was also made in kilns in the 18th century, but the experiment was soon abandoned and only attempted again on a limited scale in the middle of the next century. Kilns were only of marginal significance in the heyday of tarmaking.

Trench pits were used only to make tar for households' own use. In this method, the wood strips were placed lengthwise on bark sheets placed in the bottom of a slanting longish trench. They were then covered with more sheets of bark and peat. The bottom sheet of bark was curled to form a pipe, along which the tar flowed. The wood in the trench was ignited from the top. The fire was kept

burning by the breeze, or by waving fans if there was no wind, and the heat spread downwards. Small quantities of tar could also be made using a large iron pot. The pieces of wood were placed under an upside-down pot and the tar was boiled out by stacking more wood over the pot and burning it.

The pits used for large-scale tar production were in the shape of a rather flat funnel, with a depth about a tenth of their diameter. In the simplest type of funnel pit, the tar container was simply a barrel sunk into the middle and covered by a wooden floor. It could be retrieved only when the pit had burned out and cooled down. By contrast, in the method most commonly used for commercial-scale tar production from the 17th century onwards, the tar ran out of the bottom of the pit through a pipe. As in the case of trench pits, funnel-shaped ones were, whenever possible, built on a hillock to ensure an adequate fall in the

pipe leading out from the bottom. A secondary trench, in which the collection barrels were placed, was dug at the other end of the pipe, which was a hollowed-out pine log. To prevent the tar from flowing anywhere else than through the pipe, the bottom of the pit and the joint where the pipe entered it were sealed by applying a layer of clay or mud and compacting it. A covering of fir bark sheets was laid on top of this. An additional refinement used in the Hyrynsalmi district involved placing a layer of birch switches in a frame around the edge of the pit to support the ends of the wood strips. The strips themselves were arrayed in a radial pattern in the pit, with their thinner ends in the centre. This meant that the outer edge of the woodpile rose faster as it was stacked up, and the tar flowed towards the centre of the pit when the pile was set alight. As the wood was being placed in the pit, it was rammed with piles to ensure that it was the

3. The first stage of charging the pit. The bark sheets covering the bottom and the switches around the edge are still visible.

4. Final preparation of the pit. On the right, the master tarmaker hammers the woodpile into shape.

5. Igniting the pit. In a few moments, the ring of fire around the base will be covered with peat, but the fire will smoulder on and up along the edge of the woodpile.

6. The pit after it has been burning for more than a couple of days. The tar is now flowing into the barrels.

7. Two tar barrels set into a frame and with axles driven into their ends act as their own wheels.

8. A tar boat carrying 23 barrels approaches a set of rapids.

shape of an upturned pot. Berry bushes torn up by the roots and with peaty divots attached were then placed around the edge of the pile, their roots out-

wards. Thanks to the bush stems, there was enough air between the tar-bearing wood and the peat to ensure even ignition. A belt about twenty centimetres high around the bottom of the pile was left uncovered to facilitate ignition, but it, too, was covered once the wood had been set alight. A pile of clay on a deep layer of moss on top of the pile was used to control the fire while the pile smouldered.

Burning

Burning a large pile was a very demanding task. Under the supervision of a skilled tarmaker, the fire smouldered at a steady rate and the temperature inside the pile rose so high that the wood "sweated" its tar. It took five or six days to burn a medium-sized pile. When the operation was performed properly, about 30 litres of tar could be obtained from a cubic metre of high-quality wood. In the heyday of tarmaking, an average pit produced 40-50 barrels, but yields of over 100 barrels have also been reported. An average pit was approximately 9-10 metres in diameter. Some of the largest had diameters of as

much as 20-30 metres.

Transporting the barrels

A certain number of barrels were needed for each burning operation. They had to be sturdy ones, bound with eight hoops and holding 24 gallons (125 litres). Since the size a barrel had to be was precisely stipulated, a stave measure was used when it was being made. Barrel manufacturing was supervised by a crown official, whose seal of approval was marked on every barrel with a hot iron.

The tarmakers made their own barrels. As a rule, when they were stripping bark from trees in the forest, they left the straightest and smoothest pines to be used for making barrels. Wherever large knotless firs were available, they were used to save pines.

Barrel-making, too, took a lot of time: from one spring to the next. Around Lady Day in February, using boards that had been seasoning for over a year,

the coopers began making the barrels in preparation for the tar-burning season in early summer. Very close attention had to be paid to the quality of the barrels, which would have to stand the many stresses and strains of their long trips overland and then across the sea. The tar pits were seldom so favourably located that the barrels could be rolled straight to the long rowing boats moored at the water's edge. They had to be hauled long distances either on sleds or carts or, with a special frame allowing two barrels to act as a set of wheels, pulled by horses. Those trips were often kilometres long.

The tarmakers had to earn their money hard, because it took 10-15 days of hard work to make a barrel of tar. But the annual rhythm of the work fitted in well with the demands of agriculture. Income from tarmaking was a useful supplement that enabled people in districts like Kainuu to cope in years of major crop failures.
EN

Fire Renews the Forest Environment

Esko Männikkö

Fires have been an inseparable part of our forests' development, and every one of our heath-based forest environments has had a conflagration at least once every 500 years on average, in some cases much more often.

Most of the forest blazes during the first half of our century were caused by careless handling of fire. In older times they were often deliberately started, especially near villages, in order to provide pasturage for cattle. And that does not include slash-and-burn operations to convert forest for agricultural use. But lightning has also been a major cause of forest fires, which have played a significant role in the development of our environment.

Ground fires and crown fires

When a forest fire breaks out, the flames can advance in two ways. When they remain close to the ground and do not rise very high up the tree trunks, one speaks of a ground fire. In such a case, the devastation is relatively slight and patchy in its effects. The trees and undergrowth in the areas skirted by the flames remain unchanged. Even the areas that are burnt over are affected to different degrees. A ground fire is usually of such low intensity that most pines survive it. Fir, with its thin bark and shallow roots, is almost always destroyed.

When a fire is so powerful that it rises to the tops of the trees and spreads from one to another, it is called a crown fire. Its impact on both trees and undergrowth is devastating, and in practice everything is destroyed. The only exceptions are some outstandingly large pines, which have a chance of surviving.

Fire can also spread across a bog. It can penetrate the peat and smoulder on in places, sometimes erupting into flame again weeks after a blaze has been extinguished.

A forest fire can spread only if the forest is dry and the plants are susceptible to it. Mixed stands of pine and spruce catch fire easiest of all.

Blazes in forests of this kind can reach great intensity, because the volume of material to burn is so large. The intensity of a fire also determines what state the forest and its undergrowth will be in after the flames have swept through it. A ground fire can sometimes sweep through an area and do hardly any damage, but after a severe one it may take a very long time for the undergrowth to re-establish itself. Some areas in Lapland have remained permanently in an unforested state after a fire.

There are clear differences between regions with respect to the frequency of forest fires. The verdant heathland forests of southern Finland, often covered in deciduous species, are much harder to ignite than the dry, bleak heathlands of northern Finland. There are also major differences from one year to another, because the danger of fires is obviously much less during rainy summers than when there are long periods of hot dry weather and vegetation becomes as dry as tinder.

Recovery of burnt forests

The most important factor in the natural recovery of an area after it has been swept by a forest fire is how many trees survive. If all the trees are destroyed, the proximity and character of a neighbouring forest have the greatest effect on the development of the new generation of trees. Species with light seeds, such as poplar and birch, spread over greater distances, whereas the heavy seeds of coniferous trees can travel no more than a few trunk diameters from the parent.

If pines survive a fire, as they often do, the burnt area is reaf-forested relatively rapidly. Pine seeds germinate well in the soil exposed by the fire and soon a healthy stand of young trees has established itself. On bleak, dry heathland the seedlings grow into dense stands of trees with straight polelike trunks. If left undisturbed, they eventually become suitable for use as saw logs.

If the growth substrate is fairly dry or fresh heath and if

there are seed-bearing birches nearby, birch begins growing among the pines. This kind of mixed forest follows a growth pattern in which the birches may initially outgrow the pines, but later develop slower than them. However, if the pine gets a head start early in its development, both species can grow at more or less the same rate overall. Some time later, fir appears in abundance as undergrowth, and the result is soon a mixed forest with pine and birch the dominant species, but fir waiting to take over, eventually, the dominant role. However, even a small fire can end this development, with only pine benefitting, and a new cycle begins. Literature dealing with the major forest fires in the beginning of the century mentions them as the reason for the abundance of young pine stands in this country.

The greening of the black land

The development of new life in burnt-over areas begins from roots that have remained unscathed in the soil. The first to reappear are bilberries and cowberries (red whortleberries), two shrubs which spread well on other fairly dry and fresh heathland also. On a moist growth substrate, the soil protects their roots from even the most intense fire.

In places that have been severely charred, the return of vegetation follows a completely different pattern. Here, growth stems from wind-borne seeds or spores. The most common mosses, also the first to arrive, are cord moss and related varieties, and then hair moss, which is somewhat longer-lived than the other two.

Of the grass plants, fireweed spreads just as fast as mosses. It thrives very well in areas that have been burnt and quickly forms dense coherent stands. In time, however, these new plants go into recession and typical forest species regain their lost ground. The return of trees promotes this development.

On dry heathland, where the dominant species is heather, fire wreaks greater havoc than on semi-dry or moist heaths. The moss carpet, which is relatively thick in places, can remain virtually unscathed, whereas the heather is destroyed quite thoroughly. The areas that have been well charred are soon invaded by mosses and fireweed. But the heather, by means of wind-borne seeds, fairly quickly regains its status as the dominant species and soon re-occupies the whole burnt area, where it reigns supreme until trees move in and, overshadowing the heather, stunt its growth. Now feather moss, too, re-occupies its former habitat and the pattern of vegetation once again begins to resemble what it was before the fire raged through it.

On bleak heaths, where the vegetation largely consists of lichens, large expanses of soil can be completely exposed after a fire. New growth mainly depends on seeds and spores carried in by the wind, and it can sometimes take years before clear signs of vegetation re-establishing itself are visible. The mosses that begin growing are of the same species as in other burnt-over areas, but their period of dominance is clearly longer than elsewhere. About twenty years after the fire, the first vegetation to have established itself goes into clear decline and the species that ordinarily belong to bleak heathlands reclaim their old habitat. A noteworthy feature is that Iceland moss, the most highly developed of our lichen species, becomes abundant again only about 50 years after a forest fire. EKu

Charred stumps remain as reminders of a forest fire for decades, until they too are covered by vegetation.

Aimo Halteri

Antti Leinonen

Few primaeval, or virgin, forests exist in Finland nowadays. The ones that remain are largely inside national parks and strict nature reserves. In them live the vestiges of the wealth of insect life that inhabited Finland in the 1800s when primaeval forests were extensive.

Some of the species present then have since vanished — probably forever.

The insect fauna of commercially managed forests differs considerably from that of the old virgin forests. Although many of the commoner species occur in both types of habitat, many species which are rare in commercial forests are as a rule rather common in the primaeval forests. Certain important groups of insects, like butterflies and moths and orthopterans (grasshoppers and bush crickets) are present in very small numbers in virgin forests. Species that have accompanied man as he has replaced the forest by arable land, road verges, and gardens, do not occur at all in untouched forests. Primaeval forests constitute the last remaining strongholds of the original boreal coniferous forest insect fauna.

Primaeval forest habitats

From an insect's standpoint the most important features of a virgin forest are microclimatic stability, humidity, shade, and particularly the wealth of rotting wood, much of which is in the form of large tree trunks. What species live in a particular rotting log depends on several factors, including the species of tree, the stage of decay, the saprophytic fungus that is breaking it down, the type of forest, the soil properties, local humidity conditions, and the size and position of the trunk. It is only natural for such a diversified environment to support a wide variety of insects.

Parasitic and saprophytic fungi growing on dead wood are also correlated with a specialised insect fauna, while these fungi themselves harbour a number of species confined to virgin forests. Insect life is enriched, too, by the deciduous tree species that are scattered

Endangered Insects

among the conifers, in particular old sallows and giant aspens. The algae, bark, bark-clasping mosses and lichens, and wood in various stages of decomposition, all provide important sources of nourishment, as well as shelter, for many insects and other invertebrates. By contrast, the field layer in primaeval forests is only weakly developed. It is, moreover, dominated by dwarf shrubs like bilberry, cowberry and ling.

Troops of decomposers occupying decaying wood at various stages fall into four main regiments. As soon as a tree dies it is visited for a brief period by

a small platoon of insects living in the bark: these include bark beetles, as well as 'hangers on' who live in the tunnels made by these and many of whom turn out to be parasites or predators. At the next, similarly short stage, a company of insects specialised in living under bark and within the surface layer of the actual wood, or alternatively grazing on saprophytic fungi, moves in. At this stage the loosened bark starts to drop off, exposing the wood beneath. During the third stage, which usually lasts for several decades, the tree is occupied by insects whose job it is to get

Deadwood in ancient forests (above) offers an ideal environment to a range of insect species, many of them beetles (below).

Kari Heliövaara

down to the business of tackling the actual wood. This particular regiment consists of species that are considered to have declined most drastically over the past few decades. Finally, the decayed wood starts to crumble away into soil and its inhabitants are replaced by soil dwelling insects. In addition to the latter, many other organisms, for instance other arthropods, snails, slugs and many small soil animals, now play their part.

Few butterflies and moths

Few species of Lepidoptera inhabit primaeval forests. There are almost no butterfly species, the green hairstreak (Callophrys rubi) and cranberry blue (Vacciniina optilete) being notable exceptions. On the edges of swampy areas the number of species is greater, and especially in North Finland many of the peatland species also regularly fly in the forest. The rare Xestia borealis occurs only in a very narrow area of comparatively open virgin forest with a carpet of moss in eastern and western Lapland. Certain other types of noctuids also appear to favour primaeval forests. Typical geometers of the darker parts of such forests, where the herbage is sparse are Jodis putata, Chloroclysta latefasciata, a pug moth Eupithecia conterminata, Eulithis populata and a carpet moth Lampropteryx otregiata. All of these species are also found in commercial forests. While many of them feed in the caterpillar stage on dwarf shrubs and conifers, species like Scardia polypori, a 'micro', have more unusual pabula. S.polypori feeds on bracket fungi. Perhaps the most well-known of Finland's virgin forest species is Borearctia menetriesii. Details of the life history of this yellow and green tiger moth, which is now almost certainly extinct, having been last seen in Pyhä-Häkki National Park in 1943, are incompletely known.

Beetles to the fore

Most of the typical members of the virgin forest insect fauna belong to the Order Coleoptera. Some of them have already vanished from Finland, including the blood-red Cucujus haematodes and the large Cerambicid, Leptura thoracica. On the other hand, the commoner ancient forest species like the turtle-shaped Ostoma ferruginea and the flattened Dendrophagous crenatus, which has a habit of retreating backwards when it feels itself threatened, can with luck still be found in rotting wood in commercially managed forests.

A close relative of C.cinnaberinus which, as it its name implies, is cinnabar red in colour, lives in dead aspen trunks just under the bark. Like many other primaeval forest beetles it is in imminent danger of disappearing from the Finnish fauna. In the same situations one can also find Hololepta plana, Hylochares cruentatus, and the buprestid Ipidia sexguttata sexguttata whose abundance is in inverse proportion to the length of its name: it has been seen just four times during the present century!

First discovered at Kolva, Yläne in the early 1800s, Pytho kolwensis — a flattish, black beetle 1.5 cm in length — lives only in the decaying trunks of exceptionally large spruce trees that have been vacated by battalions of bark beetles. The larva (illustrated above) bears a pair of pincer-like appendages at the end of its abdomen. There are few suitable habitats for this international rarity outside national parks and strict nature reserves. Tragosoma depsarium is a magnificent brown cerambicid that attains a length of three centimetres and whose larva burrows into decaying spruces which in life are typically candle-shaped owing to heavy winter snows. Ditylus laevis by contrast favours soggy spruce trunks.

The list of species unable to come to terms with today's manicured, carefully controlled forests is extended by Boros schneideri, Peltis grossa, and Finland's largest buprestid, Chalcophora mariana — if indeed the latter still exists in Finland. Last seen in this country in 1953, the species has been discovered in Sweden living — much to the amazement of coleopterists — in untreated railway sleepers! Under normal cir-

Kari Heliövaara

A narrow-waisted bark beetle, Pytho kolwensis, whose larva is shown above, breeds only in fallen, rotting spruce trunks. These are rare in managed forests.

cumstances the beetle inhabits rotting Scots pine trunks and roots. Although many kinds of staphylinids are also confined to virgin forests, the biology of these is regretably very poorly known.

Lack of facts

Details concerning inhabitants of primaeval forests from other insect groups are even more scanty. The habitats and habits of certain bracket fungus hemiptera suggest that these, too, belong to the original primaeval forest fauna. Cixidia confinis, a relatively large and butterfly-like plant hopper, and its northern relative C.lapponica, crawl about under the bark of rotting Scots pines, where they live off the juices of fungal hyphae. When faced with danger, the adults take a flying leap distinguished not only by its length but also by its direction, which is almost horizontal. C.confinis is known only from Finland, Sweden and Estonia, C.lapponica being found in addition in Siberia.

The wide variety of fungi found in virgin forests has encouraged specialisation among the fungus gnats. While most of these are of gnat-like dimensions, Keoplatus sesiodes excels in having both the build and appearance of a wasp. Sadly, it appears to have vanished from Finland. As a larva it preys on other insects which it captures with the aid of a web spun underneath a bracket fungus. Solva interrupta and Europe's only member of its family, Pachyneura fasciata, also number among the ancient forest rarities.

It is highly probable that each of these species is parasitised by some other species. Unfortunately, we know almost nothing about the latter.

Protection of primaeval forest species

Elucidating facts relating to the fauna of primaeval forests is now imperative. Even in protected areas, the insect fauna is slowly but surely dwindling. Decimated by adverse environmental factors, insect populations have no chance of establishing themselves elsewhere, as there is simply nowhere for them to go to. Acid rain also takes its toll of virgin forest wildlife. Moreover, there is a gradual influx of the species accompanying the manmade environment surrounding the preserves.

Forests are no longer renewed due to natural forest fires. Species confined to burnt forests, e.g. Agonum bogemanni, Aradus anisotamus and A.signaticornis) are vanishing from Finland and indeed may have already disappeared.

Forest fires pose a major problem for nature conservation: with protected areas being so small, one fire could conceivably wipe out the primaeval forest of an entire preserve. It is thus not possible to consider burning areas artificially. Besides, virgin forests regenerate themselves over a period of time, albeit slowly. RV

THE BACKWOODS OF KUHMO

Despite the drastic effects of forestry and quest for energy Kainuu has retained its reputation as an undeveloped commune. Many enthusiasts of primaeval forest, rapids and pure water lakes direct their steps towards Kainuu summer after summer. However, if one simply sets out in no particular direction, one soon comes across large clearfellings, for the areas still in a natural state are of limited extent and may easily be passed by.

As elsewhere in Kainuu, the forests of Kuhmo commune consist largely of clearfellings, young plantations and drained peatlands. However, the true backwoods of the region are nothing short of unique. Without a doubt Kuhmo contains the most magnificent virgin forests in Finland. There the rambler suddenly experiences the sensation of having being spirited away to another world. While these are now of small extent, they contain one of the northern Europe's richest faunas.

Forest wildernesses in the north are generally almost as silent as the grave, but at Kuhmo the forests teem with life: brown bears, wild deer, gluttons, wolves and pine martens, cranes, geese and whooper swans. Black kites hover overhead, Siberian jays grow fat in the spruce forests, and capercaillies still gather in flocks at the junctions of streams and bogs. Many species are present in higher numbers than they would normally be, owing to the fact that clearfellings and a network of roads prevent animals coming over the eastern border from penetrating any further west.

A SUMMER HIKE TO LENTUA

Lentua is Kainuu's only large lake that is not these days subject to water level regulation at the hands of man. The Lentuankoski rapids are also still in an untouched condition: rapids shooting trips are organised for visitors under the direction of local experts. As if this were not enough, the dozens of islands and islets on the lake, which are owned by the National Board of Forestry, have been left in a virgin state. Almost everywhere these islands are surrounded by sandy beaches; in just a handful of places broken rock faces rear straight up out of the lake. Lentua offers the whole family unequalled opportunity for hikes lasting several days.

Upon arriving at the main Kuhmo-Suomussalmi road, the rambler is faced with several choices. It is easiest to travel by boat down the River Isojoki. After only a couple of kilometres rowing, Multisärkä is reached. This is a

Gazing sleepily out from the depths of the forest, this great grey owl could well be taken for a goblin. Such owls should never be approached when on their nest, as they will readily attack.

Antti Leinonen

sandy esker laid down during the last Ice Age jutting out like a large finger into the lake on the southern side of the island of Multisaari. Its shores are composed of the finest sand, sloping up to Scots pine woods that are very dry underfoot and support little undergrowth. Multisaari is also the first place at which one may spot the rare wild forest reindeer, the nearest relative of Lapland's domesticated reindeer.

Despite the beauty of Multisaari, it is Kotasaari that takes the prize. This appears on the western side of your boat as you head north, its sandy beaches stretching for several kilometres. The sand almost everywhere bears the hoofprints of the wild forest reindeer. With respect to spotting the animals themselves, the quieter the better — and there is nothing less obtrusive than a canoe. Deer and elk seem to regard as perfectly natural a thin crocodile-like shape gliding silently through the water. But watch the wind — the human scent is a different matter altogether!

The deer at Lentua in summer are almost all bucks, as the entire lake and its islands are strictly speaking the deers' wintering grounds. Outside the rut, which takes place in October, deer herds tend to be doe-dominant, the does and calves hiding away in the shady spruce forests on the eastern fringe of Kuhmo. The emotions cannot fail to be stirred in summer by the sight of a group of bucks, their antlers jutting proudly, swimming across a sound in the evening sunlight.

In winter some five hundred deer gather on Lentua island and on the lake's shores. On open lake ice, with a good view all around, the wild forest reindeer, the fleetest of foot of all the Nordic animals, feels itself safe. This behaviour is indicative of an earlier adaptation to predation by wolves, for even in winter these days a wolf is a rarity at Lentua. This difference in behaviour makes domesticated reindeer an easy prey for wolves, in comparison to their wild relative.

The sheer size of the herds at Lentua can be judged by the lack of the globular species of reindeer lichen, whose thalli once covered the sand spits and barren heaths in an off-white carpet. So great is the effect of these deer on the reindeer lichen growth that the deer herds will be obliged to seek their food further west. This, in fact, has already occurred once, in the 1970s, when the WWF, working in cooperation with the authorities, transferred some wild forest reindeer to Salamajärvi National Park. This introduction succeeded and a healthy herd of some 60 head now exists in the park.

RUSSET TRIP TO ELIMYSSALO

On a road map Kuhmo resembles a fishing net. It seems impossible that the country's most famous wilderness, Elimyssalo, could be ensconced in this area.

From the hiker's point of view, Elimyssalo's main point is not its size but its character, for it is a unique snippet of eastern forest taiga. During the past few decades the extent of the forests and trackless wilds of Elimyssalo have been reduced by about a half.

What, then, makes Elimyssalo so valuable today?

Elimyssalo is not Finland's oldest and wildest primaeval forest, the darkest, deepest forests being located in Ylvinsalo Strict Nature Reserve. Neither is Elimyssalo the only locality at which the rare wild forest reindeer breeds, as during the three decades in which they have radiated into Finland from the region of the White Sea these deer have become tame and adapted to Finnish conditions. Nowadays they live and multiply as well in the small tracts of forests that survive in Kuhmo.

Elimyssalo's value lies in the forests themselves and in its fauna as a whole. There is no other place in Fennoscandia in which all the large animals of the original taiga fauna continue to live together. Elimyssalo is still Kuhmo's best locality for the breeding of the wild forest reindeer. Bean geese guide their progeny to its pools, and whooper swans nest every year hither and thither on its peatlands, as well as on Lake Elimysjärvi. Beavers have dammed the River Elimysjoki into a series of stepped sections. Innumerable cuckoos vie with each other on early summer evenings; in the winter capercaillies feed silently in the twisted peatland pine trees.

Elimyssalo is a watershed, the kingdom of the spruce and Scots pine, a forest of beard moss and thousands of dried 'snags'. While the contribution of deciduous trees to the forests is minimal, Elimyssalo is far from being monotonous. Behind dim spruce forests the land opens out into fens and sphagnum bogs with, here and there, a small pool or two. Streams and springs have paved the way for rather luxuriant vegetation. Lines of dried grey 'snags' delight the eye on the otherwise open fens. Elimyssalo is a beautiful forest. Its details combine to form every Finn's conception of an untouched wilderness.

The backwoods are at their most splendid in autumn, when the leaves of the vegetation along the stream banks, and of the aspens and birches, turn golden yellow, and the Chamaedaphne and dwarf birch bogs in parts turn a delicate shade of purple.

Owing to the continental climate, snow often falls directly on top of such russet tones. On mornings following snowy nights in the autumn it is difficult to believe that the view is real. This explains why most hikers and naturalists come here in the autumn.

A few years ago the National Board of Forestry established a trail, complete with planks and logs over the wetter situations, starting at Viiksimo and skirting Lake Elimisjärvi. At the same time a real log lean-to was erected on the lake's Saunaniemi promontory for the purpose of providing hikers with a base camp from which to explore the heartlands.

Even though the number of visitors has steadily grown, the wild animals have not withdrawn over the the eastern border. This is probably because most hikers follow the well-marked trails and the animals have thus learned that they have nothing to fear from them.

Owing to its shrunken size, Elimyssalo is unsuitable for the usual form of hiking. Many people arrive there just to get a glimpse of mammals and birds in their natural surroundings. Such needs have been catered for by

The River Elimysjoki offers the region's beaver populations ideal surroundings.

Mauri Rautkari

conducting vehicles to Viiksimo, whence visitors leave on foot for the Saunaniemi camping site. With a base camp firmly established, the rambler is able to make sorties into the wilds. Everyone has a good chance of seeing a wild forest reindeer. The larger carnivores are something else again, as they remain carefully hidden from prying eyes.

ULVINSALO — DARK AND MYSTERIOUS

Most of Ulvinsalo lies on the border zone, to which access (especially for foreigners) is very restricted. This makes the strict nature reserve unique in the sense that it is Finland's only guarded reserve! Access to any strict nature reserve is by special permit only, and permission must be obtained well in advance from the National Board of Forestry's Kuhmo District Office. Ulvinsalo in places consists of very old, mature forests. A first-class view of really ancient Scots pines can be had almost from the trail itself. Along the stream courses there are large spruces hung with beard moss half a metre in length. Both spruces and Scots pines lie rotting in natural

disarray on a carpet of moss. Owing to the barrenness of the habitat, the animal life at Ulvinsalo is not as rich as the Elimyssalo fauna. The wild forest reindeer is rare there, since there are no peatlands of a type able to furnish the animal with pastures on which to browse. Among the larger mammals, it is the brown bear that has most frequently crossed the writer's path. The elk, whose meat is a great favourite of the bear, has a route going right through Ulvinsalo. One day in late summer I was slowly creeping upwind towards a bear's kill, when I stumbled upon the fellow himself sound asleep. Rudely awakened, the bear reared up on its hindlegs and let me know in bear language exactly what it thought of a person who had the effrontery to disturb its afternoon nap. Stumbling irritably off, it turned after a hundred metres or so and treated me to another outburst of bad language.

The glutton at one time had a much-used path running from the southeast to the northwest on both sides of the reserve's northern border.

As at Elimyssalo, black kites circle the open peat-

93

lands and the clearcuts surrounding the reserve. These birds are glimpsed much more frequently than the golden eagle, which in fact nests regularly within the confines of the reserve.

THE ISO-PALONEN TRAIL AND RUINED JUORTANANSALO

In order to promote tourism, the National Board of Forestry some time ago established a marked trail around Lake Iso-Palonen, leaving the forests around it intact. It was soon noticed, however, that back-packers tended to head for Elimyssalo rather than to come here.

Some people, however, do make use of the trail. The nearby old Ryti-Palonen cabin is much in favour as a place for holding courses and summer conferences, and the trail provides the most convenient means of exploring the local forests. The National Board of Forestry also issues hunting permits for tourists in the Iso-Palonen area. On autumn weekends there is thus quite a large influx of visitors intent on bagging mountain hares, and in some years game birds as well.

The fact is, however, that the Iso-Palonen trail is admirably suited to exploration by the whole family. There are plenty of ready-made lean-to's alongside the trail, where it is convenient to brew up coffee or tea. The trail meanders for the most part along the backs of high sandy eskers, from which many small lakes, gleaming invitingly, can be seen.

Right up until the mid-1970s the sandy areas of the Iso-Palonen lake area constituted the wild forest reindeer's most important, indeed almost their only, winter pasture. Only when the deer had browsed away most of the lichen, turning it to the characteristic black 'beans' that mark the animals' presence in an area, did they begin to migrate to Lentua for the winter as an alternative to starving to death. The situation has now deteriorated at Lentua to the extent that the deer are being forced to seek new pastures from even further afield.

The multitude of small bogs and mires ensconced in the wild forests of Iso-Palonen are popular with wild forest reindeer during the summer. In the warmer parts of the year, the deer eat mire and fen plants, obtaining enough vitamins from these to last for the winter as well; when the snow is on the ground they are forced to eat lichens, a diet which can be alikened to eating nothing but very white bread. In the summer at Iso-Palonen one can see both large bucks, with a good spread of antlers, and does with their calves. It is most probable that a large proportion of those Finns who have seen a wild forest reindeer actually in the wild have seen it at Iso-Palonen. The Iso-Palonen landscape is of such an open kind that even ramblers on a conducted tour usually have little difficulty in spotting a wild reindeer or two.

While Iso-Palonen fails to reach the standard of Elimyssalo, it does harbour the diversity of animal life that is the hall mark of the remote Kuhmo reaches. Towards the end of the autumn it is possible to find the spoor of a wolf, there is an osprey's nest in a large pine tree close to the trail, and the streams are dammed by beavers,

who live on the watercourses in conspicuous lodges.

There has been no attempt at attracting visitors to Juortanansalo, in the northeastern quarter of the commune. As recently as ten years ago there was a growth of sturdy trees near the eastern border extending without interruption for about three leagues from Juortananjärvi to Suomussalmi. This lovely tract of forest was broken only by the road running to the idyllic Karelian village of Kuivajärvi.

The systematic dissection of this forest began with the building of the road and railway to Kostomuksha, in the USSR, where Finns were working under contract on a large project. In the present decade these fine backwoods have been split into innumerable tiny pieces by a large complex of logging roads.

Juortansalo provides us with a unique opportunity to see the effect of modern forestry policy on ancient stands of Scots pine.

Apart from the decimated virgin forests, Juortanansalo boasts a wide variety of water-logged treeless bogs and mires, as well as a collection of streams and brooks on a scale unequalled by any other locality in Kuhmo. These are to come under official protection. Many kinds of birds nest on the extensive peatlands of Lapinsuo and Valtasensuo. Lake Saarijärvi, surrounded by brooks, treeless Sphagnum bogs, and pools, has a wealth of birdlife that is unusual in Kainuu. There is a marked nature trail running right around the lake.

A small tract of intact wilderness has also been spared on the western and southwestern side of the road lying between Vartius and Suomussalmi. This area being supplied with few paths, the rambler will find a map and a good compass essential.

Although modern forestry has made great inroads into Juortanansalo, there is still more wildlife at the latter locality than at any other in the Kuhmo district. Large herds of wild forest reindeer move around in it in summer. It seems highly probable that these animals have become crossed to a certain extent with the herds belonging to the Halla reindeer herdsmen's association.

Despite the scant cover provided by clearfellings, wolves and brown bears continue to prey on Juortanansalo's large elk populations. On large peatlands bounded by a solid wall of trees the rambler is unlikely to consider it strange for a golden eagle to suddenly swoop down, causing fledgling − and even adult − cranes, geese and swans to scatter in panic. On the other hand, he might be forgiven for rubbing his eyes at the sight of a white-tailed eagle, with its massive two-metre wingspan (the largest of all Finnish birds), flapping down to perch atop a silver-grey pine 'snag'. This is because the white-tailed eagle is associated in most people's minds with the sea.

In actual fact this species originally nested on large lakes as well, and it has simply remained on the great lakes around Kostomuksha, letting the world go by it. Saarijärvi and Juortanansalo are among the westernmost strongholds of this majestic bird in the White Sea area of Karelia. JLu

Wild Reindeer and Reindeer Forests

Pauli Nieminen

The wild reindeer (Rangifer tarandus fennicus) developed into a distinct species in Siberia during the Ice Age about 20,000 years ago and has lived in the Fennoscandia area for at least 5,000 years. Paintings found on cliff faces near the mouth of the River Uikujoki contain depictions of deer, presumably wild reindeer. The deer depicted in other rock paintings at Tsalmnevarri on the Kola peninsula in the Soviet Union and Alattio in Finnmark, northern Norway, would seem to be wild reindeer, as would the animals in several other ancient paintings on rock faces elsewhere in Norway.

Habitats

The earliest historical records relating to wild reindeer in Finland date from the first half of the 17th century, when they were reported to be living in the region north of a line between Kyrösjärvi and Hiitola. However, numerous place names with connotations of wild reindeer, especially in the Turku region, show incontrovertibly that the animal once ranged throughout Finland. As recently as the 18th century, they were numerous in Ostrobothnia and in the Suomenselkä wilderness, from where they migrated en mass to the Savo lakelands every winter. Another well-documented migration route led from the headwaters of the rivers flowing into the northern end of Lake Ladoga to the islands in the lake and was still followed in the 19th century. Large lakes have always provided the best winter homes for wild reindeer and especially in years of heavy snowfall many of the animals have been drawn to Lakes Inari and Pielinen, in addition to Onega and the large lakes near the White Sea. The good visibility on open lakes and the firm, wind-compacted snow on their ice are even more important factors determining the animals' choice of winter habitat than the Iceland moss lichen generally growing in abundance on the bleak lakeshore heathlands and rocky islands. Predators, mainly wolves, were another important reason for choosing lakes as a winter habitat. Wild reindeer usually lie on the snow with their rears to the wind. They can see wolves approaching from ahead and smell them if they come from behind.

Not even intensive hunting could make the wild reindeer abandon the areas around lakes Njuokkijärvi and Kuittijärvi near the White Sea in the 19th century. In the 17th century, Olaus Niurenius, the Vicar of Umeå in Sweden, reported that once, when the reindeer did not happen to be in the forest because of deep snow, "they migrated by the thousand to the huge Lake Inari and to several other lakes, where they preferred to die than to return to the forests to be killed, but in any case they fell prey to the Lapps."

Lake Lentua in the Kuhmo region is now the most important wintering area for Finland's wild reindeer. Although the Iceland moss reserves on the heathlands fringing the lake and on the islands in it have been greatly depleted and experts have many times predicted that the reindeer would seek new winter homes further west at least the following year, the animals have so far remained, hunger and disturbances by fishermen notwithstanding.

Extinct, but protected

The rarer the wild reindeer became, the more frenetically it was hunted. Some small herds were still found around Kihniö and Pyhäntä in the Suomenselkä district in the 19th century, and the animals were found in the Vuolijoki area as late as the 1880s. It was also reported that they had calved in the Liusvaara and Ilaja wilderness dis-

95

tricts of Ilomantsi around the same period. By the turn of the century, however, there were no wild reindeer left in Finland, with the exception of a few that had wandered across the Russian border. Few hunters comprehended that the animals had gone because they had been hunted to extinction. As they saw it, the animals had just "disappeared" mysteriously.

The explanation in Lapland, from Sweden to Sompio, was that wild reindeer had disappeared from the backwoods when they were disturbed by herdsmen who had come from Finnmark and Enontekiö to the forested zone of southern and eastern Lapland with their domesticated reindeer and introduced the "scent of humans" to the wilderness. It is true that the pressure caused by herds of thousands of their domesticated cousins may have helped push the wild reindeer back beyond the Russian border, but intensified hunting and more efficient weapons also took their toll, especially south of the areas where reindeer were herded.

In 1913, the authorities in the autonomous grand duchy that Finland then was declared the wild reindeer to be a protected species "until further notice". In all probability, not a single pair of antlers waved on a head within the borders of Finland by then, but there were still some of the animals just to the east, around Lake Onega and south of the White Sea. Visitors to the Onega region brought handsome sets of antlers back to Finland as souvenirs even later than that. When Finnish reconnaissance aircraft began flying over the wilderness forests surrounding the small village of Pieninkä, the crews spotted dark, narrow paths criss-crossing the bogs in an apparently aimless fashion. At first they were thought to have been made by either elk or people, until it dawned on the observers that they must have been made by wild reindeer. Finnish commando groups who penetrated the area soon afterwards confirmed that it was indeed so.

They came back

In 1956, Border Guard patrols began discovering globular droppings on paths near the Soviet frontier. At first it was thought that they had been left there by sheep. Soon, however, haystacks on bogs began to be torn asunder and, when some of the culprits were caught in the act, the truth emerged: the wild reindeer had returned to Finland. Soon they began to be sighted more and more often around Maariansärkät and near Palonen in the Hutunsilmä district. When Jorma Kauko, a clergyman interested in wilderness fauna and a keen photographer, was examining a pair of swans nesting on Karilampi pond close to the frontier, he became the first Finn in modern times to capture a wild forest reindeer bull in his camera sights.

Year after year, the animals expanded their range on both sides of Viiksimo. In Elimyssalo in 1966, some males were seen in spring, females and fawns in the summer months and by autumn, with a little luck, one could come across some small rutting herds. In spring 1967, at least one doe calved and shed her antlers in Elimyssalo. Only three years later, calving in the area had become as common an occurrence as such an event can in general be. Elimyssalo had become so exclusively a summer grazing area for does and fawns that not a single bull could be seen there in June-August.

Those bulls that did not go back across the border for the summer spent it in the lake district around Irkku, Veräinen and Ryti-Palonen, which also served as the animals' winter habitat. Some animals were also observed further north, around Lake Kuivajärvi and even up to Martinselkonen, the last remaining trackless wilderness in the Suomussalmi district. A small number also grazed around Ruunaa in the Lieksa district and the odd individual was occasionally seen grazing on Patvinsuo Bog.

Gradually, the animals spread along the ridges stretching from Viiksimo to the eastern shore of Lake Lentua, and Lentua is now practically their only winter habitat in Finland. Wild reindeer come there from as far away as Kuivajärvi. Lentua is the best place in the whole world to observe them in winter, as the famous deer researcher W.O. Pruitt has commented. As many as five hundred of the animals can congregate on the frozen lake. That is almost as many as there are on the Finnish side of the border at any one time.

Protection, research and farming

From 1966 to 1973, I spent a couple of weeks each year in Elimyssalo during the peak calving time. My intention was to find out as much as possible about how wild reindeer calve. The gravid does usually began arriving in the area from the north about 10 May, accompanied by the previous year's fawns. They had a particular preference for northwards-sloping hillsides. I kept a couple of does under special observation every spring.

My goal was to find a newly-born fawn still unable to move. I found the antlers of the two does that I was keeping under observation in a deciduous grove and saw their fawns many times, but never managed to be in the right place during the few hours that the fawn's legs are still incapable of supporting it. Finally, at Whit in 1971 and on the last day of my trip that year, I managed to find a newly-born fawn.

It was lying low beside a patch of snow and only twenty or so metres from the edge of the bog. Its neighbour calved so close to a nest on which a crane was hatching her eggs that the indignant bird screeched angrily at the intruder that had staggered into her home.

In my belief, that area then contained the most precious hectares of forest land anywhere in Finland. Unfortunately, the National Board of Forests shared my opinion of their value. Already the following spring, plastic tapes indicating that trees would soon be felled were in place close to the grove. Since the nature conservation authorities apparently lacked the power to protect the wild reindeer's best calving area, I marked it out on a map and sent it, with an accompanying letter, to President Kekkonen, who appeared to have both power and the willingness to wield it. It is thanks to him that the Elimyssalo woodlands still stick out as a black salient on pictures taken by the Landsat satellite, as Fennoscandia's last forest wilderness. The rest of the Kuhmo region has become depressingly white in the pictures. With the aid of a magnifying glass, one can easily make out the north-westwards thrusting tongue of heathland where, only 30 metres from the edge of the bog, the does and their fawns lie and rest. The precise place where the does calve can also be made out on the northern edge of the tongue of heathland.

Oulu University has since made the wild forest reindeer the subject of an intensive research programme. Experts from as far away as France and the United States have come to Finland to see Rangifer tarandus fennicus. Finnish scientists have compared the wild reindeer with the domesticated animals in Lapland and established clearly that they are distinct sub-species. When some domesticated reindeer were discovered among the wild reindeer herd near Lentua, fears for the racial purity of the latter prompted the idea of relocating them in their former habitat in the Suomenselkä area. To professional biologists the scheme promised research material and results, to the National Board of Forests the opportunity to conduct fellings in Elimyssalo, provided it could be shown that Suomenselkä had a separate wild reindeer population as a guarantee of the species' future.

If I had been as confident as many others of the wild reindeer's ability to cope with forest fellings, I would have preferred to leave the decision about moving west to the animals themselves. There would not have been much to prevent them bounding through forest clearings to Suomenselkä, especially since the availability of lichen in their wintering grounds in Lentua has been giving cause for concern for many years. However, they were not granted that opportunity. MMo

MARTIN-SELKONEN

Martinselkonen, or Martinkaira, must surely be one of the remotest, wildest places in Kainuu — which in turn is one of the wildest, remotest parts of the country. Martinselkonen is situated at a point where the eastern border at the level of Juntusranta (in Suomussalmi) bulges into the Soviet Union. The region consists of typical Kainuu wilderness far from the nearest metalled highway.

Martinselkonen can best be reached from the Lehtovaara road lying on its northwest boundary. The scenery along this road is typical to Kainuu: flattish country, with

Veikko Vasama

little variation in altitude and a conspicuous absence of fells and uplands.

When, at the end of the road, you heft your pack on to your shoulders and set off on foot, you immediately enter a landscape that has remained unchanged for centuries. Martinselkonen comprises six thousand hectares of unspoiled spruce forests, transitional forest Sphagnum mires, bogs covered with stunted Scots pines, and narrow treeless bogs in low-lying heaths.

PEACE NEAR THE BORDER

Rivers and other water bodies form natural boundaries to the area. On the west side there are the rivers Taivaljoki and Karttimojoki, while the actual frontier with the USSR conveniently establishes a horse-shoe shaped boundary to Martinselkonen on the northern and eastern sides. A large part of the area, almost one-third in fact, consists of the border zone, to which access is restricted, particularly to foreign nationals. On the Soviet side there are uninhabited backwoods.

Few places these days are as peaceful as Martinselkonen. The harsh engine noise and tyre howl of motorised vehicles is absent and few aircraft pass overhead. The rambler may sit where he or she chooses and, cocking an ear, listen to the sounds of the wilderness undistorted by our modern world. Martinselkonen has not always been so tranquil, however, as the area is not completely untouched. Thinning operations have been carried out on its most important heathlands, the largest and finest trees carted away. Stumps and even giant 'snags' cut into sections and for some reason left on the ground, are silent testimony to such devastating human impact.

A PATCHWORK QUILT OF SMALL MIRES AND DRY LAND

Bogs and mires in the Martinselkonen district occur almost everywhere: in the seasonally flooded places flanking watercourses, as floating masses of peat and vegetation surrounding pools, and as diminutive treeless mires wedged in between heaths. And even on the slight inclines you will find transitional forest mires and pine bogs. Peatlands are continually being produced, Sphagnum moss spreading out on to any area that is sufficiently damp. Indeed the region is considered by many biologists to be a natural laboratory of peatland formation! The bogs and mires are mainly oligotrophic (having sparse nutrients), lusher examples being found only in the neighbourhood of springs and constantly dripping water. There are no large open aapa mires in the area at all. Martinselkonen lies within the coniferous forest zone. The spruce dominates most of the area, with Scots pine very much the loser. In the absence of forest fires Scots pine seedlings are not very common, spruce seedlings and saplings being in evidence everywhere. It seems obvious that in today's climate the entire region is becoming heavily dominated by the spruce. Only a fire, started for instance by lightning, could conceivably halt this trend. The spruce forests have an undergrowth con-

sisting largely of bilberry and crowberry. Labrador tea grows on the drier patches of ground, as well as on the peatlands, and serves to underscore the region's northern affinities.

Several rivers and streams dissect the area. The largest watercourse is that of the River Karttimajoki, which flows down the western edge of Martinselkonen. In the old days Lapps used to journey to the river banks to cut hay. Their hay barns and even saunas remain as monuments to this ancient form of land use. Meadows from which at one time a rich harvest of hay were reaped have become overgrown with birch.

Most of Martinselkonen's ponds consist of peat-stained pools, but in the centre of the region there is a clearwater pool on the shore of which stands the Teeri-lampi cabin.

AN ANIMAL SANCTUARY

With its dirth of roads and untamed forests, Martinselkonen naturally provides many large animals with an ideal refuge. Once the metre-deep snow has melted in the early spring, there is a rapid influx of little buntings. The brambling's whirring cries resound from every belt of trees and the call of the snipe is heard repeatedly from the flooded bottom meadows flanking the streams and rivers. The Siberian jay and Siberian tit are among the birds that regularly nest here. Greenshanks, wood sandpipers and whimbrels take up residence on mires and along river banks. Even larger birds arrive in the peatlands in spring. The bean goose is frequently present in large numbers, rubbing shoulders with cranes and whooper swans. At this time of year, too, the woods resound to the hooting of the great grey owl. Game birds like capercaillie, black grouse, hazel hen and willow grouse, also find sanctuary in this forgotten corner of the country.

Big mammalian game animals are by no means uncommon either. Large herds of elk wander around the area, their trails clearly demarcated across the soft ground of bogs and river banks. Martinselkonen also represents Kainuu's finest surviving 'bear country', brown bears being regularly encountered there. The best time to search for them is in the cloudberry season (August), when they come out on to the bogs to stuff themselves with ripe berries.

Steps to preserve the beauty and wildness of Martinselkonen were first taken in 1969, with the drafting of a preliminary proposal to this effect. In 1973 the Environmental Protection Committee included Martinselkonen among a set of new national parks it considered ought to be established. Although the proposal was sent to the National Park Committee in 1977, the State's forestry authorities have repeatedly blocked the plan. While the latter has its devotees, their voice, for some obscure reason, fails to be heard.

Martinselkonen is one of Kainuu's last surviving wildernesses in the full sense of the term. It is not large, but it is adequate. All that it lacks is the blessing of official protection. UH

Deadwood Pines Tell a Tale

The old farmers of Sompio described to Samuli Paulaharju how standing pines gradually dry up and die: "In its advanced years, a pine stands bare, its foliage shed, with woodpeckers chipping at its bark. Later, the woodpeckers have peeled away its bark, then drilled holes in the tree. Finally, it stands as a dry deadwood, full of woodpecker holes, and sometimes as the gaunt skeleton of what was once a majestic primeval tree."

A genuine deadwood pine, or "kelo" as it is called in Finnish, is more than just a tree that has dried up and died where it stands; its trunk must also remain unrotted. Thus poplars or birches never develop into proper kelos, and fir kelo is also quite a rarity. Besides pine, the only species growing in Finland that can develop into kelo are larch, oak, yew and juniper.

Mortal pines

Although a pine can reach quite an advanced age, over 700 years in Lapland, its cells have a fairly limited lifespan. Most of the cells in the trunk live only a few years, after which they are replaced by new ones produced by the cambium, the layer inside the bark. The cells conduct water and nutrients from the roots to the green crown, whilst the bast — the layer on the outside of the cambium — takes the photosynthesis products created in the crown to the branches and root system.

As the tree ages, the cellular tissue which transports photosynthesis products increases, although the number of needles in which photosynthesis takes place remains the same or even declines. Growth in the diameter of the branchless part of the tree begins declining once middle age has been reached. As the supply of nutrients dwindles, cells in some parts of the tree become inactive. These parts can be seen when one saws a tree trunk across and notices that some of the outermost annual growth rings do not complete a full circle. The root system begins suffering from a dearth of photosynthesis products and is no longer able to take up enough water and nutrients. This, in turn, has an

Hannu Hautala

Swifts in northern Finland depend entirely for nesting places on holes drilled in trees by birds, mainly woodpeckers.

adverse affect on the crown. Needles turn yellow and whole branches began drying up.

Pine needles drop off 3-5 years after the cambium has stopped functioning. Smallish branches wither after 10-15 years, and within 18-22 years most of the bark has gone. The full transition from living pine to silvery gleaming kelo takes 35-40 years in Lapland. Even after that, the tree can still stand for well over a century.

Fragrant resinous wood
The woody tissue, or xylem, of pines contains two kinds of cellular material: on the outside is living and water-conducting sapwood and on the inside dead heartwood, which is saturated with resin and various other secreted substances. The

low-viscosity golden-yellow liquid which flows in sapwood is a mixture of two substances: volatile turpentine and sticky resin.

When a tree is damaged, it secretes large amounts of resin into the wound. One could imagine that this is its way of doctoring itself and accelerating occlusion of the wound, but in fact a strong flow of resin impedes occlusion. On the other hand, the coating of resin prevents the spores of fungi that cause rot from penetrating the wood tissue inside the tree. It also keeps air out. Enhanced secretion of resin plays quite a decisive role in preserving heartwood, which is dead and highly susceptible to rot.

Although the stumps of branches growing out of the resinous heartwood can be seen here and there, the opposite phenomenon is more common, and also of more essential importance in the creation of kelo trees: an uneven layer of hard tarry wood a couple of inches thick surrounds a rotten or even hollow core.

When a pine dies, neighbouring trees can keep its trunk alive for several years, because individual trees are linked to each other via their roots. Even the stumps of felled trees can grow branches and increase in thickness. The wood produced by a tree in this way after it has died itself is very resinous — resin can account for as much as half of the wood's dry weight — and thus highly resistant to rot. Tarry stumps that have survived for over a century without rotting are not unusual even in southern Finland.

Why are kelos twisted?
Twistedness is such a common feature in trees that a completely straight-grained softwood trunk is a downright rarity. Softwoods are generally twisted to the left when they are young. When they are a score or so years old, the degree of twist lessens and gradually turns towards the right. The older a tree becomes, the more obviously twisted its trunk becomes as the sharpness of the angle constantly increases.

Strongly-growing trees are generally less twisted than slow

growing ones. Likewise, trees are generally more twisted in hilly areas and near the margins of forest-supporting land than in ordinary tended forests. However, it is difficult to say whether twisted trees are attributable to severe habitat conditions or whether it is just that they are more noticeable in old forests where no felling has occurred.

Among various other environmental factors, the strength of the wind eddying around the crown of a tree has most commonly been put forward as an explanation for why tree trunks become twisted. A twisted trunk is a lot stronger than a quite straight one. Thus it is clearly genetic selection that encourages a twisted form in places exposed to the wind.

The sun's daily passage across the sky has provided the basis for several theories intended to explain why trees are twisted. Since the direction from which its radiation arrives is continuously changing, it would seem natural for a tree to keep turning its crown towards the light. But this theory is undermined by the branches, which always point the same way. Nor does it explain why branches and trunks are often twisted in the opposite direction to that in which the sun moves across the firmament.

Cambium the cause
The structure of the cambium layer from which a tree's tissues grow and the slanted direction in which its cells characteristically divide have maintained their status as the most plausible explanations. A tree ought to add cambium cells at the same rate as the circumference of its trunk increases. However, the cambium cells in softwoods always form new cells laterally in a slanted fashion. An old cambium cell splits into two new ones, between which new cells grow. The new cells always assume a slightly slanted orientation in relation to the long axis of the tree. In this way, they create sideways-slanted tracheids, the water-conducting elements in the wood. As time goes by, the tree become more and more obviously twisted. ML

Beard Mosses and Beard Lichens

When I was small and lacked facial hair, I used to go into the forest, pull off some of the handsome beard moss hanging from firs and put it on my head. Now I have a beard of my own, but the firs in my home district do not; if I want to see some adorned with beard moss, I have to make the long trip to the backwoods of Kuhmo.

Several species of beard moss grow in Finland. Some grow on stones, others on pines, birches or dead wood, but those that grow on firs have made the most important contribution to the landscape. True beard mosses are not found any further north than the Kuusamo district.

Of the many lichens collectively described as beard mosses, some really belong to the Usnea family of lichens. They can be identified by means of the tough internal sinew beneath the brittle surface layer. If one stretches a piece of this lichen, the surface layer cracks and exposes the sinew. Other "beard mosses", also actually lichens (Alectoria, Bryoria), as well as a cartilaginous lichen resembling beard moss also grow on the branches of firs. Beard lichens grow throughout Finland and in Lapland are the only component of the shaggy coats that cover firs. All of these mosslike lichens were formerly much more common. Few people distinguished between them, either. In southern Finland, both were called "beard mosses", in the north "beard lichens".

Both beard mosses and beard lichens have been used for medicinal purposes, as raw materials for pharmaceuticals, as cushioning and insulating material and in places even as

The Siberian jay, whose coloration gives it good concealment in dense growths of beard moss, is a typical denizen of old forests. Fragmentation of mossy forests, clearfelling and air pollution are making life more difficult for this bird as well.

Hannu Hautala

or seek refuge in the mini-jungle. Many of them stay there for the winter, and when the spring sun wakes them and they groggily stagger out of their hiding places, they make a big contribution to ensuring that birds like tits, tree creepers and golden-crested kinglets have a supply of food as early as March. Beard mosses, lichens and other lichens that grow on tree trunks and branches obtain the water and nourishment they need directly from the air. Thus they are only guests on the trees, and not parasites. The fact that trees in poor condition have the heaviest lichen encrustations does not mean that it is the lichens that impede their growth. A healthy tree grows so fast and its bark peels off so frequently that a thick coat of lichen can not form on its surface.

Since lichens draw their nourishment from the air, they also absorb harmful substances. Foremost among these is sulphur dioxide, to which many species are very sensitive. Air pollution has made nearly all tree lichens rare, with only a couple of exceptions: the grey, scablike Lecanora conizaeoides and Bacidia chlorococca, which coats trees in an even green layer, both thrive in polluted air and take over trees from which other species have vanished.

Air pollution is the main cause of beard mosses' and lichens' disappearance, but silviculture has also been a contributory factor. Drainage of backwood forests and wetlands has deprived beard mosses of their best habitats. They do not thrive in young fir forests where the trees are all of the same age, growing strongly and are of consistent density. Nature preserves far from industrial plants and traffic are a refuge for beard mosses, but for how long before pollution spreads there as well? SV

bedding in cowhouses. In North Karelia, yellowish-grey fir beard moss was used to stop feet perspiring; if one walked around for a week with moss in one's socks, foot perspiration was no longer a problem. True, the skin of one's feet were dyed yellow, but that disappeared in time. There was no element of popular witchcraft involved, either. Some beard mosses contain high levels of usnic acid and other substances which kill bacteria. Several lichens are used as raw materials by pharmaceuticals manufacturers abroad.

When a thick, hard blanket of snow or a strong crust of ice beneath it makes it impossible for reindeer to get at the lichens on the ground, the animals graze the growths garlanding the branches of trees or the pieces stripped off by the wind and lying on the snow. If the snow and ice crust persists for a long time, the reindeer are hungry and travel long distances to forest clearings in the hope of finding a more abundant supply of beard lichen. In the old days, reindeer herdsmen used to fell lichen-clad trees to provide emergency feeding.

"A grey, warm bunch of lichen nested at the base of a branch half way up a tree was a squirrel's home, one that it had built itself. And there it lived contentedly, and its little heirs were snug as well." Thus did Samuli Paulaharju describe a squirrel's nest in his book Sompio. Since those days, squirrels have had to change their nest-building habits, especially in southern Finland. In the absence of beard moss, they use whatever they can find in the environment to give their nests soft lining: moss, bark, paper, plastic and even mineral wool insulation material.

Many animals smaller than squirrels also benefit from tree lichens. Some tiny creatures eat beard mosses, but many much more numerous insects, spiders and mites prey on each other

LITOKAIRA

A wilderness of peatlands, the only extensive uninterrupted and roadless area south of the Arctic Circle, is situated on either side of the junction of the provinces of Oulu and Lapland, in the communes of Pudasjärvi and Ranua. It comprises something like four leagues (40 km) of trackless wastes extending from Heinisuo, at Ranua, to Iso Saarisuo, at Pudasjärvi. Nature conservationists from the south speak of the 'Lapiosuo wilds', while the locals know the area as 'Litokaira'.

ACCESS ROAD OR NOT?

Litokaira is the antithesis of the traditional wilderness ideal. Its highest hill is an impressive mound rising all of five metres above the surrounding open bog! In short, the entire several square kilometre wilds consists of very flat land lying hardly more than 150 m above sea level. Half of the surface area is practically treeless Sphagnum bog, and the rest terrain that is just plain boggy.

Jorma Luhta

While the area is thus largely covered by dismal treeless bogs and mires, it is in one respect unique. The central parts of Litokaira are still in a completely natural condition. Many roads have been planned for both the central and northern parts of the region, but Litokaira has also been brought before the public eye as being worthy of our protection.

A hike into this peatland wilderness is best begun from the south along the Oijärvi-Liekokylä road. With the passing of the gnat and mosquito season, at the end of summer, the peatlands are one of the nicest places in which to ramble. The extremely varied peatland birdlife is best observed, of course, in the spring, but at that time this wilderness with its multitude of rivers, streams and brooks, is extremely difficult to negotiate. Besides, the rambler may well disturb nesting birds.

FROM SOUTH TO NORTH

When the hiker coming from the Oijärvi logging road towards the west has crossed the Vitmaoja bridge the large Iso Saarisuo bog is suddenly revealed on both sides of the road. From the easily negotiated heath, which forms an obstacle to view, he can observe the life on the water-logged, treeless mires. Some of the large birds of the peatlands, the crane and bean goose, can be seen at the appropriate time of year where the road is no longer visible. The highly spruce-dominant heaths are not entirely natural, as this locality saw rather heavy logging on both sides of the war, an event that came in for a lot of criticism at the time.

After the hiker has walked a few kilometres north and crossed a couple of rather ordinary treeless Sphagnum bogs, he suddenly finds himself at Vitmalamminkorpi, in one of Finland's most magnificent transitional forest Sphagnum mire districts. Where the Vitmaoja stream splits into a large number of tributaries, the sedge growth is especially dense and there are many old hay barns lying along the river's course, forming monuments to the exploitation of these wilds by past generations.

Hikers who have chosen the easternmost route will find themselves faced by the River Litojoki. It would otherwise be easy to cross this river, but the private plots along the riverside — the old, disused hay meadows — were cleared of trees by fearful landowners very shortly after the National Park Committee in 1977 had proposed that Litokaira be designated a national park. Searching for a crossing point by labouring through the 'slash' left by the loggers and now hidden in the undergrowth, high hummocks, and wet areas lining the watercourse in the evening dusk is a quest calling for both stamina and patience. However, the humble River Litojoki, like the Kivijoki, which bisects the centre of the region, is a surprisingly good place for large pike! Fishermen use large spoons in the hope of catching one of these prizes.

On the east side of the Litojoki stretches five-kilometre long Isosuo, which is a typical Ostrobothnia open aapa mire. The monotony of the large sedgy, water-logged, treeless bogs, dissected by their never-ending lines of hummocks, is only relieved by a few pools which,

however, serve to improve the number of habitats available to the birds. In the vicinity of the Kuivauslammi pool, the northernmost of the group, the reindeer herdsmen have a cabin which they keep in good order. This offers the hiker a chance to rest his weary bones, overnight if necessary. There are in fact a number of cabins in the Litokaira district, some of them very small but a few of more generous dimensions. Unfortunately the ones marked on the map will almost inevitably be found to be those that have fallen into disrepair!

Alongside, or at least close to, the Litojoki alone there are five very serviceable unlocked huts or old saunas as once used by the haymakers. Refreshed, the lover of virgin forests will now bend his steps towards the provincial boundary and then on to the series of open woodlands which continue on northwards. Old silver birches and a scattering of spruces on this drier soil soon give way to aged Scots pines. Seen from a distance, the latter form a greyish forest at the edges of mires and pools.

WILDERNESS LAKES IN MINIATURE

At the hub of the wilds on the southern side of Ranua commune, and hence also of Lapland Province, there is a small-scale watershed which is one of the loveliest parts of this region. Its primary feature is a series of small lakes stretching out over a distance of about ten kilometres. The surrounding terrain is composed of small treeless Sphagnum bogs which, as is usual in the neighbourhood of a watershed, are very low in nutrients. The trees, which by and large are Scots pines, are around two centuries old. Signs of the presence of human beings and civilisation are visible only on the lake shores. Here the rambler will also find wilderness cabins, of which the most charming is the small example on the shore of Litjo. According to entries in the visitors' book, this edifice has been considered "the centre of the universe" and "the nicest place in the world"! While the floodwaters reach up to the floor in both spring and autumn, it is no problem to stay high and dry in the small hours on the sleeping loft. Although tales of gnomes and fairies rightly belong to the nursery, many of those who have slept at Litjo on an autumn night tend to hold a different view.

LIMITLESS LAPIOSUO

Setting out north again from the lake area, one is obliged to cross three brooks running in an east-west direction. From the western side of the Tervokangas primaeval forest a very extensive series of peatlands begins, of which the first is the Pieni Lapiosuo bog, whose title of 'Pieni' (= small) seems to be a gross Finnish understatement — until, that is, one compares it with neighbouring Lapiosuo itself.

While the back-packer will find it expedient to progress along the edges of the treeless bogs from one grove of ancient trees to another, if one is to appreciate the wide-world vista of the peatlands, at the latest at Lapiosuo one should plunge straight into the heart of the bog. In the Lapiosuo area there are several raised bogs whose network of hummock lines is as easily crossed as a heath. The dozens of small but well-wooded comparatively mineral-rich high points on the Laipiosuo bog form excellent natural camping sites and provide an opportunity to survey the surrounding wildlife through binoculars or a telephoto lens.

Roadless — and almost trackless — Litokaira is the home of large birds and other distinctive wilderness wildlife. In this area all the peatland, wilderness lake, and rugged country, species nest. A glimpse of a golden eagle, peregrine and whooper swan is highly probable, as one passes quietly on one's way through these wilds. Here, too, also nest two pairs of ospreys. Among the smaller bird rarities, the little bunting, velvet scoter and common scoter are worthy of mention. In recent years the brown bear has established itself among the Litokaira fauna.

REMINDERS OF A BYGONE WORLD

The Näätähaara house is perhaps the one house worth seeing among the handful of derelict dwellings lying along the banks of Litokaira rivers. If the rambler fails to make a detour to Näätähaara, he will miss a worthwhile experience. Moreover, in the cold of winter Näätähaara provides an excellent sleeping place at which in the welcome warmth from the stove one may permit one's mind to dwell on the folk who used to frequent this wilderness. The descendants of the original inhabitants, to their great credit, have restored the main building almost as a museum. Old tools are all in their proper places and where their use is obscure there is an apt description.

The last, unfortunately not easily navigable, trail leads the hiker from Näätähaara east-northeast to the road serving the old Heinisuo settlement area. Before long, the virgin forests give way to commercially managed forests, clearfellings, plantations, and ploughed forests. The open aapa mire, which has consisted alternately of waterlogged treeless areas and hummock lines, suddenly merges into artificially drained peatland with deep ditches. The rambler will note how light the going is in the notorious peatland wilderness, if this is compared

A brown bear has excavated this wood ants' nest, on which a bean goose has proceeded to nest. The bird has chosen this site because it is one of the first to be exposed by the melting snow.

Esko Männikkö

In times of blizzards the golden eagle may well go without food for several days. Fortunately a good meal of a hare satisfies the bird's appetite for a week or so.

with Finland's modern managed forests, with their fur-rows and heaps of discarded 'slash' lying hither and thither, a thousand hurdles in the new grass. At last, the much-anticipated Heinisuo road hoves into view which transcribes a circle leading directly to the Ranua Animal Park. Whichever way you set off along this circular route, you cannot fail to arrive at the park.

To cap the hike, the hiker coming out of the peatland wilderness can now view all those large carnivores which have remained unseen during the past day or so. The mind will return, however, to the wilderness of aged Scots pines, lines of 'snags', brooks and rivers, peatland pools, lonely ponds and lakes, and above all the large open aapa bogs, the entrance fee to which is paid for in sweat and determination.

THE WILDS

No trails cross the heartland of Litokaira. There are no guides; the map does not include many of the forest huts, and even the name of the entire wilderness is not marked! This explains why hikers even from other parts of Finland are very rare these days. The visitors' books in the cabins tend to repeatedly bear the names of an inspired and stalwart few. The reason for their coming is embodied in this entry: "Unforgettable days in the peace of the mighty peatland wilderness."

People who have slept in forest saunas, or have simply visited them, tend to make the following kind of entries in the visitor's book: "The pike were not biting." ; — "Two teal shot." — "Some geese seen but not bagged." — "We were looking for reindeer." — "We were looking for the spoor of pine marten." — "Spent the day looking for cloudberries and all of us picked two plastic bucketsful." — "I collected a whole haversackful of cloudberries, and a hundred haversacksful remained on Lapiosuo bog."

THE RAMBLER'S YEAR

Litokaira in December becomes covered with snow that for vast distances in every direction in all probability will remain unmarred by ski or snowmobile track. Only the roads leading to some occupied or useful dwelling or other are kept open by the snowplough. Cock capercaillies boldly parade about on the surface of the snow, tugging the needles off the crowns of wizened Scots pines in the bogs. Voles, weasels, stoats, red squirrels, foxes, reindeer and elk all leave their distinctive tracks in the snow. On the lovely, virgin surface the running pine marten leaves its broad spoor.

Pine marten hunting involves skiing, and not easy skiing at that, as the fresh fall of snow calls for the use of a heavy three-metre long ski. Leaving the snugness of a cabin for air made brittle by frost, the hunter may need to ski for one kilometre, or even ten kilometres, until he comes across a track made the previous night. A pine

Antti Leinonen

marten can lope easily over a distance of three leagues in a single night, so that it is possible that darkness will descend on the hunter before he reaches his quarry. Litokaira's pine martens hide away during the daytime in old black woodpecker nesting holes, in the nest of a red squirrel, golden eagle or goshawk, in hollow fallen trunks underneath the snow, in ant mounds, or among piles of stones.

A snow shovel, an axe, humane traps, and a shot-gun are among the pine marten hunter's accoutrement. Digging out a valuable fur-bearing animal at the end of an exhausting ski trek is thus exceedingly hard work. Pine marten hunting continues up until March, but before that the snowmobiles start to race over the open bogs. Hooks and nets are rarely carried by fishermen on skis nowadays since the blessings of technology and motor power are so generally available. Pike and burbot come to hooks baited with roach or Baltic herring. At the same time, the more energetic reindeer herdsmen will search for their animals, which are in a condition of semi-starvation owing to the low amount of beard moss in these wilds. A few reindeer die each winter and a golden eagle or two will descend on to the carcass.

The hard crust on the spring snow attracts the first ramblers, as well as a few winter fishermen who fish from a hole drilled through the ice. Nowadays, too, it lures

reckless snowmobile drivers with nothing better to do than to break the law by aimless weaving to and fro with no hint of purpose. Litokaira with its apparently limitless bogs at this time of year offers easy going to the skier. A full range of 'essential' equipment is often transported these days in a fibreglass sled, rather than in a rucksack on the skier's back.

After May-day the spring slush and floodwaters arrive speedily and the whole wilderness becomes uncrossable. Just then, with the floods rising, more is happening among the wildlife than at any time of year. Capercallies and black grouse call almost incessantly day and night. Cranes and bean geese, as well as the smaller birds of the peatlands, arrive in their flocks. A whooper swan pair call and splash about in the slush.

The spring clamour dies down long before it is possible to actually walk through these wilds. From late spring onwards people are almost entirely absent from these parts. With the emergence of the gnat and mosquitoes a bird ringer may study the nesting sights of golden eagles, ospreys and peregrines; the reindeer herdsman seeks out the new calves for marking; the pike fisher tramps the river courses, and canoe enthusiasts shoot the rapids along the Kivijoki.

But at the end of July more people than ever are to be seen in the wilds. The Arctic cloudberry crop brings the inhabitants of the Litokaira region thousands of Finnmarks of welcome additional income. The advent of the cloudberry season drives the bean geese, so tame and so obvious in the spring, into the heartlands to moult. When the crop is finished and the berry-pickers have gone home, the geese move back to the open peatlands.

Goose hunting, which starts on the twentieth of August, is a national 'sport'. It is not shooting for the pot, the pot and the need to fill it being forgotten. Indeed it is rather like salmon fishing in one respect: It's worth a try even if you don't catch anything! Very rarely, with shotgun and rifle, does the hunter come back with a goose in his haversack. At the latest by the return trip the eiders and teal will fall prey to the shooters, as legal alternatives to a plump wild goose.

With the start of the real hunting season at the beginning of September, there is hardly a shot fired nowadays in the whole of Litokaira, as after many years of unsuccessful nesting the numbers of forest game birds have dwindled drastically. Furthermore, hares are now more common in the neighbourhood of villages and detached houses than out in the open.

So, if a man travels to Litokaira with his gun and dog as the leaves on the trees begin to turn yellow, it is not because he envisages a good bag, but simply because he delights in just being there. JLu

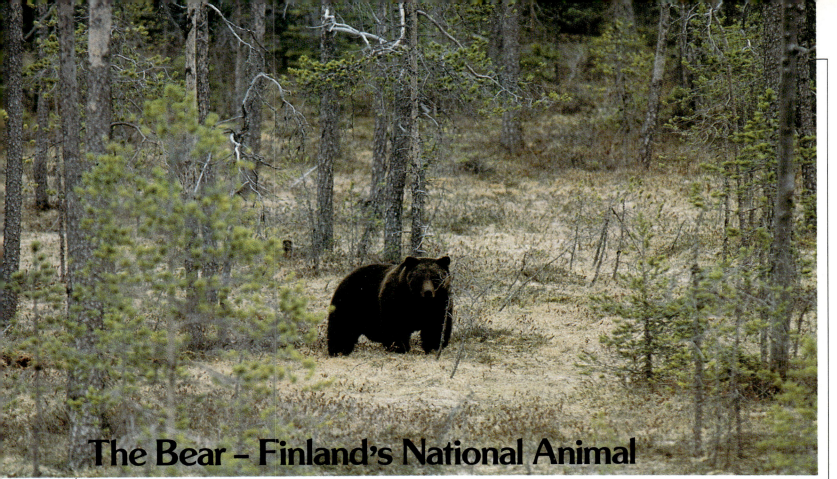

The Bear – Finland's National Animal

Eero Kemilä

The bear differs from other large predators in that it spends half the year in hibernation, neither eating drinking nor defecating during that time. However, even in this state of rest it consumes energy, which it must store up during the active period prior to hibernation. This energy is stored in fat tissue, which the bear has plenty of beneath its fur and in its stomach cavity. There is usually enough of it to last the animal not only while it is hibernating, but also for several weeks afterwards.

A wanderer without territory

A bear's life consists of either recovering from hibernation or preparing for it. The ground is still partially covered in snow when it emerges from its den and there is little food in Mother Nature's larder. Although the animal is not yet able to eat, it immediately sets about finding itself a source of food. Its appetite is as massive as itself. Thus it is particularly interested in any large "accumulation" of food, such as an elk or deer carcass, an animal carcass left as "bait" by a nature photographer, salmon or trout in their shallow spawning grounds, or even a good patch of berries.

A bear does not have an individual territory to defend against other bears. Several can wander the same smallish area at the same time. Naturally, all try to get their share of whatever food is available and the result is competition to establish a "pecking order" among the various animals in the area. This can involve violent combat.

Although bears do not have a system for dividing up territories and food resources on the basis of individual bailiwicks, each population does seem to have a saturation point. Surplus individuals have to go elsewhere in search of food and living room. Both food and females capable of reproducing are limited resources in such cases. There can be as many as five or six females of cub-bearing age within the area in which a large male lives. Any other males in the area try to mate with her.

Male bears are generally more mobile than females. Alone for this reason, more males than females are likely to be found on the periphery of a habitat range. Those higher up in the hierarchic structure steadfastly claim their first right to whatever food is available, especially if it is scarce, whilst those lower down the scale have to move off elsewhere to feed themselves.

Reinforcements from the east

Things were going really badly for Finland's bears in the 1960s. Spring hunting expeditions using snowmobiles had decimated the population in Lapland. Hunters along the eastern border had used sleds, but with equally devastating results. By the end of the decade, there were only about 150 of the animals left in Finland — and most of them were males. The population in Kainuu and North Karelia consisted almost entirely of males; cubs were seen only extremely rarely.

Later, hunting was curtailed, both by restricting the variety of methods that could be used and by reducing the length of the open season. The number of permits issued to kill bears fell from about 150 a year to between 20 and 30. At the same time, the bear population of East Karelia, just across the Soviet border, reached saturation point, which is somewhere between 2,500 and 3,000. The surplus bears had to move away in search of food. They went to Finland, which has had net immigration of 50-60 bears a year since the beginning of the 1970s.

Since the influx of bears from the Soviet Union has been constant, they have not stayed in the border region, but wandered further into the heart of the country. The strongest migration from the east has been in Kainuu and North Karelia, and it is also from those regions that secondary migration deeper into Finland has been liveliest. Now, the only "bearlesss" parts of Finland are the Enontekiö panhandle, which juts north-westwards between Sweden and Norway, Utsjoki in the extreme north, the south-western corner of the country, Åland and the other Baltic islands.

Bears can be hunted for a limited period of the year in eastern and northern Finland; those in the rest of the country are protected. In fifteen years, the number in Finland has risen from about 150 to nearly 500 and the bear is no longer a threatened species here. EPu

The Birth and Development of Bogs

Finland is a land of bogs. Nowhere else in the world do they cover such a relatively large proportion of the land area. If peaty heathlands are included, bogs cover 11.8 million hectares of the country. However, more than half of this area has been reclaimed for agricultural use or drained for forestry, and drainage work is continuing.

In the biological sense, a bog is a vegetation complex that forms peat. A bog in a natural state is constantly growing upwards. The rate of growth depends on the type of surface vegetation and the height of the water table. The faster dead vegetable matter is buried in anaerobic peat, the less it can decompose. The rate of decomposition is determined by both the bog's nutrient level and the amount of water in it. In bleak sphagnum moss bogs, where there is little oxygen and few of the microorganisms that promote decomposition, the vegetable matter rots very slowly. Peat is created relatively fast in proportion to the amount of biomass produced each year. However, the largest accumulation of peat is achieved in low-lying bogs that are permanently waterlogged and have fast plant growth rates. Bogs grow upwards at a rate of 0.1 — 1.5 millimetres a year. Measured against a human lifespan, peat is therefore a non-renewable natural resource, although in the geological sense it is renewable.

How they come into being

Finland's bogs were created through three main processes: paludification of forest land or flood plains, plants proliferating until they completely filled the low-lying water bodies in which they grew or through primary bog development, in which a blanket of peat gradually covers land that has emerged from under water, without an intervening phase of afforestation. Only some 5-10% of the bogs in Finland are the result of water bodies having become choked up with plants.

About one-third of Finland's bogs remain in a natural state. This picture is of Tolkansuo, a waterlogged aapa (Nordic concentric ring bog) in Utajärvi.

Pertti Kalinainen

Eero Kemilä

On geologically old land, which emerged from beneath the continental ice sheet at an early stage, paludification of forest land was the beginning of nearly half of our bogs. On younger land, the most common factor leading to the creation of bogs was waterlogging.

Immediately after the Ice Age, 9,000-10,000 years ago, the rate at which water bodies filled up with plants was fastest in relation to the area of bog that existed then, but its importance declined rapidly. The importance of primary paludification also declined as land aged and continuing uplifting reduced the proportion of it that was waterlogged. Forests became bogs at the fastest rate during a relatively warm climatic period 7,000-3,000 years ago. When the cooler period that followed it ended about 2,500 years ago, bogs covered about 60% of the area that they do today. Often, the various parts of the largest bog basins have developed at different times and in different ways. The bottommost layers often contain mud or sludge, indicating that the development of the bog began when plants proliferated and choked up a lake or pond. Later, as the land fringing it became waterlogged, the bog grew outwards into the sur-

rounding forest land. Paludification of the forests was usually preceded by a forest fire. After the fire, evaporation from the mineral soil declined and the amount of water running off into the boggy depression increased.

Development of bogs

Bogs are not static vegetation complexes. They are in a constant state of change. As the peat layer deepens, the nutrients and water conditions in the bog change, and this is reflected in the vegetation growing on the surface. The general tendency is for a bog to become dryer and bleaker. Land rising from the sea can be marshy to begin with, but gradually turns into swampy forest or mossy bog. As waterlogging proceeds, it may become an open fen and then, due to sphagnum growth, a dry ombrotrophic fen or marsh. In large areas of peatland, these can merge to form extensive "raised bogs".

During the early phase of their development, bogs have usually been nutrients-rich lowlands forest or quagmires, because only some of the mineral-laden soils have been leached off. Decomposed peat found in low-lying wilderness forests often contains the re-

Most of our bogs have been afforested or drained to facilitate industrial production of peat fuel.

mains of common alder and even hazel, revealing that their vegetation cover during their early phase consisted of luxuriant plant communities, some quite different from anything found on today's bogs. In the course of time, as mineral soils were leached out and the sphagnum blanket deepened, the bogs became bleaker. Sphagnum mosses have the ability to retain huge volumes of water, but also acidify their environment. With these two factors to aid it, a bog is able to increase its height, even if it has to depend entirely on rainwater, and to spread into the surrounding forests. Silver-flanked deadwood pines standing on the edges of bogs are proof of sphagnum's lethal ability to spread.

Raised and aapa bogs

Climate and topography dictate what macro form, raised, aapa or palsa, the development of bogs in a particular area will lead to. Development in the large bogs of southern and central Finland has mainly produced what are called "raised bogs". These require a climate

wet enough to ensure that they can grow above the groundwater level and go over to existing on rainwater and meagre nourishment.

A well-developed raised bog is surrounded by a sedgy peripheral zone with a mineral soil underlay. The shallow edge of the bog supports pines, but as the peat deepens and slopes upwards towards the centre, the surface become barer and is eventually almost completely open. On the central "plateau", mossy hummocks alternate with drier flat patches. On the handsome raised bogs of the Satakunta and South Ostrobothnia regions, these hummocks and level patches are arrayed in approximately concentric rings around the centre of the bog. On gently sloping raised bogs in the interior of the country, the hummocks and depressions are arrayed sequentially and laterally against the direction in which the water flows. The peripheral zone and sloping edge in these bogs are poorly developed or completely absent.

The borderline between raised and aapa-type bogs runs at approximately the 63rd line of latitude in Finland. However, there are some aapa bogs south of that line, too, especially in watershed areas. Likewise, raised bogs exist where conditions have favoured their development as far north as Lapland.

Aapa bogs have developed in the northerly cold and moist climate in places where water running out of mineral soils continuously brings a rich supply of nutrients and where there is an abundant flow of water, especially in spring. Low narrow ridges supporting rushes and sedges and drier ones that are either treeless or support the occasional birch and run in the same direction as the main water flow form netlike patterns or sometimes run in long lines for kilometres. The basic character of aapa bogs has remained unchanged throughout their existence. Most of Finland's raised and aapa bogs have already reached a mature age, and only a decisive change in the climate could begin another round of development. PHu

Veikko Vasama

KOILLISMAA REGION

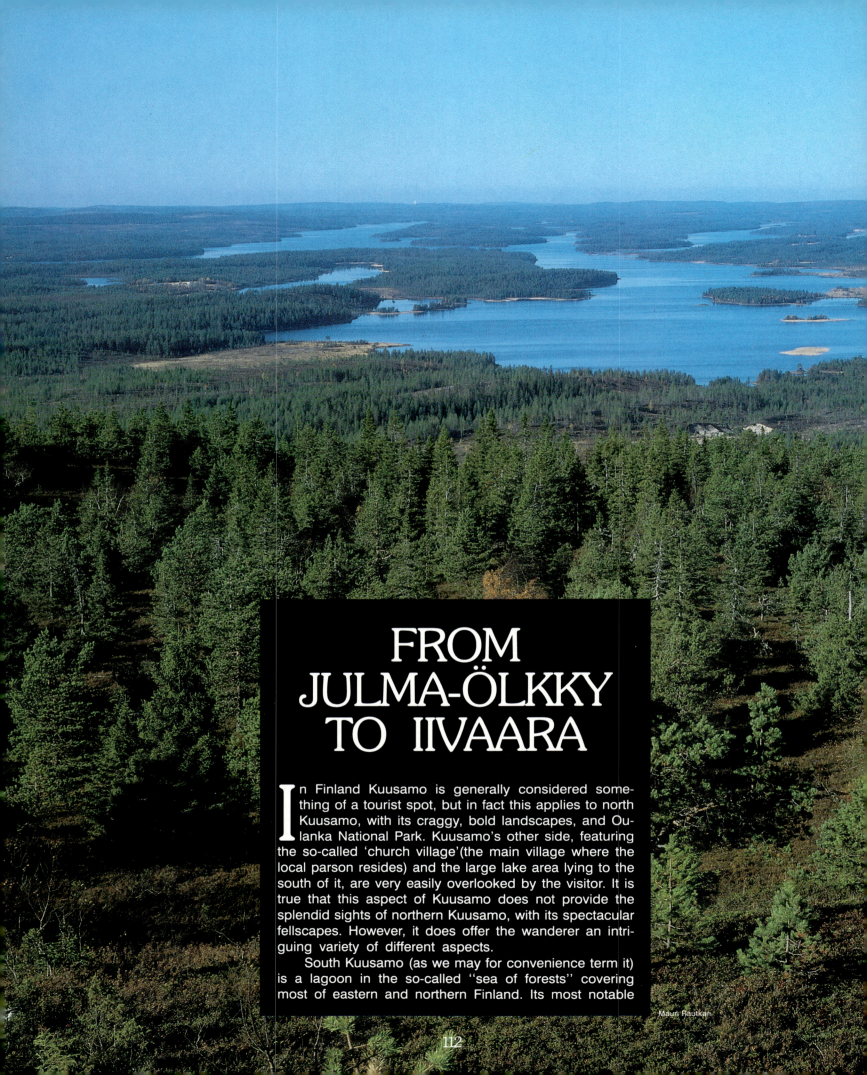

FROM JULMA-ÖLKKY TO IIVAARA

In Finland Kuusamo is generally considered something of a tourist spot, but in fact this applies to north Kuusamo, with its craggy, bold landscapes, and Oulanka National Park. Kuusamo's other side, featuring the so-called 'church village'(the main village where the local parson resides) and the large lake area lying to the south of it, are very easily overlooked by the visitor. It is true that this aspect of Kuusamo does not provide the splendid sights of northern Kuusamo, with its spectacular fellscapes. However, it does offer the wanderer an intriguing variety of different aspects.

South Kuusamo (as we may for convenience term it) is a lagoon in the so-called ''sea of forests'' covering most of eastern and northern Finland. Its most notable

Mauri Rautkari

112

and desirable feature is the sheer scale of its scenery. The region forms part of the Kuusamo watershed uplands. From here the waters flow away in no less than three directions — and how many parts of Europe can equal that? The water-sheds of the rivers Iijoki and Oulujoki, on the Hyrynsalmi route, and the River Pistojoki route flowing towards the White Sea, are all concentrated here. An esker, which for the most part is here uncommonly flat and undistinguished, separates the watercourses debouching into the White Sea from those draining into the Gulf of Bothnia. The patient hiker will discover many places well worth exploring and which in many respects reward the effort required by a long hike.

Since the war, many roads have been built across this previously untamed terrain and these greatly facilitate movement in the area and make it possible to explore the southern part of Kuusamo by means of several minor treks rather than a single major expedition. These roads for the most part are logging roads and the consequen-ces of an intensification of the road network are the same here as elsewhere — the peace of the wilds has been replaced by large clearfellings, while ditches slice through what used to be mires wallowing happily in moisture.

HOSSA — ÖLKKY — IRNIJÄRVI

Lake Iijärvi, at the junction of Suomussalmi and Kuusamo, has been given one of Finland's most common lake place names. Finland has a lot of locality names in which the word "Ii" appears. According to one school of thought at least, these names date from the time when the Lapps (Same) lived in these areas — in their tongue "ii" was equivalent to the Finnish "yö" (= night). The headwaters lake, the Iijärvi, on the Hyrynsalmi route, is located south of Hossa in a long chain of eskers. It is a clearwater sandy-shored lake whose shallow inshore waters support the eye-catching blue blooms of Lobelia dortmanna, which testify to the purity of the water. On the

Formed millions of years ago during a major upheavel of the earth's crust, the Julma-Ölkky gorge was later gouged out by the great glaciers to form a lake bed.

shore of the lake the quaint village of Teeriranta has also sprouted.

From the south side of the village near Ahvenlahti bay a narrow road separates off the road (number 913) between Suomussalmi village and Kuusamo's Murtovaara. The road is a convenient passageway to Julma-Ölkky. It runs for a start westwards between picturesque esker terrain. This delightful scenery formed here at the end of the last Ice Age between two major continental ice sheet lobes. Meltwaters from the glaciers transported with them vast quantities of sand and gravel, grading the material and grinding the stones smooth. Thus, ten thousand years ago these gravel eskers came into existence which today delight the human eye with their lichen-covered slopes.

From the northern side of Kalettomanlampi pool a road smaller than the one going to Vaaraperä winds away towards the spur between lakes Ala-Ölkky and Julma-Ölkky, approximately five kilometres away. Today's tourist, with his motorised transport, can if he wishes travel right up to these lakes. Arriving on the narrow spur between the two "Ölkky's" the visitor will find a shelter in the form of an unlocked cabin.

The more southerly of the two lakes, Ala-Ölkky, is a slim clearwater esker lake. North of the spur runs Lake Julma-Ölkky, an almost three kilometre long body of water having the appearance of a narrow fjord. At its widest point this lake is less than 100 metres, at its narrowest barely 20. Steep cliffs rise 20 – 30 metres on either side of the lake along almost its entire length.

The Ölkky-Irnijärvi region encloses a large number of steep-sided canyons. Particularly spectacular is the long, narrow Vaaraperänlahti. Most of south Kuusamo is underlain by gneiss-granite, which is the basic bedrock of Finland, being something like 3000 million years in age. Later, during periods of orogeny, this bedrock was greatly stressed and many rifts appeared in it. Today the latter are the steeply-walled canyons or gorges of south Kuusamo. Their bases, of course, have become covered with water. The granitic rock is characterised by perpendicular fracturing, resulting in just this kind of sheer-walled gorge.

CLIFFS AND ROCK PAINTINGS

This type of cliff has traditionally fired people's imagination. The Old Stone Age people – hunters and fishermen – who once inhabited this region regarded these desolate cliffs with awe and felt the need to honour them in some way. Rock paintings that are red in colour are generally found in Finland close to water. Such paintings have been discovered on the cliffs fronting the eastern shore of Lake Julma-Ölkky. They take the form of three relatively modest sized paintings, of which two represent people and the third an elk. At Ölkky in summer it is possible for visitors to obtain transportation to the site of these paintings.

Nature herself has also decorated these cliffs. Plants have wedged themselves into the tiniest cracks and on to the faintest of protuberances in the rock. Wizened Scots

Reijo Juurinen

The northern crowberry subspecies hermaphroditum forms an important food source for many animals.

pine trees, wispy grasses and other small plants now project colourfully here and there. Aside from harebells, sheep's fescue, and delicate ferns, the cliffs also support the small white-flowered saxifrage Saxifraga nivalis. Sometime towards the close of the last Ice Age the latter plant arrived here and it has continued to thrive in these extremely specialised growing conditions for thousands of years because other plants have been unable to oust it by competing with it.

The Ölkky hiking route merges naturally into the Hossa scenery in the northern parts of Suomussalmi. Lake Somerjärvi, which lies on the borders of the two communes, drains into the southern end of Lake Ala-Ölkky. Like the "Ölkky" lakes, this also has an elongated, narrow form. Its shores are once again partly formed of steep, high cliffs.

On the Suomussalmi side there is a protected tract of primaeval forest surrounding part of Lake Somerjärvi. Here it is also possible to fish, so long as one makes sure to procure the requisite licence in advance, as the area forms part of a recreation area managed by the National Board of Forestry. The protected area encompasses part of the outstandingly beautiful wilderness of the Kuusamo-Suomussalmi region close to the border, with its lovely old Scots pines.

Värikallio, a cliff dropping precipitously into the water at the eastern end of Lake Somerjärvi, bears one of this country's richest collections of rock paintings. Consisting of a grand total of 61 works of ancient art, this unique relic has suffered a form of vandalism. Somebody apparently hated the idea of rock paintings and thus proceeded to cover them with tar. Fortunately it is now quite clear that these Stone Age masterpieces are perfectly able to withstand such harsh treatment, as the Värikallio pain-

Adders, or vipers, can often be recognised by the diamond patterns on their backs. However, in dark specimens this may be poorly defined, causing them to be confused with the grass snake.

tings have started to slowly reappear. Anthropologists have suggested that these pictures are associated with the desire to succeed in the hunt, as they include innumerable pictures of the elk — in this area the most important game animal for Stone Age peoples. No less than half of the paintings at Värikallio depict this beast.

THE IIVAARA ROUTE

Iivaara, southeast of the village of Kuusamo, is south Kuusamo's most popular vacationing area. Beyond the main stretch of Lake Kuusamojärvi in good weather one can see the unmistakable hazy blue silhouette of Iivaara fell from as far away as the village itself. Lake Iijärvi is one of the watershed lakes of the River Iijoki, which debouches into the Gulf of Bothnia. The watershed at this point is very shallow and virtually hidden.

Shallow, clear River Rajajoki, marks the site of the Treaty of Täyssinä made almost four centuries ago and serving to unite the Lapp (Same) settlements in the Kuusamo district with the Finland of the Finns. "Raja" is Finnish for 'border' or 'boundary'.

As Kuusamo's lakes go, the small, rather shallow Rajalampi pool is an outstandingly eutrophic water body. Its vegetation is thick and luxuriant, with a great diversity of species, and its fish stocks are large. Once again we must look to the bedrock for the cause of this exceptional natural wealth. Iivaara geologically speaking is very young. Something like 300 million years ago magma pushed up through the Earth's crust and when it cooled future Finland was left with this fell. The rock type fell, which geologists call "iyolite", is related to the famous nepheline cyanite of the Kola peninsula.

In the Hiipinä fell districts in association with nepheline cyanite there is a great deal of apatite which is quarried there to form the basic ingredient of phosphorus-based fertilizer. Iivaara itself has been much studied with a view to exploiting it commercially but so far the fell has been saved from mining activities — as is the way of such things, making some people happy and others indignant. Iivaara's peculiar rock type is associated with a profusion of vegetation, both in the water bodies at the foot of the fell and in the small woods and spring dells on the slopes. The path to Iivaara goes along specially laid logs and planks (to stop you getting your feet wet) across the bog on the far side of the River Matalajoki. It then proceeds to skirt the fell through a spruce forest with thick mats of moss underfoot. The modern world has penetrated even this far and we find ourselves walking at times through clearcuts, but where the terrain attains a sufficient altitude, the machines have baulked and the trees are still photosynthesizing by day and turning out carbon dioxide by night. The track in

116

places is steep but for all that it is a pleasant one to toil along.

In places on the upper slopes, right beside the path there are hollows containing small groves of trees. The lush flora in some cases extends over fairly large areas, rather than simply forming narrow bands.

Gradually the forest thins out and towards the summit we suddenly reach very low-growing birch forests. On a small scale these resemble the fell birch woods of Lapland. On the northern slope there is a thick cover of moss under birch trees, but the southern slope by contrast is clothed in dryish Scots pine woods.

ATOP IIVAARA FELL

Concentrating on the steep ascent, the hiker is unlikely to be interested in looking keenly about as he ploughs on towards the summit of Iivaara fell. But when he has finally reached his goal, he will undoubtedly consider the climb well worth the effort as he admires the magnificent scenery that is spread out all around.

The scenery is stripey rather than chequered, with lakes, peatlands, and fells, oriented in a series of lines from the west-northwest to the east-southeast. The orientation reflects the progression of the great glaciers. This pattern is interesting from the point of view of human movement, it being the local custom to speak of walking 'across the landscape' or 'along the landscape'.

As Iivaara rises to some distance above the timberline, its summit is covered by a dwarf shrub fell heath on which there are a few low-growing spruces and Scots pines dotted about. This higher altitude vegetation — seen here in one of its most southerly locations — consists of a very low number of species, just as it does further north.

Dick Forsman

The wind up above will soon cool the hiker's perspiring skin and drive him down to a more sheltered spot. It is possible to return, if one wishes, by the same track and to take shelter in one of the small gullies leading east. On the descent, first moist hollows, and then larger areas of seepage begin to form themselves into brooks. It is in these diminutive hollows and small springs that the River Iijoki — one of Ostrobothnia's most distinguished rivers — has its humble beginnings.

AT THE HEADWATERS OF THE IIJOKI

The topmost brook becomes increasingly bolder and well-defined, babbling joyously down a stoney gully through a sheath of verdant vegetation. It settles down in a small boggy meadow, before finally debouching into the highest pool on the River Iijoki watercourse — Pieni Näätälampi.

Näätälampi is an extremely clearwater pool located at an altitude of almost 300 metres. A long trip and an equivalent descent are undertaken by the waters of the Iijoki before it arrives at the sea. A large proportion of the light ooze lying on the bottom of the lake is covered by an underwater meadow formed of spiked water-milfoil. Owing to the crystal clarity of the water here, this is clearly visible. The brooks beyond Iivaara cross one-time hay meadows. Abandoned hay barns and foundations remain as a memento of bygone forms of agriculture, as do the skeletons of dams crossing the brooks.

With the aid of the dams, water was backed up on to each side of the natural watercourse, drowning the mosses and reviving the sedges and grasses. Well in advance of the haymaking season the water was let out. Making hay on these boggy meadows was a time-consuming occupation. People would arrive here on a Monday and not return to their villages until Saturday.

At the foot of the fell there are innumerable small woods and moist hollows with spring water oozing into them. In one of the springs Angelica archangelica, a shoulder-high northern relative of the wild angelica, living here at the extreme southern tip of its range, cannot fail to excite interest. This is in reality a native of Lapland and the northernmost areas of northeastern Finland, but it has succeeded in establishing itself here at the foot of Iivaara fell. A. archangelica has been utilised in Finnish Lapland, and indeed in other parts of Scandinavia, for its succulent leaves, stalks and roots, from which an aromatic substance can be distilled. An attempt has recently been made at cultivating it, mainly to supply raw material for the Finnish liqueur industry.

Before very long, the Rajalampi pool comes into view between the trees and our trek up Iivaara fell comes to an end. Aside from enjoying the distinction of being one of Finland's most southerly located fells, Iivaara has a lot to offer those who take the trouble to climb it. YV

The close-set, rounded infloresences of Viscaria alpina *make it easy to distinguish from the commoner* V. vulgaris.

Finland's National Bird

Hannu Hautala

The swan was apparently a very important bird to the ancient Finns. Representations of it appear frequently in Karelian rock paintings. It has been depicted beside a sun motif, which may indicate that its sacredness is of old origin.

When cultures are undergoing transformation, old beliefs and customs can be forgotten. Thus, in the first half of our century, the Finns forgot the special status of the swan. The bird was hunted, even in spring, and its eggs and cygnets commonly collected.

The prominent ornithologist Professor Einari Merikallio pointed out in 1949 that the swan had disappeared from most of Finland As recently as the late 19th century, it nested in North Karelia and, further west, in the Suomenselkä district. By the 1940s, the only places where it could be found were close to the Soviet border and in the northernmost recesses of Lapland.

While working as a veterinarian in Muonio, Lapland in the 1940s, the writer Yrjö Kokko searched for swans in the surrounding district. After a long period of work, he produced his acclaimed book "The Whooper Swan, the Bird of Ultima Thule". This, together with his second book "They're Coming Back" aroused a sense of conservation in the Finnish people. Once again, the swan became Finland's sacred bird.

Yrjö Kokko was able to see the fruits of his work. When he died, at the age of 74, in 1977, swans were once again nesting all over Finland. The bird of Ultima Thule, the furthermost north, had become the bird of all Finland. It also became a symbol of nature conservation in Finland, and a few years ago was proclaimed the national bird.

Spring migration

Towards the end of March, swans leave their winter homes in the straits of Denmark and southern Sweden and begin their migration. Fully-grown birds fly quickly to their nesting areas. Younger individuals, not yet capable of reproducing, travel much slower and do not reach southern Finland until the end of April.

Swans can be observed near Inari in northern Lapland as early as the end of March, and by mid-April there can be as many as 150 of them there. These are nesting birds, which wait on the unfrozen part of the river for 3-5 weeks until the bogs and lakes thaw out. In the Kuusamo and Peräpohjola districts, nesting may begin only in mid-May, when floodwaters loosen up the ice on the rivers and create areas of open water near the banks.

Swans on rivers are described in several connections in the Kalevala and Kanteletar, Finland's two major epic works. Perhaps the Finns took special notice of the swans resting on the open flowing waters early in spring. As it happens, swans spend hardly any time on flowing waters at other times of the year. Lemminkäinen hunting a swan on a river in Tuonela, the ancient Finns' netherworld, is one of the key episodes in the Kalevala.

Nesting

Lakes with lots of reeds are the swan's favourite nesting place. A family needs only a small area to get through the whole summer. A lake as small as 50 hectares is enough if there are enough horsetails and submerged vegetation. A family that lives on a hummocky bog ranges over an extensive area. Especially in the north, swans have to nest on bleak lakes or hummocky bogs. That is why they often feed in lakes that are the habitat of other water fowl, and march their cygnets there almost as soon as they have hatched out, often distances of several kilometres. It must be an arduous trip for the little ones, which are only a few days old. If there is no such lush lake in the vicinity, the swans may spend the summer migrating from bog to bog or visit several lakes.

The stack on which a swan's nest rests is 40-80 centimetres high and 150-300 centimetres in diameter at the base. The bowl of the nest is about 30 centimeters wide. Since the birds use the same stack year after year, it grows as time passes. Even when one is already rather big, the birds lay new materials around the nest every year.

When the ice melts around the nest stack, the swans immediately set to work putting it back into condition. The water around it has to be unfrozen to provide protection from land predators, such as foxes. Eagles are obviously not among swans' worst enemies, because in Lapland both species nest in

the same areas.

There are usually 4-5 eggs in a swan's nest. As many as nine have been counted, but a clutch of seven is quite rare. Sometimes there are only two, and it has been calculated that the average for Finland is 4.4.

The female swan hatches the eggs herself. She leaves the nest for ½-1 hour 6 or 7 times a day, eating avidly during these periods. During her trips away from the nest, the eggs are covered to keep them warm and make them harder for predators to detect. Hatching takes 31-38 days. Since egg-laying begins in southern Finland right at the beginning of May and in the north about two weeks later, the cygnets hatch out between the beginning of June and Midsummer, three weeks later. If they do not hatch until early July, nesting is behind schedule.

It has been estimated that 10% of clutches are completely destroyed, whilst 75-80% of the eggs in those that are a success produce cygnets. A pair nesting for the first time is slightly less successful in rearing cygnets than an experienced pair. The first weeks of a young swan's life are very dangerous. Their mortality rate is about 10% a month. The rate is slightly lower (3-6%) in southern Finland than in the north (10-14%).

A swan is a fairly big bird. It takes cygnets 80-100 days to develop to the point where they can fly. The full nesting period from egg-laying to the time when the young ones take to the air lasts about 130 days. This is such a long time that swans must begin building their nests as early as possible in order to ensure that when autumn arrives the young are strong enough to cope with their long southwards migration. Their behaviour in spring is geared towards early nesting. In years when spring is usually late they do not nest at all.

Observations made in the areas where swans spend the winter indicate that the number of cygnets varies considerably from year to year. It is obvious that when an early autumn takes them by surprise, most of the cygnets in northern Finland perish. Further east, in

northern Russia and Siberia, harsh autumn weather can be more likely than in Finland. Studies conducted in southern Sweden have shown that cygnets account for only about 7% of the swan population after a poor nesting year and for 24% after a year in which conditions have been good.

Food

An adult swan is a vegetarian. Lake horsetails are quite an important source of nourishment in early spring. However, this plant apparently becomes too hard as the year draws on, because swans first stop eating the main stem, and by the end of July have stopped eating the fresher branch shoots as well. Underwater plants, especially drowning lily shoots on the bottoms of lakes and ponds, are an important source of nourishment in late summer and early autumn. Reaching down with their long necks, swans can peck shoots as much as 60 centimetres below the surface. First, they pump with their feet to wash silt off the shoots and then pull them to the surface with their beaks. The shoots are washed at the same time, because the swans keep their heads below water for 10-12 seconds. It has recently been observed in wintering areas that swans also eat on dry land; they graze grass on pastureland.

Cygnets eat insects for the first 30 days of their life. This food is richer in protein than vegetarian fare. The cygnets also eat reeds for a brief period, but by the time they are 45 days old they are eating the same vegetarian diet as adults. When the cygnets begin dipping their heads below the water to pull shoots, they keep them submerged for only a few seconds. During their first winter, their ability to gather food is inferior to that of adults.

The autumn migration

The first birds to depart on their autumn migration are younger ones that have not nested. They set off between late September and the middle of October. Young birds can stop in good feeding areas on the way for several weeks. As many as 1,800 swans can be

seen in the area around the island of Hailuoto off the northwest coast during the autumn migration. Other known areas are around Kokkola and Pori on the west coast. Swans can remain on the southern side of the Hanko peninsula on the south coast until January. Thus the swan is the last of our migratory birds to leave Finland.

Nesting birds and their young head south only when shallow small lakes and the water near the shores of larger ones begin freezing up. Those families fly to their winter grounds via southern Finland quite quickly in late October and early November.

The future and protection

Censuses conducted in wintering areas in the past decade show that Europe's whooper swan population is stable at about 20,000 birds. The Finnish population has grown strongly during the same period and the swans have expanded their range of distribution in this country. It is estimated that the nesting population grew at an average annual rate of 11.5% between 1950 and 1987. When the population was small, an average increase of 11.5% did not mean very much, but now that percentage means ten or so more pairs each year. The last time the number of nesting pairs was estimated was in 1974-79, when a survey of all birds nesting in Finland was conducted. It showed that there were 179 nesting pairs of swans in Finland. Now, in the 1980s, there are several thousands of these birds in our country. About 30% are old enough to reproduce and the remaining 70% birds under five years of age.

The Finnish swan population could increase to several times its present size, because there are plenty of suitable habitats. There are several times as many swans in Iceland as in Finland, although the country is only about a third the size of Finland in area. The density of the swan population in the Murmansk region and East Karelia, both just east of the Finnish border, is also higher than in Finland. AH

RIISITUNTURI

The name Koillismaa is very often given to the area whose hub is the old commune of Kuusamo, but this area also includes Posio, Taivalkoski and Salla. The name "Posio" is connected with Lapland; it is a relic of those times when these districts were still part of the Lapps' (Same) territories before the arrival of the Finns. The name actually means the end of a tepee, or more precisely the entrance at the end of a tepee.

Over Lake Kitkajärvi, as seen from the east, the landscape is dominated by the curvy silhouette of Riisitunturi fell. Even from this distance it is possible to see

Aimo Holtari

that the crown is bare, thrusting well up above the timberline.

RIISITUNTURI NATIONAL PARK

The ascent to Riisitunturi fell is almost imperceptibly gentle. The hiker can reach the top without being out of breath and the climb, usually to one's intense surprise, is accomplished without one being aware of it. No great vista unfurls before or behind the climber. Even the crown of Riisitunturi for most of the ascent is hidden from the hiker's view. For once we can say something good about clearfellings — the rambler can admire the entire expanse of Yli-Kitka instead of facing a solid wall of trunks and foliage! This is only a temporary situation, however, as the national park soon unsportingly swallows one up in its own forests.

Spruces are rather rare in the latter and the tree stands have a tendency to thin out the higher one climbs. At the same time the number of birch trees steadily increases. There is an abundance of bilberry and in 'good berry years' (as the Finns say) the crop seems limitless and impossible to pick in its entirety — some berries always seem to remain to be nipped by the autumn frosts. The spruces are of the typical Nordic kind, known in these parts as "candle spruces", owing to their emaciated trunks and vestigial, downtrodden branches. The latter come right down to the ground to form small dens which fire the imagination — surely these are the homes of the legendary denizens of the forests, elves, gnomes and the like? According to legend, the "people of the midnight" take offence if you light a fire in the middle of the path!

Many of the original spruce crowns have broken and become ramified, so that they now bear several younger growths at the top, rather like a crown of thorns. The heavy winter snows ("tykky") have snapped off the primary growing point of these specimens. Nature was ever the artist and in the case of these spruce trees her imagination seems to have run riot. Sometimes the lower branches of the trees trail along the ground, only to bend upwards when they reach an obstacle such as another trunk. Alongside the Riisitunturi trail the hiker cannot fail to notice an anomaly known as "Tapio's Table". This is a spruce tree whose crown is completely absent and whose branches have begun to curve downwards to form a striking resemblance to a tabletop — or, if you happen to be of a nervous disposition, to an upturned witch's cauldron.

In a rather wet gully by a brook there is a cabin which is very new, neat and robust, in keeping with Finnish tradition. This hostel of the wilds offers the hiker protection against the weather, the chance to put his feet up, and even the opportunity to spend a comfortable night indoors. The fell actually has two summits, the cabin been located in the hollow between them. One could, for instance, first head for the more southerly of the summits. Standing at the summit, at the base of the spot height triangle, the hiker may be interested to hear that he is now standing at an altitude of 466 metres above sea level, or 226 metres higher than the surface of nearby Lake Kitkajärvi.

BOGS ON A SLANT

The climb to the summit is not very long. On a clear day, once one has arrived there, the view will be found to be breathtaking. Towards the east, Lake Ylä-Kitkajärvi gleams in the sunshine like a sapphire speckled with islands and promontories. In general the islands, promontories and bays have an elongated shape, conferring this pattern on the whole landscape. They betray the direction of movement of the continental ice sheets during the last Ice Age (west-northwest).

Over to the west the landscape is dominated by the neighbouring fell, Nuolivaara, whose over 400-metre high crown, like that of Riisitunturi, is treeless and wrapped in a fell heath.

The two fells are separated from each other by Riisisuo bog which lies in a cleft gouged out by glaciers and along which now flows the Riisijoki, a river containing water stained brown by humus.

The slopes of all the fells are clothed in bands which serve to break up otherwise rather bland scenery. These are blanket bogs which nowhere in Finland occur in such abundance and to such a high degree of development as in the Riisitunturi area. It is mainly because of the presence of these that Riisitunturi was made into a national park.

The blanket bogs further up the slopes seem to merge imperceptibly into the heathland-type vegetation clothing the fell summits. This, Riisitunturi's special feature, i.e. the extraordinary amount of peatland formation, has been studied since at least the beginning of this century. Professor Väinö Auer, who gained considerable renown for his studies of Tierra del Fuego, began his research career there. It has been shown that these several thousand year old bogs are of an unusual kind for Koillismaa. Their nearest equivalents are found in the treeless heaths on the western shores of Europe — the so-called blanket bogs or blanket mires. The Finns, who have a word for everything, term their blanket bogs "slope bogs" to distinguish them from these western counterparts. Their presence is an indication of an abnormally humid climate which has no equal elsewhere in Finland. The bald patch at the top of Riisitunturi is exceptionally large for so southerly a location.

The Norwegian lemming, an animal of the tundra which has attained pop-star fame for its migrations, at least twice during the present century has attempted to reach Riisitunturi fell. On both occasions the lemming population, however, has 'crashed' within a comparatively short space of time. The reason for the extinction has most likely been an inadequacy of winter food, since the Norwegian lemming requires damp vegetation on which to feed in places with prolonged snow cover and Riisitunturi is rather miserly in this respect.

THE RIISITUNTURI YEAR

Early winter, the time of dark nights, brings a thick mantle of snow to the ground-hugging vegetation near the summit. When, as though festooned with cotton wool, the slim Nordic spruces stand sentinel beneath a silent sky and the stunted trees on the fell heaths sport dazzling white caps, the scene is right out of a children's book.

Autumn on Riisitunturi is a time of glowing splendour, the birches and aspens, yellow as buttercups, betraying their numbers even to the weakest eye. The blanket bogs at this time of the year acquire a rusty-red hue. The dwarf-shrub layer turns flame red, the leaves of the ptarmigan berry Arctostaphylus alpinus being a particularly eye-catching scarlet. Upon close examination of this autumn jewel, one discovers that each red leaf bears a fine tracery of veins. Succulent-looking black berries dangle down between the leaves.

Visitors to Riisitunturi today may well feel that they are in a true wilderness far from the hustle and bustle of the modern world. Even here, however, signs of human impact are in evidence. Here and there stretch the foundations of a hay barn, or the crumbling remains of some construction or other. The River Riisijoki used to be dammed in order to raise the water level and thereby kill off the moss growth and promote that of the sedges and grasses. At one time people came here to spend several weeks hay making, collecting the extremely sparse hay from these natural meadows, frequently working up to their knees in the water, at the mercy of irritating gnats and horseflies, and spending their nights in lean-to's or saunas. They returned home only for Sunday each week, to rest, to charge up their batteries in the sauna, and to replenish their food supply.

The hay was eventually carried home over the winter snow, being hauled from the more difficult, inaccessible places by reindeer.

Martti Rikkonen

In northern Finland the bilberry crop is generally good and its size less subject to variation than in southern Finland.

PLACID LAKE

Lake Kitkajärvi, which so obviously dominates the scenery spread out at the feet of Riisitunturi, is one of the lakes lying along the great watercourses which flow away from Finland towards the White Sea. The watershed runs on the western side of Lake Kitkajärvi along the Karitunturi — Tolvanvaara — Riisitunturi — Noukavaara fell chains. Lake Kitkajärvi, half of which lies in Posio commune, used to be a place where fishermen stretched out their arms to describe a catch. Historians say that one of the most important reasons for the arrival of the Finns in Koillismaa around 350 years ago was the necessity to catch pike. Recently deceased pike is receptive to drying and thus constituted valuable merchandise, as well as being a protein-rich food. Kitajärvi was one of the most renowned pike waters. Its red trout, grayling, whitefish and vendace populations did not lag far behind. The pike stocks have declined drastically, as have those of the grayling and trout, both in the waters draining into Kitkajärvi, and in the lake itself. That small mercy, the vendace, continues to provide fishermen with catches best-described by those with loose sleeves, as does indeed the whitefish.

In recent years a great deal of effort has been put

into reviving the valuable fish in the lake, and the aim is to raise the level of catches and hence the profitability of commercial fishing by making use as far as possible of the natural stocks. Clearwater Kitkajärvi, made up of three separate basins, is unique in the sense that its waters are still almost one hundred percent pure and that no water level regulation has taken place there. It thus has a very good chance of one day becoming Finland's most valuable inland fishery location.

THE ERAUSPOIKA TRAIL

Aside from Riisitunturi and Kitka, recognition for Posio has also been earned by Korouoma. Around Korouoma the National Board of Forestry has established the Lapiosalmi-Korouoma recreation area in order to serve the needs of hikers and other fresh-air friends. With the back-packer in mind, a 26-kilometre long trail — the Erauspoika Trail — complete with resting and campfire sites, has been set up. More trails radiate off this to other recreation areas.

Let's start off along the Erauspoika Trail from the south, i.e. from route 941 at Lapiosalmi, between Posio and Ranua. The region is lovely, dry esker terrain. The ground is covered with a light mat of reindeer lichens speckled with crowberry and cowberry dwarf shrubs. Pink-trunked Scots pines disperse their tangy scent into the air. Ensconced among the eskers there are a vast number of clearwater, sandy-bottomed lakes and pools.

In this area lies the watershed between the River Kitkajoki, which flows east, and the other watercourses, which flow to the west. In places this watershed is very narrow, being only the width of an esker.

The trail winds along the Jaakkokangas heath down a line of eskers on the northern sides on which can be made out lakes Laivajärvi and Pahajärvi, and on the southern side lakes Iso Kuuleajärvi and Pikku Kuuleajärvi. It is well worth visiting the Kuuleajärvi lakes and seeing for yourself the reason for their name, which is derived from the Finnish word "kuulea", meaning "clear" or "transparent". Rarely can one see such water so unencumbered by suspended solids. All the minutiae on the bottom near the shore with its sprawling tree trunks and fine sand are revealed in pin-sharp detail.

We are now in the Korouoma recreation fishing area, which spans a total of 346 hectares. Perch and pike, together with brown trout and migratory sea trout, are among the area's attractions.

It is no great distance from Lake Aimojärvi — a little over one and a half kilometres — over Kivimaankangas to Lake Koronlatvajärvi, where a lean-to has been built. Lake Koronlatvajärvi is located on a watershed from which water flows into three watercourses, that of the rivers Kemijoki, Simojoki and Iijoki. It would seem that the water has difficulty in deciding in which direction to flow and while it is pondering this problem Lake Koronlatvajärvi is obliged to sit there without an outlet. Local inhabitants, however, believe that there is some kind of connection, possibly a subterranean one, to the River Korojoki and then on to the Kemijoki.

On Kivimaankangas the trail crosses a logging road, while just a mite further west there is another logging road which the recreation area boundary follows for some distance. On the edge of this road running along the southwest bank of the Korojoki, at the junction with Lake Koronlatvajärvi, the Koro cabin stands on the shore of a small pool. This cabin is available for hire — which means that if you arrive on the off-chance you will probably find it locked. If you are thinking of using it, enquire in advance at the National Board of Forestry's Taivalkoski District Office, in Kuusamo.

THE KOROUOMA RAVINE

Although the River Korojoki flows from an esker region, its channel fairly quickly changes into a steep-sided ravine known as Korouoma. The sheer walls in places are vertical, rising up for several dozen metres, leaving the river at the bottom of a narrowish ravine. In places this ravine is very narrow indeed, in others rather broader. Where it broadens out there are slim meadows. The shallow and rather narrow river meanders a lot.

The main tributaries are the Pajupuro and Auttijoki, both of which originate on the eastern side. They flow in their upper reaches through peatlands, before plunging down over a jumble of rocks into the Korouoma ravine. Flowing water continually bathes some of the rock faces, bringing a steady supply of nutrients to their bases and paving the way, so to speak, for luxuriant, copse-like vegetation. In this rather specialised habitat grow large ferns and bushes including, in places, wild cherries. At these latitudes the wild cherry is a great rarity.

The precipitous cliffs lining the ravine are virtually rock gardens. Since Korouoma is a rift valley which has formed from acid, low-nutrient granitic bedrock, it is unable to support a great variety of species. In this, it differs sharply from the lime-rich cliffs of northern Kuusamo (see chapter on Oulanka National Park). Among the flora with northern affinities there are the insectivorous butterwort, the white-flowering Saxifraga nivalis, and the tiny Draba norvegica. A surprising touch of the south is added to the ravine by the large and magnificent male ferns, found here growing at the foot of the cliffs and growing nowhere else in Koillismaa.

Wherever the sheer walls give way to more gentle slopes, the river banks are occupied by green meadows. Especially at the time around midsummer, with globe flowers in full bloom in these meadows, the scene is spell-binding. Sludge brought down by the river fertilizes these so-called bottom meadows and promotes hay growth. Years ago haymakers used to come along to cut the hay standing along the river banks, as testified to by the presence of hay barns and crumbling dams crossing the river.

These haymaking activities formed part of what might be called the 'natural economy period' and when it became the custom to grow animal fodder on one's own fields this back-breaking and low yield method of keeping the stomachs of domestic animals filled in winter was (perhaps to the accompaniment of sighs of relief) abandoned. This change in land use has had certain repercussions. Meadows which originally produced hay have become overgrown by bushes and have virtually been wiped from the landscape.

The Lapiosalmi-Korouoma recreation area ends in the north at the mouth of the river Kurttajoki. At the northern end of the area there are some very interesting points worthy of exploration including Karhunpesä, the Pirunkirkko gully, and the Koivuköngäs rapids on the River Kurttajoki. YV

Riisitunturi National Park

Posio, 76 km²
Established: 1982
Under National Board of Forestry management.

Connections: Coach connection to road on southern side of park, from which there is a 3-km hike to the park boundary. On the western side the Posio-Maaninkavaara road, from which there is a 9-km hike to the park.

Services: Marked hiking trail. Unlocked cabin.

Map: Basic map 1:20 000 nos, 3533 04, 3633 07, 3633 08, 4611 04 and 4611 05.

Further information: National Board of Forestry, Ranua District Office, tel. 960-51 341 (Ranua).

The only species that can live permanently here in the north are those with the ability to survive our long severe winter. Our summer is brief. There are only a few months to reproduce, grow and prepare for the winter. That requires adaptability.

Migratory birds have solved the problem by flying south. A question worth pondering here is whether they have adapted to the winter or simply fly north in summer to nest.

All animals in the north are active in summer. By contrast, only some of them are on the move during the winter. Most put their metabolic systems on economy mode or hibernate.

The means and problems of the tiny

Most invertebrates, such as insects, spiders, molluscs and various wormlike creatures, spend the winter as eggs or larvae. They slumber either in the mild temperature of the soil or in protective coatings that shield them from the chill of winter.

Among those that spend the winter as adults are some beetles and butterflies as well as many crustaceans and isopods like wood louses. The small tortoiseshell, Camberwell beauty and several other butterflies, which fly about in the spring sun, have developed into adults already the previous summer.

Among wasps and bumblebees, only queens that have mated hibernate, but all castes in a community of common ants do so. Bees introduced from further south do not become benumbed even in winter. By eating honey sparingly and producing heat with their muscles they keep their buzzing spherical communal dormitory at a temperature of over 15° C, and as much as 30° C at the centre of the sphere.

When the temperature drops below freezing, small hibernators face two dangers: freezing and dehydration. Freezing water ruptures cells and dehydration kills them. The cells of some cold-resistant insects have been found to contain small quantities of an anti-freeze substance, glycerin, in winter. Other small species have developed

another way to cope in that their cells have the ability to combine water with proteins for the winter. This water neither freezes nor evaporates. The shells in which various invertebrate animals as well as eggs and larvae spend the winter have impermeable linings to prevent evaporation.

Adapting and regulating

Some animals have body temperatures that go up or down with the temperature of their environment. The main ways in which they can regulate their temperature are behavioural, i.e. by exposing themselves to sunshine, going into the shad-

ow or, in winter, by digging deep enough into the soil.

Birds and mammals have fairly unvarying body temperatures, which they keep more or less stable whatever the surrounding conditions. Some species have sophisticated regulation systems, which enable them to lower their temperatures in periods of inclement weather, during their daily sleep periods or when they go into hibernation.

Economically and hand-to-mouth

The basic problem in coping with winter is where to get enough energy to keep the

flame of life flickering until the new spring dawns. This energy problem has two aspects: supply and demand.

Many animals save energy within their own bodies in preparation for winter. This is mostly in the form of fat tissue, which has an energy content about twice as high as the sugar burned in their cells in summer. Our birds and mammals are, without exception, at their fattest when winter begins.

Another and more common way of getting energy is, of course, to eat enough in winter as well. That is what most of our birds and mammals do, although their bodies, too, con-

Life All Winter Long

The long hairs of its white winter coat protect the arctic fox from the wind, while the soft fluff beneath insulates its body effectively.

Seppo Keränen

tain substantial stocks of fat to help them survive the leanest periods.

Lowering body temperature

The greater the difference between an animal's temperature and that of its environment, the faster heat is dissipated. Hedgehogs and bats, which settle down for the winter at the end of autumn when their bodies are well bolstered with fat, are able to minimize energy consumption by lowering their body temperature virtually to zero. This reduces their metabolic rate to a slight fraction of what it is in summer and they sink into a completely comatose

Pauli Nieminen

state.

Tits employ more or less the same principle in winter. They bustle briskly about the gloomy winter sky, but when night falls withdraw to a hollow somewhere, puff up their feathers and drop their body temperature from over 40 to as low as 32 degrees Celsius. If one peeps into their hiding hole and shines a lamp on the bird, the round ball of feathers does not move, although its eyes are clearly open.

This brief torpor is an example of short-term adaptation to cold.

The ability to adapt metabolic activity to short periods of

cold is also an advantage if the summer is cool. Swifts, which have originally nested in holes drilled by woodpeckers in the trees of primeval forests, can fly hundreds of kilometres to avoid rainy weather. Their young can survive in the nest for days on end without food, lowering their temperature nearly 20 degrees as that of the surrounding air falls at night. Their bodies warm up again during the day. This energy saving notwithstanding, the chicks can lose as much as half their original weight. Young mammals, which can remain in their nest for a long time without their mother, have the same ability to adapt and survive.

Winter sleepers and vigilants

Bears, badgers and raccoon dogs differ from animals which go into a torpor to hibernate in that their body temperature hardly falls at all during the winter, although they spend long periods in their nests. When the weather permits, raccoon dogs and badgers get up and investigate the environs of their nests.

Animals that remain active all winter have their means of enduring the cold. As their body temperatures drop, mammals can quickly produce heat by shivering. This is a deliberate contraction of their muscles, a

form of exertion which releases energy and raises their body temperature.

Brown fat, or thermogenic tissue, is found in mammals, especially between their shoulders. Its function is to produce energy exceptionally efficiently. The heat given off as the fat is consumed is rapidly carried to the other parts of the creatures' bodies by blood. This type of fat plays a central role in the way that all young mammals generate heat. It is activated in adult mammals in emergency situations, when their body temperature falls.

It pays to insulate

Lowering body temperature is

The events of the previous night are recorded in the snow: a small mammal's nocturnal ramble ended in the talons of a preying owl.

only one way of conserving energy. Without proper insulation of the body surface it would be pointless. The difference between the air temperature and that of the bodies of mammals and birds which remain active during the winter can be as much as 70-80 degrees.

To cope with the cold of winter, animals can regulate blood

circulation to prevent the parts of their bodies exposed to air or water from being unnecessarily warm. The feet of duck and gulls cool down almost to zero. The toes of large mammals have a temperature of less than 10 degrees Celsius in winter.

Lowering the temperature of the body surface also has its dangers, because cell tissue can be frozen and destroyed. Of course, fur and feathers reduce heat loss without the skin cooling too much.

The purpose of fur and feather coverings is to keep a warm insulating layer in place against the skin. The outer hairs and feathers are mainly for protection against the wind, whilst down and fluffy hairs close to the skin keep in the body heat.

The more immobile air there is close to the skin, the better the insulation. Birds and mammals shed their summer coats and replace them with their winter garb in autumn. A sparrow's new winter plumage weighs 70% more than its summer outfit.

Structure and behaviour

A large body has less surface area in relation to weight than a small one. Animals living in the north are larger on average than members of the same species living further south. A smooth surface dissipates heat slower than an uneven one. Northern populations of various species have shorter bodily appendages than their southern kin.

Behaviour and living habits also enhance thermal economy. Rolling up into a spherical shape and tucking snouts, beaks and feet inside the body's protective coat are common ways of reducing heat loss. Animals spend the night in holes or burrowed into snowdrifts for the same purpose.

Snow protects and insulates, but it also hampers movement and access to food. The white winter coats of many species camouflage them from their enemies. On the other hand, the whiteness of wolves in the Arctic region and of polar bears is probably meant to make them undetectable by their prey. MSo

Trees' Winter Burden

Hannu Hautala

The hilly landscape in Kuusamo is truly white in the heart of winter. Not a single speck of black can be detected on the Arctic fells, because snow covers the trees from top to bottom. It differs from the snow that blankets forests further south in that it has not fallen from the sky, but rather formed directly on branches and any other object projecting from the smooth blanket on the ground. Telephone and electricity poles, blades of grass, radio and TV antennas, snow barriers and buildings become encrusted with snow in exactly the same way.

Snow encrustation is not limited to hill forests. Just as totally, it covers any protuberance on the surfaces of open Arctic hills: stones, berry shrubs, solitary trees, trail markers. When the winter darkness is at its deepest, snow coalescing in the frigid air attaches itself to even sheer rock faces and clothes their dark surfaces in a white mantle. The prevailing wind can give snow encrustations on

exposed buildings asymmetrical forms: at times it seems that the Creator plays with His snow brush and paints the figures of elves, mountain trolls, goblins and gnomes, which in the gloomy twilight of winter seem eerily real.

Snow encrustations can form anywhere if the weather conditions are right. The air must be moist and at just the right temperature to ensure that the moisture in it freezes so slowly that it neither forms a fog nor precipitates as snow, but rather creates a static mantle of mist. Encrustations usually form rather poorly in southern Finland and the mist lays only a thin coating of hoar frost. But the only difference between hoar and snow encrustation is in the thickness of the layer.

Winter conditions in the hills and Arctic fells of Lapland and the adjacent Koillismaa region often favour snow encrustation. The borderline between the areas in which snow forms crusts and falls as precipitation can be quite sharp. From a certain latitude northwards the forests on

the hill slopes are totally white, south of that glimpses of other colours can still be seen.

Encrusted forests contain far more snow than those on lower slopes. Just as much snow falls on them as elsewhere, and the volume that forms directly from the air can be as much again. The mantle clinging to a single tree can weight tonnes.

The trees on slopes where encrustation occurs are mainly firs. The same climatic factors that cause encrustation in winter have effects in summer as well. Areas above the encrustation line are damper in summer than forests lower down; now vegetation receives some of its water directly from the air in the form of dew condensing from mists. The tops of hills often support firs with heavy moss coatings, whereas the lower slopes of the same hills are more likely to be dry-looking pine heaths. Dogwood, which thrives in moist, maritime conditions, is commonly found on many of the slopes where snow encrustation is most likely in winter. In autumn, fog can

hover above the upper slopes for days at a time.

In March, when the sun begins giving warmth, the snow crusts begin clodding and falling. When the trees shed their burden and the forest begins greening, it is a sign that winter's back has been broken.

Burdens of tonnes of snow can shatter and mutilate trees. Forests that are heavily encrusted in winter look ragged in summer, with bent crowns, dead leaders, twisted trunks, multiple crowns and clear signs of decay in places. Most of them are of insignificant commercial value. When winter conditions cause exceptionally heavy encrustation of tended trees lower down the slopes, the sight revealed when the snow disappears the following spring resembles the result of an artillery bombardment.

However, old hilltop forests make an important contribution to the diversity of nature. They are home to many mushrooms and insects that have long since disappeared from tended commercial forests. SV

Candle spruces

It is not only the Arctic fells that announce that one has arrived in the north. One can also see it from the shapes of the spruces, which become more and more slender, more and more like pillars or tapering knobbly candles. As one goes northwards, slender candlelike spruces become a common feature at Kajaani in the east, but if one goes up along the Gulf of Bothnia in the west, one does not find many of them until one has reached the uplands fringing the valleys of the Tornio and Kemi rivers. However, individual short-branched spruces can be found in the very south of Finland.

Good stubby-branched Lapland spruces look taller than they actually are. They are rarely over 20 metres, a height that some in the south reach in only a few decades. Short branches can be considered a means of adapting to heavy snowfall; less snow can accumulate on a tree with short branches than on one with long branches. This theory is supported by the fact that also the pines in Lapland have very short branches when they are young; indeed, they rather resemble spruces when seen from a distance.

It's actually Siberian

The slender-crowned spruces of the north are different from those in southern Finland in other respects, too. Their cones are smaller and shorter and have scales with rounded points, whereas the scales of southern spruces taper to a fairly sharp point. The young branches of northern spruces are "furry", but those in the south are bare. However, these differences are gradual and there is no sharp dividing line between different types.

Spruces in different parts of Finland represent several subspecies. As the Ice Age descended, spruces had retreated in two directions, south to Europe and east to Siberia. When the ice eventually melted, they once again advanced towards the north. They reached Finland from the two directions in which they had long before receded, swinging around the Gulf of Finland from the south and coming directly from Siberia in the east.

During their separation, which may have lasted hundreds of thousands of years, the European and Asian spruces had managed to develop into somewhat different types. When they met again here in Finland, they intermixed again on an extensive scale. The slender-crowned pillarlike spruce of the north is a fairly pure Siberian variety, whilst the one that grows in southern Finland is the joint descendent of the European and Siberian wings that converged here. That may explain wide variations in the character of the species in that part of Finland.

The area in which Siberian spruces grow extends into Sweden, and in the east all the way to the Pacific coast. Most of the European spruces growing on mountain slopes in Central Europe are now suffering from the effects of acid rain.

Quite many plants (and perhaps also animals) in northern Finland are of different origin

Hannu Hautala

from the equivalent populations in southern Finland; they "wintered" in different regions during the Ice Age and made their way back to Finland via different routes when the ice retreated again. Most of the species in Lapland returned from the east, but some species probably managed to find a refuge on the unfrozen Norwegian coast, at least during the last glaciation, and eventually came back to Lapland from the west and even from the north.

Mossy spruce forests

With the exception of the rare few growing in the lushest areas along streams, the spruce forests of Lapland are not very dark. The trees are well spaced and their short branches further emphasize the feeling of spaciousness.

Spruces dominate on waterlogged fine moraine soils. As a forest ages, the moss carpet on the ground become thicker and thicker. Since the trees are thinly spaced, grow slowly and are damaged by rot, their annual growth increase is not particularly interesting from the commercial viewpoint. Nevertheless, they do not deserve the name given them by professional foresters: "suicide spruce forests". There are always new seedlings coming along to replace the dying trees. In decades of travels through the wildernesses of Lapland, I have never once seen a stand of spruce that died where it stood. Although these trees are of little importance for commercial wood production, the beard lichen growing on them is an important source of food for reindeer in winter.

It is in these forests that highly controversial clear felling and ploughing schemes have been conducted. Although violent efforts have been made to replace the spruces with pines by ploughing up the ground and replanting, success has been very limited. After it has been ploughed up, the soil settles again and is simply too dense for pines, whose roots suffer from lack of oxygen. A spruce's root system is much closer to the surface than a pine's. That is why spruces are much better equipped to grow in the cold, waterlogged soils of Lapland.

Pests

Just as spruces tend to make forests and landscapes rather one-sided when they are the dominant species, they signif-icantly enrich the forest environment when they are mixed with other species. Hardly any larger animal eats the long resinous needles of spruce, nor are very many insects attracted to them. But these trees give shelter to many birds and their seeds make much better eating than their needles.

In mid-summer some years, the shoots on spruces turn yellowish brown and dusty: a fungal growth has transferred from another host, wild rosemary, to the spruces to develop its spores and destroy the needles.

Fungi find it easy to attack the wounds caused by snow damage. The worst enemy of spruce stands in southern Finland is a root fungus that does not thrive in the north. But trees there are highly susceptible to several other fungi. SV

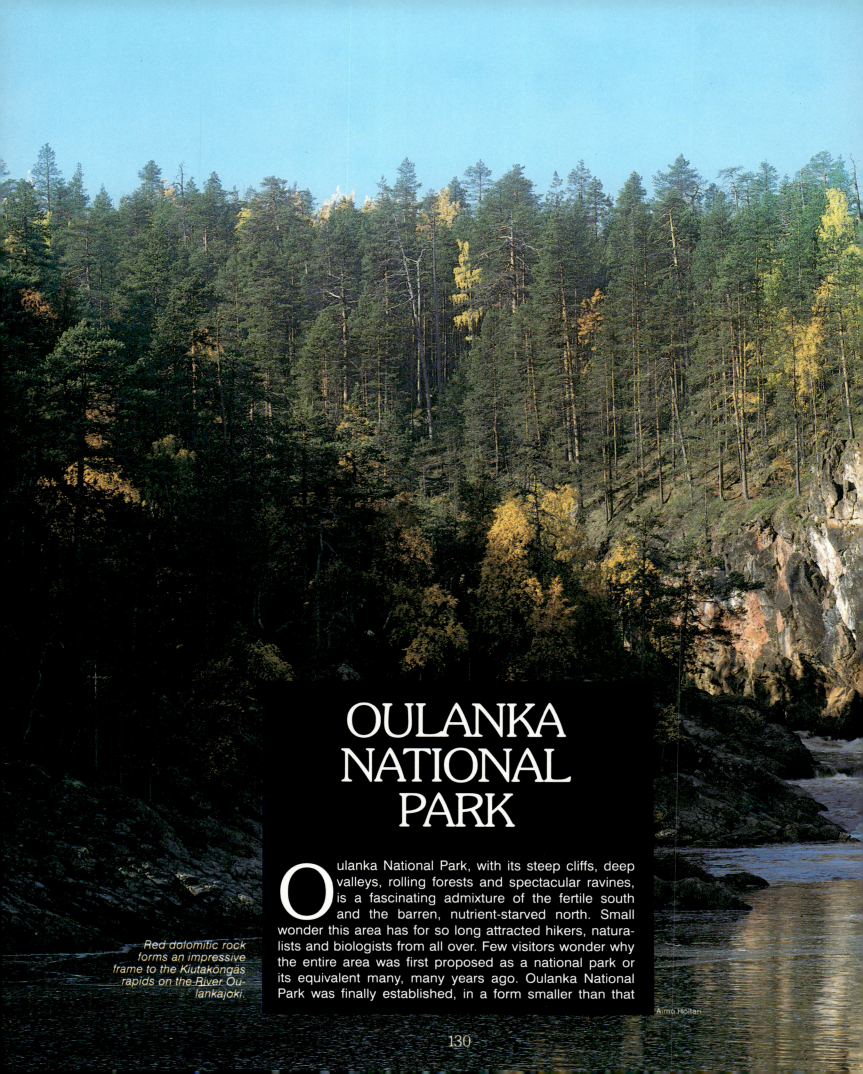

OULANKA
NATIONAL
PARK

Oulanka National Park, with its steep cliffs, deep valleys, rolling forests and spectacular ravines, is a fascinating admixture of the fertile south and the barren, nutrient-starved north. Small wonder this area has for so long attracted hikers, naturalists and biologists from all over. Few visitors wonder why the entire area was first proposed as a national park or its equivalent many, many years ago. Oulanka National Park was finally established, in a form smaller than that

Red dolomitic rock forms an impressive frame to the Kiutaköngäs rapids on the River Oulankajoki.

Aimo Hoitari

Seppo Keränen

The teal — a bit of a pip-squeak among ducks — is one of Finland's commonest waterfowl on forest and peatland pools.

envisaged and campaigned for, in 1956, since which time it has been extended (in 1982) by the addition of the peatland area lying between the old park and Finland's eastern border. Its original surface area was thereby doubled.

In 1987, after a long and bitter struggle, Kitkanniemi was joined to the national park, expanding the preserve by a further 60 square kilometres. It is very easy to reach the national park nowadays, as it is flanked on both its western and southern sides by roads. Additionally, the road going to Liikasenvaara runs right through the park across the River Oulankajoki. The most famous of all the Koillismaa hiking routes, known as Karhunkierros ("The Bear's Route"), runs through the park. Despite its Finnish name, this is not a complete 70 km circuit (= "kierros") as the route begins alongside the Salla road and ends at Rukatunturi fell, site of a famous skiing resort.

FROM THE BEAR'S ROUTE TO TAIVALKÖNGÄS
Back-packing along the Bears' Route usually begins at the Salla road, just slightly north of Lake Ollilanjärvi. At this starting point we are almost at the average altitude for Kuusamo, i.e. 250 metres above sea level, but for the whole walk we shall be journeying almost imperceptibly downhill. And when we finally leave the park there are only some 140 metres left above sea level (but, it might be added, there is still a considerable journey to the briny

itself). However, the descent is by no means continuous and in places the going is hard due to the uniqueness of the landforms. There are flat, level heathlands, but there are also deep ravines enclasping the rivers, since the entire River Oulankajoki valley has formed along major fault lines.

For a start the going through Scots pine forests is a novice's dream. Only in some of the brook gullies is the vegetation more luxuriant. On the bank of the foaming Aventojoki river there is the first resting place, where it is possible to brew up a welcome cup of some beverage. Remember that inside the national park the lighting of campfires and camping are permitted only in specially marked places.

Afterwards the trail forsakes the River Aventojoki and winds through the forest to Ristikallio. The impression of a vertically walled, but in some respects graceful, eminence is added to by the quiet dark river. Despite its near nudity this idyllic, tranquil ravine scenery has been photographed thousands of times.

The Bear's Route continues from Ristikallio due north through variable Scots pine forests. After slightly over a kilometre the rushing river Maaninkajoki is crossed immediately above the rapids. The river rushes through a steep-walled ravine and it is well worthwhile leaving the path to visit the calm pool below the rapids.

The trail skirts the Vaalulampi pool to an old reindeer

herdsmen's hut, the Puikkokämppä cabin, which has been renovated for the use of hikers. There are reindeer within the national park and reindeer husbandry is also practised here. The visitor will not see reindeer in large herds, but singly and frequently seeking shade on sweltering hot summer days in the bottom meadows lining the river. However, signs of reindeer will be found almost everywhere in the terrain. One metre high stumps represent the remains of trees felled by herdsmen in the pre-national park days to enable the reindeer to obtain beard moss during the winter when other food has been scarce. At that time timber was not accorded the value that it is nowadays. In addition there are still at least five reindeer fences in the park.

From now on in the vegetation becomes more lush as we arrive in a limestone district. The calcium in the bedrock and the moist nature of the slopes is manifest in the sheer abundance of plant species, as well as in the verdancy of the mossy carpet underfoot. Spruce becomes dominant, with bilberry covering most of the glades, and other herbs becoming much commoner. In places there is a striking resemblance to the deciduous woodlands of the south, with fewer dwarf shrubs and more larger shrubs. At its best, this luxuriance occurs at the mouths of streams, where metre high ostrich ferns or lady ferns overshadow the lower vegetation.

Taivalköngäs is the second of the park's great rapids. At midsummer the water flows along two main channels and at the same time its level drops by six metres. During the spring, due to the floods, there is a third channel between the other two which takes the form of a small brook. The term "taival" (= a rough road) refers to the problem of making progress. It used to be necessary here to make a porterage when going up- or downstream, in order to avoid the rapids.

The names also refer to the fact that relations between the Lapps and the people encroaching from the south were relatively peaceful. Many Lappish names have been preserved right up to the present day, without any attempt at eradication. These include some of north Kuusamo's most magnificent sights: Juuma, Konttainen and Kiutaköngäs.

THE STEEP OULANKA CANYON

At Taivalköngäs a small trail from the north joins the Bear's Route, along which we now journey towards the park's steepest ravine, the Oulanka canyon. The route deviates slightly from the river's course and one finds oneself walking through rather monotonous terrain. The effort required, however, is amply repaid by the stunning beauty of the River Oulankajoki scenery. The river flows from the Savilampi pool towards the northwest in a very modest form, but some distance upstream the panorama abruptly changes. Mighty cliffs enclose the river, which meanders through a narrow channel between the sheer walls. Here the effect of the micro-climate is emphasised

by the fact that the flora on the cliff faces varies according to the light reaching it. On sunny south-facing vertical walls, those plants capable of withstanding dryness thrive, whereas on the opposite side, where it is shady, the northern fell plants grow. Among the flora here are some real rarities this far south, including the mountain avens, and Arnica angustifolia on the shady side, and Saxifraga cotyledon on the sunny side.

The slope ledges, which might also be dubbed a 'hanging garden', contain many other northern species, together with plants which are very common in Finland even in gardens!

The trail leads up to the top of these sheer walls and from there a vista opens out over the gorge right up to the Savilampi pool. The large, so-called candle-shaped spruces on the river bank are far below us. Rocks rise sheer for 50 metres or so above the water level and there time and the variations in the weather have taken their toll, cascades of gravel having fallen down from the rocky surfaces to the foot of the cliffs. Water that has seeped into the cracks owing to changes in temperature has slowly but surely fragmented the rock.

Plant rarities here include relics, many of them dating from the last Ice Age almost ten thousand years ago and now occurring far from their other growing places. The nutritious nature of the rocks and the cool microclimate have made it possible to survive in conditions equivalent to those of the treeless tundra. Snow does not disappear from these places until well into the summer and water trickles down them keeping the habitat cool and moist throughout the summer.

We return to the shore of Savilampi pool as the cabin beckons invitingly from the far bank of the Oulankajoki. In front of the cabin a path disappears once again north

Reijo Juurinen

This lovely Arnica angustifolia, a native of the fell uplands, is one of Kuusamo's surprises, growing in one of its ravines.

towards Savinajokivartti.

The entire route from the Salla road via Ristikallio and Taivalköngäs and then on to Savilampi and the end of the Urriaapa road is some 17 kilometres long. It can be undertaken without any great deal of effort within a couple of days, including one overnight camp.

FROM TAIVALKÖNGÄS TO KIUTAKÖNGÄS

The two-storey cabin at Taivalköngäs rapids is an old loggers' hut whose function has been changed to serve the needs of hikers. Alongside this building the trail runs via suspension bridges on both sides of the main forks of the Oulankajoki, firstly along the foaming reaches of the fork and on the other side of the island lodged between the forks over the fork nearest the canyon. There is a camping site in a sort of meadow.

Some distance away on the northern side of the path the river Kiekeröjoki rushes along its own small ravine. The bottom meadows lining this river attract reindeer. At one time hay used to be cut here for use as animal fodder. Upon reaching the water from the northern valley slopes, the Kiekeräjoki ends in a pool of the same name, after it reverses its direction. The trail crosses the river via Ruusulammenkangas, with its Scots pine trees, to the Hepokoski rapids, where there is another area set aside for camp fires and camping. It is highly probable that here the rambler will be visited by a Siberian jay or two looking for food.

Continuing the walk, one finds the scenery observed alongside the track more level. Scots pines are rare, those present being something like 130-150 years old. In places there is an extremely dense growth of young trees marking the sites of old forest fires, and if one looks around carefully, one can see more signs of such fires, including burnt stumps, fire scars on the boles of trees, and even charcoal on the ground.

Old records tell us something about these fires. In 1907 the assistant forester for the district made his written report: "On the fifteenth or sixteenth of June a fire broke out in Kitka area I alongside the River Oulankajoki above the Kiutaköngäs rapids, probably started by a fisherman's fire. The fire raged on both sides of the river, partly as a ground fire and partly as a crown fire, over an area as estimated by eye totalling 4500 − 5000 ha. Fortunately the fire was brought under control within three or four days after concerted fire fighting efforts, otherwise it might have caused untold damage. A small part of the area including a (tree) crop meant for cutting purchased by consul H.Åslund last autumn also burned. The reason for such a large area having burned was the low number of fire fighters, as the nearest houses are located a full league (c. 10 km) away and there is but a handful of these buildings in any case."

On dry heaths very little wildlife is visible. There are few species and also few individuals. The redstart may bob its tail from its nest hole in a dried tree, and the spotted flycatcher may, while hunting for flies, appear very tame. If during the course of the day you also hear the brambling's whirring call, you have now already seen or heard all of the commonest birds of this biotope. During the evening chorus you may become slightly better acquainted with the area's birdlife. The mistlethrush's melancholy series of notes and the redwing's repeated ditty resound in the pine forests.

In the younger pine forests while there is a greater number of both species and individuals, the list of birds does not extend very far. Only in the more humid forests or alongside the brook courses are there other species to be found, but even at its best the bird density of the national park is low, being something like 120 − 130 pairs per square kilometre.

The same scarcity applies to the mammals as well, in spite of the fact that taking into account the national park's northerly location the number of species is surprisingly high: 28 species including several closely related species in competition with each other. Some concept of mammalian life − hares, stoats, weasels, foxes − can be obtained, of course, during the winter, when prints are left in the snow.

NEAR THE KIUTAKÖNGÄS RAPIDS

Many visitors to the mighty Kiutaköngäs rapids arrive by road. Something like 30,000 people a year arrive by private transport and coach to see the rapids, whereas only about a tenth of this number actually hike along the Bear's Route. For this reason, in the neighbourhood of the Kiutaköngäs a variety of facilities for visitors have been provided. These include parking and camping places, together with a kiosk, an information centre, a park ranger's residence, and the Oulanka biological field station belonging to the University of Oulu. There are two nature trails, one going to Kiutaköngäs and the other to the vicinity of the new camping site from the Haaralampikangas heath, and both of these are less than five kilometres long.

One can walk along the Rytisuo Nature Trail in dry weather in ordinary walking shoes, as walkways have been laid down in the wetter situations. Alongside the trail information boards tell the visitor something of such interesting features as blanket bogs, the sites of old fires, forest pests, hole-nesting birds and mammals, the ancient hay making culture, plant and animal life of the peatlands and transitional forest mires, and the old cabins.

Bordering the trail one of the flood meadows has been restored as an example of a one-time "fattener" of the cattle of this district. Alongside a stream, the meadow plots with their underlay of moss were inundated by artificially raising the water level, which brought in nutrients and at the same time killed off the moss. A wooden dam was closed in the early summer and then opened just before the hay was harvested. This type of land use was quite normal right up to the Second World War, when the growing of fodder as a field crop effectively brought redundancy to these remote meadows.

In the slope forest alongside the Rytisuo Nature Trail the fellings of the 1910 period are also visible. Signs of forestry take the form of both the topography of the trail

Like the common coltsfoot, Petasites frigidus (a relative of the butter-bur), flowers before its leaves come out. By the time the latter have unfurled, the flowers have already wilted.

Dick Forsman

itself, which runs along an old logging 'road', and more obvious signs like old tree stumps and some felled trunks which were discarded because they were already rotten within. Since only the oldest and most perfect trees were felled, the forest has retained its different age classes and it is difficult now to divine the effect of this kind of 'friendly forestry'. Something like 80 years have passed since these fellings took place. The wind has felled some of the spruces on the river banks very often such that the butt tears loose from the ground to reveal wood rot. The bases of old spruces are very often swollen to a bottle shape. Such trees are suffering from a rot caused by fungus attack, which the large carpenter ants then proceed to make use of. Their labyrinthine nests are clearly visible in trees which have become torn open.

DOWN THE BROILING RAPIDS

After a short stretch the trail reaches the Kiutaköngäs rapids. The noise of the latter is not audible for any great distance as the rock walls and the waterfall lower down tend to obliterate the sound. It is only when one stands right at the brink that the noise is disclosed for what it is — a thunderous roar. The 40-metre long rapids through the sheer rock walls have carved their way down through two kinds of rock and are continually eroding a channel along the oblique fault line. The southern side is hard

quartz, while on the northern side lies reddish brown dolomite, a relatively soft, and hence easily eroded, material. Impurities in the form of iron present in the dolomite stain the walls reddish brown. Where the dolomite has been just recently exposed, its russet tone is much brighter.

The old rock walls, now grey with age, offer a refuge for many specialised plants. Early in the summer the walls are covered with mats of white flowers. This is the time of the low-growing mountain avens. There then follow the saxifrages and a species of Draba, as well as many warmth-loving plants. Fortunately these are well out of the reach of visitors, as such plants have almost completely vanished on the island side.

Kiutaköngäs has been a meeting place for many people. On its banks implements from the Stone Age have been discovered and the camping sites of log floaters can still be found among the vegetation on the banks. There are even the floors of cabins and fishermen have for long lit their fires on these sandy banks.

A relic dating from the early part of this century can be discovered by the observant hiker in the shape of a large Ice Age boulder (technically known as an "erratic") lying under a spruce in the vicinity of the track going to the island. This bears the initials HM and the year 1901. The boulder's inscription almost certainly represents the beginning of the log floating era.

The whole magnificence of the rapids is appreciated best from the eastern point of the island. The cliff is at its highest and there is an uninterrupted view over the lower pool and of the small rapids which succeed it. When the floodwaters have receded, small pot holes formed by water action on small stones are exposed. The whirling stones gradually carve out perfectly symmetrical cauldron-shaped pits in the bedrock, their own surfaces becoming ground down to gemstone smoothness as they do so. As the pit deepens, the stone can no longer be forced out by the water and there it stays until it is one day ground down to nothing.

The Oulankajoki is a river subject to periodical flooding. Its name derives from the word "oulu" or "oula", which is Häme dialect for floodwater (Häme is in fact located much further south, in the region around Tampere and Hämeenlinna). For a couple of weeks after the middle of May the river proceeds to live up to its name. Water gathered from the open peatlands and forests in the upper reaches serves to raise the water level surprisingly rapidly by a matter of more than three metres. The Oulankajoki thus differs from the neighbouring Kitkajoki, in which a large basin prevents a sudden surge of spring water, thereby naturally regulating the flow lower down.

In the thousands of years since the last Ice Age, the river valley has been infilled and eroded so that stages in the river's history are visible as strata exposed to view by fresh cycles of erosion, as valley flats and as ox-bow lakes left stranded as the river has shifted restlessly in its never-ended quest to find a new channel. The thick stratified sandy deposit has its origins in a sandy bank about a kilometre away alongside the trail, the slopes of which are criss-crossed by reindeer tracks. The river erodes and continually alters its channel. Bends become deeper, sandy banks disappear and reform elsewhere, and history repeats itself time and again, though perhaps with slightly less vigour than at the end of the great Ice Age.

KITKANNIEMI'S BROWN MOSS FENS

Kitkanniemi remains as a triangular area between the rivers Oulankajoki and Kitkanjoki. It has been incorporated in the national land conservation programme ever since steps were taken to establish the Oulanka National Park. Owing to its calcium-rich bedrock and variable topography, it has acquired an extremely diversified flora since the Ice Age. It even supports several very delicate plants which are not found elsewhere in Oulanka. On lime-rich rock and cliff faces the species diversity is particularly high. In many places there are rich brown moss fens, springs, transitional forests along stream courses, and small woods. Collectively, Kitkanniemi is among the most important sites of endangered plant species in Finland. There is no primaeval forest here, as the logging activities at the turn of the century encompassed Kitkanniemi as well. Fortunately, the method of tree harvesting was far less severe than it is today.

Let's now walk along this section of the Bear's Route. When the path finally leaves the Oulankajoki, it rises towards the Kulmakko stream course. At the south end of Lake Kulmakkojärvi stands Jussinkämpä, a new cabin intended specifically for hikers (as distinct from being a fishermen's or loggers' cast-off). East of this, beyond a protracted esker, lies one of the area's most lush brown moss fens, Pitkäsuo. Fens of this kind at Kitkanniemi vary considerably, their flora consisting of a unique combination of northern and southern species.

On many of the fens there are considerable numbers of lady's slipper orchids, while in the copses one finds ostrich ferns with fronds fully a metre long. Further into Kitkanniemi there are so-called large herb copses showing no signs whatsoever of human interference.

The trail continues from Jussinkämpä due south to the southwestern tip of Lake Pesosjärvi. It then progresses to the Saaripuro valley, where there are a number of fertile brown moss fens and sedgy meadows. Since the stream was at one time dammed in connection with hay making, the peat layer is extremely thin. With such activities now a thing of the past, Sphagnum mosses are encroaching over the area and producing thicker layers of peat.

RARE PLANTS

Saaripuro descends in a swift rush of water down a tightly walled ravine to the Kitkanjoki river valley. Mezereon, Actaea erythrocarpa, and a species of red currant grow in the copses at these lower levels. Ferns and grey alder are also very much in evidence.

The Kitkanjoki ravine narrows immediately after the point named Päähkänänkallio, and the trail is forced by circumstances to run right alongside the water. The latter is exceptionally clear, which is in direct contrast to the situation in the Oulankajoki, whose waters are stained tobacco-brown by peat. A succession of cliffs harbours a northern flora adapted to a high concentration of calcium. Many of the species are not found in Finland outside Kuusamo. Others occur at their nearest point on the lime-rich fells of Enontekiö; these include certain ferns. The wall rue spleenwort, however, is a southern species that occurs around Lohja and in Ladoga Karelia, now behind the border.

Not to be outdone by this prolificness of rare plants, the bottom meadows and sandy banks also have a unique collection of their own. There is, for example, a close relative of the honeysuckle that is not found anywhere else in Finland.

The trail keeps to the river bank as far as Petäjikkäpuro where, after rising steeply, it descends just as abruptly to the river again. The cliffs here have been eroded away by moss growth, although they are nowadays quite dry. Many uncommon fell plants, relics of colder climatic periods, have taken advantage of nooks and crannies forming in the rock.

After reaching the eastern end of Jäkäläuoma, the trail continues for three kilometres along the edge of the cliff. From the western end it is but a short walk to Jyrävä, but as the trail in that direction is not marked you will need a map. Clearfellings appear just before the second Putaansaari island on the Kitkanjoki. On the opposite of this island a suspension bridge connects the path to the western bank of the river. From here it is possible to continue the hike right up to Rukatunturi fell, the alternative being to turn back towards Juuma village and thus gain the road.

Oh, and don't forget Jyrävä, where the Aallokkokoski rapids race and foam down a several hundred metre gorge, losing ten metres in altitude and giving you an opportunity once again to witness the forces of nature at work in this lovely national park. JV

Oulanka National Park

Kuusamo and Salla, 206 km^2
Established: 1956, extended 1982.

Connections: The Käylä-Liikasenvaara road runs right through the national park. There is a coach to the western side of the park, at the start of the Bear's Route.

Services: "The Bear's Route" hiking trail runs through the park right up to Rukatunturi fell (70 km). Additionally, there are two well-marked nature trails (4.5 and 4.8 km), as well as other marked trails. Cooking and camping places have been set up alongside the trail; there are five unlocked huts. Information centre alongside the short trail leading to the famous Kiutaköngäs rapids.

Map: Outdoor map 1:50 000 Rukatunturi-Oulanka.

Further information: National park information centre and warden, tel. 989-46 104 (Kiutaköngäs), or National Board of Forestry, District Office of Taivalkoski, tel. 988-52 221 (Taivalkoski)

Motto:
What other plants do,
orchids do
it better.

The motto is correct in almost every respect, but not in the most important: the struggle for life. Hardly any orchids are the dominant species in their habitats. Rarity is the characteristic feature of many of them and they feature prominently on lists of endangered species both in Finland and elsewhere. Apart from that, they are achievers. They represent an extraordinarily large

Martti Rikkonen

Two beautiful deceivers: the lady's slipper (above) and the fairy-slipper (or calypso) orchid. Neither offers the insects that visit it any honey. They have to carry the pollen without reward.

Hannu Hautala

family of plants, encompassing perhaps as many as 30,000 species in an enormous variety of habitats on every continent except the Antarctic.

Pollination tricks

Several of the 33 orchids which grow wild in Finland could easily hold their own in a beauty contest with some of their more renowned tropical kin. The most beautiful and striking is the superb lady's slipper. Its flowers, over 10 centimetres long, literally capture their pollinators. If an insect that gets inside the pouchlike flower is too large or too weak to push its way through the small opening between the stamens and the base of the lips, it is trapped and dies inside.

The calypso or fairy-slipper, which grows in fir groves in northern Finland, rivals the lady's slipper for beauty. Its honeyless flowers deceive bumblebees. It even has false yellow stamens painted on the outside of its liplike petal.

The fly orchid, which grows in meadow groves on the Åland Islands and in the Parainen district in the south-western corner of the mainland, fools its pollinators in another way. Its flower resembles a shiny black insect complete with eyes, wings and feelers. It also emits a fragrance imitating that of the female cicada wasp's to attract males, which alight on the flower and try to copulate with it. In doing this, they get pollen on their heads, and when they are tricked into trying to mate with another flower, the orchid's love letter reaches its address and a new generation is on the way. The spotted orchid is another species that cheats

Seppo Keränen

pollinators, because its flowers contain no honey to reward them. It is particularly attractive to colourful Leptura and Ano-plodera butterflies, which are often seen mating on the blooms.

There are also orchid species which reward their pollinators well for their honest labour. The lesser butterfly orchid, which emits its fragrance at night, contains ample honey, which provides fuel for the hawk moth as it hovers about like a helicopter. When it tanks up, lumps of pollen stick in its suction snout and are deposited on the next orchid visited. A closely related species, the weak-fragranced greater butterfly orchid, is different in only one respect. Its pollen lumps are further apart, and thus stick in the visiting butterfly's eyes rather than its suction snout. This means that collecting honey from different species does not generally cause hybridization, because the pollen is not deposited in the right place.

The lesser twayblade, which grows in small wilderness forests has an insect-sized flower and feeds fungus gnats, whose gentle touch releases a pressurized drop of glue at the base of the filaments supporting the pollen anthers. The glue splashes onto the insect's head and the pollen dust adheres to it. Only when the pollen has been taken away does the flap covering the stigma fold aside to facilitate pollination.Quite apart from their fascinating pollination methods, orchids have several other special features. They have the smallest seeds of any flowering plants. Those of the creeping lady's-tresses, for example, are so tiny that half a million of them would weigh only a gramme. Ten million of them could be sent by post at the ordinary letter rate!

Cohabitation

During their life as seedlings, all orchids are completely depend-ent on mycelia, fungi which penetrate the cells of the germinating plants. Within these cells, the mycelia are absorbed and provide the orchid with nourishment. It is often only in its third or fourth year of life that the orchid forms its first green leaves and begins living like an "ordinary" green plant, in part at least. Several species of orchids, such as the ghost orchid, coral-root orchid and bird's-nest orchid, all of which lack chlorophyll, remain completely dependent all their lives on their internal fungi.

This cohabitation of fungi and orchids used to be considered a symbiotic relationship, but it would probably be more accurate to say that the orchids are parasites on the fungi. However, it is obvious that the fungi do obtain some vitamin-like substances from the orchids, which also produce other substances that inhibit the fungi's growth, thus keeping them in check. At least some of the

The pallid ghost orchid has no chlorophyll and hides like a fairy. It can live beneath the soil for years and only thrusts its flower shoots above the surface for two or three weeks during favourable summers.

fungi in the roots of orchids belong to the stereaceae family and cause root rot in trees. Many orchids have very particular demands with regard to the habitat in which they grow. Some of them have become rarer as a result of environmental changes, but so far only one — the musk orchid, has beome extinct in Finland. The most threatened are the delicately red, large-flowered red helleborine and the bog orchid and fen orchid, which, as their names indicate, favour waterlogged habitats. SV

Jorma Luhta

EASTERN AND NORTHEASTERN LAPLAND

Tapani Vartiainen

FROM PYHÄTUNTURI TO LUOSTO

Pelkosenniemi's Pyhätunturi and Sodankylä's Luosto are both visible from main roads and are easily accessible. The area remaining between these two fells has traditionally been considered by hikers and others of their ilk as some kind of a wilderness of economic importance offering very little to the outdoorsman in the way of original wildlife and habitats. However, this — Lapland's southernmost true fell region — encompasses tens of thousands of hectares of very variable scenery and ideal hiking terrain.

THE PYHÄTUNTURI FELLSCAPE
When Finland's first national parks were planned, the objective was not to single out habitats or even entire landscapes representative of Finland and thus worthy of preservation but to conserve something unique. Hence,

Pyhätunturi National Park, which was established as long ago as 1938, was limited at the outset to the seven kilometre long fell chain itself, thereby excluding peatlands and forests typifying this particular region. At the beginning of 1982 the 30 square kilometre park area was extended by a further 11 square kilometres.

Pyhätunturi itself is an unusual landform for southern Lapland, fells typically being found much further north. The highest of its five peaks, that of Noitatunturi, rises to 540 metres above sea level, putting it just 375 metres above its surroundings. Extremely deep gullies between these peaks help the scene to resemble the picture book mountain chains of Central Europe rather than the gently curving Finnish fells. The most spectacular places during the height of the tourist season are rather heavily populated by visitors, but this should not be allowed to detract from their beauty.

Especially in the summertime, the Pyhätunturi landscape seems to be dominated by dull grey piles and broad expanses of shattered quartzite on the slopes. Needless to say, it is best if at all possible to avoid walking across these. One's first impression is that there is nothing alive at all in these desolate wastes of stone. This is not, it has to be admitted, very far from the truth. The quartzite, which is made almost entirely of quartz, provides a very nutrient-poor growing medium for plants, aside from which it is hard in the extreme and does not easily crack to make space for questing roots. Quartzite has formed on the beds of ancient seas and in places in the national park it is possible to find wave prints on the surfaces of boulders. Such natural artwork would, of course, make an admirable souvenir were it not for the national park regulations, which forbid the collecting of geological specimens.

In particular on grey, drizzle-soaked days, the Isokuru ravine appeals to the photographer more because of its faintly sinister appearance than for any intrinsic beauty. At the end of the ravine lies what must be the park's most photographed entity, Pyhänkasteenlampi pool — into which water cascades from the higher pool of Karhunjuomalampi.

The park-like Scots pine and spruce forests clothing the lower slopes of the fells become flatter as one proceeds upwards — the conifer timber line is situated at under 400 metres. This is not the result of climatic factors but of the precipitous and infertile nature of the upper slopes and the physical presence of masses of shattered rock offering no purchase for plants. An irregular birch zone continues up to almost 500 metres. The flattish fell tops are almost entirely treeless and for the most part are devoid of other kinds of vegetation into the bargain. Here and there one may come across a low-growing juniper, bilberry or ptarmigan berry. In places dwarf shrubs also occur that are typical of localities further north.

From the summit it is possible to see a long way over the surrounding area of southern Lapland and to appreciate its peculiarities. On almost every side lies forest and peatland; only in the north and east do fells protrude above the horizon. Luosto's lonely, nearby summit is the single exception to the rule. Immediately west of the fell chain, in the extended area of the park, there are typical open aapa mires. Only when one actually sees the flatness of the country here and the extent of its forests and peatlands with their small pools, will one appreciate why the ancient people called the area Pyhätunturi ("pyhä" = sacred).

FROM PYHÄTUNTURI TO LUOSTO

In its northwestern corner the national park practically touches the southern extremity of the so-called 'natural state forests' of Luosto (the term 'state' here being synonymous with 'condition'). The boundary between the national park and privately owned land is only too obvious here. What in the winter one may well consider to be the treeless side of Huttutunturi fell, in the summer is revealed for what it is, a large clear-cut. It is possible to gaze out from this bare area right across Pyhäjärvi village to the Savukoski fell group.

In both summer and winter the hiking route heads up Huttutunturi, running along the western side of the fell summit. In places very steep, the slope provides an excellent view over the large dappled Siuronaapa mire towards the west. Through the mire the River Siuronjoki winds sluggishly along on its way south to Javarus. The eastern side of the mire is very exposed, consisting of brown moss fens and treeless Sphagnum bogs. This area is partly covered with water and as a consequence it is an important breeding ground for peatland birds. Very few ramblers under summer conditions will wish to push their luck by setting out across its quaking hum-

Dick Forsman

Alpine sow-thistle is very conservative in its choice of habitat: it is confined to gloomy stream gully thickets.

A golden plover pair stands guard over its young on a collapsed hay barn on a sedgy meadow.

mock lines. In the western sector of the mire, aside from the open bogs there are also small patches supporting a tree growth. In this difficult boggy terrain most of the common peatland bird species live.

Siurunaapa mire is clearly visible from a distance as one toils along the slopes of Huttutunturi, Kapusta or Latvavaara. All of these are quartzitic fells whose bare tops are caused by the stony nature of the ground. The forests near the top consist of fell birch. While the hiking routes reach quite high elevations, there is nothing to stop the walker from remaining at a lower level alltogether.

A VISTA OF LUOSTO

As one descends from Latvavaara to Pyhälampi, Luosto is in view like a framed masterpiece. On the western side of Pyhälampi pool Ruispelto opens out whose name ("ruispelto" = rye field) tends to create the impression that some prospective new inhabitant has at some time or other stumbled on this place and decided to settle down in it. Legend has it, however, that the name derives from the dense local spruce forests, with their trees of identical age, for which the old Finnish adage of "Spruce forests like a field of rye!" seems to be particularly apt. The shores of Pyhälampi pool are not only low and boggy, but are also practically treeless. Whooper swans

nest beside the pool and the swan families may remain there right up until the autumn.

The River Pyhäjoki, which has its origins in the Pyhälampi pool, adds a certain variety to the topography. Its banks are extremely lush, generally consisting of transitional forest Sphagnum mires distinguished by a large growth of ferns. Familiar, but perhaps rather surprising in its abundance here, is the red currant — the hiker who arrives at the right time may treat himself to handfuls of small red, delicious berries tasting as good as (some might say better than) currants from his own garden. In good years there are so many that the hiker can take on a large, tasty supply of energy within a few minutes. He will have a use for his sandwiches later on, when the first Siberian jays arrive at his camp.

After another couple of kilometres, the time comes to leave the river and bend one's steps north again, if the intention is to explore the mighty Rykämäkuru ravine. Many hikers after a first glance down into this gorge turn slightly green and forget the flora, preferring to direct their attention to the attractions of the upper rim. A short distance on, there is a second rather deep, rocky valley, at the mouth of which one can sit listening to a brook babbling way down below.

The highest point in the immediate area is Rykimäkero, which is choked with broken rock and on whose

Hannu Hautala

One of the far north's rarest songbirds is the brightly coloured redstart, whose cheerful ditty can even be heard during the light midnight hours.

western side there is a small Lapp tepee village. The latter is not a real one but is constructed so as to resemble the real thing as closely as possible.

When one has reached the vicinity of the Pyhäjärvi road it is worth taking a look at the managed forest area. Those who venture on to the very wet peatland with its brooks towards the end of summer will discover the bright yellow flowered saxifrage, Saxifraga hirculus and the small pink-flowering Epilobium hornemanni, allied to the rosebay willowherb. The view here tends to be dominated by Luosto fell, whose graceful curves rise above the dark spruce forests towards the northwest. On the return trip the rambler may turn his attention to geological specimens and endeavour while walking along the Rykimäselkä road to distinguish milky quartz, haematite, jasper, and other treasures.

AT LUOSTO'S SUMMIT

On the crown of the fell stands a fire guard's cabin by climbing on to the roof of which one can gain two or three metres on Luosto's 540 and thereby obtain the best available view of one's surroundings! On the eastern side

at the foot of the fell the roofs of holiday chalets and other buildings are visible in what the Finns call a 'holiday village'. The recreation fishing pools of Aarnilampi and Ahvenlampi twinkle from among the trees. On the other side of the Pyhäjärvi road lies Orresokka, which seems to be composed largely of a jumble of quartz fragments. Away in the distance, partly obscured from view by forests, flows the Kitinen, here the main thoroughfare, made remarkable by its rushing rapids and limestone cliffs.

Like Pyhätunturi, Luosto's crown is as devoid of substantial vegetation as an egg-head's bonce. In autumn the rich red of dwarf shrub leaves stand out in striking contrast to a background of grey stone. A weasel may poke its head out of some cranny, only to disappear just as abruptly and then to reappear in an entirely unrelated spot. The existence of small mammal populations is also revealed by the short-eared owl's presence. Creamy white and brown, this bird skims silently across the dwarf shrubs in the full light of the late midsummer evening, to settle quickly just a few dozen metres away and wait to see what the human interloper is going to do next. The golden eagle is no stranger to these parts, either: at least one pair nests regularly at Luosto.

Even if the incline does not demand it, looking down towards your boots as you ascend Luosto's slopes is an astonishingly rewarding avocation: the tiny pink blooms of Loiseleuria procumbens amidst tight little knots of leaves, a slab of quartz white as marble decorated with bright green lichens bright as jewels, a stonechat nestling chirping vociferously under a juniper bush — may all pass unnoticed if you keep your head erect. Lower down on the slope a mountain hare makes a dash for the cover offered by a a low-growing spruce, but stops to look back, its attitude betraying curiosity rather than alarm.

North of Luosto the untouched forests narrow to a kilometre or so. The Pyhätunturi-Luosto hiking trail continues on alongside these forests until it reaches the E4, but long before you reach the highway logged forests will have crept in to spoil the scenery. AF & PO

Pyhätunturi National Park

Pelkosenniemi and Kemijärvi, 42 km²
Established: 1938
Under Finnish Forest Research Institute management.

Connections: There is a road and bus service from Kemijärvi to the national park border.

Services: The area is supplied with hiking trails with camp fire places and a camping site. Information centre. The Luosto trail (45 km) starts at Pyhätunturi. There is a recreation centre, camping site, hotel and cabins available for hire near the park.

Map: Outdoor map 1:25 000 Pyhätunturi, or Outdoor map 1:50 000 Luosto — Pyhätunturi.

Further information: Finnish Forest Research Institute, North Finland District Office, tel. 960-15 721 (Rovaniemi).

Our Most Threatened Birds

Many of the species of birds that live in our northern wildernesses are among the most threatened in the whole country. In some cases, the situation has stabilized and the decline has been arrested, but other species have already disappeared to all intents and purposes. Owing to major changes in our environment, such as extensive clear-felling of forests and bog drainage, many species that are still common today are dwindling in numbers all the time. The selection of birds that inhabit our country is not immutable; new species move into the habitats of threatened ones, whilst others may weather a critical phase and begin recovering.

The aristocrats of predators

The most prominent examples of our threatened bird species are predators. The peregrine falcon and the sea eagle are familiar to anybody who is interested in nature. Both species hit the headlines in the 1960s, when a connection was established between environmental toxins and sharp declines in their populations.

There are now an estimated 50 nesting pairs of sea eagles in Finland. Most of them nest in our Baltic archipelagoes, but since the beginning of the 1970s some have been observed in the large lakes of Lapland as well. The population in Lapland has been estimated at 10 pairs, but there may be some more that have remained undiscovered in the vast wildernesses there.

Although there is nowadays a general awareness of the threat facing the sea eagle and that it does not harm reindeer, its future in Lapland does not by any means seem assured. As long as the golden eagle is persecuted in reindeer herding areas, the sea eagle is not safe. It is difficult to distinguish between the species and "accidents" happen.

The peregrine falcon has made a promising comeback since its numbers reached a nadir in the 1950s and 1960s. But it is still threatened by poisons and hunters along the route of its migratory flights.

Jorma Luhta

Antti Leinonen

Although they nest in the remote north, far from industry and modern civilization, Lapland's sea eagles have not avoided environmental toxins. They ingest toxins in the Baltic region during their migrations, and their nesting areas are not completely clean, either. Burbot, that delicious fish scorned by the men of Lapland, is often thrown away and is an important source of nourishment to the sea eagles as they return from their migrations south. These and other bottom-living fish have been found to contain large concentrations of mercury, which is passed on to sea eagles as a result of human winter fishing practices.

The sea eagle's future prospects are also suffering from felling of forests in Lapland and growing snowmobile traffic in nesting areas during the hatching season.

The peregrine falcon's future looks brighter. The population is now growing slowly but steadily, and clearly more chicks are being hatched and reared than during the bad years in the early 1970s.

Peregrine falcons are no longer persecuted in Finland, although a few shooting incidents have been reported in recent years. However, they are still being killed in their wintering areas in France and Spain.

The greatest threat to the future of our peregrine falcons is still posed by environmental toxins, which they ingest when they eat the smaller birds that they prey on. Although DDT is now banned in Finland, it is still entering our environment through the medium of our falcons and the birds that they eat in their winter habitats.

A denizen of the most remote reaches of the north, the gyrfalcon has traditionally been considered an endangered species in Finland. However, it has probably always nested here in only very small numbers, and there is no certainty that major changes in the size of the population have taken place. Egg collection during the first half of the century may have reduced local populations, but is unlikely to have had permanent effects. Thus it still nests in places where it was known to nest a century or so ago, in addition to which the increased popularity of hill hiking has led to the discovery of many new nesting sites, some in quite recent years. The number of gyrfalcon

pairs that now nest in Finland can be estimated at 25-30.

Nesting gyrfalcons depend for their food on ptarmigan and willow grouse and their success in breeding fluctuates from year to year with the availability of nourishment. In years when ptarmigan are scarce, gyrfalcons do not nest at all. However, they do remain in their nesting areas, living on ducks and waders.

Since it remains in the north all year round and its nourishment mainly consists of unpolluted local birds, the gyrfalcon is not as susceptible to environmental toxins as species like the peregrine falcon. The main threat facing it at present is the disturbance caused by hikers, although this can still be considered relatively slight, and, a much greater problem, nest robbery, of which there have been numerous instances in neighbouring countries.

On the brink of extinction

Old Lapland veterans still remember a time when white-fronted geese were a more common game bird on the Utsjoki bogs than ordinary wild geese. Today, however, they are

a prime rarity everywhere, and it is doubtful whether any of them nest in Finland. In practice, therefore, this species has become extinct in Finland. The causes of this catastrophic decline in population have been pondered at length, but fruitlessly. One explanation advanced is overhunting in former years, and especially raids in which whole flocks of moulting birds incapable of flying were bludgeoned to death in their nesting areas. There is an old tradition of this kind of poaching in the north, but even so it can hardly be the sole reason for the rapid decline in the white-fronted geese population. Current theories attribute it to environmental changes along the birds' migration route and in their winter habitat.

Breeding in nurseries has recently been resorted to in Sweden in an effort to revive the Scandinavian white-fronted geese population, which has fallen to five per cent or so of its former level. Some birds have already been released into the environment and they are now being bred in Finland as well.

A lesser species that has likewise suffered from hunting is the familiar snipe's larger relation, a bird called the whole, whose future looks just as gloomy as that of the white-fronted goose. Some wholes are still observed migrating south each year, especially near the south coast, but there is no evidence that they have nested in Finland in the last 35 years.

Although overhunting has been put forward as one of the main causes of the virtual disappearance of the whole, there must also be other reasons. These might include the disappearance of many of the marshy meadows in which they prefer to nest, as well as climatic changes. DF

PEATLANDS OF SOUTHERN LAPLAND

Wildernesses in Finland are generally well off the beaten track, with the peatlands in particular being located far from the nearest roads. At Pelkosenniemi, however, the situation is exactly the opposite. Here we are right in the middle of an extensive peatland wilderness. Settlements and the road network are confined to the narrow river banks, the rest of the terrain being occupied by peatlands, in the form of spruce swamps, wet sphagnum bogs, and wet brown moss fens.

If one arrives at Pelkosenniemi by road, the region does not in fact appear particularly boggy. The river bank

Veikko Vasama

147

Dick Forsman

The brown-tinted fluffy white blooms of a sedge, Schoenus ferrugineus, dot the Sokka aapa mire.

scenery on the northern side of Kemijärvi is composed of extensive cultivated areas, beyond which rise small hills and fells. A similar setting greets the traveller coming from Sodankylä, since the road follows the high fell regions. Only on the northern side of the actual village is it possible to gain an impression of peatlands even being present, when the road crosses a few kilometres of sphagnum bogs notable for their cloudberry crops.

In Kairala, too — which according to the road map, is surrounded by peatlands and in which one has an uninterrupted view reaching out as far as the most distant fells — it is difficult to believe that peatlands exist. The visitor finds himself surrounded by an extremely luxuriant landscape. The broad channel of the River Kitinen curves away along a magnificent valley, with human settlements located on elevated banks looking like elongated ridges. Cattle browse in the sedgy meadows and swallows curve through the air.

But if one drives from Kairala to the Luiro road, one at long last begins to get the feel of the peatlands. The ferry trip over the Kitinen in summer is an experience not easily forgotten. The logs which fill the river are first collected together with a boom pulled by a tractor.

After the ferry, it is a good idea to stop awhile on the high banks and look back. Kairala is now visible as a postcard scene backed by the summits of the Pyhätunturi fell range and more distant Luosto. Old-fashioned, decorative log houses with their quite formidable dimensions, artistic cornerpieces, and quaint porches, are a delight to see. Stretching out before you there is an idyllic scene straight out of Finland's past. For some reason the village was overlooked when the enemy

systematically destroyed Lappish villages during the last war and its hundreds of years old architecture remains untainted even by the modern age.

The road continues from the Tallavaara settlement down towards Nevatunturi fell, which dominates the northwestern sector, and finally peatlands hove into view. Without warning one is suddenly plunged into the middle of the flat, open Kairanaapa mire, which at a league or so in length (10 km) ranks among the country's largest of its kind. The peatland scenery opening out towards the north is one of the most magnificent to be seen from any roadside in Finland.

After a few kilometres, the road ends at Luiro, where houses line the roadsides, backed by fields and finally a broad and glistening brown moss fen. Everywhere one looks there are only peatlands and yet more peatlands. Over the river, towards the northeast, lies the Sakkala-aapa mire sprawling out over several hectares. The southeast is dominated by the impressive Sudenvaara-naapa mire and the south by the impenetrable Sokanaa-pa mire. Away towards the north stretches the lovely Lampanaapa mire, while the entire western horizon is underscored by the Kairanaapa mire which the hiker has just crossed.

From the slopes of Luiro fell, higher only than old Sompio fell, there used to be a first-class view of totally untouched peatlands.

GETTING TO GRIPS WITH THE PEATLANDS

The peatlands can be approached by the rambler from a variety of angles. Those with a bent towards traditional foot-slogging will find it difficult to choose a route. One can set off in a northwesterly direction, towards Sodankylä, north towards Luiro, east towards Kotala and Kelloselkä, or even southeast towards the Vuotos Pahkakumpu settlement. In all of these cases the rambler will stride for days through the loveliest kind of peatland scenery.

However, those lacking the energy, boldness, or simply the time to tackle the peatlands in this way, will find it preferable to devour these unique landforms in smaller portions. Even in the course of a single day, one can expect to see quite a lot and this has the advantage of permitting one to cut down considerably on the weight in one's pack.

When planning the daily itinery, one should remember that advance estimates of the time required to trace a specific route are often well off the mark where peatlands are concerned. Experience has shown that the average speed of progress in boggy terrain is only around two and a half kilometres an hour. While this rule-of-thumb allows for coffee, tea, and food breaks, small diversions from the main route, halts to view one's surroundings, identify plants, observe birds, or take photographs, time taken crossing brooks and streams, it also presupposes a lightly loaded rucksack. It is possible in this case to walk for twelve hours a day without risking a state of utter exhaustion and in so doing to cover a healthy distance of some twenty-five kilometres.

KAIRANAAPA MIRE

The peatlands on the western side of Luiro lead south. Lines of tussocks and pools have developed against the current, so that longitudinal progress, both on Kairanaapa mire, with its large pools, and Lämsänaapa mire, made up of large water-logged patches, is difficult. The best plan is to skirt these bogs as far as possible from Luiro, Puljunpalo, or Härkäjoki.

Kairanaapa mire at its southern end is very barren and difficult to negotiate, although its birdlife is prolific. The northern end is much more interesting from the floristic and scenic aspects. It has a particularly noteworthy feature in the shape of a pool, Kairanaapalampi, which although a kilometre or more in length, is only some twenty metres wide, and lies right in the centre of the mire. The upper end of the lake is bordered by a narrow fringe of birches, but in other places the lake is flanked either by wet fens or by pools containing water stained almost black by humus. Not only is the pool always brim-full of water, its water level actually appears to be higher than the rest of the mire.

Kairanaapalampi pool is a bird paradise. When the spring meltwaters spread right over the mire, surrounding the pool like some glorious lake, hundreds of pairs of ducks fly in. The dominant species are the tufted duck and teal, but there are also many golden eyes, mallards, pin-

A familiar bird of the larger lakes and archipelago, the herring gull also nests in the peatlands on hummocks surrounded by water.

Eero Kemilä

tails, and eiders. Geese, whooper swans and smews also occasionally drop in. Indeed, that southern rarity, the shelduck has even from time to time put in an appearance.

Just as abundant are the waders, especially the shanks, snipe and red-necked phalarope. The broad-billed sandpiper and lapwing also occur in places. The most prominent birds of prey are the hawk owl, great grey owl, and short-eared owl. In abundant vole years the great grey owl is generally found in the untouched heathlands between Kairanaapa and Puljunpalonaapa, where it then builds comparatively large numbers of nests. Aside from the rough-legged buzzard, hen harrier, and merlin, the buzzard and honey buzzard add a dash of southern spice to these northern wilds.

Puljunpalonaapa, which for six kilometres follows the western fringe of Kairanaapa, consists of a collection of wet fens, covered at the southern end with graceful birch woods. Orchids are among the most prominent and interesting of the fen plants, but the moss cover on the bogs is just as dazzlingly colourful, glowing in shades of carmine, gold and copper.

LÄMSÄNAAPA MIRE

On the northern side of Kairanaapa mire, from behind the small Hietäjoki river, unfolds another gigantic peatland, the Lämsänaapa. This raised mire is one of Finland's most representative of its type, corresponding to the Kesonsuo mire at Ilomantsi, in eastern Finland. On the western edge the mire is continuing to increase its height, as indicated by the gradual death of large areas of Scots pines. The raised mire offers few obstacles to the determined hiker, so long as he keeps to the lines of tussocks running in an east-west direction. Should the rambler in a surfeit of over-confidence attempt, however, to cut across the tussock ranks and their intervening wet patches along a northerly or southerly course, he will soon find himself in difficulties.

That familiar bird of the Finnish lakes and Archipelago, the herring gull, is one of the mire's more spectacular denizens in summer. Here the gulls nest in safety on hummocks standing high and dry above surprisingly deep pools. Considered from the climatic aspect, Lämsänaapa is a rare natural masterpiece that will remain indelibly etched on the memory of all who cross it.

THE VASANIEMI BOGS

Between the Kemihaara and Luiro at Vasaniemi lies one of the country's largest unbroken tracts of peatland. The main road from Pelkosenniemi to Savukoski and Sokli crosses the southern tip this complex, between the Jänkäläisen aapa and Sokanaapa mires which once again remain hidden, as though put away by magic, from the roadbound traveller's eyes.

On the northern side of the causeway, the Sokanaapa mire is a renowned locality for birds, but unfortunately a singularly inaccessible one. Ridges of springy Sphagnum hummocks, already discontinuous at the edges, come to an abrupt end just short of the centre of the mire. Resisting the urge to view the sea gull colonies,

flocks of arctic terns, whooper swans, waders or smew may prove difficult to the ardent ornithologist, but it is highly recommended, as there is no quicker way of dampening the enthusiasm than by falling repeatedly into peaty water imparting a foetid odour that will advertise one's presence for the remainder of the day.

One can explore Sarkanaapa mire by following the path from Jänkäläisenpalo. Keeping to the edges of the mire, this trail leads between a bevy of pools known as the Sokanlammet, to ridge-like Sokanharju, which in reality is an esker. Here the view northward arrests the attention so much that few will take the trouble to investigate Sokanaapa mire. A fairy-tale landscape opens out towards Sudenvaara fell, where one suddenly comes upon an unbelievably elegant birch wood, slender trees forming narrow ribbons in an apparently never-ending stream towards the north.

For a peatland, the density of birdlife on Sudenvaaranaapa mire is unusually high. The prolificacy of perching birds is especially noteworthy. The commoner species here include the yellow wagtail, reed bunting, meadow pipit, and in some years the redpoll. The reed bunting exhibits a preference for the more barren Sphagnum bogs and thickets, but the bluethroat is more catholic in its choice of habitat. One may be lucky enough to glimpse the little bunting, as this Siberian rarity's favourite terrain appears to be just this kind of birch-covered fen.

More abundant than normal, too, are the wood sandpiper, ruff, and snipe. If one bases observations solely on their cries, some other birds would seem to be very common indeed, but their total populations are actually far smaller than those of the species mentioned above. These noisy species are the spotted redshank, greenshank, crane, jack snipe, curlew and whimbrel.

SAKKALA-AAPA MIRE

One can reach Sakala-aapa mire either via the water route from Luiro, or from the east via the small road circumnavigating the lower slopes of Matalainen fell. In this case one should cross the Verkko-oja stream before reaching the mire. Innumerable spring floods have turned the stream's banks into an almost impenetrable thicket of shrubs, clubmosses and grass, and sedge tussocks.

The best parts of Sakkala-aapa lie on the northern side of Karhunpesäsaari island, but several kilometres beforehand the mire changes from being a brownish water Sphagnum fen into a pale green sedge fen. Beyond Karhunpesäsaari island the mire continues as a birch fen, but its general appearance is quite different to Sudenvaaranaapa, being much more diversified and intresting.

Many waterbirds inhabit this mire. Almost every pool in July has its complement of ducklings, and sometimes more than one family is present. The red-necked phalarope, however, is the commonest bird on these pools, having apparently adapted itself very well to the wetter areas of the birch fen habitat.

Sakkala-aapa is also popular with some of the larger birds. Cranes, bean geese and whooper swans are to be found there during the breeding season. The golden eagle

King of the mire, the crane is very shy during the breeding season. It keeps to the fringes of the peatlands, where it can make a quick dash into the safety of the trees.

and great grey owl hunt over the mire. The eagle-owl, now a great rarity in Lapland, also patrols the near territories, coming down from its nest sites at the tops of gullies.

KILPIAAPA MIRE

Without a doubt, Kilpiaapa is among this country's most picturesque bogs. It is also extremely large, extending for about a league and a half (some 15 km). Kilpiaapa is easy to reach because all the paths and trails leading west both from the main village and from Kairala end at its borders. The vista opening out in front of the experienced rambler brings to mind the vastness of Ostrobothnia, with its dominance of sky and far-flung horizon.

For the peatland researcher the Kilpiaapa mire represents a treasure, as many of the bog and mire types characteristic of the open aapa mire zone of southern Lapland are conveniently clustered in it.

THE VUOTAS RESERVOIR REGION

The threat to construct the Kemihaara reservoir hung heavily over Pelkosenniemi inhabitants for something like a quarter of a century. This third reservoir on the upper reaches of the River Kemijoki would have inundated the entire eastern side of commune, in addition to parts of Salla and Savukoski. To make matters worse, the village of Luiro would have lain underwater, just as had occurred at Sompio some years previously. The uncertainty surrounding Luiro ended in the 1970s. Extremely strong local resistance and the fact that the peatland wildlife of this region was demonstrated to be unique, together with the wide variety of known adverse effects of similar reservoirs already in existence, finally persuaded Council-of-State to relinquish its plan for a new reservoir.

Nowadays, following the demise of the master plan, people tend to speak of the lesser "Vuotso project". Stiff resistance from all quarters, the over-production of electricity, and the Government's penurious state, put paid in 1982 even to this considerably less ambitious plan. Nature lovers could once again breathe freely, while local inhabitants could start to look ahead with optimism.

The exploration of Vuotos begins — appropriately enough in the local tradition — with a ferry trip. The River Kemijoki, which has swollen to become a torrent, is crossed at the church. It is possible to approach the heart of the reservoir area from the new, now metalled highway from Aavaspuoli to Ahvenvaara, whence in a dry summer one follows the base of the winter road as far as Rutivaara fell. At this point one is finally forced to proceed on foot, since Rutivaara forms part of a large southeast-northwest oriented elongated esker which would have become the western bank of the reservoir.

Beyond the esker seemingly limitless peatlands begin, but there are heathlands, eskers, hollows, river courses, lakes and pools hidden in these peatlands.

The most delightful region of all lies between the Jaurujoki and Siiamosseljä rivers, in the neighbourhood of Neulikkoaapa mire. Thin-layered brown moss fens, orchid-filled meadows, and the bottom meadows with their thickets and old hay barns along the water courses all tend to soften the severe countenance of the wilderness. The area's most significant entity from the natural historical aspect is elliptical Säynäjäjärvi, which is one of those very rare places in the forested zone of Finland where the velvet scoter nests. Like other lakes in the area, this one is shallow, rather straight-shored and broad. Aside from around a dozen pairs of velvet scoters, the district is very popular with other waterfowl, including tufted duck and smew.

BEAN GEESE AT VUOTOS

Ornithologists visit Vuotos mainly, however, for the geese. The bean goose density in this region is one of the largest in the country and owing to the limited size of the bogs and mires the birds are rather more approachable. The geese are at their most obvious in May as soon as the snow melts off the peatlands. Bean geese recently returned from the south cavort and fly ceaselessly around the flooded bogs, their joyful cries resounding everywhere.

By mid-May, however, there are far fewer geese in evidence, as the older birds will have dispersed to their breeding grounds on the fringes of the mires. It sometimes happens that an irate male bird suddenly takes to the wing, to fly in circles over the hiker's head, giving vent to its piercing alarm cry. Most of the birds encountered will be young individuals born the previous summer. These tend to feed in small flocks in the centres of open mires. When frightened, they will frequently take off and then fly in very close to inspect an interloper. By midsummer these flocks will have vanished as though removed from the face of the globe. Numerous studies indicate that they retire to the furthermost fells of the White Sea area in order to moult.

The annual moult which entices the geese away from the open mires serves to let in nesting pairs. The change in life brought about by the inability to fly forces the parent birds out of the thickets lining the brooks and off the mires with higher vegetation, where predators are able to steal up on the unsuspecting birds with ease. At the latest by mid-July the geese families will move out into the open centres of the bogs. It is surprisingly difficult, however, to spot these geese, since with the loss of their flight feathers they become extremely shy and practically mute. The joyful hubbub of spring is forgotten.

The geese collect in social groups around some remote mire pool where they are constantly on their guard and ready to flee at the merest hint of danger into the shelter of the forests or on to the safety of the pool.

While there are several such gathering grounds in the vicinity of the Kokonaapa mire, and while the best of these may contain a hundred or more geese, only very rarely does one succeed in coming upon the birds unawares. Unless one has been lucky enough to spot a bird before it has been put on its guard and to creep up on it, one may conclude that there are no bean geese about. On the other hand, the leavings of these large flocks in the centre of the mire will be clearly visible. After a long sojourn by the birds, the fringes of the pool will be full of moulted feathers, down, and piles of droppings, while the mire for several hectares around will have been trampled as though the defence forces had been carrying out manoeuvres on it!

If one examines these signs carefully, one may well come across other tracks as the brown bear, for example, is extremely partial to a square meal of bean goose. Bears are consequently regularly to be found in the neighbourhood of these large goose gatherings. At Vuotos such a creature has for some years taken its toll of geese, the tracks it leaves showing that it is an extremely large individual.

This bear does not always go hungry. Each year the remains of a goose or two are discovered on the mire. Indeed two of the author's ringed bean geese have been killed by a bear, the remains of one of them lying at the end of a set of tracks impressed in the mire by this large animal.

At the end of July, when the geese have already grown new feathers, people begin to appear in the peatlands as the cloudberries start to ripen. At Pelkosenniemi cloudberry picking and marketing provide an important additional source of income for many people and as such constitute one of the more environmentally acceptable ways of earning a living. The fly in the ointment here, however, is the advent of the snowmobile, which can just as easily be driven over a soft mire as over soft snow. Men from Kemijärvi searching for cloudberries criss-cross this area with these new 'toys', leaving unsightly tracks.

While the snowmobile fraternity is a nuisance, inundating the entire area by a reservoir would have constituted a major catastrophe. Regretably, when it became known that a reservoir was to be built, loggers quickly moved in to chop down the trees, scything right into the region's heartlands. The shelving of the plan has not brought back the trees.

Has the project in fact permanently been shelved? Who knows. The attitude of certain high-up people is well reflected by a statement made by a Minister of Trade and Industry not so long ago as he flew over Vuotos: "A hopeless mire". PK

Aimo Holtari

Winter Gloom and Midnight Sun

The majority of our planet's inhabitants live in areas where days and nights are of approximately the same length all year round. Every day is succeeded by a dark night, which in turn yields to another bright day. For a good few degrees north and south of the equator, the length of the day varies by only a few minutes all year round.

The situation is different here in the far north: light summer nights are balanced by dark winter days. Just north of the Arctic Circle, the sun shines round the clock for several days each summer. Only a hundred kilometres further north, it remains continuously above the horizon for thirty days.

At the Arctic Circle on Christmas Day, the sun pops briefly above the southern horizon at midday, but only a hundred kilometres to the north it remains below the horizon for several days on end. The midnight sun in summer and the midday gloom in winter are only different sides of the same coin.

The earth's inclined axis
The varying length of the daylight period is caused by the rotation of the earth around its axis. The side facing the sun is day, the other side night. As the planet rotates from west to east, the illuminated and dark zones move westwards in a cycle that lasts 24 hours. Variations in the relative lengths of the day and night as well as seasonal changes are due to the earth's inclined axis and its orbital movement around the sun. If the axis were not inclined, the situation would always be the way it is at the spring and autumn equinoxes. All over the world, the day and night would be exactly the same length, about 12 hours.

The earth's axis is inclined at an angle of about 23.5 degrees. This figure fluctuates slightly, but only very slowly. At the spring equinox, the axis is inclined exactly sideways from the perspective of the sun and day and night are of exactly equal length. From either pole, the sun is just visible above the horizon. At the North Pole, it heralds the beginning of a day that will last half a year, whilst a six-months night is beginning at the South Pole. As summer approaches, the days lengthen in the northern hemisphere and the nights shorten. The sun illuminates a larger and larger area around the North Pole as the earth's axis gradually tilts further and further towards the sun. Finally, when the summer solstice (or midsummer) arrives, the North Pole is inclined at an angle of 23.5 degrees towards the sun. Now, everywhere within the Arctic Circle is in sunlight round the clock. During the day, the sun climbs to a height of $90° - \alpha + 23.5°$ (α is the latitude of the locality). At night it is at a height of $90° + \alpha + 23.5°$. Thus, for example, it is

The sun shines on Saariselkä at midnight for more than 50 days in summer.

45.5 degrees above the southern horizon in Muonio in northern Finland at noon on Midsummer Day and 1.5 degrees above the northern horizon at midnight. In the Antarctic, it will not be seen for months.

But the earth retains the same tilt as it proceeds along its orbital path. After Midsummer, the illuminated area around the North Pole begins shrinking again. By the time the autumn equinox arrives, the illuminated "skull cap" on top of the world has become so small that only the North Pole is in sunlight. Once again, day and night are the same length everywhere.

The period of gloom
After the autumn solstice, the North Pole sinks into six months of sunless gloom. The

sunless area around the pole continues to grow until the winter solstice, by which time it has spread to the Arctic Circle during the day. The entire area within the circle, including most of Lapland, falls into a gloomy state that the Finnish language calls "kaamos". By contrast, the area within the Antarctic Circle at the other end of the

see how long the "nightless night" is in summer and how long the sun remains out of sight in winter can cause us astonishment. The midnight sun period lasts 53 days at Muonio in summer, but the winter gloom only 23 days. Further north in Utsjoki, the midnight sun shines for 72 days, but the winter gloom lasts only 53

with navigation. During it, many stars are visible and the horizon can be seen clearly enough to determine their height above it.

Although the sun does not rise above the horizon even at midday during the winter gloom, there is a long period of twilight every day. Even on the shortest day of the year in the

ground. The nights are pitch-dark, especially when there is heavy cloud cover. In northern Finland, these times are in October and part of November. In the south, they continue on into December.

The moon is an important "lantern" during the midwinter darkness. It follows almost the same path as the sun as it passes across the sky. A new moon is in the same quarter of the sky as the sun and is thus not visible. A full moon, on the other hand, is in the opposite direction to the sun, i.e. is at approximately the same point where the sun was six months earlier. In the heart of winter, when the sun is invisible, the full moon shines round the clock and does not set even in the north (except on the rare occasions when the moon's orbit deviates five degrees or so from that of the sun). In summer, when the sun is high in the sky, the full moon is hardly ever visible above the horizon.

During the darkest period, the full moon is at its highest point in the wintry sky of the north. When pure snow blankets the landscape, open land and hills alike, so much light is reflected in the northern sky on a cloudless night that it is bright enough to work outdoors or ski in safety.

Martti Rikkonen

world is bathed in sunlight, even at midnight.

In mid-winter, the angle at which the sun hangs above the horizon at midday is 90° — a — 23.5° and at midnight -90° + a — 23.5°. Thus at 68°N, Muonio's latitude, it is 1.5° below the horizon at midday and 45.5° below it at midnight. Bright summer nights and sunless winter daytime gloom succeed each other year after year and the whole pattern is very symmetrical.

When the sun is above the horizon, we have daytime and light. But when it sinks below the horizon, the darkness of night does not fall at once. The atmosphere diffuses sunlight, and darkness descends only after a period of fading twilight. Even when the sun has set in the mathematical sense, the atmosphere diffracts or "bends" its light to the extent that it still seems to us to be entirely above the horizon.

A glance at an almanac to

days. These discrepancies are due to the atmosphere's ability to diffract light and to the fact that when the sun rises or sets is determined according to its upper edge. The sun itself is half a degree in apparent diameter.

The midnight sun and completely sunless winter days can be experienced only within the Arctic and Antarctic circles. Everywhere else in the world, the sun sets and rises every day. The zones within which there are bright summer nights and fairly gloomy midwinter days stretch 500-1,000 kilometres towards the equator from both poles.

The dimness when the sun is below the horizon is divided into three categories: bourgeois (0°-6°), nautical (6°-12°) and astronomical twilight (12°-18°). There is still enough light during the bourgeois twilight to work or read a newspaper outdoors. As its name suggests, nautical twilight is associated

The kaamos winter gloom lasts just under a month at Lake Inari. Only the moon lights snow-clad Ukonkivi Fell.

northernmost part of Finland, the sun comes to within 3.5 degrees of the horizon. The bourgeois twilight lasts about four hours then. There is about one and a half hours of nautical twilight before and after this. Thus the total length of twilight during which there is enough light to work outdoors is roughly seven hours. The gloom of winter is not absolute in Lapland.

The eerie lights of winter

The actual length of the daylight period does not in itself determine how much light there is in the north during the winter. The darkest period is probably in the autumn, before the snow falls and covers the

Even during the darkest period and moonless periods, Nature has not left the north completely without light. Quite often, the Northern Lights (Aurora Borealis) wanly illuminate the bleak landscapes of Lapland. Sometimes they flare up so intensely that they momentarily light the landscape as effectively as the full moon. They remain rather dim for long periods, but can be seen almost all across the sky for hours on end.

The Finnish word for this period of winter gloom is kaamos, which probably once meant a thick, ground-hugging blanket of mist rising from river valleys and enveloping everything in darkness. Today, the word means the sunless time of winter, which in cloudless weather can clothe the splendid scenery of Lapland in a superb satiny costume.

KK

The Golden Berry of the Bogs

Jorma Luhta

The cloudberry is a northern plant. The southern limit of the zone in which it lives in Europe cuts across the eastern shore of the Baltic and runs through southern Scandinavia and northern England. It grows in the same latitudes in North America, and is thus found throughout the frigid zone of the northern hemisphere.

A bog plant, or is it?

The name by which the cloudberry is called in southern Finland indicates that it is a bog plant. It grows on open mossy bogs and pine-studded blanket bogs, both of which are bleak and poor in nutrients. Consequently, it is rather odd that the runners grow in dense clumps also in well-shaded wilderness spruce forests that are rich in nutrients.

It would appear that nutrients are not as important a factor to the cloudberry as the absence of competition from other plants for living space. The gloominess of wilderness spruce forests prevents many of the cloudberry's competitors from thriving, as does the low level of nutrients in mossy bogs. In northern areas of Finland, where there are fewer competitors and more moisture than in the south, the cloudberry can also grow on forested heathlands or seashore meadows.

The cloudberry thrives best on open mossy bogs. Night frosts in early June often reduce the crop.

Pertti Kalinainen

Close to the Arctic Ocean, it can even grow on sand dunes or rock outcroppings.

Strong roots

Even in summer, two-thirds of a cloudberry plant's weight is hidden beneath the peat, and it goes underground completely for the winter. A square metre of land surface can contain 150 — 300 metres of ground runners, with dozens of metres of roots beneath it. Most of the roots penetrate 5-30 centimetres into the earth.

The plant owes its welfare and ability to spread to its strong root system. In spring, when the ground thaws and the temperature rises, it uses the nourishment stored in its root system to make its aboveground shoots grow rapidly. In late spring and early summer, the root system expends its energy capital. Only after midsummer do the overground shoots get back to themselves and begin storing the new energy produced by the leaves. Most of this is for use the following spring and summer, although some of it is consumed already during the autumn and winter. During the autumn, the plant grows new runners to replace the old decaying ones and occupy new growth sites.

The cloudberry mainly spreads by means of its land runners; seeds play a relatively minor role in reproduction. An extensive patch of plants can, in fact, be a single "clone", i.e. stem from a single mother plant. In most cases, however, a patch consists of several intermingled clones.

The root system begins consuming energy immediately the ambient temperature rises above freezing point, be it summer or winter. The leaves dry out when they are 3 — 4 months old, regardless of temperature. Thus the cloudberry can not thrive in areas where the winter is short and warm, because its roots would consume more energy in a year than its leaves are capable of producing.

Leaves not fond of sunshine

The above-ground parts of the cloudberry plant grow anew every year. These mostly consist of kidney-shaped leaves, of which there can be 1 — 3 per shoot. There is only one flower per shoot, but most of the shoots are flowerless.

The size of a shoot depends decisively on where the plant is growing. The plant remains small on an open bog; its stem is often no more than five centimetres long or even shorter, and the leaves are unlikely to exceed five centimetres in diameter. In shaded places, by contrast, the stems can stretch to twenty centimetres or so, with leaves as much as ten centimetres across. Leaves in shaded spots also have a different structure from those exposed to sunshine; those on open bogs are thicker and harder than those in shadowy woodland areas.

The leaves are well adapted to northern conditions. They photosynthesize, i.e. bind energy, even when there is little light and heat, a period that can last virtually uninterruptedly for up to two months north of the Arctic Circle. Photosynthesis is intense when the temperature is around fifteen degrees Celsius. The leaves do not like hot sunny weather. When the temperature rises above 18 degrees, energy production declines sharply and a protracted period of hot weather will keep photosynthesis at a low level for a long time. The leaves of plants on open bogs begin turning brown already in July and the plants are often an attractive red colour by August. Where trees and shrubs provide shade, they stay green until September. They drop off in August-September, and only withered stems remain above ground until the next summer.

Two kinds of flowers

When cloudberries are in full bloom in early summer, their flowers can cover large areas of bog in a white blanket. But this beautiful sight can not be enjoyed for long. Each flower is open for only two or three days, and the full glory hardly ever lasts more than a week on any one bog.

The cloudberry flower has four or five white petals, each about a centimetre across. There are several dozen yellow stamens in the centre of a male flower, whilst the centre of the female flower contains 5-40 greenish carpals.

Naturally, only the female plant produces berries, so one can know as soon as the plants are blooming what kind of crop to expect. Male plants outnumber female plants, although the ratio between the two can vary greatly from bog to bog.

Pollinators needed

Colourful hover flies and insects resembling ordinary house flies pollinate most of the cloudberry blossoms. Bumblebees and wild honeybees visit the blossoms less frequently, but pollination succeeds well when they do stray onto them. The number of drupelets in a berry depends on how thoroughly pollination takes place; small insects pollinate only some of the carpals and the berries are small.

The mobility of the pollinating insects depends on the air temperature: when it is below

Cloudberries fetch a good price. Picking them provides people in Lapland with substantial supplementary income.

Jorma Luhta

fifteen degrees, they mainly stay where they are. Thus cold weather at the time the plants are blooming lowers the pollination rate.

Berry crop a matter of luck

Night frost is an unwelcome visitor to cloudberry bogs. Experts have discovered that a temperature of minus two degrees is a critical threshold during the blossoming period; if it is colder, most of the flowers are destroyed. The critical point for unripe berries is about the same, but their susceptibility to frost varies from one stage of ripening to the next.

Bumper cloudberry crops do not come often, but only once or twice in a decade. A good seed crop once a decade is quite adequate, because the plant concentrates most of its energy on reproducing through suckering, i.e. via its root system.

In some places, however, the plants produce a good crop of berries almost every year. Shady woodlands and banks overhanging water are relatively well shielded from frost. Those are among berry-pickers' favourite spots. Female plants are usually lush and strong in such places, so regular abundant crops do seem to be too much of a burden on them. Berries on plants in shady woodland are usually large with plenty of globules.

A berry usually consists of 5-15 drupelets, but the number can be as large as 35. It varies in weight from one to three grammes. In bad years, berries with only one or two drupelets represent a large proportion of the crop. Large berries are the first to ripen; the small ones growing beside them can take as much as a week longer. A ripe berry is as rich in Vitamin C as blackcurrants and well ahead of most other wild berries.

The northernmost municipalities in the province of Lapland are empowered to seek permission from the Ministry of Agriculture and Forestry to prohibit non-residents from picking cloudberries and have frequently exercised this right. However, hikers are still entitled to pick as many as they can eat. JKo

Seppo Koponen

The Bane of the Cloudberry

A good cloudberry crop is important to the livelihoods of many families in northern Finland. Therefore it is understandable that in the early half of the 1970s brown, withered leaves on cloudberry plants and "black cloudberry worms" attracted widespread attention. At its worst, the area of destruction extended from south of Lake Oulujärvi to the northern limit of pine forests, and in places on into the Arctic birch zone. The pest manifested itself mainly on open bogs, often the most productive in the area, but only seldom in forested or shrub-covered areas. It appeared that anywhere that the surface of a bog had been disturbed was in increased danger of destruction; the banks of bog drains and fringes of winter roads were particularly vulnerable.

Small roundish holes and larger weblike "windows" had been eaten in the leaves of the cloudberries that had turned brown. The culprit turned out to be a greyish-brown beetle about half a centimetre long and with yellowish sides. The leaves were being eaten threadbare by both the adults and their larvae, which were glossy black on top and partially yellow underneath. The pests be-

longed to the genus Galerucella, the leaf beetle family.

In spring, as soon as the first cloudberry shoots rose from the ground, the beetles arrived and laid their matte-yellow eggs on the leaves, in clusters of a dozen or so. Each female laid hundreds of eggs. The black larvae that hatched from them immediately began nibbling the leaves. After a feast lasting three or four weeks, the larvae went into the chrysalis stage. The next generation hatched out towards the end of summer and ate leaves for enough time to accumulate energy to get them through the winter.

The beetle is known as a cloudberry pest only in Finland and adjacent areas of Norway and the Soviet Union. Just why it afflicts this particular region is not known. The plague was at its height in the early 1970s, after which it waned dramatically. It has been gradually increasing again since the beginning of the 1980s. When the numbers of beetles were at their lowest in Lapland, damage caused by them was also noticed elsewhere, especially further south in the Kainuu and Peräpohjala regions.

The zone in which the beetle is found in Finland is the most continental part of the country.

This moment augurs destruction of the berry crop: cloudberry beetles mating on the leaves of their host plant.

The species clearly likes warmth, as is manifested by its particular prevalence on open bogs and broken bog surfaces. There appears to be a clear correlation between weather conditions and fluctuations in the beetle population. It proliferates when several very warm summers succeed each other. The summer of 1975 and those following it were cold and, at least in the northern parts of its distribution range, the beetle's larvae failed to live to maturity.

When beetle numbers are very large and many leaves are eaten, the cloudberry crop can be disappointing for a couple of years after the one in which the actual destruction takes place. However, it should be borne in mind that the beetle is not the only nor even the most common cause of poor crops. The weather when the plants are blooming and its effects on pollinating insects and their mobility as well as the weather while the berries are ripening, especially night frost, play a key role in determining how good the crop of berries will be. SK

IN THE WILDS OF SALLA AND SAVUKOSKI

Split into segments bounded by old roads, the Salla and Savukoski districts up until the 1960s were otherwise trackless wilds. Little tree-felling took place until then. At present the network of logging roads is slowly intruding on these fell chains and the forests have now been heavily logged. Today's hiker will have to seek solstice in the national parks.

Craggy Värriötunturi fell constitutes one of the snow bunting's southernmost breeding places.

Veikko Vasama

Dick Forsman

NARUSKA

Between the Naruskajoki and Tenniöjoki rivers lies a wilderness of fells in which the lakes and pools are typical of the southern part of the Salla region. During the summer this terrain is very easy to walk in, there being only a handful of peatlands, but plenty of Scots pine forests, especially in the extreme south of the region.

The Tenniöjoki river is a very special one. At its headwaters it lies close to the eastern border, diving into the deserted wilds on the Soviet side, flowing through Lake Tenniöjärvi, a lovely lake, and then forming a series of rapids of which Liinahattu is the most spectacular and violent rapids of the entire Kemijoki waterway. It loses a rare degree of altitude during its descent. Changing its course towards the west-northwest, the river then finally comes home to Finland.

The southern part of the fell chain on the Finnish side is so narrow that it is best first to ascend the rapids on the river Naruskajoki — channelized for log-floating purposes — but nowadays also renowned for the excitement it offers experienced canoeists.

A VISTA OF FELLS

Following the generally northerly direction from Kenttä-lampi pool, one skirts Vasavaara fell, going down into the ravine and then climbing up again to Toresvaara fell, at whose southwest extremity, where there is a rocky cliff, one can turn northeast and undertake a long ascent towards Salla's highest point, 629 metre high Sorsatunturi fell. Right at the very end the ascent becomes steeper. This fell has a very sharp peak in comparison to the surrounding fells, which have more pate-like summits. From the rubble-covered summit there is a very spectacular view towards fells lying in the south and west, as well as towards the northern fells and eastern fell masses. It is in this splendid but rather sterile landscape that the snow bunting nests.

The fell chain on the northern side draws the hiker. There is no more extensive undulating fellscape outside Saariselkä. First, however, one is forced to descend on to a narrow bog, Sorsavuotso, compressed into a gully. If one is fortunate enough to arrive in the cloudberry season, one can fill one's stomach here with this northern delicacy. One now has to choose between heading north via Kaunisoiva or heading in roughly the same direction via Jäkälätunturi. Both of these have smooth sides blanketed in lichens and dwarf shrubs where reindeer browse and on which the lonely cry of the dotterel plucks at the heart strings.

Along the Saapakko-Oiva summits continuing to the north one's gaze is drawn to the right as though by a magnet: a fell to which a section has apparently been added later. This is Takkaselkätunturi fell, which bears a rocky protuberance on its posterior. This hump is composed of a different type of rock to the fell itself — an ultrabasic rock containing large amounts of amphibolite and chlorite — and the nose-like prominence of this as interesting as a botanical garden. Arnica alpinus, Potentilla nivea (one of the cinquefoils), and a variety of other unusual species in this fascinating 'garden' have remained steadfastly in their stronghold since the latter phases of the Ice Age.

After crossing the Kuskoiva slope the topography begins to feature more boulders. Gullies full of rushes tend to make the going a bit more strength-sapping. The hiker will not fail to note that there has been a fire at the southern tip of Tuntsa. On the Nuolusoiva fell it ascended even as far as the bare summit.

THE HEADWATERS OF TUNTSA

Even before the war, Tuntsa was a celebrated spot among fishermen, but few people from the south, other than geologists and forest researchers, ever bother to go quite so far up the river's course. It was only after the Tuntsa fire that the way was opened to tourists.

There are now only some 30 kilometres of Tuntsa actually within Finland. Three-quarters of it was ceded to the Soviet Union after the war. The river flows into Lake Koutajärvi and finally its waters flow along the River Koutajoki to the White Sea. Lower down in the water-course salmon and migratory sea trout are encountered.

From the mouth of the Nuolusoja rise burned fells and smaller hills. During the hike one can observe the way in which nature has recovered following the fire and to estimate on the right behind the fells the position of the border towards Puitsitunturi fell. This fell represents the place at which the present borderline differs from the pre-war one. Once probing out into the USSR near Kantalahti, Finland these days has a hole in it at this point.

From Jänisvitsikko rises the cone-shaped silhouette of Sauoiva. When turning towards this, one is obliged to cross deeply-scored gullies. These ancient faults were full of water at the end of the Ice Age. In the summer of 1917 a geography student studied the route down which the waters had made their escape, as well as the esker formations. By the autumn the study was complete, consisting of a set of maps and a lengthy text. The researcher presented it at the university, but then took it away with him. When changing trains at Viborg station he accidentally left his thesis on the luggage rack of the carriage he was in. Next day the revolution broke out and the train, as one might expect, never came back. Sadly, the gullies in the headwaters of the Tuntsa have not been studied since.

Sauoiva is a prominent fell not unlike a pyramid sloping up to 615 metres. In the near distance its clearly delimited shape becomes rather coarse. The fell's pink granite has become split into large fragments which now cover the bedrock, they themselves being clasped in turn by surface-hugging lichens.

From the summits of Sauoiva and Pulkkatunturi, located on the former's northern side, an interesting and varied panorama opens out towards the east: in the northwest skirting Nuortti fell, but crossing a large valley with a backdrop consisting of Saariselkä, here a delicate shade of blue. Towards the northeast extends over the border the Alinen Nuortti valley from which on the right stand out the kilometre high Siiulutaldi-Vuojimi fell chain

Jorma Luhta

The northeastern wilderness has few lakes but numerous rushing streams and rivers bring variety to the forested landscape.

with its snow covered summits. Towards the east the land falls away to become the Juonnijoki valley, whose backdrop is formed by more than 800-metre high Tsuinatundra. This is the real wilderness which keeps Finland supplied with a steady input of large carnivores and a large part of which has been set aside as the Laplandiya National Park (USSR).

THE STEEP-SIDED GULLY OF VÄRRIÖTUNTURI

In the west stands the very elongated Värriötunturi fell which in summer is seen to be covered by a dry, scanty heathland. Snow melting on this fell and its upper slopes forms water that disappears into the ground, only to reappear at the foot of the fell as springs whose waters are destined for the Gulf of Bothnia, the Arctic Ocean, or even the White Sea.

The northern end of Värriötunturi is cut by a mighty rift valley whose walls fall precipitously into the pools and crevices below . Owing to the depth of the gully the snow in places remains up until midsummer, so that alongside small brooks flowing through the broken rocks there is an uncommonly cool micro-climate. In it, right in the middle of these forests, have survived some of the plants normally associated today with the high fells, but which in fact are relics of the last Ice Age. By contrast, the south-facing slope warms up so much in the sun that it suits, for example, the wild strawberry. The raven nests on high ledges on the cliff, while in winter the wolverine leaves its tracks along the valley floor.

North of Värriötunturi fell lies the University of Helsinki "Värriötunturi Research Station" which is specialised in the study of large carnivores, all species of which occur in this district. While the research station is well-equipped, even making use of television cameras, the main prerequisite for this kind of study is peace. For this reason the researchers try to discourage hikers from walking in the vicinity. To assist this need, the Värriö Strict Nature Reserve has been established in the vicinity of Sauoiva.

NUORTTI

The River Nuorttijoki, which for a start flows southwest, starts at the foot of Nuorttitunturi fell. Soon it begins to curve to the left, eventually flowing northeast over the Soviet border. The area within this sweeping curve is one of Lapland's many interesting corners.

From the latitude of Sorsatunturi fell northward right up to Saariselkä there are very few lakes — few, at any rate, by Finnish standards. The scattered water bodies that exist are more in the nature of peat-fringed pools than actual lakes. In such surroundings, Lake Ainijärvi, with its steeply sloping shores, is a novelty. Apart from sedge, reed and horsetail beds, the lake supports no substantial aquatic plants. However, a high plankton production maintains food chains important from the fisherman's point of view, the most vital link being the trout.

The lake is bounded on the south side by the Ainijärvi eskers, which are clothed in spruce. This hilly situation represents Finland's northern limit of growth for the wild strawberry. Ferny copses line the brook, their special attribute being a peculiarly pacifistic strain of the common stinging nettle — these plants have no stings! With leaves longer than that of the normal barn facade and garden nettle, this variety grows wild in lush gullies. The stinging variety in these parts occurs only around the ruins of buildings, a specialised habitat to which it was brought by mankind.

Northwest of Lake Ainijärvi the dominance of spruce dwindles, with a consequent increase in birch. However, at the southern foot of the Rouvoiva fells there is a large treeless tract. The forests in the neighbourhood of Soklioja are primarily birch woods, with a field layer contrasting sharply with that of the surrounding forests. The occurrence of these intrigued natural scientists for quite a long time, until one day it was discovered that the area's characteristic rocks, which are carbonate-based, were overlain with apatite. This, as is the way of such things, is to be quarried commercially within the next few years.

The unusual features of the Sokli scenery are most clearly discernible in the neighbourhood of Lake Loitsojärvi: park-like stands of birch, treeless valley floors, a single bluewater lake, stark cliffs that have been blasted out experimentally and now stand before a jumble of shorn-off apatatitic boulders the unsavoury colour of excrement. Once quarrying gets into full swing, within the next few years, the landscape will change even more dramatically. The peace and dignity of the wilderness in the Sokli area will be destroyed, the fell chains echoing to the clamour and blasting associated with converting this new source of phosphorus into Finnmarks.

Finns now export phosphorus for making fertilizer, but it has been estimated that by the turn of the century, when Finland's own meagre reserves run out, they will have to consider importing the same commodity. Or, to be more accurate, their children will have to.

In the interior of Nuortti the terrain, while being ideal for hiking, tends to improve as one journeys east — to be faced before long with a yellow notice-board marking the border zone. It is impossible to obtain permission to visit this area simply for the purpose of rambling about in it. In fact, the foreigner would do well to forget about the border zone altogether, there being plenty to see in Finland without going outside it!

CIVILISATION DESCENDS

Coming out of the wilderness into Tulppio produces something of a culture shock. After the tranquillity, it seems absurd to stand in a phone box inquiring about coach times while the roar of a rising aircraft drowns out the voice coming down the wire.

There is slight compensation. Tulppio has always been a pioneer of technical development. In a shed you can still see one of the first traction engines which, imported from the United States in the 1913-1916 period, hauled log rafts from the River Nuorttijoki. This river unfortunately flows in the wrong direction (i.e. towards the Arctic Ocean) over to the Vuohtusjoki and Kemijoenhaara, which conversely do Finns the favour of flowing in the right direction (i.e. in roughly the direction of Helsinki). This — the ego-bolstering plan of one Hugo Richard Sandberg, who was the forestry chief at the large Kemi corporation — failed in the face of natural forces and world events (the reader will remember there was a World War). Large quantities of timber, comprising according to the records some 150,000 logs, were hauled out, however, in that short space of time. Apart from the engine, the ruins of cabins and even deep furrows in the ground, remain as mementos of Sandberg's bold plan.

Today Tulppio forms a base camp for sports fishermen; tomorrow it may well be a booming mine town.

This ultrabasic area has about it something of the barrenness of the desert. Stony ground, together with only minute traces of chromium, nickel, cobalt and copper, combine to make conditions very inhospitable for ground-hugging plants. A plant typical to these ultrabasic conditions is a small fern whose name sounds like an anatomy lecture: green-ribbed spleenwort (Asplenium vi-

Despite its bright colouration, the bold pine grosbeak is one of the less easily seen birds of blanket bogs.

ride). It is particularly adept at growing in small cracks (or should we say fractures?). The fern spreads easily through the agency of very fine wind-dispersed spores and hence has taken up residence wherever ultrabasic rock is exposed.

HISTORY OF THE WILDS

West of the Tulppio district one can choose between taking and ignoring the road. A suitable compromise is reached by making use of an old track that is neither road nor rough terrain. In some places you will able to see the road from this track anyway. Heavy log sledges in winter were given impetus by a downhill grade at Suttikämpä, where a man was permanently in attendance whose job it was to scatter hay and other materials to increase the friction and reduce impetus.

Sotataival, a spur lying between the rivers Sotajoki and Vuohtusjoki, is a thoroughfare of historical interest. All 'traffic' heading northeast passed along this route right up to the turn of the century. In summer boats were poled up the Kemihaara and Vuohtusjoki, then carried to the River Sotajoki, whence they were guided downstream to Nuortti, and where necessary on down (or up, if you prefer it) to the Arctic Ocean. Even in winter this route was in constant use.

The rivers saw a good deal of activity at the beginning of this century when Lapps of the local tribe brought fish down from the Arctic Ocean to the work site by reindeer in winter. Sotataipale, which boasted cattle, met milk needs. There was a second herd at Tulppio. The traveller par excellence was the company's bull who, kept in trim on a diet of hay, spent his time plodding from one harem of cows to the other. Nobody knows whether he preferred actually getting there to the less demanding task of simply placing one foot in front of the other.

The River Värriöjoki gradually builds up from a set of small streams and eventually drains into the Kemihaara at Martti. In spite of its remoteness, the valley of the Värriö has seen much of significance in the history of Finland. After the furore of the First World War had died down, the Kemiyhtiö concern undertook large-scale clearfelling in this area. A mutiny broke out in one of the lumber camps on 2.2.1924. Its leader, one Jahvetti Moilanen, read the Nordic Partisan Battalion's manifest standing on a box that had contained lard from America. During the next few days this company of a few hundred men commandeered the villages of Savukoski and Salla — without a shot being fired — before fleeing over the eastern border.

Both this mutiny and the original clearcuts have been wiped away by time. Logged in order to produce the first spruce pulp for paper-making, the forests had time to recover before the large-scale construction of logging roads of the last few decades. TR

The Russian word "zavoda" means factory, but also — and especially — a work site in a forest. "Savotta" is the Finnish version of the word, which was borrowed when the first logging camps were opened in this country in the early 19th century. Savotta culture and all the romanticism involved in it was at the peak of its flourishing in the first half of our century, when the only forces that battled with the forests were living ones: men and horses.

The wildernesses of Lapland have undergone very strong mechanization since the 1950s. First, chain saws replaced crossbows, bow saws and axes. Then tractors, which had already replaced horses on farms, inevitably appeared in the forests, complete with logging accessories. The accessory equipment was hammered together on farms and in village smithies to begin with, but soon found its way onto the metal industry's product lists. The traditional leisurely annual rhythm of horse-powered logging operations was no longer enough for machines, whose efficiency reduced the need for both men and horses.

The culture associated with logging camps reached the peak of its development in the 1950s. They now had more atmosphere and were homelier than ever before. The frequency with which trees were felled had speeded up, as a consequence of which the need for accommodation had declined, but camps were of a more temporary nature. All important now was the ability to move fast from one logging site to another. Building log cabins had become a thing of the past. Barrack-style huts replaced them, but were soon themselves replaced by mobile cabins and caravans. Eventually, increasing car ownership meant that workers could travel to the sites each day from their own homes.

Mechanization in forestry had a major impact on the wilderness environment. Roads of various standards now fragment vast areas of formerly trackless wilderness and the effects of mechanized logging operations

Savotta – the Culture of Logging Camps

are clearly visible in many places. Powerful machines have scarred what horse-powered logging left of the forest environment. Anybody who walks the forests today can still see the traces left over half a century ago.

Off to the forests

Before setting off to their camps in the forests, logging teams had to make thorough preparations. As a rule, the forests had been surveyed and evaluated by their owners, usually the National Board of Forests. There had to be at least a rough general plan so that camps, roads and floating routes could be located as purposefully as possible. The idea was to select the stands to be felled in places that would enable camps and roads to be used for as long as possible The stands marked for felling were often bordered in such a way that they sloped down towards the trunk roads.

Camps and main access roads had to be located close to sizable waterbodies with

A logging camp in the 1920s.

plenty of places along the roads where logs could be dropped into rivers almost every night during the winter.

Camps

The camps had a mystique all their own. They were where loggers spent the whole winter, and to some vagrant souls they were the only home they knew.

The earliest logging camps were semi-underground, dug into hill slopes with only a few round logs forming a wall above ground. The roof was of

split logs, slabs and chips. The huts had dirt floors, simple porchless doorways and bunks built onto the rear walls. Heating was provided by an open fire located by the door. The men slept in bunks attached to the rear wall. The horses had to make do with a rough shelter knocked together from softwood poles to protect them from winds and blizzards. Two or three teams of horses and at most a dozen men would create all that in only a few days. They were paid a lump sum for

164

A tracked steam locomotive pulling logs on sleds in 1912-16. The locomotive, complete with sleds, is still on view in Tulppio. A similar one is in the Forest Museum in Rovaniemi. Above right: a temporary wooden track in Savukoski.

the job and were free to decide for themselves what standard of amenities they wanted. There was no trouble keeping the hut warm, day or night; whoever felt cold got up and put some wood in the stove.

Camps built and maintained by employers became more common in the 1920s. The huts were of jointed round logs, with moss between them as insulation. The floors were half logs, which had been split with axes or hand saws. They were insulated only around the walls, by means of a layer of compacted earth. A stove or open fire provided heat. The men cooked their food and dried their clothes in the same rooms where they slept and lived.

Only after the Second World War did logging camps become more "luxurious". Now they were built of logs split with a buzz saw and had plank floors and heat-storing stoves. The kitchens and clothes-drying rooms were separated from the rooms where the men slept, and double beds replaced the earlier primitive bunks. There was also an attendant to keep a fire on at night.

Roads

The roads in Lapland were very poor in those days. In summer, supply roads twisted and turned through the terrain, following solid ground and avoiding bogs. They were mainly created by the traffic that passed along them; the ground was smoothened only where absolutely necessary. Since there were no earthmoving machines to deal with rough spots, the roads went around them and were very serpentine.

Winter roads were straighter, following level land and avoiding only steep inclines. Forest, even sparse stands, protected the roads from wind and blizzards, for which reason they rarely crossed large open bogs. They were clearly marked to ensure that any stranger could find his way to the camp. This was done by cutting conspicuous notches into trees on either side of the road. Where roads had to cross large open expanses, they were usually marked by means of pine logs with boards set crosswise into notches in their upper ends to indicate the way.

Quite separate roads were needed to transport the wood itself. In winter, they came into being "of their own accord" as load after load was hauled down from the upper edge of the felling block to the trunk road running along the fringe of the bog in the valley below. Trunk roads were carefully built and maintained. Their beds were smoothened with axes and hoes during the summer and with snowploughs and road planes in winter. A so-called road engineer, usually an older man, was in charge of maintaining trunk roads. Wielding a pick, he filled in ruts where the blade of the road plane had not bitten deep enough and stood by to help when a load went off the road.

Floating

Using horses to haul wood fairly short distances — up to ten kilometres or so — to the water's edge had long been a tried and trusted method. Floating was the most common method for longer distances, because the headwaters of the Kemi and Tornio rivers reached deep into the heart of Lapland. Full-length logs were floated down surprisingly small streams. Sawing them into shorter lengths in the forest became common practice only after the First World War. Using small streams and creeks to float logs was the only natural way of reducing relatively expensive horse haulage to a minimum.

Schemes to improve log floating channels in Lapland began at the same time that wood-processing industries were developed along the Gulf of Bothnia coast, i.e. in the early years of our century. When necessary, watercourses still in a natural state had to be regulated to facilitate log floating. Small dams were built in suitable places, usually just downstream from small rapids. In places where the water flowed strongly, stones were removed from the bed near both banks to direct the flow into the main channel. The hardest places to deal with were rapids, where the absence of a real channel made the water spread in a shallow sheet from bank to bank. Here, logs were used to build sluices, which forced the water into narrower and deeper channels.

The biggest concern in the headwaters of rivers and streams was that there would be enough water, because means of regulating the flow were quite limited. Even temporary structures so far from main roads represented a considerable cost factor.

Experiments with mechanical wood transport

Thus a natural interplay between horses and the forces of nature enabled wood to be transported from the places where it grew to the processing plants. However, the idea of using mechanical power to get wood to the floating channels began to develop in the 1910s. This was particularly necessary in places where the distance from the felling site to the river was too long, or where the logs had to cross a watershed. Large tracts of forest in northern and eastern Finland lie in areas where the rivers flow into the Arctic Ocean or the White Sea, outside Finnish territory.

Several of the big wood-processing companies operating in Lapland came up with mecha-

The remains of a 1920s logging camp.

nization schemes at the same time. Arthur Lagerlöf, managing director of the Raahe Company, and the Kemi Company's forestry manager Hugo Richard Sandberg, were open-minded men with an innovative approach to development. In the former company's experiment, a zinc-coated steel hawser was spanned from an intermediate wood depot to the river's edge. A motor sled was attached to the hawser and moved along it, drawing a load of timber behind. One line ran 16 kilometres in the Alakitka area of Kuusamo in 1913-14 and another 9 kilometres in the Perunkajärvi district near Rovaniemi in 1920-21. The first attempt, in the Ailanka district of Kemijärvi in 1911-12, was a total failure.

The Kemi Company tried a different approach in the Tulppio district of Savukoski in 1912-16. It used a steam loco-

motive fitted with caterpillar tracks to haul sleds loaded with logs distances of 30-45 kilometres. The method was already in use in the United States, where the locomotive was purchased. Getting it from the railhead in Rovaniemi to the Tulppio wilderness about 220 kilometres away was quite a feat in itself.

Both companies' systems proved successful in the technical sense, and the equipment and work methods involved were developed at the same time. However, the experiments proved expensive and were eventually suspended for a decade or so. Now it was the turn of trucks, which were developed to transport heavy loads of logs. Motorized transport of wood made its advent on a large scale in Lapland in the 1930s, and after that technical development reached its peak.

Traces still visible in the environment

Once a road has been built in a forest, it stays there forever. Formerly a wide-looking thoroughfare, it may now be only a narrow path, which inexorably draws the hiker to it. "No path is so small that it cannot be walked," is how an old saying puts it.

The already partly decomposed logs of an old camp draw the wanderer to them; a place to draw water is always close by. A cabin corner still stands, its jointed logs in place, and five-inch pines near the

fireplace cast one's thoughts back to the twenties.

Once the nervous chord of the camp, the trunk road can now be made out as no more than a deteriorating rut fringing the edge of the bog. In summer, the reindeer plod it as they seek momentary relief from the torments of the mosquitoes and blackflies. Worn or not, the road is still there, as is the marker post, however much it leans.

In the forest, one still sees the rotting stumps of trees felled by axe some time in the twenties. Further down the slope, knee-high fir stumps are the remains of trees that fell to reindeer herdsmen's axes. They were felled for the beard moss and lichen growing on them. The Finnish word for cutting those trees also means the period of idleness while the men waited for the log-floating season to begin.

A stream or river headwater that year after year carried logs on their way to the mills is an inspiring sight for the hiker to behold. It brings one in touch with the romanticism of log-floating, about which so much has been written. Clad in its summer garb, a streamscape looks modest compared to the mighty log-floating channel that it is when in spate in early spring. The stones dragged out of the middle to create the channel are still there, as are the logs that formed the sluice walls, although they have now subsided into the stream bed. The cabin has been removed, but the sauna is left for the use of anybody who happens by.

By the bank of the stream stands a makeshift shelter, which fishermen have improved at some stage. Nestled under the branch of a stately pine near the water is a box once fashioned by a fisherman in the hope of attracting a scaup duck, whose eggs would bring greater variety to his diet.

Now, as we approach the end of the twentieth century, the culture of logging camps has gone and most of those who helped shaped it have gone beyond the treeline from which there is no return. Many characters who were legends in their lifetime are now irrevocably part of history. MM

The acrid smell of smoke had been hanging in the air for weeks. At that time of a hot summer in the village of Salla, it was more the rule than the exception in those days. It came both from forest fires and controlled burning for silvicultural purposes. Early that evening, when the local fire chief came to wake me up, I did not immediately associate his call with a fire raging out of control in some backwoods district.

The alarm had first been raised by three foresters returning from a fishing trip. They noticed clouds of smoke hanging over Tuntsa. An aircraft was

The Tuntsa Fire

Veikko Vasama

sent out to survey the situation, but the pilot concluded, wrongly, that the fire was on the Soviet side of the border. Some firefighting teams already on the way to the scene were ordered back. This error was to delay efforts to fight the blaze by several days.

Firefighting

Once the alarm had been given, the operation got under way at a brisk pace. Shops were opened in the middle of the night to provide the firefighters with food and equipment. It was a motley crew — not every household sends the most able-bodied to fill its firefighting quota. Crouched on the back of a truck, we were well up in the headwaters of the River Naruskajoki by the small hours of the morning. At Kota-Antti, we dismounted and, stiff and covered in grey ash that made us look like mill gremlins, we continued on foot.

It was a long march to the fire. The day was hot — the summer of 1960 was the second hottest recorded at the Sodankylä weather station this century — and the butter on many of the men's sandwiches melted and streamed from their knapsacks and down the sides of their boots. By midnight we had reached the fire front. A controlled fire had been started on Takkaselkätunturi Fell in an effort to deprive the menacing conflagration of fuel.

In fact, there were two areas of fire. The northernmost — in the Papuoiva — Puitsi — Peuratunturi districts had started weeks earlier. The fire had seemingly begun on the Soviet side of the border and eventually swung round and burnt its way back there. Now, 130 Finnish border guards were fighting it on the northern front.

The southern front, in the Nuolusoiva and Kuskoiva districts, was tackled exclusively by civilians, who numbered 484 at the peak of the operation. They

The Tuntsa forest fire raged in the Salla district over a quarter of a century ago. The scars that it left are still clearly visible.

were divided into seven groups, each led by an experienced firefighter. We green boys formed ourselves into a group of about ten altogether. Theories as to what caused the fire varied from lightning through shooting to arson. Whatever the cause, it was advancing rapidly along the ground. There was nothing much that could be done during the day, but at night, when the blaze was somewhat subdued as it glowed

Kemi Oy

in roots, hollows, anthills and hummocks, the menace was easier to tackle. At first there were surprises. Once, even the large fir in the shadow of which we were curled up and trying to sleep during the day, burst into flames. Soon, however, the situation had stabilized to the point where we could even permit ourselves some diversions. The large moraine ridges in the area, with their abundance of mushrooms, made an unforgettable impression on the minds of boys with a feeling for the great outdoors.

A helicopter had been brought to the area to survey the situation and ferry in supplies. The firefighters had been told to take along provisions for a week, but most of them had set off without anything, which caused major problems before the arrival of the helicopter.

They fought the fire from 8-28 July. The helicopter pilot reported on 14 July that the fire had been confined to a limited area, after which about 300 men were sent home. The last firefighters proper departed on 19 July, with only some reindeer herdsmen staying on until the 28th to mop up the remaining fires and see that no new ones broke out.

Damage and benefit

The area over which the fire raged totalled 19,570 hectares, of which 9,570 was healthily growing forest, 5,050 retarded forest and the remainder scrubland. Fir stands, of which the forests in the area mainly consisted, were destroyed right up

Even when the fire had been beaten on the Finnish side of the border, it still raged across Soviet territory.

to the treeline. In predominantly pine forests the damage was mainly confined to seedlings, some of them fairly strong ones, but in places where the flames could climb up to the tree crowns, even the sturdiest old trees perished.

The fire caused damage estimated at at least 2 — 2.5 million finnmarks. The losses caused reindeer herdsmen by the destruction of beard moss and lichen have never been properly estimated, but were certainly considerable. The reindeer herding association in the northern part of the Salla district had to cut the maximum permitted headage from 7,000 to 5,000 at the beginning of the 1970s. However, cuts on a similar scale were made in other parts of Lapland around the same time.

Another result of the fire was that logging began in the primeval Salla forests earlier than would otherwise have been the case. To facilitate logging some 40 kilometres of forest roads suitable for heavy vehicles and 200 or so kilometres of lighter roads were built in the district. This opened remote and formerly more or less primeval forests to several forms of exploitation. By 1967, about 275,000 cu. metres of wood had been felled in the area swept by the fire. Trees other than those scorched by the flames were also harvested whenever practical. About 8,000 hectares of land has since been ploughed and re-planted in the area, but establishing new dense stands of seedlings in places higher than 300 metres above sea level has proved difficult. Pine stands in which good seed trees were spared have recovered moderately well, especially in the northern part of the area. Trees resulting from natural regrowth now cover about 2,000 hectares.

The Tuntsa fire was probably the last major forest blaze in Finnish history. But we were not aware of that when we returned, soot-blackened and smelling of smoke, to our homes. EP

The area of the Tuntsa fire.

Arctic Circle

5 km

Papuoiva
Sauoiva

Tuntsajoki

Peurahaara

Peuratunturi
Rakitsaiset

Kujaselkä

TUNTSA

Värriöjoki

Tuntsajoki

Nuolusoiva

Kuskoiva

Vatuskajoki

Takkaselkätunturi

Teuvo Berggren

KOITELAIS-KAIRA

In olden times Koitalainen had a thoroughly bad reputation. At a time when what is now the Sompio reservoir was still an unfettered wilderness tract the Kotelaiskaira region was surveyed. Standing at the summit of the Nattaset fells and regarding the wilds of Sompio with the keen eye of a writer, Samuli Paulaharju also made out the brooding hulk of Koitalaistunturi fell. But the eminent author discovered nothing about the

Jorma Luhta

Koitelaiskaira region beyond the fact that it was the domain of the Devil and witches. The Sompio people were able to tell hair-raising tales about it.

It seems probable that the Sompio folk tried to pull the inquisitive visitor's leg but Paulaharju included the goblins, earth spirits and gnomes in his stories. Valter Keltikangas, from south Finland, also explored Sompio. In his opinion the Sompio people greatly exaggerated the difficulties of travelling through these very wet peatlands for a reason that is as old as the hills: they could up the price for their services as guides! It was no strain for the richer visitor to find a guide who would boast of being able to cross the most difficult, wettest areas "in daylight and in darkness, sober or drunk".

Koitelaiskaira also attracted Aarne Erkki Järvinen, a forester and writer by profession, and a person well able to portray life in the forested area of Lapland. Järvinen crossed the Koitela peatlands on skis in the depths of winter during the very short twilight days. He filled his sled with so many capercaillies that today's hunters read his stories with their lower jaws slack. It is a fact, though, that this bird was abundant in the old Lappish wilds (it is now uncommon over almost the entire country). On winter days blackcocks would sit in flocks of ten or more picking at the tops of stunted Scots pines in the mires. If some hunter or other shot more than he ought to have done, it made little difference, as there were birds aplenty elsewhere and the gap was soon filled.

On the threshold of old age, Järvinen brooded on the disappearance of the forest wildernesses. He began to make proposals for the protection of that part of Koitelaiskaira remaining on the southwestern side of the reservoir. His efforts have finally borne fruit: the central part of the wilds surrounding Koitelaistunturi fell is now under official protection.

OASIS FOR WILD ANIMALS

Since the 1970s extensive geological surveys have been carried out in Koitelaiskaira. In the neighbourhood of the fells there is a large ore deposit in which nearly all the valuable elements, including platinum, have been detected in small quantities. It is to the benefit of wildlife that these minerals are present in strata that are too thinly spread to be of much use commercially. Thus, it seems highly probable that for economic reasons no mine will ever be established here.

Finland's densest whooper swan population nests in Koitelaiskaira. For instance, at least ten pairs of whooper swans nest on the peatlands on the western side of the fell. Aside from birds with nests, young unmated swans wander around from one set of pools to another during the summer. Smaller water birds, from the medium-sized bean goose to the small smew, nest here too.

The golden eagle pair inhabiting Koitelainen has three nests in good condition which it uses in rotation. The last brown bear, on the other hand, was shot during

Jorma Luhta

the 1960s, when it became possible to use snowmobiles for hunting purposes. Since then one or two young bears have immigrated into the remote spurs of land between the large open aapa mires. Wolf and wolverine cross this area only very rarely, but foxes are commonplace.

HIKING THROUGH JOUTSENKAIRA

What is the best time of year, you may ask, to explore Koitelaiskaira. Saturated in summer, the peatlands are easier to ski across in the winter, but a large proportion of the Koitelaiskaira wildlife takes to the air in the autumn and travels to warmer climes. Even permanent residents like bears do not wake up until May Day.

When the snow turns to slush and then to spring floods the aapa mires for a long time remain unnavigable and crossing smaller streams, not to mention normal rivers, is a major problem. As conditions for hikers improve, nesting birds are most sensitive to outside disturbance. There again in June and July the wilds are visited by small armies of berry-pickers. Therefore — to answer the question — I would suggest a hike during the russet time, which generally takes place in the first week

of September. Then there is a complete absence of horseflies, ordinary settle-round-the-mouth-and-eyes flies, gnats, buffalo gnats, mosquitoes and those diminutive yet virulent pests, no-see-'ums. Birds and mammals tend at this time of year to move about more freely than they do in the middle of summer.

In Koitelaiskaira there is no tourism at all and hence there are no facilities aimed at making conditions more comfortable for the visitor. The National Board of Forestry permits hikers to burn fallen wood — apart from during a general fire danger alert (always broadcast by radio and TV). One must not, however, burn standing wood, however dry and combustible this may appear.

By far the best plan is to follow a U-shaped course from Moskuvaara to Lokka, as both of these locations boast a bus service. Round about the turning point of the State-owned post, or mail, coach there begins a trail leading to Käyrämö. After rain the logs that have been laid down to make the going easier in wet situations may well prove to be treacherous and slippery. All in all, though, the going is fairly easy on this particular trail. It must be remembered that a sleeping bag and (for the

entire loop) a week's supply of food will need to be included among one's gear. Obviously the food weighs much more at the start of the trip than towards its end.

When, on the left side of the track leading northeast, a small peatland pool comes into view, one should turn north towards Satovaara fell. At this point most people will want to sit down and brew up coffee or tea. The pool also offers the first opportunity to see whooper swans and family groups of bean geese. The cygnets are still unable to fly, so that if you sit still, you can observe them from fairly close.

Satovaara fell is an outstandingly beautiful hill covered with candle-shaped northern spruces. It is very rare for a Lappish spruce forest to attain its climax. Forestry officials are always staring hungrily at this kind of tree stand. The naturalist cannot fail to notice that the trees which at first sight appear to be clones take on a highly individual appearance if one spares them more than a casual glance.

After autumn's first frosts, the cloudberry cover under the spruces glows an incredible shade of red in places. On the western side of the fell there is a lake, Satojärvi,

Jorma Luhta

After the breeding season siskins move about in noisy flocks. Isolated individuals are much quieter and often bolder.

which has acquired its name from the fact that it has traditionally been the moulting site of the local bean geese and whooper swans ("sato" = moult). Lake Satojärvi is an excellent place for birds and it is possible at this time of year to see dozens of whooper swans gliding gracefully over its surface.

If you take the trouble to climb into the crown of a tree on the northern summit of Satovaara fell, with the assistance of a pair of binoculars you will be able to see part of one of Europe's densest whooper swan populations. The aapa mire in front is one of the wettest of its kind in Europe. Towards the west, on the other hand, some of the Nordic area's most destructive logging has taken place, with trees removed right up to the timberline. One of the most distressing examples of the latter mode of destruction is the slope of Keivitsatunturi fell, now in view on the far shore of the lake.

When the wonderful world of spruces, Siberian jays and pine grosbeaks on Satovaara fell is left behind, much more difficult hiking terrain abruptly appears. Towards the left lie treeless Sphagnum bogs and in front the hiker is now faced by bogs dotted with Scots pines, wet heaths, and the high sedge vegetation near the River Allimanjoki. It is with a feeling of relief that one finally enters a dry heathland in the vicinity of the Joutsenlampi pools. Now, in autumn, the russet tones of Loueaapa mire blaze out through gaps in the foliage of the conifers.

I would not recommend on the first stages of the hike tramping over wet aapa mires encumbered by a fully loaded backpack. It is much more sensible to explore Loueaapa mire and its wonders without carrying very much at all, and then to transfer one's lean-to camp a few kilometres away towards Loueselkä, which is a particularly beautiful spot. From Loueselkä's cliff there is a wonderful panorama spreading out in the direction of

Koitelaistunturi fell. In the patchwork of treeless bogs lying below, whooper swan parents guide their cygnets and it is possible to glimpse a bear there, as well.

Loueselkä is also a good place from which to make a small one-day trip relying on what one is able to pack into a small haversack or shoulder bag. Travelling from morning to evening one can comfortably make a rewarding circuit taking in the Loueaapa, Kiviaapa, Iso Kiviaapa and Porkkausaapa mires. At small lake Kivijärvi, over towards the northwest, after a cup of coffee or tea, one turns about and begins the trek back to 'base camp'. This kind of what I might call unencumbered hiking is often accompanied by sights of whooper swans, cranes, bean geese, ordinary ducks, common scoters, smews, capercaillies, Siberian jays, and tits.

PRIMAEVAL SCOTS PINE FORESTS

After spending a couple of nights in the neighbourhood of Loueselkä, one will probably feel like moving on. There now begins a day's march, the final objective of which is Koitelaistunturi fell.

Even though Koitelaistunturi (over 400 m) does not seem formidable, its lower slopes are clothed in some of the most splendid and oldest Scots pines in the forested part of Lapland.

From Koitelaistunturi's crown textbook examples of the large open aapa areas typical to Lapland radiate out in all directions. The wetter treeless bogs shimmer over to the west. Behind Rovapää the Lokka reservoir is a polished silver platter and beyond this again the shapes of the fells of the Saariselkä hiking region can just be made out, their outlines blurred by distance. Their actual position, as the crow flies, is five leagues (40 km).

Having spent the night in one of the reindeer herdsmen's cabins, one sets out along a fairly easy trail towards the village of Lokka, passing through the heathlands of Rykimäselkä, Koitelaisenselkä, and Kustruotomankuusikko, with their ancient spruces and pines, silvery 'snags', and rotting logs. After the shade of such awe-inspiring forests it is refreshing to become lost in the undergrowth filling the hollows and dells ensconced within them, into which the Creator seems to have cast all the malformed, bent, twisted, gnarled, blighted and blemished trees of the wilderness with their branches enclasping one another.

Koitelaiskaira was never meant for those wishing to walk briskly, head high, boots flung out, arms pumping, with the wilderness flashing past unseen and unheard. It was intended for those wishing to expend time exploring its beauty spots. The Rovapäänlampi pools, with their surrounding spruce heathland and their collection of geese and swans, constitute the final wonderland to which the inspired hiker will desire to go.

On autumn days between the reservoir and the treeless bogs on the western side of Koitelaiskaira there exists an air bridge for water birds, making it necessary to look up as well as down. In these particular reaches there is also the best chance one will ever have away from the coast of glimpsing the white-tailed eagle. JLu

Hannu Hautala

The Wolf, Better than Its Reputation

The wolf has been one of the most persecuted animals in Finland for the past one and a half thousand years. That is people's fault, not the wolf's. In the first half of the 19th century, Finland's deer and elk populations were decimated almost to the point of extinction. Small game, too, had become very rare as a result of excessive hunting. That made winter a hard time for wolves. They entered villages and towns to scavenge refuse heaps for food and even got into barns via the openings through which manure was emptied out. This did not endear them to people. Nature did not offer much more food in summer, so the beasts had to resort to livestock and other domestic animals for their nourishment.

The persecuted persecutor

Most accounts of attacks by wolves on people are founded on quite vague reports and records. The only really reliable accounts are from the Turku region. Between the end of 1879 and 7 November 1881, a total of 23 children were reported to have been killed by wolves or animals resembling them. However, even in these cases there is no complete certainty that the culprits were actually wolves; a theory that has gained ground in recent times is that the animals were a cross between wolves and dogs.

In any case, people became fed up with wolves in the 19th century. By the 1880s, the animals had been hunted to extinction in the southern, central and western parts of the country where they disappeared.

The area to which wolves had been confined remained largely unchanged for the next century. Populations of the animals fluctuated in northern Finland and in the eastern strip fringing the Russian border from Kainuu down to North Karelia. On occasions, they ventured further west into the interior. They always chose the easiest route, following roads and paths, running along the open crests of moraine ridges and crossing open bogs via the long dry hummocks on them. The long moraine ridges that cross Finland from east to west have brought them to the Maanselkä and Suomenselkä regions not far inland from the Gulf of Bothnia and even to the shores of the Gulf itself and as far south as Turku.

The wolf is a social animal that lives in packs. These wolves live in the Ähtäri animal park.

Finland's own wolf population was hunted to extinction everywhere except the Enontekiö and Inari districts, where some still survived in the 1950s and 1960s. One reindeer herdsman in Tsuukiskuru was not as committed to wiping out the predators as he seemed to be; he "cheated" a pair of wolves by raiding their lair every year, taking their cubs and collecting the not inconsiderable bounty. Eventually, the parents were killed as well, and the same happened to all the other wolves in the Inari region. The last cubs in Lemmenjoki ended up in a furrier's shop in Helsinki in the early 1960s.

Reinforcements from across the frontier

On the other side of Finland's eastern border, things had been going less miserably for wolves, and at times even well. Large tracts of forest were felled in the years immediately after the war. New stands of hardwood species and softwood seedlings sprang up in the cleared areas. These are excellent food for elk, which increased and multiplied. For the wolves, in turn, this meant more food, and their population also burgeoned.

The basic units in which wolves live are called packs. Each pack claims a territory of its own and defends it against other packs. Thus a given area contains only a certain maximum number, usually 5 — 7 per thousand sq. kilometres. That is also usually the number in a pack. Surplus individuals have to go elsewhere in search of food and living space.

The wolf population of Soviet Karelia reached saturation point in the 1960s. The surplus animals had only one direction to go — west across the Finnish border. There was talk of a "wolf invasion", a "westwards expansion".

This expansionist drive did not lead to the re-conquest of Finland. People saw to that. About 150 animals were killed. Culls in Soviet Karelia reduced the population there to the point where there was no further pressure for migration.

By 1974, however, the population in Soviet Karelia had again reached saturation level and all pack territories were fully occupied. Once again a suitable "vacuum" was found across the Finnish border. Some of the wolves migrated deep into the Finnish heartland and soon established a presence almost everywhere in the southern half of the country. Only Lapland remained free of wolves, with the exception of the occasional "vagrant".

After 1977, the number of wolves on the move in Finland declined again. The population in Soviet Karelia then numbered 600-650, and 150 or so were being shot each year. Obviously, wolves do not migrate without reason. When the population falls to the saturation point or below it, the need to migrate no longer exists.

A gloomy future

From the viewpoint of wolves, the food situation in southern Finland is now completely different from what it was a century and a half ago. The elk population is approaching ten per thousand hectares in places, and there are thousands of white-tailed deer in the southwestern quarter of the country. There is also an abundance of small game, especially hares. In many places, open-air dumps and rubbish heaps provide an additional source of food. Although wolves now roam by the dozen in summer, they do remarkably little harm to domestic animals. In this respect, of course, it should be borne in mind that whereas livestock once grazed in open pastures, they are now mainly in fenced enclosures under the watchful eyes of their owners.

The fear that the wolf population would "explode" in the near future has been expressed in many quarters. However, this fear is completely unfounded. No major "invasion" can be expected from across the Soviet border. Most of the wolves on the fringes of a population are males; about eight in ten. This fact alone mitigates against invaders from the Soviet Union breeding in Finland. Cubs reach puberty only at the age of 22 months or later. Many sustain injuries, and others are killed on the roads.

The future of Finland's wolves depends, naturally, on people's attitudes to them. The species is unprotected in reindeer-breeding areas. Permits to hunt them from snowmobiles are easy to obtain, so hunting is quite efficient. As a precaution against rabies, they can be hunted in a zone along the Soviet frontier from autumn to spring. They are a protected species elsewhere in Finland, but it is not very difficult to obtain permits to hunt them — by whatever means. Applicants for permits have only needed to say that they have seen several wolves together — overlooking the fact that living in a pack is the essence of a wolf's lifestyle. EPu

The Aurora Borealis – the Celestial Light Show

Kari Kaila

The Aurora Borealis or Northern Lights have a strange name in Finnish: "revontulet". It means "fox's fire".

The name has a folk origin. When red foxes run through the forests and backwoods of Lapland, their bushy tails brush shrubs and leave a trail of powdered snow hanging in the air. It is also said that when a fox runs through high grass its tail fur generates static and sparks. When it runs in the dark, the red glow of its tail can be seen from afar and lights up the surroundings like a lantern.

The tale of the fiery fox is charming in its originality. Thus, although we modern people know what causes the Aurora Borealis, the belief that the mysterious flickering lights in the northern winter sky are caused by a giant fox brushing its tale across the firmament still determines the word we use in Finnish to name the phenomenon.

What causes them?

The Northern Lights are produced by solar particles striking the earth's atmosphere. The sun is a massive ball of gases, mainly hydrogen and helium, with a diameter 109 times that of our puny planet. Under the enormous pressure and temperature at the centre of the sun, hydrogen is constantly fusing to create helium — and huge quantities of energy. The energy flows to the surface of the sun and radiates out into space as both electromagnetic and particulate radiation. The former we see as light and feel as warmth. The latter are electrically charged solar particles, mainly electrons and protons.

Solar activity fluctuates in intensity. This manifests itself most clearly in the number of sunspots — dark flecks on the solar surface — which follow a cycle of eleven years or so. Once they have reached their peak, they decline gradually and may even disappear com-

pletely at the minimum, which comes seven years after the maximum. The next maximum comes about four years later. When solar activity is at its peak, there are also numerous solar flares or enormous eruptions from the surface.

The earth is a huge magnet, but not a very strong one. When solar particles reach the vicinity of our planet, some of them are drawn into its magnetic field or magnetosphere. There they gain more energy and plunge, guided by lines of magnetic force, into an almost circular zone of the atmosphere about 2,000 kilometres from the magnetic poles.

The region in which the Aurora Borealis is seen most frequently runs through the northern part of Finland. Its southern limit continues on through the northern parts of Siberia, Alaska and Canada, southern Greenland and Iceland back to Scandinavia. When solar activity is high, the northern lights can be seen in this zone on as many as 200 nights a year. There is a corresponding zone around the southern pole, but most of it is in Antarctica and the Antarctic Ocean. Although Aurorae can be regularly seen in very large regions of the world, they are a rare phenomenon in that those regions con-

tain only one per cent or so of the global population. If an Auroral display is studied at any given moment, one can see that it appears in an almost circular zone, the so-called Auroral ellipse, which is located asymmetrically in relation to the magnetic pole. Within this ellipse, the lights are closest to the magnetic pole around midday and furthest from it around midnight. The ellipse remains in the same position in relation to the sun, and the earth rotates between the northern and southern ellipses.

Since the Aurora is at its southernmost point at midnight, it is often shifting southwards

The most common colour in the Aurora is yellowish green. Late in the evening, the lights are often visible as arcs, several of which are superimposed on each other in this picture. At its brightest, an Aurora can illuminate the landscape as completely as a full moon.

during the hours of late evening and withdraws northwards again with the coming of morning. Even at times of only moderate solar activity, there are still Aurorae. Although not visible to the human eye, they can be detected by satellites and ground-based instruments almost always, as weak glows within the ellipses. During solar maxima, when the flow of particles from the sun is many times greater than during minima, powerful Auroral eruptions are often measured. The earth's magnetosphere is subjected to strong disturbances at such periods. This even affects compass needles, which quiver slightly.

Kari Kaila

Forms of Aurorae

A calm ribbon-like Aurora, which appears in the northern sky as a glowing arc, is the most common type of display early in the evening. It may be pallid and rather colourless to begin with, and so matte that even a little diffuse background light prevents it from being noticed at once. It gradually shifts southwards and can brighten to the point where it is clearly visible. More arcs can appear close to the original one, and then disappear again.

Later in the evening, one or other of the arcs may develop folds and grow brighter. Rays begin protruding from it and its characteristic yellowish-green colour begins to become recognizable with the naked eye. The rays can be very high and their upper extremities are sometimes a beautiful red. They gradually move along the arc, after which the Aurora can again fade.

As midnight approaches, an arc moving fairly rapidly southwards can herald the beginning of an eruption. The arc slows in its southward movement and brightens strongly. Now the Aurora expands rapidly to the east, north and west, gains strongly in brightness, and new ray-like arcs and shapes appear in the sky. The movements of the rays and changes in the

A rare sight: a green Auroral arc with a belt of bright red above it. Both colours are produced by oxygen atoms.

folds of the arcs can be momentarily quite abrupt. If the eruption has begun to the south of the viewer, he may for a time notice an area overhead from which the rays appear to have disappeared. An Auroral corona or crown has been formed, with clear forms whirling wildly and several colours visible at once. This is the high point of an eruption, its brightest and most colourful moment. By now the display has taken over most of the sky and ray-like forms can be seen everywhere. But it soon begins fading. Within half an hour, the bright, sharp forms have disappeared and all that remain are scattered clouds, fragments of the Aurora pulsating at different rates. These patches often grow dim, only to regain their earlier brightness a mo-

ment later. They can continue to pulse for hours.

That is an Auroral eruption at its finest. However, it is just as likely that the display will not be anything more spectacular than a brightening arc and the development of a few rays. Several eruptions can take place during the same night, each lasting an hour or two. Pulsating patches of light are a typical feature during the latter part of an eruption as well as towards morning. If bright lights are visible early in the evening, really magnificent eruptions can be expected during the night. A black cloudless sky in Lapland can be completely covered in Auroral colours for as long as several minutes.

When do the lights flare?

The Aurora Borealis flashes in the sky all year round, winter and summer. The lights flicker slightly more often in spring and autumn than in summer and winter. The reason for this is not known, but in Finland — and especially Lapland — the summer nights are so bright that the Aurora would not be visible even if were ablaze. It flares virtually every night in Lapland, but is invisible when there is heavy cloud cover (and the weather is in consequence relatively mild). This has caused the widely held misconception that there are dazzlingly handsome displays only during periods of severe frost.

As electrons penetrate the atmosphere, they collide with atoms and molecules, and the denser the layer they are entering, the more frequent these collisions are. An electron adds energy to every atom or molecule it hits. Some of this surplus energy is soon discharged by the atoms, with each kind of atom emitting light of a characteristic colour. When such collisions and energy discharges occur by the million every second, we see the result in the form of the Aurora.

The colourful splendour in the sky

Nitrogen and oxygen are the most abundant gases in the atmosphere, both at sea level and in the extremely rarefied

layers where the Aurora flashes. At altitudes of 100 kilometres, of course, most oxygen is in the form of atoms rather than molecules. The most common Auroral colour, a greenish hue, is produced by oxygen atoms releasing their energy charges. Greenish Auroral fires generally blaze at altitudes of 90-150 kilometres and their lower limit is often quite sharp.

The red colour visible above the green belts also comes from oxygen atoms. Its altitude is 200 — 400 kilometres and when it is strong it gives the Aurora its finest splendour. Reds can also appear when no green hues are visible, and then the sky seems to be on fire. It is hardly surprising that the sight of such lights in the sky has inspired fear in people who did not know what they were. In fact, these reds are caused by fairly low-energy electrons.

Reds of a different kind are produced when very high-energy particles strike the atmosphere. They cause a purplish stripe along the lower edge of a green light band. The purple is produced when particles strike nitrogen molecules, and this happens at relatively low altitudes, sometimes only 70 kilometres. Only extremely rarely do Aurora occur any lower than that. That is also why no audible sounds can be heard from them on the surface of the earth, no matter how wildly they dance across the sky. The only sounds that one hears from an Aurora are created between one's own ears, as the imagination is stimulated by the gyrating lights that strike the eyes. Anyway, if any sounds did come from them, they would reach one's ears only three minutes or so after the lights, and the video and audio spectacles would be completely out of synchronization.

Nitrogen sometimes produces also powerful blue and violet discharges. Thus an Aurora features many hues, greens, reds, blues and violets, in addition to numerous dim glows of many colours. It is the balances between all these colours that determine what the Aurora looks like to the viewer below. If an Aurora is dim, the eye sees it as only a pallid grey grow. KK

176

KOILLISKAIRA AND SAARISELKÄ

Saariselkä is one of the best known parts of Lapland. Its the kind of place which you've either visited or will visit. The kind of place some say they'll never visit again, because "it's been spoilt by hundreds of cottages and is as crowded as a market place", while others say they won't go there "until there are roads and services and you don't need to trudge around lost with only the wolves for company". Although for a long time there were no roads in northeast Kaira, there were ancient routes, natural trails winding through the region. Rivers lead from the region in two main directions: the Nuortti, Jauru and Lutto rivers to the east;

Veikko Vasama

the Kitinen, Luiro and Kemi rivers southwards. Not that travelling would have been a popular pastime for the locals; if you lived in the wilds you mainly stay put with the occasional trip to Sodankylä church for the major festivals and to bury the departed in consecrated ground.

As a tourist area, the region long remained in the shadow of western Lapland. The intrepid few who wandered in Saariselkä proclaimed the beauty of its countryside and the ease of getting around. The number of their disciples however grew slowly until the 50's and 60's when Finnish author Kullervo Kemppinen's book about it caused a rush to this "travellers' paradise". With the influx of visitors the services grew, huts sprang up in the wilderness and the reindeer trails between them became wider. Travellers' hostels, hotels, restaurants, holiday apartments and souvenir stalls, in fact everything the modern tourist could ask for, were built within easy reach of the main highway. In its wake came the rubbish and spoiling of nature that has become a problem in Saariselkä and other Lapland tourist and fell regions so that the World Wildlife Fund in conjunction with travel organizations and officials has launched a clean-up operation.

Aimo Holtari

The Nattanen region is nowadays a nature reserve and in summer you can only explore it along the marked trails. In winter you can ski there freely as there is no danger of disturbing the nature or ruining the land. In summer as well as in winter camping and campfires are only allowed in certain places.

For those who love distant vistas a short path runs from the Sompiojärvi road to the top of Pyhä Nattanen. Most travellers journey along the thirty kilometre Ruija path which starts from the shore of Sompiojärvi lake.

SOFT FEATURED RAUTUTUNTURI FELLS

Generally speaking, the slopes of the Raututunturi fells are the gentlest of Nattaset although this difference is not apparent in the height: Kiilopää soars skywards a full 546 metres and many others are in the same class. The soft shapes are a result of age: granulite is one of the oldest types of rock found in Finland. The influence of the ice age in shaping the surface was quite modest as the continental glacier did not really move in Lapland. In the Raututunturi fell country the signs of the final phases of the melting of the glaciers are visible as edge formations of the Baltic ice lake and in the beds of the river outlets on the slopes of Kiilopää and Ahopää, the lateral moraine at Kutturapää and the saucepan shaped hollows gouged out by the ice at Ahopää.

Small changes take place on the land surface all the time; the effects of frost cause, and will continue to cause the formation of so-called network lands; perhaps the most beautiful of which can be found in Kaivoslakso north of Kutturapää. Open holes do not appear frequently making it easier to travel around the Raututunturi fells.

The flora in this region is sparse. The coniferous forests are flat, Scots pine heathlands. Black crowberries grow abundantly making those southerners unused to its taste believe in a new adaptation of Murphy's Law — tasteless berries crop heavily! Knowledge of the fact that this berry makes an excellent wine simply intensifies the thirst which can be extinguished from the winding brooks.

Above the pine level on most of the slopes is a belt of fell birch, there are some exceptions however — on Iisakkipää Scots pine forms the forest border. The most common forms of ground vegetation here are mosses, lichen and crowberries; during the autumn there is an abundance of blueberries, bog bilberry and especially black bearberries.

Around Kiilopää you find the fell birch. On the bare patches the less demanding fell plants thrive — club mosses, blue mountain heather, black bearberry, diapensia, creeping azalea, tiny cassiope, and on the damp upper slopes and patches where the water trickles you find mountain avens.

If spring doesn't lead to a second winter, May and June are busy times. In the pinewoods of the valley the grouse call and the redstarts and redwings warble. Just a

NATTASET — GATEWAY TO THE TUNDRA

Driving along Route 4 you surely know when you have arrived at the Koilliskaira boundary: Nattaset looms suddenly on the horizon, its appearance changing according to the weather and lighting conditions.

Although no great distance from Nattaset to the Raututunturi fells, the landscape and geological aspects are totally different. This many-peaked fell chain is of red Nattaset granite, where the peak areas are split into large slabs. The highest summit is Terävä-Nattanen at 544 metres.

A small, but healthy white-tailed eagle population nests in eastern Lapland.

Hannu Hautala

slope joining the district border both in the east and in the west. The separation fence is three kilometres south of the summit on the west side of Niilanpää. During herd gathering time wanderers might be advised to avoid certain trails. Reindeer separation takes place around midsummer, as well as in late autumn and in midwinter.

Kiilopää is one of the best places for admiring the massive Saariselkä fell. On the horizon, peak after peak rises into the air and the gaps in the distance become bluer and bluer. In clear weather, if you don't look at the map, the trip seems to be just a short distance; however it's at least a day's journey on foot to the Saariselkä side — and a long day at that!

The Suomujoki river in its valley flows between the fells. In the lower reaches there are no spruces; on the low eskers the ground underneath the Scots pine is covered with an unbroken field of lichen making an excellent winter grazing ground for the reindeer. In certain places on the Vaara slopes you can find lush dells with hoary alders growing, although generally speaking the vegetation is somewhat sparse. The crystal clear sand and stony bottomed Suomujoki river seems at first glance to be almost sterile, you can see many metres to the bottom although there doesn't seem to be any life there.

Or is there? Judging from the presence of the Arctic tern, merganser and black-throated diver you might be tempted to purchase a sport-fishing license — there are fish in the Suomujoki, whitefish and grayling, salmon and pike, perhaps not to the extent of richer waters, but, with luck quite enough. On the river bottom clams sulk in their own protected peace. The winter scenery brings life to those places where the current is rapid in the form of fast flying dippers, elk also gather in the valley area during the time of snow.

Suomu's Kotajärvi lake shore is a Koltta-Lapp settlement area which, despite its relative youth, is a valuable area culturally. The Semenoff Koltta family from Suenjeli lived here during the summers of 1946-1947 before moving on to Sevettijärvi lake. The settlement area is nowadays the finest example of the Koltta building tradition in Finland. At the same time several Koltta families overwintered at Oskarinjärvi by the Lutto river. The Suomu flows into the Lutto over some fine rapids almost ten kilometres before the national border. The colour of the water and the nature of the shore doesn't change significantly; the Lutto flows on between its barren banks.

THE BLUE FELLS OF SAARISELKÄ

Saariselkä Fell begins in this corner of Koilliskaira immediately south of Lutto and Suomu, practicing first for three hundred and fifty metres at Karhuselji and a hundred metres higher in Kiertämäpää rising then into real fell country. Peuranampumapää exceeds 525 metres, Hirvaspäät about a hundred metres higher with the summit of Kuikkapää reaching an impressive 678 metres.

The rock formation of Saariselkä does not differ from the Raututunturi fells; the stones are just more visible as blisters on the upper slopes. The flora varies

little higher in the fell birch the bluethroat is the clear winner of this springtime song contest, but the best set of tail feathers belongs to the brambling as he earnestly laps up water. The whimbrel's observation post is in the branch of a dead tree at the edge of the marsh. In the mires and on the fell heathland the golden plover whistles his melancholy life story — with justification too, as nest and chick robbers depress even the brightest nature. Voles and hares aren't keen on making noise whereas the stubborn Norway lemming proclaims its existence with a great performance, not worrying, at first anyway, about the buzzards circling in the sky above. Plovers may be seen on the barren tops, this is their southern limit. If you have enough time and are sufficiently interested, it's worth sitting quietly in the dell and studying the surroundings — after a short while you may notice out of the corner of your eye a stone starting to move: a ptarmigan has decided to continue its search for food without caring about the watcher.

FROM KIILOPÄÄ TO SUOMU

At the top of Kiilopää the wanderer will recall that reindeer husbandry is a primary feature of land use in these regions. The border fence between the Lapland and Ivalo Reindeer Owners' Associations runs along the northern

Jorma Luhta

Distinctive Korvatunturi fell lies right on the Finnish border.

enormously in the different parts of the area. Spruce in the south, in places growing together with the fell birch to form the forest border. In the southwestern border the spruce woods take on a deciduous appearance. Here, as in the Raututunturi fells, you find some arrogant species on the banks of the brooks or in the dells where they can get enough moisture for the whole short summer.

Certain rare sedges and grasses will not be familiar to the ordinary wanderer, but during the flowering season he'll certainly recognize the mountain avens on Vintilätun-

turi fell and maybe in some small gully a small plant which looks and tastes like wood sorrel which, according to the conservation rules of the national park, should not be picked. Among the rarer plants growing here are the bright blue alpine veronica, the pink flowering moss campion, and the yellow wood violet whose bright yellow colour distinguishes it from its relatives.

The fauna is principally the same as in the Raututunturi fells; on the eastern border the occasional wolf and wolverine taking a look westwards — although they generally regard the unpopulated and unused wildernesses behind the border as a healthier place to live. Saariselkä fell is regarded as the northern limit for vipers although a few individual sightings have been made in the northern part of this area.

Pikku-Luirojärvi has been a reindeer round-up station for at least a hundred years. The oldest fences are now so rotten that their location can be seen mainly from the lush vegetation growing there. All that's left of the oldest peat cottages are just some circular earthworks. The newest cottages — and these are nearly 40 years old — are still used in summer for marking the calves.

LAND OF AAPA MIRES AND SPRUCE THICKETS

The southern edge of Saariselkä fell is a watershed: the waters of the northern and eastern side flow into the Arctic Ocean, while those of the south and west belong to the upper water-course of the Kemijoki river. Thus the Luiru river with its tributaries and the Jauru river which flows over the border belong to the Koilliskaira forest and marsh wilderness. This is perhaps the least known part of Koilliskaira and at the same time the richest in terms of nature conservation. No grand landscapes here — unless you regard the huge, difficult-to-traverse aapa mires as such — and so the traveller is usually satisfied to simply cross the area without making any great detours.

The birdlife of the mires and brookside thickets is plentiful and varied. Rare, even endangered species nest on the aapa mires; species whose natural habitats are decreasing due to environmental change. To ensure protection of the nesting birds it is forbidden to enter the areas of Lamminaapa, Pajuaapa and Repoaapa from 15.5 to 15.7. So we must believe without seeing how the bean goose shepherds its downy chicks and how the peregrine falcon dives on its prey at two to three hundred kilometres per hour.

By the middle of July this critical time is over, in some years this area bears an excellent crop of arctic cloudberries which the locals pick to augment their income. In the spruce woods on the edges of the mires you probably won't spot the great grey owl whose habitat this is. Despite its size, its skill at concealing itself is impressive.

In the actual wilderness there are still signs of the ancient way of life: at the mouth of the Auhtijoki river is the largest known deer trapping spot in Koilliskaira — 25 pit traps. There used to be a bear trap on the bank of the Jauru river, on the way to to the wilderness hut of Peuraselkä; a second one in fairly good condition is at Vieriharju. In principal, hunting in the area came to an end with the establishment of the national park, although for the locals this way of utilizing the wilderness has been preserved to a certain extent. Fishing is forbidden in the upper branches of the Kemijoki river in order to protect the fish population.

Undoubtedly the most famous part of this forest wilderness is Korvatunturi fell, which can only be admired from the south due to the border-zone regulations and so the only place to climb for a good view is the 427 metre high amphibolite hill, Naltiotunturi, on the west side of which a reindeer slaughterhouse was built to provide reindeer meat for export.

THE FISH-FILLED NUORTTI

On the southern tip of the Urho Kekkonen National Park is one of the most popular places — the comparatively rich waters of the Nuortti river. Its brackish water and mainly moss-covered bottom give it a dark appearance compared with the clear waters of the Suomu and Lutto rivers. The summer-flowering marsh marigolds on the banks are often completely under water. Angelica, red common baneberry, red currants and, of course, globe flowers grow around the banks of the brooks. In its lower reaches the Nuortti flows through canyons whose walls rise steeply about a hundred metres high. In places the vegetation is of the verdant coppice, cranesbill-fern type of the extreme north.

The secret of the popularity of Nuortti is only partly concealed in its beautiful scenery. From mid-June to the beginning of September hopeful fishermen trample the banks on both sides of the river in search of brook trout and grayling. Their success can be seen from the comments in the guest book of the Kärekeoja wilderness hut: some have caught the full permitted quota while for others the only fish have been tinned sardines in tomato sauce!

Boating on the Nuortti is interesting to say the least, even when the water is at its highest the rapids are shallow and stony. At the mouth of the Sotajoki river you need to keep your wits about you and let the most timid go to the shore, but on the upper courses modest skill suffices to get you to the boundary of the national park at Kärekeoja, below which motorboats are not allowed. Downwards from Kärekeoja the number of rapids and rushing streams increases; seeing Kurtsinniska will persuade many to proceed on foot; after which the Jänkakoski and Nuorttiköngäs rapids rush by. Few travel this far or further by boat or canoe: at the fast rapids the boats have to be dragged or poled upriver slowly.

The distance travelled can best be measured by the number of sandpipers and wagtails: 1 pair of sandpipers = half a kilometre, 1 pair of wagtails = 2 pairs of sandpipers. The otter is one of the original inhabitants of this area and the ever growing wild mink population began through accidental introduction at Kantalahti in 1959. In the hummocks of the shoreline woods on the upper course of the river you might catch a glance of one of the region's special animals — the wood lemming, the shiest and most inconspicuous member of its fell country family.

FROM LUIRO TO NUORTTI

To get to the hut on the southern shore its worth going around the western side of Luirojärvi lake. You can spend a while getting to know the lakeside area and even take a sauna bath in the new sauna which has been built there. Within half a kilometre of the lake shore camping is only

Siberian tits have thick plumage to protect them against the harsh winter.

allowed in certain places.

In the wilderness parts of the Saariselkä fell area camping is freely allowed, as long as the tent isn't erected on the open fell land, and fires may only be lit in certain places. After resting you can continue along Sokostinoja which lies between Sokosti and Ruotmutti-pää. From the side of the brook its worth going to Haaramaa and bearing direct eastwards to the Hammas-kuru hut which is situated on the border of the fell and forest wilderness with the nearly 700 metre high Vuoma-pää as its eastern sentinel. The easiest way to the next stage, to Siulanruoktu, is by climbing the western slope of Vuomapää and then descending to Siulaoja. From Siulanruoktu you can proceed eastwards to Tahvontupa and Peuraselkä on either side of the Jauru river. This route which hugs the southern edge of the Vongoiva pinewoods is the wildest in the national park; it's real bear country around Jauru. If you've travelled by the northern bank you can cross the Jauru in Peuraselkää. Its quite a climb from the valley to Härkämurusta, and the vegetation on the slopes changes too; you reach the Kemi-Sompio wilderness region where firelighting is permitted if conditions are favourable. The traveller accustomed to the immeasurable solitude of the wilderness is in for a small surprise at Härkämurusta — there's a telephone box at the summit — these useful items, of which there are twenty in the area, are usually to be found in the wilderness huts. After recovering from the shock and ringing your friends (make sure you only ring those prepared to pay for a collect call) you can continue in a southeasterly direction along the reindeer fence. On the eastern side of the fence, stretching as far as the Finnish border, are the best winter grazing grounds for the Kemi-Sompio Reindeer Owners' Association; the reindeer are moved away in summer to prevent the lichen

from being worn away too much. A good twenty kilometres from here are a couple of reindeer herders' huts, quite near the track, where the traveller can spend the night.

At Mantoselkä the trail leads southwards away from the reindeer fence. Just a little north of Naltiohaara is the last zone, now you are in the Nuortti wilderness where the same rules apply as for the Saariselkä wilderness. The trail first goes along the Naltiojoki river and then winds around Naltiotunturi fell on the eastern side. It may be difficult to cross the river during the floods. From Naltiotunturi fell the route again follows the fence through a magnificent pinewood. In Mettapallo your attention is drawn to the large number of anthills; you can see anything up to twenty ants fussing around in the space of one footstep. Travelling up this route you needn't worry about finding a place to brew your coffee — about every 2 kilometres on the national park side there are places where you can light a fire.

It is ten kilometres to Tulppio from the boundary of the national park; if you want to do some fishing on the way, choose the riverside route — otherwise travel along the Haukijärvi esker — whichever way you choose you may well get a chance to admire the ospreys nesting nearby. AF & PO

The Urho Kekkonen National Park

Sodankylä, Savukoski, Inari, 2550 km²
Established: 1983
Under National Board of Forestry management

Connections: Many regular buses run daily between Rovaniemi-Sodankylä-Vuotso-Tankavaara-Kiilopää-Saariselkä travel centre-Kaunispää-Ivalo. In summer buses run twice a week to Raja-Jooseppi, which is three kilometres from the park boundary by forest road. Daily bus from Kemijärvi to Ruuvaoja and twice a week onwards to Tulppio which is 15 kilometres from the park by the trail along the Nuorttijoki river. By car you can get close to the park along forest roads. The nearest airports are at Rovaniemi and Ivalo.

Services: Tankavaara information centre, Luulampi information centre and cafe, information boards at Raja-Jooseppi, Luirojärvi, Tulppio and Kiilopää. National Board of Forestry trail huts, wilderness huts, camping places and firelighting places. Marked trails in some parts, nature trails in Tankavaara and Kiilopää. Plenty of hostels and travel services on Route 4 near the park boundary, gold diggers village and museum at Tankavaara, accommodation also at Tulppio and Vuotso, boats and cruises at Lokka and Porttipahta reservoir, tel. 9693-46190, trips to the park by reindeer drawn carriage, Vuotso tel. 9693-46190 and Savukoski tel. 9692-43424.

Maps: Outdoors map 1:50 000 "Kaunispää-Kopsusjärvi" and "Sokosti-Suomujoki". Topographical maps 1:50 000 3742 2 Kopsusjärvi, 3744 1 + 4722 2 Sokosti, 4722 2 + 4724 1 Talkkunapää, 4721 2 Sorvortatunturi, 4723 1 + 4223 2 Nuorttitunturi. GT-Map 1:200 000 no. 17.

Further information: Urho Kekkonen National Park office, Sompiontie, 99690 Vuotso, tel. 9693-46241, Tankavaara information centre, tel. 9693-46251 and Kiilopää wilderness centre, tel. 9697-87101.

The Lost Fish Larder

Lake Sompiojärvi came into being thousands of years ago, when a huge ancient lake that had dominated that region of Lapland disappeared and the vast aapa-type bogs (with ridged hummocks, ponds and moss-vegetation) rose from the waters. It was swallowed up by the Lokka reservoir in the early 1960s. In its own way, however, most of it still exists, but it is no longer an independent component of the landscape. Nor is it a distinct community of creatures any longer, and it has lost its significance as a central focus of local wilderness lore.

I spent a good deal of time in the Sompio district in the late 1950s and early 1960s. The lake, then spending its last years in a natural, unhurt and living state, became familiar to me in many ways. The scenic beauty of its setting and the richness of the life forms that it supported left an indelible impression on my mind. The folk culture that sprang from the bounty of nature in and around the lake and the various methods developed to exploit it were both fascinating and rooted in everyday realities and needs. In summer and autumn, the lake captivated anybody that came to it, and those who used it were eager to make new arrivals feel at home. Tales, reminiscences and folklore were swapped by the fireside in fishing cottages in the evenings. During the day, anybody willing to pull an oar was a welcome helper and companion to an old fisherman.

Along the Mutenianjoki River to get there

For all its splendour and renown, Lake Sompiojärvi was not all that big, less than four kilometres across. But it was astonishingly round in shape, with neither promontories nor islands. Only a rock called "Old Woman's Stone" broke the smoothness of the lake as it protruded from the water bounded by a stoneless bog shore. That rock was a favourite perch for ruff and reeve resting a while before continuing their migratory flights.

The flatness of the great bog spreading to the south and the majestic sweep of the Nattastunturi Fells to the north gave the lake an impressive natural setting. It was a place where the delicate richness of a small-scale landscape combined with the awe-inspiring scale of an open wilderness view. By contrast, it had none of the mediocre charm of an average landscape. The shores all around the lake were boggy and difficult to traverse. Getting there from the nearest villages was even more laborious. There were plenty of bogs, and the dense willow thickets along rivers and streams had to be circumvented. On the other hand, the longer route via the Nattastunturi Fells was "dry" but strenuous.

The most natural, most common and most convenient way to reach the lake was by boat, following the hundreds of meanders of the River Mutenianjoki upstream from the village of Mutenia. It was always an unforgettable trip. Sometimes the Nattastunturi Fells rose from the horizon of the vast bog spreading in front of the boat, at other times the prow pointed back towards the hill on which the village stood. The river forced the boat to turn with every meander as it passed through channels cut from the peat of the bog, between walls of willow thicket and past the occasional clump of smallish birch trees. But still one made progress. The bogs were left behind. At this point there was a huge, dark, half-dead spruce as a landmark. A barn and the bases of haystacks showed where wild hay had been cut on the bog. Every little place along the river had a name, had become more and more familiar to successive generations, and was laden with memories of events that had transpired down through the years. Everything had a meaning, something to tell.

Finally, the river with all its memories and reminders of tra-

Veikko Vasama

dition approached its end. The smallish stream began straightening out, continuous stands of birch swept down close to the water's edge and finally we rose into the fast-flowing stretch where the river emerged from the lake. In front of us now was a small meadow fringing the shore of the lake, with a few fisherman's cabins neatly built of grey pine logs. Just behind them was the open shoreline and the full expanse of the lake and its fringing birch groves was in view. Further back were more bogs, fir-clad hillocks, the foothills of the Nattanens and then the majestic fells themselves, those stony cones and walls against the sky.

The bounty of the waters

The lake was astonishingly shallow, mostly only a metre or so deep, and two at most. The deeper ruts in its bed had been filled in with the passage of thousands of years of time. The bed was so soft that one sank into it, a rich layer of mud that nourished an abundance of plant life. The lake was rich in plankton and bottom-living organisms, and its fish stocks correspondingly ample. Even more important, the streams descending from the hills kept the oxygen level high in winter, when ice and snow covered the lake.

From mid-summer to autumn, large circular growths of bur reeds patterned the surface of the water. Patches of horsetails alternated with bright-green boggy meadows all around the shoreline. The waterside meadows had still been mown as late as the 1950s and the hay gathered into stacks, around which small fences had been built to protect them from raiding reindeer.

To the human settlers who came there, the lake was a virtually inexhaustible fish larder, from which they drew nourishment lavishly, especially during the autumn. But those who lived by gathering the bounty of the wilderness also looked beyond the lake, to the sky and beyond the stands of reeds. The lake, the calm river stretches near it and the surrounding bogs were home to abundant populations of water fowl, and the forests around its shores sheltered willow grouse to be trapped in winter.

Thus the lake yielded fowl, but above all fish. It contained whitefish, pike, perch, ide, dace and ruff, but no fish of the salmon family. The autumn catch was the most important. For many decades, large boatloads of fishermen made their way up the river, some from far away in the lowlands, and there was much life and activity around the grey cabins. A glimpse of how intensive the fishing had been in former times could still be caught around 15 September in the late 1950s and early 1960s, during the collective fishing effort that was jokingly called the "Ruff Market".

From the world of memories

And what about summer evenings on the lake: the background whine of thousands of mosquitoes, the chirping and whistling of the birds in the trees along the shore and the incessant mating calls of the waders! Great flocks of male water fowl enjoyed the leisure of mid-summer. A pair of whooper swans nesting on one of the bogs would come to the reedy shore for supper. An osprey nesting at the base of the Nattastunturi Fells would soar down to fetch a late night snack for its young. Some evenings, too, there would be another osprey on a fishing trip, coming from another nest further south beyond Mutenia. Rings spread out from where the fishes welled up to the surface of the lake to snatch their insect catch. The herbal fragrances of the meadows and the bogs wafted through the air.

The fragrances were more pungent in the autumn, the air crisper, and the bounty of nature even richer. The cloudberries that grew on the bogs had already been gathered and brought home for winter storage, the huge autumn fish catches completed. For all that most of the people were gone, there was all the more activity on the surface of the lake. Water fowl gathered there in preparation for their autumn migration south. Enormous flocks of mergansers in hissing lines, driving small fish towards the shore, with the wings of goldeneyes providing a background music that drowned everything else out. A V-shaped formation of bean geese, hooting and honking as it struck a southwestern course and headed off on its long migratory flight. The swans remained calmly where they were until the water began freezing. Cloudy banks of mist adorned the slopes of the fells, where rutting reindeer bulls were raising a racket. As yet, there were no signs of tree felling to be seen, no forest roads, no rising reservoir waters, none of the bustle of mass tourism. Everything was as it had been for centuries, but the era was drawing to a close. The remains of the turf huts that the forest Lapps had lived in throughout the Middle Ages and into the 17th century were still there, distinguishable as pits and small piles of oven stones dotting the landscape.

The Sompiojärvi that created those pictures is not dead, although it no longer exists in time. It now lives its life in that world that throughout history has been the best and most flawness: the bright world of memories, into which the modern forces of destruction cannot reach.

MLi

The Reindeer's Year

Reindeer are associated so strongly in people's minds with the exoticism of Lapland's remotest reaches that few travellers to the north are aware that they are in the reindeer herding region soon after they have passed Oulu or Kajaani. The southern limit of the area specified in the Reindeer Husbandry Act follows the River Kiiminkijoki in the west, continues along the Puolanka-Hyrinsalmi highway further east and is then the same as the dividing line between the municipalities of Kuhmo and Hyrynsalmi. One third of Finland's total area lies north of it.

Scions of wild Arctic animals

Two geographical breeds of reindeer live in Fennoscandia, the (Arctic) reindeer Rangifer tarandus tarandus (L) and the wild forest reindeer Rangifer tarandus fennicus (Lönnb.). It can be presumed that the two breeds met somewhere in the southernmost of the high Arctic fells. They may also have interbred, because the (semi-domesticated) animals in the Saariselkä district are known for their long muzzles and "legginess", both of which are characteristics of wild forest reindeer.

The semi-domesticated reindeer herded in Finland are descended from completely wild animals. The only external difference between them and the wild animals, which still live in southern Norway and on the Kola Peninsula, is colour. Wild reindeer are almost without exception a plain greyish brown, whereas many shades and colours catch the eye in a herd of domesticated reindeer, from white to almost black, and even some speckled or patterned coats. Those colour mutations are the result of selective breeding. The skins of white reindeer gave handsome leather coats and jerkins and the animals, reflecting light like a mirror in bright sunshine, made it easier to locate the herd in the dense scrub that covered the lowlands in summer. Nowadays, changes in clothing customs and the introduction of technical herding aids are threatening the status of white reindeer; rather than

Aarni Nummila

breeding white animals, herdsmen are more interested in normal coloured ones with better meat-yielding characteristics.

The first literary reference to reindeer dates from 1434, when peasants along the Gulf of Bothnia coast were ordered to pay part of their church tithes in reindeer calves.

Calving in the snow in May

The rule in the animal kingdom is that heirs are produced when food is abundant. The time when reindeer produce their offspring can be defined even more precisely: when the worst blizzards and severe night frosts have passed, but as much as possible of the spring and summer growth period is still to come. The saying "calving in the snow in May" is fairly accurate, because the peak period is usually around the 18th of that month, with the latest stragglers arriving in June, and sometimes not until July. The first to calve are generally choice meat animals, with young dams gravid for the first time the last to produce offspring.

As she prepares to calve, the dam leaves the herd. If she has a calf from the previous year, it attempts to follow her, but is beaten off with pucks of her antlers and kicks of her fore legs. In most cases, the yearlings then follow young dams or those which have no calves of their own.

The mosquito is the worst herder

The splendour of spring and early summer comes rudely to an end when mosquitoes and blackflies begin hatching out around midsummer. Now the reindeer are on the move. Here and there one sees individuals and small groups surging determinedly forward in a particular direction. It takes only a few days for herds hundreds and even thousands strong to form in the summer grazing areas. All reindeer with the exception of old males join the group.

Being in a herd brings relief from the torments of the insects, although the benefits are not shared equally by all. The most sheltered places in the centre of the herd go to the

Matti Mela

Reindeer husbandry is the most efficient way of converting the bounty of the northern forests and Arctic fells into food for humans. Every year, animals are rounded up and those destined for slaughter culled from the herd.

individuals situated highest in the social hierarchy. Young and otherwise "deprived" animals must stay close to the edges of the herd and bear the brunt of the insects' worst stings; for all that, they are better off than animals living alone.

Congregating in herds is a hereditary characteristic of reindeer. However, they do so only temporarily, but even in summers when there are no stinging insects. Although the peak period for mosquitoes and blackflies taxes the animals' strength, it has its advantages from the viewpoint of herdsmen. "The mosquito is our best helper," they say. The formation of herds gives them an ideal opportunity to brand calves, and larger herds are easier to find and drive into the enclosures where the branding is done.

The rutting month

In the language of the fell Lapps, the word for October is "rohkatmannu", which means "the rutting month". The first sign that it has begun is a rumbling sound emerging from

deep in the bull's throat. This is a general signal, which he uses when guarding his harem or letting other bulls know of his existence.

The rut is at its height in October, but an upsurge of sexual activity can be detected as much as a month earlier, especially in the behaviour of the males. Their antlers, which have grown under a velvety covering coat, are now exposed, bony and frightening weapons. The males strip the velvety coats from their antlers by rubbing them against wrist-thick trees; they are "polishing" their weapons. Just-stripped antlers glow blood-red in the autumn sun, but soon change to a mahogany brown.

There is a lot at stake for the bull. Unless he manages to collect a harem of does his life has been wasted in the genetic sense where this autumn is concerned. Hard battles are waged for the right to possess does. However, an important feature is that just as much attention is paid to protecting oneself as to inflicting harm on the adversary. The most unbridledly violent warriors take excessive risks, and the wounded suffer the following winter. But the rut is a taxing time for even those bulls that "play it safe" in battle. The reserves of fat that they have accumulated during the summer are consumed and their weight drops by a third.

The does do not allow the rutting season to interfere with their preparations for winter. They are in heat for only one day; if they do not become pregnant the first time, they are in heat again two weeks later, and at two-week intervals thereafter if necessary. That leaves them plenty of time to feed and their weight keeps on increasing throughout October.

Reijo Juurinen

On low power for winter

The struggle against winter does not release the reindeer from its grip for a single moment. It begins immediately in spring, when the animals begin replenishing energy reserves that have been depleted during the winter, and continues all summer, when they build up the stock of fat that will see them through the next winter. Without those vital stores, they could not survive until spring. The main components of their winter diet, Iceland moss, beard moss and beard lichen, are a little like white bread; they are rich in easily digested carbohydrates, but poor in the proteins, minerals and vitamins that are essential for healthy organs.

If the animals have stored enough of those essential substances in their bodies, their "white dough" diet also has advantages. It is a known fact that when the protein and trace element contents of food increase, the animal also needs

more water. Reindeer satisfy their thirst by swallowing snow, which has to be heated to a temperature of +40 C in their stomachs. This takes a lot of energy, as does rooting out food from underneath the snow. Every opportunity to save energy has been used.

Reindeer do not dig blindly into the snow in search of their

Reindeer nowadays rarely find such amply-stocked larders as this lichen-covered heath in the Inari district.

favourite lichen Iceland moss. They rely on their sense of smell, thrusting their noses into the snow and digging only when a strong smell of lichen assails their nostrils. Their sense of smell is reliable even in snow as deep as 90 centimetres.

A reindeer digs into the snow with its foreleg, changing from one leg to the other every now and then. When the snow is thin, the holes are small in area and round in shape, but when the snow is deeper than half a metre the animal digs long and narrow passage-like trenches. This, too, is intended to save energy, because extending an existing hole is easier than opening new ones.

The social character of the reindeer also helps them in their winter digging for food.

When one animal has managed to break through the hard snow crust, others join in to expand the hole in all directions. This creates large snowless patches, where they can feed for weeks or months, because the more the patch expands, the more open rim there is to expand with a minimum of effort.

That notwithstanding, competition for food is intense on these open patches. Supremacy in the herd belongs to the mature does, whose antlers drive away both the bulls that have lost their antlers in early winter and young does. The does' privileged position in the social hierarchy benefits both the calves that they have borne the previous spring and the foetuses developing in their wombs. The situation is so frustrating for bulls that they often head off on their own to have some relief from the does' antlers.

Impact on vegetation

The animals' winter attacks on the lichen that they uncover from the snow leaves clear marks on the heath: Iceland moss is their favourite winter food, but it grows less than five millimetres in a summer.

The difference between a virgin lichen heath and one that has long been grazed by reindeer can be seen most clearly near the southern limit of the reindeer herding region. South of the line, dry heaths have thick continuous carpets of lichen. The dominant species is an almost globular one that is also popular with florists as a decorative material. The living part of a lichen is usually 30 – 40 millimetres high, but the dead and only partly decomposed stem means that the carpet is usually more than 10 centimetres deep. A lichen carpet in this climactic stage of development is the result of a long process of growth; if it is destroyed by a forest fire, it can take as long as a century to reach the same stage again.

After a carpet has been grazed hard, its average depth is less than 10 millimetres, and the lichen covers only a fifth of the soil, if that much. An area that has been picked clean contains only about one-hundreth as much biomass as a virgin

carpet. The large globular lichens are quite a rarity in the southern and central parts of the herding area, because their tolerance for intensive grazing is low. In northern Lapland, by contrast, they are on the increase. Especially in the Enontekiö district and on exposed fell slopes, more meagre types of lichen are more common than the dense globular one.

It is more difficult to notice other vegetation changes caused by reindeer; one needs a trained eye to spot them. One sign is the virtual absence of beard moss and beard lichen any lower than about two metres above the ground on trees.

In stands of Arctic birch or the birch-overgrown bogs of central Lapland, the observant eye notices that the trees have living branches only from 1 ½ metres or so above the ground. The branches gradually die if the leaves on them are grazed year after year. Reindeer have an important role as a natural means of controlling undergrowth in reforested areas.

Reindeer husbandry as a livelihood

Any Finnish citizen resident in the reindeer herding region and a member of a paliskunta, a kind of co-operative herding association, is entitled to own reindeer. There are now 7,300 owners, who belong to 5,400 households. Since there are about 190,000 reindeer (only those aged over 1 year are counted), the average number per household is 35.

Sales of reindeer meat bring in about 60 million finnmarks a year, but the social significance of reindeer husbandry is greater than the amounts of money directly involved would suggest. First and foremost, it provides employment in areas where other opportunities to gain a livelihood are hard to find.

Even more difficult to quantify is the importance of reindeer husbandry to the rural culture of northern Finland. Although not all Lapps even own reindeer, their identity is largely based on these animals. It would be difficult to imagine an old northern village community without these animals. TH

Martti Rikkonen

INARI
LAPLAND

LAKE INARI

From the top of Tuulispää, between Ivalo and Inari, a unique vista opens out encompassing over 100,000 hectares of good fishing waters, as well as innumerable islands. The River Ivalojoki delta opens out as a labyrinthine green area against the backdrop of the Nanguniemi fells. Around the multitude of lakes can be seen isolated fells. Several score kilometres distant are the extensive fell chains feeding the rivers Ivalojoki, Lemmenjoki, Vaskojoki and Kaamasjoki with the meltwater running off their slopes. The highest streams in the watersheds of the Vaskojoki and Kaamasjoki reach the Norwegian border well over a hundred kilometres away from Lake Inarijärvi.

The waters begin their journey from the fells at an altitude of 300-500 metres. They may momentarily slow down at one of the lakes — Paatari, Mutusjärvi or Solojärvi — but they then continue to flow on until they reach

Aimo Holtari

191

Lake Inarijärvi, which is still around 120 metres above the level of the Arctic Ocean.

BOAT TRIP ON INARIJÄRVI

At the Inari fishing harbour the loading of a boat fitted with an inboard motor takes about half an hour. We have only a couple of cardboard boxes of supplies, as the intention is to live on fish for about a week. Optimistic, to say the least. Buckets holding our nets are lifted into the boat and finally three spoon fishing permits are stored safely away on board.

Signs of the Ice Age are visible everywhere, with shattered rocks and large "erratics", huge boulders hauled along, and eventually discarded, by the great ice sheets. The shore line looks rather peculiar. The shore is steep and constantly lapped by the water. There are a lot of dead roots and battered greyish tree trunks, providing enough fuel for at least a century.

WATER LEVEL REGULATION

In connection with the Petsamo nickel mining activities (now behind the border) almost a 150 years ago, there was a sudden desperate need for extra electric power. Alongside the mine flowed the mighty River Paatsjoki, whose long series of rapids a decision was taken to harness. The drop in altitude from Lake Inarijärvi to the Arctic Ocean is over 100 metres, and the water flows along practically all the year round at a rate of 100-200 metres a second. The lake's natural flow rate variation was, however, a challenge to the constructors of hydro-electric power stations. Unfortunately, in the late winter there was comparatively little water in the river and this was the time of year when the most electricity was required. A decision was made to raise the surface level of Lake Inarijärvi in the summer and autumn to an appreciable extent.

This engineering had the effect of inundating the forests lining the shore, thereby asphyxiating the roots of plants. In the autumn the water froze at a much higher level than normally, but the water level then fell more than two metres during the ensuing winter. Metre-thick ice, weighing millions of tons, began to pound the shore, and the combined effect of this and the artificial raising of the water level thus had an impact on everything within a vertical zone three metres high.

Almost half of the benthic animals incorporated in food chains close to the shore disappeared, leading to slower fish growth. Inarijärvi's famous char was adapted to spawning in shallow, rather than deep, water in the autumn. With the commencement of artificial water level regulation, most of the lake's burbots were left high and dry, crushed between the ice and the lake bed. Brown trout populations crashed.

The fate of Inarijärvi's most important fish species was even more saddening. The Riga whitefish, the mainstay of spring and summer fishing on the lake, feeds on large zooplankton, which disappeared, probably owing to a lowering of the temperature caused by the raising of the water level. The whitefish started to grow thinner and their spawn changed from being a bright yellow to an undistinguished, lifeless shade of grey. The Riga whitefish was obviously unable to adapt to the regulation. The same fate awaited the sticklebacks which in the shore area form the most important food of the migratory sea trout. These changes were extremely radical and depressing.

It was not until the mid-1960s that any attempt was made to investigate the damage caused to fish by man's interference with the water level. The process of law in this particular case — an excellent example of the ponderous nature of officialdom — took no less than forty years (the same holds true for the River Kemijoki case). Nowadays whitefish, migratory sea trout, lake trout, and brown trout are being stocked in Inarijärvi, with the consequence that catches are improving and fishermen are beginning to face the future with a new optimism.

OVER OPEN WATERS

Up above, a lesser black-backed gull observes the travellers from rather high up but an emboldened Arctic tern follows the boat from a distance of just a few metres. After following us for some distance, it heads back to its nesting site on a small skerry. Evening is already on the way and the red-throated divers begin their eerie cries on the open water. A red-throated diver flies over in the direction of the pools on Varttasaari, where it has its nest on a pool surrounded by an island that in turn is completely encircled by Lake Inarijärvi!

The open water of Kasari is so large that many of the Arctic Ocean passage migrants stop off there. Shags, for instance, can be seen there quite often, but the large white-billed diver which was unfortunately discovered, too late, entangled in a fisherman's net, is a very rare visitor indeed to these parts.

The speed of the boat has to be reduced because of the many shoals at the mouth of the Suovannuora. We are now in an area where large peled whitefish roam the shallow shore waters searching for the bigger bottom-living animals. Caddisfly larvae and mayfly nymphs, as well as small shellfish, provide food for these fish. We cast a few nets before going to the cabin.

FISHING ON THE FRINGES
OF SAMMAKKOSELKÄ

The outboard engine attached to the rowing boat puffs away at low revs. The rod rests will easily stand up to the casting of three spoons simultaneously. Since we are in an area good for brown trout, the depth chart and sounder are indispensable. The brown trout must be at a depth of about 15-20 metres, but migratory sea trout may well be close to the surface, or at a moderate depth. The spoon which is being trolled deep in the water is the first to catch a char, which rises to the surface kicking lazily. This species was brought over from North America in 1955. It is a predatory fish of clear, cold and deep waters. It is said to live for a decade and to grow to a maximum weight of 40-50 kilos. The first specimens were stocked in Inarijärvi in the late 1970s. The largest char that have

Kasariselkä, on Lake Inarijärvi, in a January blizzard.

been taken here have weighed 6-7 kilos. There is as yet no absolute evidence of successful spawning by this fish, but many fishermen believe that this has taken place in recent years.

The following story has been told about the spread of vendace into Lake Inarijärvi. At the beginning of the 1960s vendace spawn was brought down from Sodankylä to Inari and in the spring the newly hatched fry were introduced in, among other places, Lake Alajärvi, on the southern side of the local airport. A certain proportion of these vendace escaped through a grill at the hatchery into the River Juutuanjoki. Lake Alajärvi began to develop its own vendace stocks from which fish, upon reaching a certain age, began to migrate along the River Alajoki, and to pass thence to the Ivalojoki. At the end of the 1970s winter fyke nets were used in the estuary of the Ivalojoki. The main catch consisted of a few hundred kilos of reeska but among them were a few kilos of vendace. In the 1980s vendance begin to spread very rapidly over the whole of the great lake, and now they are encountered everywhere.

With spawning by the vendace being very successful over a couple of autumns, rather intense competition between the reeska and the vendace took place with respect to the available plankton food. The reeska may well end up taking only a silver medal in this interspecific competition. Migratory sea trout and lake trout stockings may now succeed better than previously since these fish consume vendace.

As dusk begins to descend, the fishing rhythm starts to slow down. The migratory sea trout and brown trout cease feeding now, to resume it in the early morning.

Our return to Kärppätupa takes place through labyrinthine sounds, going along very quietly. When the fish soup has been eaten and the raw trout fillets have been placed in salt, we go to sleep in our sleeping bags without bothering to construct any kind of lean-to.

FISH AND CLOUDBERRIES FROM SAMMAKKOSELKÄ

The sun is already well up by the time we fishermen awaken. A few Siberian jays investigate the surroundings of the camp thoroughly. Nature's dustmen are extremely efficient. Near the boat a feral mink has taken care of the tidying up of the beach. Swifts curve through the air a couple of hundred metres above us. These birds have their nesting holes in old aspens on Varttasaari island. A black-headed gull also keeps to the shore, looking for something to eat. Its fledglings ought to be large enough by now to fly.

On the edges of the great northern open waters of Lake Inarijärvi there are hundreds of islands in which only low-growing dwarf shrubs or two metre high fell birch grow. The core and interior of these islands may consist of rock or of closely packed moraine, but the surface resembles a beret in shape, covered with dwarf shrubs the fringes of which extend almost to the water. The moisture content is ideal for Arctic cloudberries. On some of the islands or peninsulas on the eastern shore many of the cloudberry bogs extend right down to the shoreline. The banks are clothed in such a dense growth of cloudberry plants that it is difficult to force the boat's prow into them or to jump on to the shore without breaking some of the plants. This kind of situation is not encountered

Marti Rikkonen

Lake Inarijärvi's wide open waters have attracted even the Arctic skua. The turnstone is one of the most vociferous of the latest inhabitants.

anywhere else other than on Inarijärvi. When the first half of June is favourable to flowering, when the cloudberry flies form dense clouds, and when there are sure signs that masses of gnats and mosquitoes are on the way, then the berry crop may well reach high proportions. Small bogs are completely choked with cloudberries. The proximity of the large lake serves to protect these from minor frosts, and only an extremely cold north wind at the height of the flowering seasons may result in the berry crop on unprotected islands being almost non-existent that year. In this case one has to be content with berries found in transitional forest mires, which are protected somewhat by their tree cover.

'AS DEEP AS IT IS LONG'

Open stretches on Lake Inarijärvi, which are scores of kilometres long and almost as broad, convey the impression that the lake is very deep. The same can be said of some of the steep shores fronting many of the islands; these plunge into the depths as though into a well. The song about Lake Inarijärvi, which maintains that it is "as deep as it is long", seems to have stemmed from this particular concept.

Lake Inarijärvi's depth ratios are in fact no different to those in any other large lake in this country. Erosion flattened out the landscape over hundreds of millions of years and the late Ice Age with its vast land and water masses evened out the scenery so much that there are few altitude differences amounting to hundreds of metres within a small area.

The open water areas of the lake reach 50-70 metres in depth for quite long distances. However, depths in excess of 100 metres have yet to be recorded there. At Vasikkaselkä, in the northern part of the lake, a depth of 97 metres has been recorded. Inarijärvi's deepest troughs remain well above sea level.

A large proportion of Inarijärvi's life exists at a depth of under 20 metres, even in the open waters. Life needs light and this goes down only 20-30 metres, however clear the water is. In the shore waters down to a depth of

2-3 metres the bottom is completely devoid of growth owing to the artificial water level regulation. There are few benthic animals. The depth between 5 and 10 metres is the most productive zone. Organic material consists of a thin layer on top of mineral deposits. This is inhabited by caddisfly larvae and mayfly nymphs, as well as large numbers of mussels and water snails. Most of the benthic fauna biomass consists of chironomid larvae and oligochaetes. At lower depths of 10-15 metres lake ore covers the bed in the form of up to palm-sized reddish brown plates. This has at one time almost certainly been mined on a small scale as a source of iron.

At a depth of 20-30 metres in the daylight the light is blue, darkening to blackness just a little lower down. The bottom is covered in the level areas by bluish grey ooze containing humus and the dead parts of both plant and animal plankton which have slowly settled into the depths. There is very little life even in the bottom ooze; pale microdrilous oligochaetes and small red chironomid larvae occur, however, down to 60 metres.

In these open waters the medium is well oxygenated and clear. The cold water is much favoured by chars, which occur from time to time at depths of several dozen metres. For food intake their normal swimming depth is 15-30 metres, at least in the summer, when the surface water is too warm to permit them to remain there for very long. "Too warm" in this case means at a temperature of around 10 degrees Celsius. In the winter, with a metre of ice coating the whole lake, the chars disperse into shallow water underneath the ice. Catches of many kilos of brown trout are best sought at depths of about ten metres. This fish species is happiest in the blue twilight or in complete darkness.

On the return trip there is time to stop at "Ukonkivi", a rocky island rising to several dozen metres from the depths and continuing above the surface of the lake for another dozen metres or so. Ukonkivi is pock-marked with hollows and tunnels which the water has most probably dissolved and eroded out over millions of years. The place is striking and it is no wonder that the Same (Lapps) considered it the sacred home of the gods and went there to sacrifice those whose deaths they believed would help to establish good relationships with the deities in the matter of hunting and fishing.

In the vicinity of Kalliosaari, there is another rather special island on which past generations buried their dead (the Finnish name "Hautuumaasaari" means 'burial ground island'). This burial place was left in peace until the artificial regulation began. The erosion caused by the latter began to eat away the sandy island and near the shore bones — even skulls — suddenly began to appear. Technology and the need for energy had interrupted the peace of centuries.

The only course of action possible was to protect the island's shores in order to prevent the entire mass from subsiding into Inarijärvi's depths and vanishing forever. This has been successfully carried out — although the original peace with this generation of mankind has gone for good. OT

VÄTSÄRI

Towards the east and northeast of the Inari basin there lies a large tract of wilderness representing Finland's northernmost coniferous tree limit. The northern part of the area lying between lakes Nammijärvi and Sevettijärvi is known as Vätsäri. Vätsäri is an entirely protected area where no forestry is carried out.

The Vätsäri wilderness can be approached from three different directions: from the north at Sevettijärvi, from the south at the village of Nellim, while from the west enthusiastic canoeists or rowers would do well to explore Vätsäri via the deep fjords and indentations lining Lake Inarijärvi's eastern shore.

Jorma Luhta

BARREN WILDERNESS

Vätsäri has no mighty fells to offer, neither does it boast primaeval forests. The region comprises the watershed between the Inari basin and the Arctic Ocean. Its oldest Scots pine forests were logged in the 1920s-30s period. The signs of this relatively delicate treatment of the forests have already been obliterated by the elements and plant growth. Here and there are some loggers' cabins now overgrown by moss.

On the other hand these wilds do offer peace and 'atmosphere' in unlimited amounts. Their fauna includes some of the most retiring of the backwoods animals. As the scenery for the most part is very barren, it is to the smaller details that the naturalist must look if he is to benefit fully from a sojourn at Vätsäri. Myriads of pools and brooks lie between the larger lakes, of which there are but a handful. Dryish mineral poor heathlands are patched with small bogs, while silver-grey screes bedeck the inclines.

TOWARDS THE CENTRE

A trek through Vätsäri may well be begun from the village of Sevettijärvi. Once one locates the trail leading north from Lake Suolisjärvi, the first part of the trip is very easy. At the end of this trail the real wilderness begins, with its many inhabited trackless Scots pine forests.

The trip is well worthwhile, as beyond Lake Surnujärvi rears Surnupää, the area's large, two-peaked fell. From one of the summits a view is to be had right over the heartland of this wilderness, making it possible to select one's route more carefully. A look at Surnupää serves to entice the hiker still further towards Mellalompolo, whose sandy shores are almost without equal. Finding a suitable camp site here is only hampered by the large variety of spots available!

Old wild deer traps can still be found at the top of the esker above Mellalompolo. They are slowly becoming overgrown and serve to remind us of the time when deer hunting was essential to the survival of wilderness folk. There were many ways available to them for trapping deer, these large pits, dug alongside the deers' migration routes, requiring more effort than any of the others. However, the energy expended was well worth it, as the pit traps caught large numbers of animals.

Continuing south for several kilometres, the esker rises to an impressive height. Hiking up there is very pleasant, not the least owing to the splendid views that open out at regular intervals along the way, now towards the east, now towards the west. The esker curves through small lakes to the western side of the Surnu house.

SUBTLY CHANGING SCENERY

The next points of interest for the rambler are bare-capped Nammivaara fell, on the north side of Lake Nammijärvi, and Mustavaara, which stands next to it and is noted for its lovely Scots pine forests. Here the scenery begins to change, the pine forests becoming thicker, the individual trees older and taller. There are fewer birch woods and the peatland lakes are more eutrophic.

These changes in habitats are accompanied by an increase in the abundance of animals. The rambler will notice in particular the birds, and especially the loud-voiced waders. In the middle of summer the large wilderness birds (swans and geese) ae very quiet and they lie hidden away with their broods in some remote place. By August gatherings of bean geese become prominent as they constantly come into view flying from one favourite feeding ground to another.

Whooper swans will be seen if one keeps one's eyes open and treads warily, so as to make the least noise. These birds are very frequently to be seen on lakes in transitional forest sphagnum mires, and if one is very lucky the smew may also remain in the near vicinity, undisturbed by the strangely garbed visitor's progress. A male smew viewed at leisure against the dark waters of a peat-stained pool is a sight not easily forgotten.

While both the golden and white-tailed eagles may occasionally be observed soaring up above, most of birds-of-prey flying over or circling in search of a quarry will be rough-legged buzzards or ospreys. The thought of 'bumping into' a bear causes some to lick their lips in anticipation, others to go weak at the knees. This inhabitant of remote areas is very adept at avoiding people, so that encounters with it are few. A moist mound of dung or scratch marks on the trunk of a pine are as much as one can expect to see on most treks.

NAAMAJÄNKÄ — MATALAJÄRVI

On the southern side of Lake Nammijärvi, the River Naamajoki leads the hiker to Vätsäri's largest peatland complex, marked on the map as the Naamajänkä — Matalajärvi area. Here the large mires unfurl to become great bogs tens of hectares in extent which, however, are not overly wet, so that they offer no obstacles to the wanderer once the spring floods have subsided. These peatlands can be circumnavigated on the western flank and then one can cross at the narrowest point by following the path from Kessivuono to Lake Kessijärvi.

Those who are interested in wilderness wildlife ought not to pass up the chance of exploring these peatland habitats. A fascinating assortment of birds seek out bogs and mires and their fringes in the spring. Both the whooper swan's ringing call and the loud trumpeting of the crane will be heard here. There is an abundance of waders and in willow thickets a choir of small birds employs a wide range of octaves under the leadership of a bluethroat.

On the south side of Majavaselkä the hiker gradually becomes aware of the close proximity of human habitation. The trail network becomes denser and there are several houses prominently set out along the shore of Lake Inarijärvi. If time permits it is worth walking from Lake Juggerjärvi west up to Inarijärvi.

Following the shores of Inarijärvi eventually brings one to the Paatsvuono river mouth — and here the trek ends. HW

Hannu Hautala

The Arctic Tern – The Bird of the Long Days

The Arctic tern spends most of its life in daylight. It is the only bird that sees the midnight sun in both the northern and the southern hemisphere. It spends 2 – 3 months of the year in its nesting area, three months or so in its winter grounds and the remaining 6 – 7 months on its long migratory flights. It nests along Arctic shores, on islands and in tundra throughout the northern hemisphere. Its range of distribution is divided into two distinct sectors in Finland:

in general, it nests all along our Baltic coast as well as in the Arctic upland and forested regions of Lapland. There is also a small but stable population in the large lakes of the Peräpohjola region, in addition to a tiny community on Lake Oulujärvi.

The Arctic tern's light soaring flight and its whistling "kee-kee" with rising inflection are familiar anywhere near fish-rich rivers, hill ponds and large open lakes. In the uplands and forested regions of Lapland, the birds nests everywhere except

on the bleakest hilltops and in the shallowest headwaters of rivers. It quite commonly nests even on open or hummocky bogs where ponds or bogholes are found. Most nesting pairs are isolated from each other in Lapland, but there are distinct nesting communities in coastal areas. Small concentrations comprising several pairs are also found on sandbanks in large rivers as well as on rocks and islands in lakes.

In early summer, Arctic tern put on an impressive and high-

ly audible display as they perform their flying mating rituals. This includes the so-called fish flight, in which the male carries a fish in his bill and, whistling excitedly, tries to entice the female into his territory. Since both sexes are identical in appearance and size, the behavioural patterns associated with the fish flight have an important function in determining the birds' sex. Birds that have already mated put on a display of high-altitude flying, using long strokes of their wings to

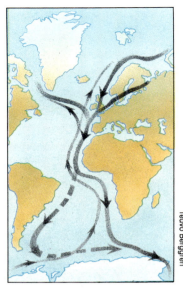

The Arctic tern's migratory flight extends from one polar region to the other. The alternative routes southwards are along the coasts of Africa and South America.

soar, one after the other, to a considerable height and then descending in a long glide with their wings stiffly held downwards at an angle. This kind of flight often involves carrying a fish and is generally performed throughout the nesting period.

The male's task is to feed the female while she is laying. The birds' diet is not confined to fish; in the Baltic archipelago, at least, they commonly skim insects from the surface of the water and plunge into it to gobble tadpoles. It is probable that insects are a more important part of their diet in Lapland than in coastal areas. When the weather is cold and windy, food is difficult to obtain and what the male can manage to forage is not enough for the laying female. In such cases, young pairs nesting for the first time easily abandon their nests. The large flocks of idle birds that one sees in Lapland during unfavourable summers are one clear sign of this.

The Arctic tern is a long-lived species. Ringed birds over 20 years old have been observed nesting in our Baltic archipelago. Individuals over 30 years of age in other parts of the world hold the longevity record for the species. Thus the number

of offspring produced need not be high each year for the population to remain strong. Nesting is a failure from time to time, but in a good year a pair can rear two chicks to the point where they can fly away.

The Arctic tern's nest is a shallow depression in the ground. The birds sometimes drag dry grass, lichen, straw and similar materials into it, but in places where there is no vegetation, on sand, in reed beds or hummocky bogs, it is left unlined. The female usually lays two eggs, but sometimes only one or, more rarely, three. The chicks remain in the nest for a couple of days after they hatch, but then venture into the immediate vicinity and hide in vegetation when danger approaches. As larger fledglings, they like to go swimming. The mother defends the nest against intruders by diving at them and can also hit them nastily on the tops of their heads with her bill. Winged raiders like crows and other predatory birds are warded off long before they get near the nest, whereas smaller mammals like foxes, mink and stoats are attacked with blind fury. By contrast, reindeer can come quite close to a nest without provoking an Arctic tern into the air. The fledglings take to the air when they are about three weeks old and rapidly develop their flying skill. The whole family sets off on the autumn migration together. For at least the early part of the trip, the fledglings still depend on their mother for food.

The Arctic tern's migratory flight is the longest in the bird world. The northernmost populations have to cover 18,000 kilometres to reach the fringes of the Antarctic pack ice. They do not arrive there until October or November. They begin moulting in December, and at the height of the southern summer change the wing feathers with which they have made a round trip of 36,000 kilometres. In March, now clad in fresh new feathers, they are ready to set off north again. The summer migration is faster and more intense than the autumn one: in 60 days, doing some 300 kilometres a day, they return to the north. MH

Protected but Still Endangered

The freshwater pearl mussel is an endangered species throughout Europe. There seems to be little room left for it even in the remotest backwoods, much less in Central Europe, where the number today is only a tenth or so of what it was at the turn of the century. Unfortunately, the little creature is not able to adapt flexibly to rapid changes. Its fate is sealed and it dies away sooner or later when the hand of man has swept over the river where it lives.

Protected, but not safe

In the early decades of our century, it was still permitted to catch the mussels in Finland. Many a poor resident of Lapland or other wanderer in the backwoods could add a little margin to their lives by finding a pearl now and then. Some even hit a jackpot of a kind. One such fortunate soul was the professional pearl gatherer Konrad Hollo, who in 1925 found a nine-karat specimen 10 ½ millimetres in diameter — the size of a grape. It was probably the largest pearl ever found in Finland. The hunt for freshwater pearls got out of control in the 1920s and 1930s, when divers with good equipment arrived from the "South". They emptied the largest rivers by diving and dammed or diverted smaller ones to scour them of their treasures. The mussel was declared a protected species in 1955. Until the latter half of the 1970s, it was the only invertebrate in Finland enjoying the dubious benefit of this status.

Although protection shielded the mussel from hunting, it did nothing to prevent the destruction of its habitat. Pollution loads continued to increase, especially in southern Finland and Ostrobothnia. In northern Finland, where the mussel was relatively safe until then, drainage of backwoods bogs added particulate pollution to its home waters. Pressure to harness

rivers increased further when energy prices rose dizzyingly in the early 1970s. Now, dams began appearing on even small rivers. The freshwater pearl mussel was no longer safe anywhere.

In 1978, the Finnish section of the World Wildlife Fund chose the mussel for special protection. A working group was appointed which began studying the state of the rivers in which the creature lived and the causes of changes in its range of distribution. It had taken 20 years for a study into the effects of protection to begin.

A perfect habitat in Salla

A little river about three metres wide and less than half a metre deep gushes merrily over some rocks and opens out into a calm stretch. Trees curve into a vault over it and the willow-fringed banks of the calm stretch reveal that there is shady water for mussels under the banks themselves.

The bed of the river is gravel and sand; a little further on it is overlaid with organic material, and there can be no mussels there. The rocks in the rapids have gravel between them. There are few plants, except moss. The water is as cold as that from a spring. And that is how it should be.

Old mussels live partly in rapids, partly in the deeper parts of calm stretches, wherever the water is over 2 ½ metres deep. Young ones live in the shelter of gravel and sand in the rapids and in the sand at the bottom of calm stretches, where the water plunges down from the rapids and creates a flow. Young mussels spend the first 4 — 6 years of their lives dug into the sand of the river bed. They need a lot of oxygen and food, which the water carries to them. The flow must be strong to be able to penetrate the sand. Even small quantities of bog water bring particles of peat, which clog the gaps be-

The freshwater pearl mussel in its correct habitat, a clean stream with a gravel bed.

Ilmari Valovirta

tween the grains of sand and suffocate young mussels. By contrast, those individuals that have lived long enough to rise to the surface of the river bed are able to turn their shells to ensure that the breathing aperture in its upper part is inclined at just the right angle to the direction of the flow.

We found some!

The population in this particular section of river was not very large, but still there were several thousand along a stretch of a few hundred metres. There are rivers where there used to be hundreds of thousands of the mussels. One such was the River Ähtävänjoki in Ostrobothnia. Now it has been dredged and harnessed. Every autumn, researchers go there to see how the mussels in the basins upstream from the dams are being covered by a layer of loose material that grows thicker every year.

One set of rapids in the river contains a place where there are more than 30 mussels in an area of only half a square metre. A density of over 100 per square metre can be considered a sign of a good habitat. Such places are not all that rare in the untouched rivers of Lapland.

Compared with ordinary river and lake mussels (or clams), the freshwater pearl mussel grows rather slowly. The age of a young individual (under 15) is calculated by counting the concentric growth rings on its shell, in the same way as a fish's age can be determined by counting the rings on its scale. The age of an older individual is determined by using a microscope to examine the growth zone in a cross section of its hinge. Since

Ruthless exploitation in Taivalkoski. Hunters killed hundreds and perhaps thousands of mussels to find a single marketable pearl.

this can be done only in a laboratory, one has to find some empty but well-preserved shells. By studying the soft parts of a mussel, one can measure what levels of environmental toxins, such as lead, zinc, iron or copper, have accumulated in them. We are trying to discover how well a mussel that lives several decades functions as an indicator of environmental toxins. In other words, these creatures may be able to help us as a living record of the changes that have taken place in a river's condition in the course of several decades.

The largest individual that we found was over 12 centimetres long. A mussel of that size in northern Finland is about 80 years old. For the length of a human life, this moss-clad individual has squatted here between the rocks. It has accepted whatever the stream has brought; autumn floods, the cold of winter, the surge when the ice breaks up in spring and hot dry spells in summer. Wedged between the rocks, it has not been able to move much, apart from a little up and down in the gravel or inclining its shell with or against the flow of the water. That is the lot of the mussel. Once it has found its place in the world, it does not ask for much besides time and peace.

Reproduction by chance

Today's young mussels will be capable of reproducing only around the turn of the century, when they have reached an age of 15 — 20 years. Some of them could well be alive in the year 2100 — if people give them the chance.

The animal kingdom contains few species whose reproduction and the survival of young individuals depend so much on chance as in the case of the freshwater pearl mussel. The males discharge their sperm into the water in July and August. They are carried into the females' gills, where they fertilize the hundreds of thousands of eggs that the gills contain. Naturally, this succeeds only if the males are upstream from the females. The eggs develop into small mussel-like larvae called glochidia, which temporarily become parasites in the gills of fish. Brown trout, salmon and sometimes minnows are the mussel larvae's temporary hosts in Finland.

As the shadow of a fish passes over her, the mother mussel blows out the larvae and at least a few out of every thousand are drawn in with the water that the fish breathes. Chance also plays a role in whether or not the larva manages to snap the two halves of its shell together at just the moment that it brushes the fish's gill. Once it has managed to attach itself to a gill, the larva is safe for a few months at least, because the fish secretes a protective membrane around it.

It is often only the following spring that the larvae detach themselves from the gills and drop to the bottom of the river to begin their slow growth to maturity. Chance also determines where the little one falls. If it comes to rest on a muddy bottom, its life is over, but on a sandy bottom it will be able to find refuge in a gravel bed. In a set of rapids, where trout rest, it may fall behind a sheltering rock, and this is the best starting point of all for a life that could last many decades. IV

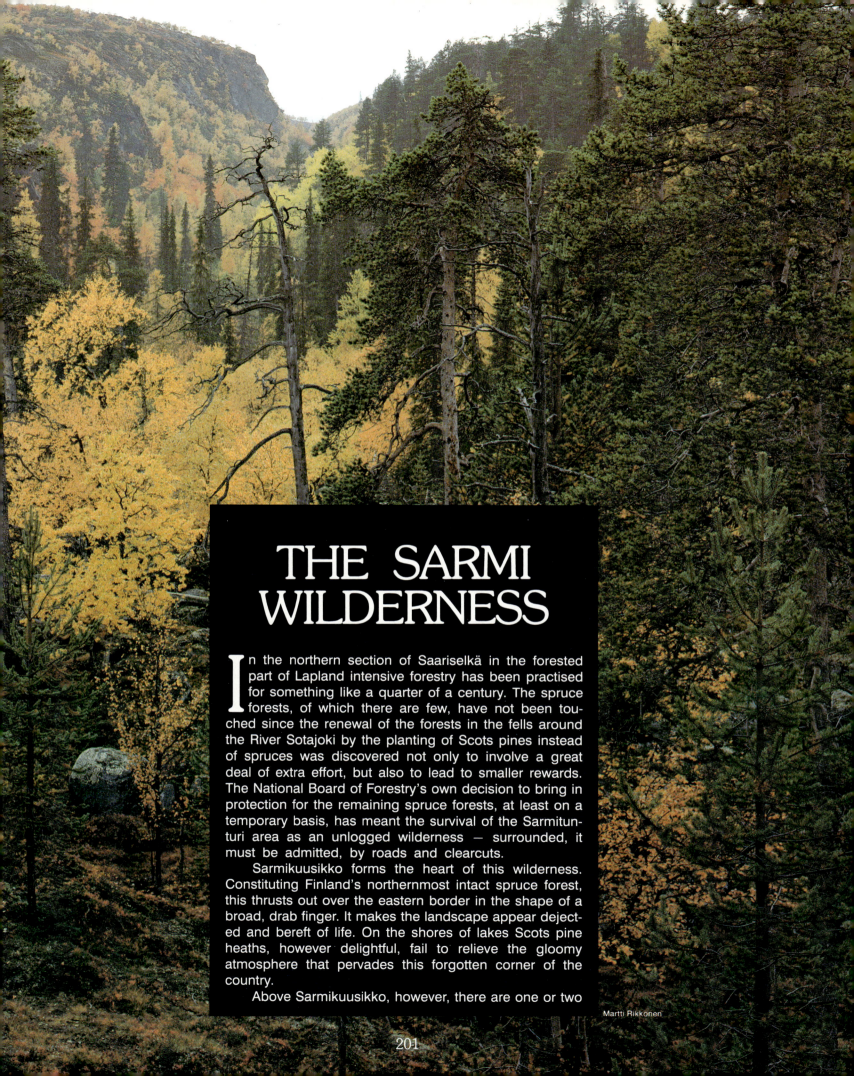

THE SARMI
WILDERNESS

In the northern section of Saariselkä in the forested part of Lapland intensive forestry has been practised for something like a quarter of a century. The spruce forests, of which there are few, have not been touched since the renewal of the forests in the fells around the River Sotajoki by the planting of Scots pines instead of spruces was discovered not only to involve a great deal of extra effort, but also to lead to smaller rewards. The National Board of Forestry's own decision to bring in protection for the remaining spruce forests, at least on a temporary basis, has meant the survival of the Sarmitunturi area as an unlogged wilderness — surrounded, it must be admitted, by roads and clearcuts.

Sarmikuusikko forms the heart of this wilderness. Constituting Finland's northernmost intact spruce forest, this thrusts out over the eastern border in the shape of a broad, drab finger. It makes the landscape appear dejected and bereft of life. On the shores of lakes Scots pine heaths, however delightful, fail to relieve the gloomy atmosphere that pervades this forgotten corner of the country.

Above Sarmikuusikko, however, there are one or two

Martti Rikkonen

Martti Rikkonen

Forest management is steadily eradicating the capercaillie's traditional display grounds.

fells whose lofty openness provides a welcome change after the dimness of the spruce forests and gullies. The topography here is fairly kind to the walker and orientation poses few problems since there are lakes and streams from which to take bearings. Moreover, the summits of either Akalauttapää or Sarmitunturi are visible from almost wherever one happens to be standing. There are about ten unlocked cabins in this area.

IN THE LAND OF THE SKOLT LAPPS

Anyone arriving without a car can reach the Sarmi wilds by, for example, hopping off the Raja-Jooseppi bus at the Kolmosjärvi road junction. Along logging roads there is a walk of a few hours to the northern side of Lake Kolmosjärvi, where the wilderness first begins to peek out at civilisation. Close by there are two very cosy cabins which will serve admirably as accommodation at this stage. One of these is a Skolt-style cabin which is in very good order. The Skolt Lapps, who during the last war were evacuated from the village of Suonikylä, endeavoured after the hostilities had ceased to return home. From Suomu to Arttajärvi houses and outbuildings were erected close to water bodies, but a few years later, when the region became too small to support the whole tribe, the Skolt Lapps were resettled on Lake Inarijärvi. A charming cabin on Lake Kolmosjärvi is one of the more beautiful reminders of these times.

From the southern side of Valolompolo an enchanting trail begins which runs along the backs of eskers northeast to Lake Harjujärvi. Between the latter and the River Kivijoki it is only something like an hour's walk. The Kivijoki is the swiftest flowing river in the region and the area's most important waterway. The winding, partly shallow, partly deep river is a wonderful companion right through these wilds. Brook trout and grayling dwell in its

waters and as the August nights begin to draw in, large lake trout ascend the river in order to spawn. Mussels thrive in its white and brown chequered sandy bottom, while on the shore sands mink and even otter footprints can be found.

Following the nameless tributary of the Kivijoki, one can fairly easily negotiate the spruce forests right up to the foot of Akalauttapää fell. When the stream disappears one sees in front the steep sides of this fell, from which it is possible to obtain the best view in the area.

REMINDERS OF BYGONE TIMES

This is the old hunting grounds of the inhabitants of the Ivalo and Sulkusjärvi districts. Since there is a distinct absence of larger lakes, no permanent settlement of this area ever took place. Hunters have traditionally sought deer and birds here, however. At least on the eskers adjoining the headwater pools on the Pahakuru and the eastern shore of Lake Kontosjärvi there are still long lines of pit traps and on the edges of Sarmikuusikko one can still find numbers of bear traps. Many of this region's local names are connected with the hunting or trapping of one game animal or fish or another. The most important game animals — deer, brown bear, capercaillie, and otter — have all given their names to places, just as have the burbot, pike, migratory sea trout and whitefish. Rarer game is implied in the name Joutsenmunalampi (= "swan egg pool").

Immediately under the northern slope of Akalauttapää fell there is the exact opposite of Sarmi, in Pahakuru, whose roughly east-west orientation creates two radically differing plant and animal environments. The northern face embodies the warm and consequent luxuriance of the south, while the southern slope is associated with damp- and shade-loving northern plant species. The raven nests are all perched on the southern face of the gorge. Pahakuru (= "bad gully") could just as easily have been dubbed 'Paradiisikuru' ("paradise gully"). The western end of the gully in particular is very easy to negotiate, being full of lush herbage and fernery surrounding brooks and pools. The eastern end, however, is full of boulders. At the end of the gully this region's most enchanting route, running from Asentolampi to Santapää, via Asentolampi, is well worth the walk for those who have the time. One can descend from Santapää towards the Finnish limit of the border zone as far as Lake Kippisjärvi, to which a logging road has recently been built. Good speed can be made along this new road back to the River Kivijoki. Following the river leads one to an excellent camping ground beside Lake Joenyhtymäjärvi. From here a rough trail along the Rytioja stream leads back to Harjujärvi.

While the Sarmi wilds themselves are uninhabited and even Sulkusjärvi has only a couple of houses on it, the shores of Lake Kivijärvi can boast the ruins of a Lutheran church destroyed by fire sometime before World War II. It was built a century or so ago, presumably as some kind of an ecclesiastical front against the orthodoxy of the Skolt Lapps. RO

POMOKAIRA
AND
REPOKAIRA

I n those places at Pomokaira in which there are as yet
no clearcuts it is very difficult to preserve one's sense
of location, even with the assistance of the newest
maps available. Variations in altitude are few. Where
dry land begins and peatland ends seems to be very
clear to the map-makers, but not to the hiker. One

Hannu Hautala

Stone chat fledglings are a common sight at midsummer alongside logging roads in Pomokaira and Repokaira.

Hannu Hautala

wanders the whole time through slowly growing spruce forests or leafy pubescent birch groves, all of which are quite indistinguishable from others of their kind. The loose bottomed shallow pools on Pomokaira bogs would tend to indicate that there have been numerous deeper pools in this area which have now become infilled by peat. This gradual process has turned the wetter areas into peatlands, while the spruce has dominated almost all of the uplands. The spruce has altered the micro-climate and the soil via the latter's fungal flora, in order to make these more closely approximate its own ideal conditions for growth.

THE EASTERN PART OF POMOKAIRA

On the northwestern side of the Karjala fell chain the large mire complex of Pomoaapa has been included in the State's national peatland protection programme. The raised bogs on the southern fringe of this area constitute a gateway to the Pomovaara fell group, which is composed of fragmented, reddish-grey Nattas granite. This fell land in general is extremely barren, although in some situations, notably alongside brooks, small tracts of grey alder forest occur. When hiking towards the south-southwest, one is obliged to cross a river — the Ylä-Postojoki — at its headwaters. The tar black water brings nutrients down from the peatlands of Pomokaira

where vast quantities of humus have become mixed with it and iron has become dissolved in it. The latter explains the jelly-like rust brown masses deposited at intervals along the river banks. Despite the darkness of the water, brown trout thrive in these rivers.

Southwest of the river stretches a series of fells, decorated with scatterings of broken rock and stones. Forests in the northern parts of the uplands, in the so-called Pomo virgin forest area, have been preserved for posterity. On the scree areas on the crowns of fells like Tenniövaara future hikers may still be able to admire ancient Scots pines with their characteristic fish-scale bark. Spruce, however, dominate in most places here. Sadly, they are even encroaching on the few remaining pine stands. We will have to skirt tall wood ants' nests which having being deserted by the ants are now moss and dwarf shrub-covered hummocks that are beginning to blend in with their surroundings. It appears that even these indomitable insects are engaged in a one-sided struggle against the Christmas tree.

AT THE HEADWATERS OF THE KITINEN

The village of Pokka, lying directly on the headwaters of the River Kitinen, is an excellent place at which to establish a base camp. From this one can set out into the Repokaira wilds, leaving most of one's supplies safely stowed away. This village has a number of camping sites run by local people, some of whom can also provide roofed-over accommodation, in addition to boat hire. In spite of these facilities, there are not enough tourists to have started eroding the loveliness of the wilds close to the village. Up above Pokka there is an area of eskers covered with heathlands that, stretching in an unbroken chain along the Kitinen valley, have obviously been cast with the hiker in mind. The forests consist of scattered Scots pine trees with an underlay of colourful lichens.

Where the Kaalimaa house stands one bids farewell to the ancient agricultural settlement and disappears into relatively untouched, and certainly unspoilt, terrain. The focal point of a way of life is Lake Taatsijärvi, on the north shore of which there is an ancient sacrificial site, Taatsinseita. The lake itself is elongated and oligotrophic in comparsion to the lakes of southern Finland. Neither water lilies nor other substantial emergent vegetation occur in it, the reason for this being the lake's altitude (280 m) and latitude, the surface waters not becoming ice-free until well into summer.

Underwater, however, there are growths of true pondweed and spiked water-milfoil, as well as large amounts of bottom-dwelling moss in the interstices of which water boatmen and insect larvae hide away from the fish. The latter comprise mainly perch and whitefish. It is also possible to go from Pokka to Taatsijärvi by boat and if one is willing to spare the time one can journey up the Rousku rapids to Kitinen's headwater lake. The hiker will normally leave the waterway and either set off in a northerly direction, crossing dry terrain right up to Taatsinpalo, or head north-northeast along a route taking him through more moist, but equally variable, country. The

Typical Repokaira scenery — solitary lakes and open aapa bogs with hummock ridges separated by shallow pools.

bogs and mires along the Takahaara for the most part feature hummock ridges bristling with dwarf birch. On the eastern side of the fell, alongside the ditches, stretch meadow-like strips aglow in summer with the blooms of the globe flower and fragrant orchid.

AT THE HEADWATERS OF THE IVALOJOKI

On a few of the slopes, white rings on some of the pine trees may attract attention: these markings indicate the extended area of Lemmenjoki National Park (see p. 217). The land begins to slope here down towards Naskama-aapa mire. The Suovuotsi becomes narrower, leaving a long, slim little pool at its bottom. In the muddy waters near the shore the mare's tail thrusts its small fir-shaped figure up above the water. The feathers and droppings of waterbirds which have now left decorate the hummocks, with eiders and common scoters lying hidden along the far shore. The green orchid Coeloglossum viride grows wherever there is seepage; the species is becoming increasingly rare in the south. As one proceeds further north, the forests begin to thin out.

Naskama-aapa mire offers a northern perspective emphasised by a sparse cover of birches on a savanna-type landscape. This aapa mire is a very typical specimen, differing from that in Pomokaira, for example, in having numerically fewer hummock ridges which compensate by covering a larger area of the mire. In the birch-covered peninsula on the eastern shore you have an idyllic camping site. It is possible to swim in one of the peatland pools by simply standing on the floating Sphagnum stretched around the pool like the iris of an eye, and then waiting until it sinks far enough to accommodate you in the water above it. The call of the jack snipe is a familar sound here. At the edge of the bog the eye is attracted by the blue flowers of the butterwort, and in hollows scraped out by the reindeer a local species of rush and a clubmoss have commenced to grow.

Water from the aapa mire is conducted away by the numerous tributaries of the Naskamajoki. While following these north at the fringes of the mire, you come in contact with a few spruce covered areas. As the river gains strength and stature, wild cherry and wild currant put in an appearance. At the confluence of the Naskama-joki and Ivalojoki, you can turn up the main river.

After about three kilometres you reach permanent, established civilisation in the form of the village of Lisma (or Salko, as it is also called). This is a typical Lapp (Same) settlement. The route we have taken lost its significance a long time ago as the sole connection between the village and the outside world. Nowadays there is a road approaching the village from the east which is attached at its far end to the main Inari highway. The Ivalojoki headwaters do not exhibit such a strong current as is normal in the gold districts. Long tracts of still water are interrupted by faster flowing stretches and the banks of the river are generally covered in a dense tangle of willows and herbage. Reminders of the spring floods are present in the form of dark brown tufts of 'hair' high up in the trees formed of dry moss that has been hung up by the raging torrent.

The effect of these floods, however, is a very mild one and during the period of low water you will have no difficulty walking along the banks close to the water's edge.

The last indigenous beaver was shot at Salla on the Enjanjoki in 1868. Individuals were brought in from North America and released at Lake Pallasjärvi, Kittilä in the 1930s. The species has now spread even into the Pomokaira-Repokaira area. In this area the Canadian beaver's descendants have discovered enough of their staple diet, aspen, to make staying on worthwhile.

THE ENVIRONS OF THE REPOJOKI

Northwest of the Jolkkavaara fell group one descends into a rift valley, the Huuva-autsi. At these northern latitudes the continental ice sheets thrust up from the southwest, tending to pot-scour the ravine rather than to dump large quantities of left-overs in it. The bed of the gully shimmers with a regiment of water bodies known as the Huuvajärvet lakes. The latter are well stocked with grayling and whitefish — a fact that has not been overlooked by poachers!

Proceeding from the Repojoki headwaters, on the western side of Repovaara fell a peatland tract closely resembling a slice of tundra is pock-marked by stony pits. The northern limit of this Sphagnum bog slopes towards the headwaters of the Tenojoki river. From this water shed it is but a stone's throw to the dry land spanning the border, but the regulations prohibit one from just crossing over. Norway's Övre Anarjokka National Park closely resembles Finland's Lemmenjoki National Park, to which it is juxtaposed. The main feature here is the river valley, dotted with large expanses of still water, in the thickets surrounding which the bluethroat pours out its delightful song. In moist areas on the river banks, northern species like the white-flowered butterwort and Thalictrum alpinum, a relative of the common meadow-rue, flower.

The return trip to Repokaira takes one through birch woods in which isolated Scots pines figuratively at least ponder on their future. In places it is the birches themselves that have suffered from the depradations of a particularly virulent pest, the caterpillar of the autumnal moth, a type of looper, or spanworm. Defoliated sometimes to the last leaf, mature trees have died off, paving the way for contingents of seedlings and saplings, which are now busily competing for space.

The Repojoki flows along the southern side of Repovaara fell down a conspicuous gully, below which, however, it resembles the Ivalojoki headwaters in rubbing shoulders with willow thickets and birch groves. If the rambler chooses to rest up during the heat of the day and to rove late in the evening and early in the morning,

he may well stumble on browsing elk and hares.

Apart from the watercourse, the peatlands on the northern side repay investigation. Cranes nest on the great flat expanse of Lemmenjänkä and a rough-legged buzzard has its nest on an 'island' in this boggy terrain. Finland's southernmost palsa bogs (see p.242) are located on the southeastern rim of Sallivaara fell.

After crossing the metalled highway running between Inari and Kittilä, the lower reaches of the Repojoki run for another five kilometres before its confluence with the Ivalojoki. In front, on a bend, there is an extremely wide river crossing, but probably thanks to its width it is possible to wade across the river in rubber boats without getting your trousers wet. It is easy to walk upstream for ten kilometres or so, past Karikoski, the Karvajoki, and Järväköngäs rapids.

Especially in the neighbourhood of the quieter pools, the banks are often clothed in willow thickets. Near the river no less than seven species of willows jostle for space. At the foot of the Kivikoski rapids, turn south.

ALONG THE HEM OF PORTTIPAHTA

On the borders of Inari and Kittilä-Sodankylä there has been very little human impact. To the east lie the remains of the old Rovanen-Kultala trail, to the west at the site of the modern metalled road, the old post route from Pokka, via Ivalo-Matti, to Inari.

Alongside this road stands Mirhamitupa, where the assizes used to take place. Legend has it that the building was erected on the border of two communes, so that accused people from Inari could sit on their own side of the municipal border, but the judge did not need to travel to Inari in order to try them: he simply had the charges read out from the Kittilä end of the room.

After reaching the Peuravaara fells, it is best to turn southwest and to cross the River Iissijoki as high up its course as possible, as the Porttipahta has inundated the river estuary. Depending on the height to which the surface level has been regulated, the water will have backed up the channel for a considerable distance, making a crossing awkward to say the least.

Southwest of the Iissijoki river mouth you reach the point at which the Kuolpujoki disgorges its brown waters into the Porttipahta basin. After the Siliäselkä crossing, you come to the path running from Pokka to Laiti on the bank of the Kitinen. Laiti village has been drowned by the reservoir, but a few of the outlying detached houses on one of the upper trubitaries are still standing. These, however, have no permanent inhabitants. You can now take the easy trail back to Pokka. The pools lying between the rivers Kitinen and Järvijoki must be approached slowly and quietly in summer, as they are usually inhabited by tufted ducks.

While it was nice to leave Pokka, it is also nice to return. And one place well worth visiting while you are there is the Kirsti Pokka museum of local arts and crafts, where you can inspect old implements and weapons. If you have not yet satiated your wanderlust, you can always hire a boat and row down the Kitinen. TR

Dick Forsman

Lapland's Summer Torment

The people of Lapland have a word for it: "räkkä". It expresses the idea of a time of summer when bloodsucking insects torment reindeer, other livestock and humans alike. True, those pests, mosquitoes, blackflies, midges, horseflies and gadflies afflict most all warm-blooded animals virtually everywhere in Finland, but Lapland seems to have been specially singled out for their unwelcome attentions. Generally speaking, the plague lasts from around the third week of June to the end of August, but there are large annual fluctuations in both timing and intensity.

Folklore has it that the räkkä period begins in Lapland just before the Midsummer festival. As one writer has put it: "The mosquito is out and about even if it needs two crutches, and that is when the reindeer congregate on their summer pastures." Another piece of folklore has it that "If you kill a mosquito before Jacob's Day (24.7), ten more will hatch; if you kill one after that, ten more will die." In other words, the mosquito population goes into decline in the last week of July. It is also around then that the reindeer herds that have formed to protect the animals from the insects begin dispersing. Around the same time as the mosquitoes, the horseflies first assault the reindeer herds, although it is at the height of the summer that they, together with gadflies, cause the most mischief. They sometimes continue to annoy the animals until September. By Jacob's Day at the latest, the blackflies are flying in dense clouds and attacking anything with blood in it. The last to make their appearance are the tiniest of the tiny, the *biting midges*, which join the feast around the middle of August. However, an early spring can bring things forward and exceptionally warm weather in May and June can accelerate hatching and cause a sudden and intense early räkkä. In such years, blackflies can take the initiative and plague reindeer calves taking their first steps or cattle that have just been put out to pasture, even in the south of Finland.

Incessant whiners

Ever since reindeer were domesticated from wild animals, the räkkä, and especially the role that mosquitoes play in it, has determined summer herding practices. The words of a traditional Lapp song by Paulaharju describe what happens: "The mosquito drives the reindeer to the hills/drives them off the lowland bogs and into a herd./We couldn't manage the reindeer/If there were no mosquitoes./It is a small creature/ but everything sure flees from it." Reindeer herdsmen exploit this behaviour, especially when they earmark calves. When the mosquito plague begins to abate, the herds break up, although the arrival of new swarms of other insects can sometimes drive them into new herds.

Of the 38 species of mosquitoes in Finland, about half are found within the reindeer herding region. The mosquito räkkä in Lapland is caused almost entirely by insects belonging to the *Aedes* genus, which contains a large number of species. Several species belonging to the genera *Anopheles, Culex* and Culiseta also have a markedly annoying role in the south of Finland.

Aedes mosquitoes live in pools of thaw water during their larval stage. There is no shortage of these small water bodies in Lapland's terrain, where a late arrival of summer prevents their drying out. The earliest of the species to take to the air is *communis*, which is flying by late May in southern Finland and 3 — 4 weeks later in the Arctic uplands of Lapland. *Cantans* and *diantaeus* hatch soon thereafter. The aggregate number of individuals representing these three species declines as one goes northwards, and by the Arctic Circle have been replaced almost entirely by three other species, *punctor, pionips* and *hexodontus*. Mosquito swarms all over the country also contain *excrucians* and *intrudens,* which hatch later, usually only in July. *Culiseta* mosquitoes, which have striped legs and mainly bite at night, appear on the scene in July and August. Those adults hibernate, which means that they can also be a torment as early in the year as May.

Whenever one is working about the yard, hiking in the forest, sitting or strolling on a lake- or seashore or on an island with bushes and trees covering it, female mosquitoes whine around one looking for an opportunity to bite and get some blood. If they succeed, they suck between 2 and 12 milligrammes of it, enabling each set of hundreds of eggs to mature to the point where they can begin growing. There can be thousands of them flying around a human being, and tens of thousands attacking a reindeer in the forest. A human being can suffer more than 400 bites a minute and a reindeer nearly 10,000.

A mosquito first becomes aware of the presence of a potential blood donor when the wind brings the smell of carbon dioxide exhaled by the mammal. It follows this to the vicinity and then homes in precisely, guided by the victim's body heat. It does not fly directly to the spot where it will bite, because more or less all bloodsucking insects need some air space to fly around their victim. By congregating in herds, reindeer can significantly reduce the number of mosquitoes that can get close enough to bite them. Exposing itself to wind has the same effect, because mosquitoes fly very poorly. The worst sufferers are creatures forced to stay in one place, such as hatching birds and chicks left unprotected in nests. When there is a really bad räkkä, some of these can perish. Since both mosquitoes and blackflies take to the wing once the temperature rises above 7-8°C, the unrelenting torture can last for weeks during the warmest periods of the year. Even reindeer can perish at such times. It has been calculated that an individual animal can lose as much as 125 grammes of blood a day, most of it to mosquitoes.

Mosquitoes are almost universally considered an intolerable nuisance. Still, there are some people who hardly suffer from them at all, or who hardly notice their bites. The explanation has to do with these individual's body temperatures, the amounts of carbon dioxide which they exhale, their pain threshold and immunity. That the latter property develops is supported by the observation that the soreness of bites declines as the summer goes on.

Eyes and ears

Blackfly larvae grow in all kinds of flowing waters. Their favourite growth habitats are the rocky beds where bogs and lakes discharge their waters into rivers. Their population density in such places can run into hundreds of thousands per square metre. The number of adults hatching in a set of rapids many hectares in size is almost beyond imagination! Males remain at the rapids where they hatch, but the females, after they have mated, fly five to six miles in search of blood. In the same way as mosquitoes, they can sense birds, people or any mammal, swarming furiously around their victim in dense clouds and every now and then landing on the skin and running to and fro in search of a place to bite. In a test conducted in Canada, 78 females landed on a square inch of skin in one minute, and 17 embarked on a meal of blood. One can only imagine the torment! The victim does not feel the actual bite, but when the female has left the painful itching begins and can last for days.

Blackflies are on the wing all day, but most intensively in the forenoon and late afternoon. In the northern summer, however, one is in danger of their bites round the clock if the temperature remains between 7 and 27°C and there is no more than light rainfall. As is the case in neighbouring countries, there are about 50 blackfly species in Finland, about a third of which (belonging to the genus Simulium) are a pretty serious nuisance to livestock and people.

Species belonging to the genus Eusimulium specialize in biting birds. Nearly all of these species breed in masses virtually every year and when the plague is at its height one has to go indoors for shelter; unlike mosquitoes, they attack only outdoors.

Mass deaths of livestock attributable to blackflies are occasionally recorded from various parts of the world. Such occurrences are rare in Finland, but there were two cases caused by blackflies in 1982: numerous cattle calves died of shock after being badly bitten by the insects in the Vammala district in early June and between 400 and 500 reindeer calves perished in the Oivanki district of Kuusamo the following month. Deaths of individual domestic animals are difficult to link to blackflies, although it is assumed that they occur rather often. That reindeer are killed by blackflies almost every summer is certain, but it is virtually impossible to determine exactly which species are the worst culprits.

People, too, have been so badly bitten by blackflies that they have had to seek medical treatment. Two particularly bad years were 1975 and 1981, when Simulium ornatum was particularly active and wreaked considerable havoc in May and June.

The invisible torment

Quite little is known about the biology of biting midges and the species to which they belong. However, most of the blood-sucking species (of which there are about 15 in Finland) belong to the genus Culicoides. Their larvae live in all water bodies and waterlogged land. They mature and swarm from June onwards, but it is only in August and September that they become very noticeable as the last symptom of the räkkä period. They bite all warm-blooded creatures, but people seem to suffer most. The insects are so small (some of them are less than a millimetre in length, but they are usually 1 — 2 millimetres) that they can reach even the most protected parts of our skin unobserved. Their sting is sore and the spot itches for hours afterwards.

The bite one feels

Of all this country's blood-sucking insects, those that attack people and livestock least are horseflies, but they can still be a nuisance. There are nearly forty species in all, but fewer and fewer as one goes north towards Lapland, where there are fewer than twenty. The larvae live in inland water bodies and waterlogged land. Some years, the adults fly as early as May, but as a rule they become a nuisance in open landscapes, fields, forest clearings, on Arctic hill slopes and close to open waters during warm sunny weather from mid-June to the end of August. They can consume anything from a few tens of milligrammes of blood to hundreds of milligrammes in a single meal. Their bite is sharp, stinging and painful. Just as we do, animals react to their sound and may even stampede. Reindeer panic easily as they cannot distinguish between horseflies and the even worse bot flies. However, when it has been bothered by them for a longer time and lost a lot of blood (as much as 100-300 grammes a day) a reindeer loses weight and eventually dies of shock. Cows, too, can be sucked virtually dry, which is understandable when several hundred horseflies dine on a single animal within the space of only half an hour.

Chrysops relictus, which can be recognized by its golden-green eyes and mottled straggly wings, has been mentioned as the most common species in Finland. However, the grey, stubby-winged Haermatopota pluvialis has been the most numerous species, representing as much as 75 per cent of the total caught in some tests. Species belonging to the genus Hybomitra and the rare Tabanus genus (which is found in southern Finland) represent at most a quarter of the population.

Genuine parasites

If their frantic behaviour is anything to go by, the insect that reindeer detest most is the warble fly, of which there are two species in Finland.

The one that specializes in reindeer is on the wing on calm sunny days in late July when the temperature is at least 13 degrees. Impregnated females lay their eggs (as many as 500 each) in the hairs of the animal's growing summer fur. A few days later, the larvae hatch and burrow under the skin. There, nourished by tissue fluids and breathing through air holes, they remain until summer, inch-long, greasy-looking creatures, whose presence is revealed by large protuberances on the reindeer's back. They eventually drop to the ground and go into their pupa state.

Another species lays its eggs in the reindeer's nostrils. The parasites weaken the animal and if there are too many of them it can die.

Protection and avoidance

People and animals have age-old methods for dealing with tormenting insects. A bunch of leafy birch twigs is still a handy thing to have in one's hand when walking outdoors. Where wood tar was once smeared on the skin, much more convenient preparations are available today. Reindeer are sometimes driven into corrals for protection. There, their urine, faeces and perspiration combine to produce a smell that confuses many insects. Horseflies hate shade, mosquitoes wind. An upward flow of air and the attraction of light forces mosquitoes and blackflies up and out through the opening in the conical points of the summer shelters built for animals in Lapland. By spending hot days lying on sandy banks, reindeer ensure that the carbon dioxide that can reveal their presence dissipates upwards rather than spreading across the landscape.

Colour is also important. Tests have shown that dark greys, chestnut brown, purple, blue and sharply contrasting patterns attract both mosquitoes and blackflies. Light green, yellow and orange are better camouflage. Animals' colouration is the result of evolution involving many factors, but it appears that insects have to some extent at least influenced the coats of Finnish landrace cattle, with lightness and contrasts conspicuously absent.
KKu

HAMMAS-TUNTURI

The Hammastunturi region is limited in the south by the River Ivalojoki, in the east by the highway between Ivalo and Inari, and in the west by the road connecting Inari to Pokka. Before the construction of the Pokka road in 1966 the Hammastunturi area, together with the fells of the Lemmenjoki and Repojoki region, constituted an extremely wide expanse of trackless wilds, in which there was only very sparse Same (Lapp) inhabitation.

Since the 1880s gold has being intricately mixed with the mysteries and legends of the southern part of the area bounded by the River Ivalojoki. The very first gold prospectors ascended the Ounasjoki river and pulled their boat at its headwaters along about a 2 km-long path to the upper end of the Ivalojoki at Lake Korsajärvi. From there they then went downriver along the Ivalojoki to below the Appisjoki river mouth as far as what is nowadays known as Kultala ("kulta" = gold). By the 1880s mines had opened up down the length of the river and during its heyday there were hundreds of men occupied in this pursuit.

Martti Rikkonen

A reindeer herd on a frozen fell-land pool in the Hammastunturi fell chain. Note the herdsmen's tepee on the right.

Nobody, however, was to become rich on this gold and the miners one after the other drifted elsewhere. However, gold prospecting has continued in some small measure (one is tempted to say 'in a miner way') right up to the present day. The hiker may alongside some lonely stream find rusted implements, caved-in mine shafts, and rotted sluices. Alongside the old gold village of Kultala, the National Board of Forestry has put up an unlocked cabin for the use of hikers and fishermen. From here many hikers continue on to the northern side of Ham-

mastunturi fell, to the old reindeer roundup fence, or to Kultala (same name, different place) on the River Lemmenjoki. Although the Pokka road in a sense makes the wilds smaller, the dimensions of the latter are still formidable. The distance from Törmänen to Menesjärvi is 45 kilometres and from Inari to Kuttura 55 kilometres.

THE CALL OF THE WILDS
The first roads to supply Hammastunturi were constructed during the war when the Germans laid down a way

Martti Rikkonen

suitable for vehicles as far up as Lake Solajärvi.

In the 1960s and 1970s the logging road network, with its concomitant clearfellings, made considerable incursions into these fell-lands. While there are now rather a lot of roads and clearcuts of various ages, the area has so far remained relatively peaceful as there is very little traffic moving to and fro.

In the early 1960s a dam was constructed across the drainage channel of Lake Hammasjärvi and for over a decade the lake served at the Kirakkaköngäs rapids,

right alongside the Inari-Ivalo highway, as a late-winter reservoir for a power station. This kind of surface level regulation ceased in 1975 but its impact is still visible along the shores of the lake.

When one sets out in the direction of the Hammastunturi heartlands from Kultala, on the northern side of the Ivalojoki, a series of bare-topped rocky fells soon comes into view. The tree stands consist of rather large Scots pine trees with, west of the Appisjoki, gloomy spruce forests. In this area the rambler may still come across extremely large ancient pine trees, some of which have already died and dried out to form 'snags'. The reason for the rather dense forest growth in this southern section is probably the ideal conditions of heat and light which obtain there. Spruce-covered slopes are typical to the Ivalojoki tributaries on the Hammastunturi side. There are very few Scots pine forests here, spruce forests being particularly common down in the river valleys. Further up, the fell slopes in addition to the crowns are clothed in fell, or mountain, birch. The northern side of the Repojoki differs appreciably from the other parts of the Hammastunturi region; namely it is characterised by the low coniferous forests typical of fell lands. From this sea of conifers a few fell summits jut proudly in naked defiance. In the middle of the forests there are large mires through which a few rivers meander.

The area of Hammastunturi bounded by the Ivalojoki is one of Finland's most notable breeding grounds for birds of prey, and especially the golden eagle. Owing to the inaccessibility of the region, local populations of the latter have remained very high. Brown bears have been increasing in recent years in the Hammastunturi district, too. In the past few years one or two wolves and wolverines have also been encountered in the area.

Within recent decades there have been a few forest fires, for example at Taimenpalo and Matinpalo, through the aftermath of which the rambler is obliged to pass when walking the Kuttura-Karvaselkä trail to the next unlocked cabin. Breaking out in 1946, the fire left as its legacy an unbroken expanse of dead forest, which so far has not been touched by the axe. From the road which splits Repokaira into two an attempt was made in the 1960s to open up a so-called 'winter road' to Kuttura. This met with failure, however, since the nature of the topography prevents even the most robust of heavy machinery from setting to work in it.

While the Hammastunturi wilds have shrunk, they still arouse admiration, especially in the river area between the Repojoki and Kuttura. The Ivalojoki, which gathers its waters from Lemmenjoki National Park, consists of a series of quiet pools interspersed by rushing rapids. Locally the river becomes compressed between sheer rocky walls to form a canyon-like channel. The appearance of the Ivalojoki changes after Hirvisuvanto, long stretches of rushing water and foaming rapids alternating with quietly flowing water.

REINDEER HUSBANDRY AND OTHER LAND USE

Permanent settlements in the Hammastunturi area are the Kuttura Lapp village lying on the northern bank of the Ivalojoki, the Senja Aikio house at Lake Hammasjärvi, and the Pentti Lehtola house at Lake Lonkajärvi, some fifteen kilometres distant. There are no other Lapp settlements or even individual houses. However, the Lapps are active year-round in this area since there are so many important reindeer grazing grounds and calf-marking stations here. Nowadays, with the deterioration in the lichen situation in the clearcuts on the fringes of this

region, the Hammastunturi reindeer migrate to tne area between Kuttura and Nuovukkapää unusually early in the autumn. In this district the reindeer herdsmen are obliged to live with their herds for a few weeks in the autumn in order to round up their reindeer, and to spend time with them again in the spring. Hence the shelters commonly stumbled on by the rambler on the slopes of fells are the remains of the herdsmen's temporary accommodation.

Calf-marking stations include Palopää, which lies on the western side of Hammastunturi fell. There are now far fewer calf-marking events than in the pre-1970 period, as it was originally believed that all the new calves could be gathered together for marking in the spring. However, the herdsmen quickly noticed that there were fewer grazing grounds for the reindeer owing to the loss of beard moss in the clearcuts. At Kulpakkovuoma, below Hammastunturi, stands the old Vuorhavaara fence, which was last used for calf-marking in 1970. The Lapps used this site as a reindeer roundup station from the 1920s right up to the mid-1960s. It sat in those days plum in the middle of the reindeer husbandry area, from which there was a reasonable distance to, for example, Ivalo, where reindeer sold during the roundup were transported for slaughtering. There are still old cabins along the roundup fence.

Before the Fell Lapps settled down in the Hammastunturi area, the Inari Lapps used to fish and hunt there. This explains why one occasionally comes across old wild reindeer pits. These are especially common on the heaths between lakes Ronkajärvi and Kaitamojärvi, as well as on the heath south of Lake Syväjärvi, and in the Lake Hammasjärvi district. Such pits were generally dug on eskers along paths normally frequented by wild reindeer.

Other signs of the traditional Lapp lifestyle are the circular scars on the slopes of fells representing rotted roundup fences. At the mouth of the River Appisjoki, at Viljaniemi (Hammasjärvi) and in the Akulahti district one can still discover the sites of the tepees of the original Lapp fishermen. According to local history, the region has been much used over the centuries for hunting and fishing by Lapps belonging to the Morottaja clan. At Lake Talvitupajärvi, four kilometres north of Hammasjärvi, there is a tepee site in which the old buildings are still visible. Nowadays in the Hammastunturi area reindeer husbandry is practised by the Fell Lapps, one or two Inari Lapps, their fennicized descendants, and even one or two people of pure Finnish stock.

The old Same people used to visit the Hammastunturi region with their reindeer in the winter, moving in the summer up to the shores of the Arctic Ocean. With the closure of the Finno-Norwegian border in 1852, reindeer husbandry here became more complicated. Towards the late 1800s tepee settlements migrated down from Utsjoki and Kautokeino (in Norway) to Hammastunturi, and these later became firmly established at, for example, Kuttura, Menesjärvi and Repojoki. The last immigrants arrived from Enontekiö, in northwestern Lapland, to take up residence at Lake Kulpakkojärvi in the early 1930s. Since

In an apparently lifeless wilderness the glow from a camp fire attracts a pair of camp guards in the shape of Siberian jays.

Hannu Hautala

home with them. With the melting of the snow in the spring the reindeer are transferred to the river valleys and peatlands in the heartland of Hammastunturi. Here the does can give birth to their calves in peace, and the young animals can develop undisturbed. As the weather gets better and clouds of gnats and mosquitoes become a nuisance, the reindeer move up into the Alppistunturi fell group.

The hiker in the Hammastunturi region will very frequently encounter the crumbling remains of some kind of hay shelter on a reed-covered river bank meadow or estuary. Just a few decades ago the Lapps used to grow fodder at these places for their cattle and the semi-tame reindeer that pulled their sledges. In order to prevent free-ranging reindeer from pilfering the dried hay, the shelters were generally surrounded by a stout fence. Not only did the Lapps cut hay for their domesticated animals, they also used it for lining their boots, hence the origin of the Finnish expression "heinäkenkäisiä" ('hay-shoe people') for Lapps living in the very remote areas.

FISH AND FISHERY IN THE AREA

In the lakes of the Hammastunturi area many species of fish abound, including whitefish, pike, perch, burbot, and migratory sea trout. In a few lakes there are also char, which have been stocked in such places as lakes Raha-järvi and Hammasjärvi.

In the rivers there are the usual running water species: lake trout, brook trout and grayling. Aside from grayling and brook trout, the local fishery is interested in pike, burbot, minnow and sticklebacks (2- and 3-spined species). In places along the Ivalojoki there are whitefish with very dense strainer teeth. In addition to this, a less dense-toothed whitefish stock feeding off bottom-dwelling animals and reaching several kilos in weight ascends from Lake Inarijärvi to the River Ivalijoki and Juutua waterway to spawn. The lake trout also moves upstream beyond Inarijärvi into the Hammastunturi area rivers. The latter are important to the lake trout of the Inarijärvi, Ukonjärvi and Paatari stocks as spawning grounds and sites for fry production.

Trout reproduce in rapids to which individuals of reproductive age migrate from the lakes to spawn. After spawning, in the September to November period, their offspring spend two to seven years in rivers, during which time in the fast-running waters local fish species, i.e. grayling, burbot and pike, are in competition with the trout smelts for food. There are local stocks in lakes Irrajärvi and Taimenjärvi which may attain a weight of 2-3 kilos. The trout of these lakes descend the rivers draining out of them in order to breed.

In the rivers of the Hammastunturi area trout are found right up to the highest pools. A local brook trout may spend its entire life in a brook and begin to reproduce while it is only a few dozen grams in weight. On the other hand, the lake trout which migrates a greater distance would appear to require for reproductive purposes a river with a minimum flow rate of 0.5 — 1 cu.m/sec. However, it is not possible to draw a distinct

then, radical changes have taken place in reindeer husbandry. A stop has been put to the traditional migrations occurring at different times of year between summer and winter pastures. Today the herdsmen are obliged to keep their beasts year round in the same areas. The slopes on the Ivalojoki side of Hammastunturi during the late winter form rather good browsing places for hungry reindeer, as the snow tends to build up there and to remain soft, making it easy for these cloven-footed animals to dig down through it to the succulent lichen food at ground level.

The Hammastunturi herdsmen round up their reindeer from the various areas during the autumn and take them to Juntinoja, at the side of the Pokka-Menesjärvi road, or to the Vittakuru roundup site alongside the Ivalo-Inari road, or alternatively to the Tupavaara roundup site on the northern shore of Lake Ronkajärvi. After the annual roundup the owners virtually take their animals brook trout and lake trout, as the former descends to the larger rivers and the offspring of the latter may ascend the smallest of brooks from the largest of rivers.

The Lake Hammasjärvi trout at one time used to swim down the Kirakkojoki in order to spawn. With the construction of the dam on Hammasjärvi, the trout were unable to reach their spawning grounds, so that the natural stocks in the lake literally became extinct. Again, the sudden setting free of the dammed waters of the lake in spring also caused considerable damage to the after-growth of the lake trout ascending the Kirakkojoki from Lake Rahajärvi.

Commercial fishing is carried out in the Hammastunturi area as a side-line to a way of life based on a natural economy, while fish are also consumed, of course, in order to vary the diet. The Lapps catch for their own needs river whitefish and lake trout which are ascending the rivers to spawn. With a reduction in catches from lakes and rivers debouching into lakes, due to water level regulation, many of the Inarijärvi whitefish and trout fish-ermen have been forced to look elsewhere for their catches: the lakes of the Hammastunturi area have provided one of the alternatives.

THE FUTURE OF THE WILDS

Today many objectives are being levelled at the Hammastunturi wilderness. Clearcuts with their concomitant dense network of logging roads, reduce the local inhabitants' opportunities of choosing a reasonably close-to-nature sort of existence. One consequence of radical clearfelling is the extreme reduction in lichen growth, particularly on trees, forcing the reindeer to move up the fells whether they want to or not. This results in food supplies at higher elevations being more heavily taxed by the animals than previously. In time there is a reduction in the number of grazers — the reindeer themselves. The network of roads lets permit-holding hunters and fish-ermen from other parts of Finland into hunting and fishing areas that the people living on the fringes of these wilds have traditionally held the right of access to.

The Hammastunturi region is not at present widely recognised as a good spot for outdoor pursuits like hiking, probably because of its close proximity to the UKK National Park and Lemmenjoki National Park. The rambler may continue up from Kultala on the Lemmenjoki by unmarked trails north to Kehäpää and the Hammastunturi uplands down old reindeer fences to Vuorhavaara and Hammasjärvi. From there he can strike out along the path leading to the Kaitomajärvi road. It is also possible to hike from Kultala to the Lemmenjoki by way of Lake Taimenjärvi, where one can make use of an unlocked hut. This latter route runs through very variable Ivalojoki scenery. Most hikers seem to prefer the forested fell lands east of Lake Hammasjärvi. Far less popular, for some reason, are firstly, the Nukkumapää fell region, where unforgettable vistas open out over the whole complex of Lake Inarijärvi and secondly, the heartlands of the Hammastunturi wilderness with their profusion of hidden pools and lakes. JK

Local names in Same and Finnish

Many names incorporating some feature of the Lappish landscape have remained almost unchanged for centuries. Common parts of names include (Same/Finnish/English): oaivi/pää/peak, várri/vaara/fell, johka/joki/river, vuobmi,vuopmi/vuoma/river and jávri/järvi/lake. These are frequently combined with words referring to the Same culture, mammals, fish, birds, or events; e.g. Loddevárri/Lintuvaara/Bird fell.

Lakes and rivers have been given names according to their location; e.g. Dievá-aljávri = lake on top of ridge or esker. Some lakes are named after fish; e.g. Dápmotjávri = Trout lake, with its river the Dáptmotjohka = Trout river. Fells are named along similar lines; e.g. Jeälgeloaivi = Lichen peak.

Points of the compass:

davvi	= pohjoinen	= north
máddi	= etelä	= south
nuorta	= itä	= east
veasta, oarji	= länsi	= west
davvenuorta	= koillinen	= northeast
davveoarji	= luode	= northwest
máttanuorta	= kaakko	= southeast
máttaoarji	= lounas	= southwest

Weather:

arvi	= sade	= rain
biegga	= tuuli	= wind
bivval	= lauha	= mild
buolaš	= pakkanen	= frost

Terrain:

avči, ávži	= syvä kuru	= deep gully
balsa, bovdna	= mätäs	= hummock
bunci	= tunturialueella jokin korkeampi kohta	= higher place in fells
čorru	= tasaisesta maastosta erottuva osa	= higher place on level ground
dievá, dievvá	= harju	= ridge or esker
dearbmi	= törmä	= bank
duoddar, duottar	= tunturi	= fell
gorči, gorži	= köngäs	= major rapids
guolba, guolbba	= jäkäläkangas	= lichen heath
gáddi	= ranta	= shore, beach
geavnis, geavnnis	= köngäs	= major rapids
guoika	= koski	= smaller rapids
guotku, guotkku	= kahden järven välinen maa	= land between two lakes, isthmus
jeäggi	= jänkä	= large bog, mire
luobbal, luoppal	= lompolo	= long, narrow lake in ravine
luokta	= lahti	= bay
maras	= karu ylänkömaa	= barren upland
njárga	= niemi	= peninsula, promontory
muotka	= kahden järven välinen taival	= trail between two lakes
oaivi	= tunturin huippu	= fell summit
rohtu	= joen- tai ojanvarsikoivikko	= birch grove on river or stream banks
skurču	= syvä kuru	= deep gully, ravine
várri	= vaara	= fell

JK

Antti Leinonen

The wolverine lives in a small "territory", but has a very extensive habitat. In fact, unlike a wolf pack or a lynx, it does not have a specific territory which it defends against other members or groups of the same species. Several wolverines can eat some of the same carcass within a short period, but each individual prevents others from getting too close. That is why the animal's territory is referred to in quotation marks. A wolverine's habitat, which is hundreds of square kilometres — and sometimes over a thousand — in extent, would be simply too big to defend against other members of the species.

Diet and nesting

The wolverine is a poor hunter. However, in late winter and early spring, when reindeer are weak and bogged down by deep snow, it has its opportunity. It can kill several animals in a small area within a few minutes, but this does not prove that it is a capable hunter. Indeed, many researchers have established that it prefers to find food rather than have to hunt for it. It can eat berries in autumn, but carrion is the dominant component of its diet. It has to have a lot of stamina as a wanderer to be able to find enough carcasses in large wilderness areas, where animal populations are usually sparse. Carcasses are frozen hard in winter, so good teeth and a sturdy neck are needed to break the rock-like meat into consumable pieces. The wolverine is well-endowed for its role as a scavenger.

This member of the weasel family is a relatively rare species of northern Siberian fauna. Its range of distribution is a narrowish band running through Europe, Asia and North America and straddling the northern fringe of the boreal forest zone and the sub-Arctic. It prefers terrain like the forested part of Lapland, which is dotted here and there with hills. In places where snowdrifts accumulate on hill slopes, it excavates its nest in February and March, creating a system of snow caves tens of metres long. But it can also dig its nest

The Threatened Wolverine

caves into the snow on bogs in the middle of coniferous forests in taiga regions.

There are usually two or three cubs, but one lair in the Kuhmo district was found to contain five. The cubs must be strong enough to follow their mother when the walls of their nest melts in spring. They can remain with her until as late as August. The species' reproduction rate is so good that it, supplemented by immigration, was long able to compensate for the numbers killed and the population remained fairly stable in northern Finland. Indeed, the population there was large enough to give several professional hunters a livelihood. But then snowmobiles arrived. Especially in eastern Lapland, reindeer herdsmen created a network of patrol routes in the wilderness. When they noticed wolverine tracks crossing or along one of the snowmobile routes, reinforcements were summoned and the animal tracked down. Soon the indige-

nous wolverine population had been virtually exterminated. Others came across the Soviet border to fill the vacuum, but suffered the same fate. Still, wolverines have been breeding in Lapland again since the beginning of the present decade.

The long-distance trekker

The area of Finland in which the wolverine lives extends in a long wedge from Lapland down along the eastern border to the northernmost parts of North Karelia. Whereas the population has declined sharply in Lapland, it has increased slightly further south in the past decade or so. In practice, this means that relatively permanent residents have replaced the "vagrants" that used to come across the border.

A typical feature of the wolverine's mobile lifestyle is that it can set off on long expeditions outside its normal habitat. Thus some from North Karelia have wandered as far west as Savo

and Häme. Individuals from the Kainuu region were last observed in the Oulu area, quite close to the Gulf of Bothnia coast, in 1983. Strangely enough, wolverines wander far from their normal areas even when their numbers in Finland are quite low.

The wolverine is Finland's most endangered species of large predator. The number remaining in Finland is between 20 and 40 individuals, depending on movement across international borders. The figure of 60 often mentioned is greatly exaggerated. Although the species is protected in theory, it is mercilessly persecuted in practice. As soon as one is detected in a reindeer herding area, a permit to kill it is immediately issued by the Ministry of Agriculture and Forestry and any means, including motorized vehicles, may be employed. In other words, "protection" has actually increased the threat to this creature.

EPu

LEMMENJOKI

The coach arrives in the early evening at the small Same (Lapp) village of Njurgalahti, at the end of the road on the bank of the River Lemmenjoki. Tied up at the bank there is an extraordinarily narrow riverboat made of exceptionally wide planks. As the passengers step out of the coach they are issued with orange life-jackets. The outboard starts up and the long slim boat arcs out over placid Lake Sotkajärvi. The Jomppanen houses, tourist cabins made of 'snag' wood, and some new settlements are soon left behind.

The boat is soon in the national park. A more magnificent gateway to a national park it would be difficult to imagine. On both sides of the boat jut up splendid Scots pine forests. On the south bank these alternate with dry gravelly terraces and steep-sided eskers. A stone-strewn hill extends out right up to the river bank on the north side. In front the mighty Joenkielinen fell is reflected in the waters of the lake: the fell's summit lies some four hundred metres higher than the lake surface.

Martti Rikkonen

Reijo Juurinen

Ptarmigan inhabit stony areas on fells, where their changing colours match their surroundings.

During a twenty-kilometre long river trip upstream towards the gold-panning district of Kultahamina the boat passes through several lakes, with stretches of fast-flowing water between them. In a couple of places the passengers are obliged to get out and walk past thundering rapids, while the boat is either piloted up the river under motor power, or poled up it, according to how high the water level happens to be. During this trip the river valley becomes increasingly steep-sided. After the Härkäkoski rapids the fells on the southern side of the river begin, as it were, to crumble into the water, their sides becoming a series of precipitous steps. Boulders dislodged from the sheer walls lie in heaps at their foot. These heaps of broken stone continue down under the water to a depth of several dozen metres. From a narrow ledge a hundred metres up a rough-legged buzzard takes wing and begins to circle slowly over the expedition.

EUROPE'S LARGEST
FORESTED WILDERNESS

Lemmenjoki National Park constitutes the largest area of protected virgin forest in Western Europe. Its impressive 2,800 square kilometres encompass besides the River Lemmenjoki many other large rivers, complete with their tributaries and catchment areas. The preserve, something like ninety kilometres long, extends beyond the

spruce and pine limits. The national park encloses open groups of fells, endless forests, and huge areas of open aapa mires. The large dimensions of Lemmenjoki National Park are supplemented by those of the wilderness over the Norwegian frontier adjoining the park. Trackless Finnmarksvidda, with its fell birches and open heaths, continues for another hundred kilometres or so in Norwegian territory. A tract of Norwegian wilderness 1,400 square kilometres in area and inhabited by thousands of reindeer has likewise been preserved for posterity as Øvre Anarjokka National Park. This area, together with Lemmenjoki National Park, forms a nature conservation area more than 4000 square kilometres in extent. The dimensions of this from east to west are 100 kilometres and from south to north 90 kilometres — good distances by any standards.

On the Norwegian side there are only scant Scots pine forests in the valleys of the rivers Anarjohka and Skiehttšamjohka. The spruce occurs in the form of a single, isolated forest far beyond the timberline.

The lichen-carpeted fell heaths and open fell birch forests which have been spared the depredations of the autumnal moth (cf. p. 241) on the Norwegian side are in pristine condition. Practically two-thirds of Øvre Anarjokka National Park is taken up by groves of birches.

On the Norwegian side of the reindeer fence erected along the frontier there exists another world. The fell

218

summits with their caps of pale lichens stand out even more clearly once the first snow has fallen on them. Even if old photographs were not available showing the luxuriant lichen growths that existed in the valley of the Vaskojoki before the Finnish reindeer underwent a population explosion, one would assume the frontier to separate two different ecosystems. Even satellite photographs clearly show the difference in the condition of the reindeer pastures on the two sides of the fence.

What we may for convenience term the Lemmenjoki-Øvre Anarjokka national park area is not only large but also exceedingly peaceful. This is partly because hiking has for long been concentrated on a very small part of its eastern sector. On both sides of the border the intention is to make the protected area even bigger. Norway's national park programme drafted in 1986 includes a proposal to extend the Øvre Anarjokka National Park far north of its present limits. On the Finnish side in Enontekiö commune there is an area earmarked on the so-called regional plan for annexing to Lemmenjoki National Park. This new area would enclose, among other exciting formations, extensive fields of sand dunes.

A FELL-LOVER'S PARADISE

Most popular with hikers is the area in the vicinity of the Viibus and Marastaktuoddarak fells, which are thrust apart by the River Leämmi (Lemmenjoki in Finnish) valley. These fells belong to the granulitic region which, starting at Saariselkä in the southeast, continues right up to Paistunturi fell at Utsjoki, in the extreme northern part of Finnish Lapland. Fifteen fell summits attain an altitude of over 500 metres, and the mightiest fell, Morgam-Viibus, fails to reach the 600 metre elevation by just one metre. The fell tops curve away in a graceful arc covered with dwarf shrub heaths over which the backpacker can maintain a good average speed without the presence of mosquitos or gnats. Here the lower slopes are blanketed by fell birch, the deeper-lying valleys with Scots pine forests. Areas of scree, or other obstacles to the rambler, are rare. Notable exceptions are the ravines of the rivers Leämmi and Vaijoki.

IN THE WAKE
OF MIGHTY FORCES

The River Leämmi valley, cutting through an otherwise gently undulating fell upland, is an intriguing sight. It is at its most spectacular as it winds away from the brink of Pushko-oaivi under an evening sun, the shadows clearly revealing the depth of the fifteen kilometre long ravine.

The River Leämmi valley was created in a rift between segments of bedrock, which happened to be in the same direction as the progress of the continental ice sheets during the last Ice Age. A visitor will find it fairly easy to discover signs of the various stages through which the valley passed during its formative epochs. In this region the ice sheet, moving up from the southwest and continuing towards the northeast, was compressed between the Viibus and Marastaktuoddarak fells. At the glacial melting stage, a tongue of ice remained in the

valley long after the upper slopes were exposed to the sun. Large meltwater rivers flowing down the margins of this tongue accumulated gravel masses between the slopes and the ice sheet to provide a convenient crossing place for the hikers of the twentieth century. Terraces clad in Scots pines indicate the position of the ice margin. Since the bed of the valley was occupied by a thick layer of ice, gravel was unable to reach it. After the ice melted, the large hollows it left became deepwater lakes.

Meltwaters thundering down into the valley from the fell summits carved out large grooves in the slopes and eventually reached the level of the ice tongue in the valley bottom. When the ice finally melted and the meltwaters trickled to a stop the mouths of many of the rivers remained 'hanging' high up on the sides of the valley. These hanging river mouths are now occupied by small waterfalls as the water descends as though from a high shelf to the level of the valley bottom. Three of these permanent waterfalls shower down from Viibus fell into the rugged mass of boulders fringing Lake Ravadasjavri.

The largest of the hanging rivers is the Ravadasjohka, whose multi-stepped, dashing Ravadaskordsi rapids with their total descent of several dozen metres during the spring floods is a very impressive sight indeed. The Ravadasjohka river valley in its upper reaches greatly pre-dates the last Ice Age and its sides have become obliquely eroded rather than steep. When the continental ice had deepened the Leämmi valley the river suddenly realised it was being left stranded high up the rocks, and so towards the end of the Ice Age it began to erode out the canyon now occupied by the Ravadaskordsi rapids. In order to protect this spectacular landform from wear and tear due to eager sightseers, the National Board of Forestry has constructed steps and safety rails in the steeper, more susceptible, places.

The lower reaches of the River Leämmi acquired a 10-kilometre long esker (a ridge-like formation) deposited by the river originating at the melting glacier head. The hiking trail from Njurgalahti follows this esker, at times keeping to its top, at others skirting the steep gravel hills that it made.

The achievements of the Ice Age can also be observed in the high fell uplands. While these parts of Lapland have not since the Ice Age been inundated by the sea, as has a large part of southern Finland, the fells Viibus and Marastaktuoddarak have once lain partly under water. Since the edge of the melting ice curved away towards the southwest of the fells, between the fells and the glacier ice lakes composed of meltwater became dammed in place. The waters flowing out of these washed over the eskers and at the saddle points frequently carved a crossing channel which even now is easy to discern. Numerous ice lakes were formed at the different stages of the melting of the glacier and these were in general of a short-term nature. In one particular period this kind of ice lake occurred in the headwaters of the River Miessejohka. Its bank can be made out today on the south side of Korhosenoja at an altitude of 395 metres. The waters of the lake poured out into the Morgamoja stream. At the edges of the tongues of ice lying in the valleys flowing water eroded and accumulated on the slopes of fells material to form fluted channels, embankments, and shelves. Many of these were created one below the other during the melting of the ice. The fluted channels resemble nothing so much as a set of permanent waves in the contours of the map. Examples of them are to be seen on many of the local fells.

VIRGIN FORESTS AND ANCIENT FELL CHAINS

Aside from its magnificent scenery and diversity of geological formations, the Leämmi valley also offers views of splendid forests. Probably nowhere else in the north are there such massive Scots pines.

According to history, all roads originally lead to Rome, the hub of commerce and culture. On the contrary, in this region today all the rivers lead away from the Lemmenjoki fell chains, the centre of the open wilderness. Many mighty rivers have their origin here, passing from Lapp country into two seas and three countries. On the international border, the River Skiehttsamjohka, which later becomes the Anarjohka, and still later the Deädnu, finds its way to the Arctic Ocean which, of course, lies not only north of Finland but north of Norway too. The famous Deädnu salmon brave this river as far as its source in order to spawn. By contrast the Fasku, Leämmi and Avveel rivers head for the Barents Straits via Lake Anar and the River Patsjoki. The southern part of the fell chain produces the headwaters of the rivers Kitinen and Ounasjoki which eventually wind up, camouflaged as the Kemijoki, in the Gulf of Bothnia. This forms part of the Baltic Sea. The common place of origin of all these rivers is a mighty plateau which underlies most of the national

Vast untouched Scots pine forests are included in Lemmenjoki National Park between the rivers Fasku and Leämmi.

Martti Rikkonen

park. In this mosquito and gnat paradise limitless flat areas of birch forests alternate with long rows of treeless bogs and fens, in the centre of each of which a brook flows. Among the low fell birches grow thick Scots pines whose multiplicity of branches in the generous space available has become wide and dense, rather like a giant witch's broom. The standing dead birch trees are a constant reminder of the large-scale destruction caused in the 1960s by the autumnal moth, a species of looper (or span-worm, as they say in North America). From the bases of each tree numerous fresh shoots have already sprung. A new fell birch forest is thus in the making.

The bog lines fringing brooks in many places spread out to become open aapa mires with alternating wet and dry areas. In the centre of the wetter mires the bean goose and whooper swan find the nesting peace they need. During the breeding season one is not permitted to walk on Navgosjeäggi mire at all.

At Repokaira, on the park's southern border the spruce forests are still common, but in the northern part of the park they are rare. Coming over the River Riebanjohka they have shrunk to fragments of forests which here and there stand out as blue masses ensconced in the fells and seemingly fighting shy of one another. The trees rise to a great old height above the birch groves as black-coated, needle sharp "candle spruces".

HAZY BLUE FELLS

Many a hiker who has walked to the top of Morgam-Viibus has been intrigued by the view west. Behind the 30-kilometre wide chain of fells rises a narrow line of crags which appear to form a bastion against Norway.

Hannu Hautala

The carrion-eating raven is the archenemy of hunters who set snares for game birds.

Lemmenjoki National Park

Inari and Kittilä. 2,800 km².
Established 1956, extended 1971 and 1982.
Under National Board of Forestry management.

Connections: Roads skirt the national park on the northern and southeastern sides and it is possible to enter the park via the road to the village of Lisma. The bus goes along the eastern side of the park, to the village of Njurgalahti and at Njurgalahti the 14 km long trail begins to the centre of Lake Ravadasjavri. In summer there is a regular motor boat service to Lake Ravadasjavri and Kultahamina.

Services: From Lake Ravasjavri marked circular trails (2 km and 23 km) alongside which there are camping sites. A few unlocked cabins. At Njurgalahti, accommodation in house, holiday village, as well as other services.

Maps: Outdoor maps 1:100 000 "Lemmenjoki" and "Inari—Menesjärvi".

Further information: National Board of Forestry, Inari District Office, tel. 9697-11 951 (Ivalo).

The dark and mysterious colour of these, the "blue mountains" is due not only to the shadows cast by the evening sun, but also to the rock of which they are composed. The Skiehttsamtuoddarak fells are composed of alkaline amphibolite, a tongue-twisting term which, however, is full of meaning for the botanist as it implies something special in the way of vegetation.

The Lemmenjoki region is generally barren. Only here and there has anything remotely resembling a dense tangle of scrub formed in a gully or on a river or brook delta. In this scrubby birch forest wild red currant compete with willows. Globe flowers, cranesbill, a thistle Cirsium helenioides, and Polemonium caeruleum enrich the habitat with their colours during the flowering season. This kind of floral oasis occurs at Kultahamina where the River Leämmi drains into Lake Morgamjavri.

While Lemmenjoki National Park stretches over the Scots pine and spruce limits, it does not, however, reach as far as the tundra proper. If he feels frustrated in this respect, the rambler in the westernmost sector of the national park may conjure up the proper tundra atmosphere by hiking across the Skierreoaivi and Peäldotuoddar fellscape. Despite their names, these do not rise particularly high above their surroundings, but they are covered by flat, open, fell heaths. HO

Nordic Gems

Although none of the more precious gemstones are known to exist in Finland, we are relatively well endowed with other beautiful minerals suitable for making jewellery. The range of attractive stones varies from helsinkite, named after the capital itself, to the minerals of Lapland. Several places in Finland are famous for their gemstones and minerals, but jewels of nature can be found in many other parts of the country as well. When one is out and about, it is worth keeping an eye open on rocky shores, in gravel pits and where soil has been disturbed. Vigilance can be especially rewarding in rainy weather, because the colours of stones show better when they are wet.

Pegmatite granite, which occurs virtually everywhere in Finland, can be very rich in attractive minerals. This is a coarsely crystalline light and often reddish rock, which occurs in veins and is clearly distinguishable from the surrounding stone. Pegmatite often contains quartzes, garnets, beryl and minerals containing many rare elements. Extensive bodies of pegmatite are sometimes quarried for the feldspar which they contain (and which is used by the ceramics industry), and these quarries can be real treasure chests for the mineral collector. One such quarry near Kuortane provides jewellery manufacturers with high-quality varieties of quartz. One of these, a brownish, completely transparent smoky quartz, is of superb quality. The same quarry has also yielded pink, blue, yellow and striped quartzes. Deep-green tourmaline and transparent beryl crystals, both of gemstone quality, have been found in the same place.

Many other beautiful minerals have been found in the South Ostrobothnia region in which Kuortane lies. One of them, a charming red rhodonite, sometimes with effectively offsetting dark inclusions, is found near

Ylistaro in an old iron mine.

A beautiful green chromium diopside, sometimes almost transparent, is found in Outokumpu in eastern Finland. When a spherical piece of this stone is polished, it can produce an interesting phenomenon, a glow of light that apparently comes from beneath the surface. Outokumpu's treasures also include uvarovite, a

1

2

3

1. As its name suggests, smoky quartz is a smoky brown transparent mineral that can be polished into pretty gemstones.

2. Spectrolite from Ylämaa in south-eastern Finland is a very popular gem mineral used to make a wide range of jewellery and ornamental articles.

3. The main minerals found in the granulite zone of Lapland are quartz, feldspar and garnet. Red almandine garnets, also from Lapland, are among the most beautiful gemstones.

4. Green chromium diopside from Outokumpu is much in demand as a raw material for ornamental articles.

5. Jaspers of several colours are found in Lapland. The green variety pictured comes from Kittilä.

brilliant green variety of garnet.

A young couple from Sodankylä were hiking in the Pelkosenniemi district in summer 1985 when the woman, who had been bitten by the minerals bug, spotted an unusual violet-coloured stone in a streak in a hillside cliff. The stone turned out to be amethyst, a variety of quartz. When she found more of the stones in the area, she filed a claim and obtained the landowner's permission to extract minerals.

Amethyst has been found in the area in clusters weighing tens of kilogrammes and also as very large individual crystals. Most of the material is opaque and rather valueless, but some crystals — or at least parts of them — are of such high quality, transparent and deep violet in colour that they are suitable for processing into gemstones. The finest are as superb as top-quality stones from abroad. However, such gems are not produced without a lot of work. Each crystal has to be laboriously extracted from the surrounding rock and then carried to the nearest road.

Cordierite, which changes colour when it is viewed from different perspectives, topaz, beryl, potash feldspar, graphic

4

growth lamellae in the crystal reflecting the light that strikes them. These lamellae or layers correspond to the changing composition of the crystal. They were created by fluctuations in temperature and pressure as the crystal was being formed and their thickness is only of the same order of a light wavelength.

Quite apart from the beauty of its landscape, Lapland is also outstanding for the wealth of minerals hidden beneath its surface. Prospectors panning for gold there may well find a consolation prize in the form of almandine, a deep-red iron aluminium garnet, which at its best qualifies as a precious stone. The stones that prospectors find in their pans have already been given one stage of processing by Mother Nature herself. As the brittle and inconsistent crystals have been washed down rivers with gravel, the weaker and inconsistent parts have been worn away. What remains is often a flawless gemstone ready for cutting and polishing.

Another mineral sometimes found by gold prospectors is corundum. This is generally opaque, sometimes a delicate reddish colour, but mostly grey or dark brown. Some polished pieces produce a beautiful starlike glow. However, these "stars of Lapland", are very rare, because the phenomenon manifests itself only on the rounded surface of a corundum polished at precisely the right angle in relation to the structure of the crystal, and most of the crystals are of too poor quality to be used as gemstones.

Lapland's other mineral treasures include Kittila's dark-red jasper quartz and red-white striped jasper breccia, both of which can be worked to make various ornamental items. Jaspers of several colours, including yellow and green, are also frequently found as loose stones almost everywhere in Lapland. A lump of jasper can be easily recognized by its smooth, rounded surfaces.

An amethyst find in Lapland provides a good example of how a formerly unknown wealth of minerals can come to light when a collector has a sharp eye — and a lot of luck. MV

granite, many other minerals and beautifully coloured and structured stones starting with common granite can be a joy to the eye when they assume their most attractive forms. However, it should be remembered that stones and minerals can be the result of a development that has taken perhaps billions of years. Think before you chip a beautiful stone out of a piece of rock. It can easily shatter, and perhaps you can capture its beauty just as well with a camera.

Finland's most important gemstone is undoubtedly spectrolite, a variety of labradorite mainly found in south-east Finland in areas where rapakivi, a coarse, well-weathered, red granite, is common. When cut and polished the right way, this greyish and completely opaque stone comes into its own, reflecting all the colours of the spectrum in the same way as a dove's neck or a butterfly's wing. This intriguing play of colours is produced by the thin

5

Lapland Gold

The 19th century saw numerous gold rushes of varying duration in many parts of the world, including Finnish Lapland. The lure of the precious metal drew hundreds of thousands to California, the Klondike and Australia. No such massive numbers were involved in Lapland, but at the height of the rush as many as five hundred were seeking their fortunes on the banks of the River Ivalojoki.

When news that gold had been found in Lapland spread throughout the then grand duchy and to the rest of the Russian Empire, Finland was in the grip of a severe famine that had lasted several years, and the government's coffers were empty. The rich goldfields of California had been found only a couple of decades earlier and now hopes of a new El Dorado behind the Arctic fells was kindled in the authorities' minds.

Officialdom took swift action. A handsome building, the Crown Goldfield Station, was erected near the river and the country's best geologists, together with inspectors and gendarmes, were despatched to the area. Their tasks included assigning claims to prospectors, inspecting their operations and buying gold on behalf of the government. The liveliest summer in the canyon through which the river flows was in

1871, when nearly 500 eager prospectors were hard at work on their claims. According to official statistics, their total haul came to 56 kilogrammes of gold. Once the most lucrative and easiest places had been scoured, without any huge fortunes being made, the rush tailed off. A couple of decades later, even the authorities had lost interest and gone away.

The search for the mother lode

Another search for gold began in Laanila around the turn of the century. This time, interest focused on gold seams in rocks rather than on placer deposits in rivers. A certain Dr. J.J. Sederholm, who was then head of the Geological Research Institute, played an instrumental role. His studies in Lapland led to the establishment of several companies intent on finding gold veins in the bedrock. Deep holes were drilled at several sites and some gold-bearing structures were discovered. Indeed, some of the samples contained incredibly high concentrations of gold, but present-day research methods place their origin in a doubtful light.

Mechanization

The search for placer gold resumed in the 1920s. Now, the prospectors were large companies relying on machines. The two biggest of them imported steam-driven machines and began using them to wash placer gravel on the rivers Sotajoki and Tolosjoki. They found little gold and both had to give up a couple of years later when their share capital was exhausted.

Lemmenjoki

A minor gold rush on the River Lemmenjoki flourished in 1946-51, with as many as 150 men digging on their claims during the summer in the peak years. Some of them stayed on after the others had left, and their names have become part of Lapland's folklore as "lifers". Only one, Heikki Pihlajamäki, is still there, working his claim on the River Miessijoki all year round. The others have all gone, either to the towns and cities or — in many cases — to the big bonanza in the sky.

Yet another rush

The latest of Lapland's gold rushes began at the end of the 1970s and is still in progress. It was sparked off when the price of gold soared from under $200 an ounce in 1978 to more than four times that in 1981.

Renewed interest in Lap-land's gold was part of a world-wide phenomenon. A couple of hundred claims were staked, mainly in places that had already been worked over in earlier years. The high price of gold made it a reasonable proposition to fine-comb what had once been combed. Most of the new prospectors had modern equipment, excavators and mechanical diggers, to help them, but most still relied on traditional methods, which did not require major investment.

Today's hikers can still see reminders of the various gold rushes along many rivers and streams, where decaying cabins and moss-clad mounds of stones are monuments to the work of bygone generations. The old buildings on the River Ivalojoki and those (now restored) at Ritakoski, rusted parts of mechanical excavators and the gaping shafts of empty mines are proof that the halcyon days of gold mining are history. The people who lugged machines weighing many tonnes into the wilderness really believed in gold. And bearded men hard at work with their pans on the banks of brooks and streams show that new chapters are still being written in the history of gold prospecting every day.

Now, a tourist attraction

The same gold fever that infected prospectors in the old days and inspired them to tackle seemingly insurmountable difficulties nowadays strikes tourists, who grasp the washing pans just as eagerly. Perhaps, if they are lucky, they will see a large nugget glittering in the pan! Folklore has it that nuggets as big as a reindeer's shoulder have been found in Lapland in the past.

Gold has been dug at Tanka-vaara for 50 years. The earliest prospectors came from the nearby village of Purnumukka and included one character called Aslak, who walked on crutches. Aslak had a dream about finding gold in a certain place near the hill called Tanka-vaara. He went to the place — and found gold! Tankavaara has had many ups and downs since then. In the 1970s, it entered a new phase of existence when it became a tourist attraction, where anyone who wants to try can, for a fee, look for gold. Some find it, too.

The Tankavaara tourist attraction was the brainchild of two Lemmenjoki veterans, Niilo Raumala and Yrjö Korhonen, who staked a claim and built a washing unit, which tourists could rent during the summer months. Several other entrepreneurs have since gone into business in Tankavaara, which has become a tourist attraction with an international reputation.

Background information on gold panning is on offer in the Tankavaara Gold Museum, which has collected a valuable fund of historical material dealing with the various gold rushes in Lapland. The few specks of gold dust, or even a tiny nugget, that one has found increase greatly in value when one finds out what enormous trouble men were willing to go to in the hope of finding gold in those bygone days.

Gold panning competitions

The major annual event in the Lapland goldfields is the Gold Championship, which has been held at Tankavaara every year since 1974.

At first the event was merely a Finnish championship and more a festival for gold prospectors and local inhabitants. However, interest grew so much as the years went by that in 1977 the first World Championships were held. That was the beginning of a process of internationalization. Nowadays, the World Championship venue changes every year, with willing hosts in many parts of the world.

Thus a trivial gold find in Finland gave birth to a major international event, because the competition rules originally drawn up in Tankavaara are still used wherever the event is arranged. IS

Reijo Juurinen

Pellervo Kankainen came to the Lapland goldfields immediately after the Second World War. This picture was taken during his last summer there; he drowned in autumn 1980. He never accumulated a fortune. "I don't want to dig gold, it's enough for me to be able to sleep on top of it," he used to say.

THE MUOTKATUNTURI FELLS

Straddling the borders of Inari and Utsjoki communes, on the south side of the road connecting Kaamanen with Karigasniemi, stand a number of very attractive fell crowns girded by distance in a blue haze. These will be visible, at least intermittently, even through the windows of a car or bus travelling along the road. If one cares to step out of one's car and to walk up a fell at the roadside, one will be able to appreciate the beauty of the scene at leisure: a sweeping area of fells with many summits and lines of eskers, a wilderness worthy of exploration. Strangely enough, most hikers have only a very hazy impression of the fell chains, which include such gems as the Muotkatunturit, the subject of this section.

Ville Halikainen/LKA

The Muotkatunturi fells lie on the borderline between Finland and Sweden. This area is completely uninhabited. From south (the River Vaskojok) to north it spans four or five leagues (50 km), while its width from west (the River Inarijoki) to east (Lake Muddusjärvi) is about the same. The Muotka area covers a couple of thousand square kilometres and in this entire area there are no permanent settlements, apart from along the roadsides and rivers.

In the uninhabited fell land wilderness of Muotka Man's handiwork is manifest only in a few unlocked huts, the reindeer fence running along the commune boundary, one or two roundup stockades, and the border guard posts.

THE MUOTKATUNTURI FELL CHAIN

The Muotkatunturi fells are high and dry, the scenery very undulating, the higher ground devoid of trees, and the lower elevations clothed in fell birch woods. Peatlands are sparse here, and generally located in the vicinity of the handful of brooks and streams down which water flows out of this district. The streams and rivers give an impression of being constantly in full spate, but the water in fact is quite shallow. Only at Peäldujuuha in the northeastern sector are the rivers so wide and deep that a boat is necessary.

The fringes of brooks in places are a tangle of scrub, but beaten reindeer paths are abundant, providing a convenient thoroughfare even through the densest growth. Altitude variations are small, the roadside being at an elevation of 200 metres above sea level, the highest peaks not quite touching the 600 metre mark. When approaching the Inarijoki, one descends to below the 200 metre contour, and the Vaskojoki at its mouth lies at something like 150 metres above sea level.

From the map one notices that the Muotka area is supplied with very few water bodies. The main ones lie in the area's heartland, taking the form of brooks flowing down gullies between the fells, which collectively form a landscape known in these parts as 'skaidi'. There is only one lake of any size, and this is the Peäldujavri of the Lapps and Peltojärvi of the Finns. In actual fact there are about a hundred other small lakes and pools, most of them concentrated in the eastern and south-eastern sectors, which dominate the scenery. There are plenty of water bodies in the northwestern quarter as well, since this area is a watershed where the tributaries and minor rivers and brooks running into both the Keilla and Inarijoki rivers originate.

HIGH SUMMITS

As we have observed, the Muotkatunturi fells do not rise to any great height, no single crown even reaching 600 metres. The highest peak is called Koarvikodds (Käyräkynsi), which attains 590.3 metres. The other three highest fells in the area are Peäldoaivi (567.2 m), Kalgoaivi

(563 m), and Avdsegasoaivi (just under 550 m).

With the normal altitude of the water bodies and peatlands being something like 300 metres, even the region's highest peaks fail to impress the onlooker. Only Koarvikodds manages to thrust up by as much again above Lake Mukkaslompolo. For example, Peäldoaivi actually juts up less than 300 metres above Lake Peäldujavri, despite the impression of loftiness conveyed by the almost vertical plunge of its southeastern face.

What the Muotkatunturi fells lack in stature they make up for in sheer numbers, so that the final impres-

sion is of a picturesque fell cluster. This undulating fell scenery constitutes Lapland at its best.

MUOTKA WILDLIFE

Only the very edges of the Muotka region are clothed in Scots pine forests in which lichen heathlands are roofed over by a rather sparse covering of old trees. Pine also grows along the Vaskojoki and Inarijoki. The deeper one plunges into the fells, the scarcer the Scots pine becomes, with the centralmost valleys of this region populated almost unvaryingly by fell birch. Isolated pines

stand out as dark smudges on the slopes right up at the northern end of the river valleys. On the warmer, south-facing slopes, the birches are so tall and sturdy that the hiker can only stand and stare in wonderment.

The uplands consist of open, bare areas with a scattering of dwarf shrubs and smaller plants. Rock-strewn slopes are also commonplace, but are no problem for the walker, as the fragments of stone tend to be flat and shale-like. Exposed bedrock dapples the crowns of many of the higher fells. Most of the fell lands consist of bare areas dissected by bush or shrub fringed brook valleys. There is a noteworthy absence of Scots pines, making conditions a bit more difficult in wet weather and in winter, as there is nothing to use for firewood. The hiker has to be satisfied with green birchwood and dried juniper bushes. The latter, which make admirable fire lighters, are particularly common near peatlands.

Rivers here are relatively well stocked with fish, and the terrestrial fauna is also interesting, including everything from otters to brown bears, ravens to whooper swans, and willow grouse to golden eagles. Especially in years of high lemming populations, one cannot help but be aware of the presence of large numbers of owls. Naturally in such a landscape, a wheeling rough-legged buzzard overhead with its piercing cry is almost a permanent fixture.

KOARVIKODDS

Koarvikodds, the area's highest fell, dominates the scenery for five kilometres or so on the southwestern side of Lake Peäldujavri. It stands alone slightly to one side and has a more craggy outline than any of the other fells. Especially when viewed from the south, it seems to be lying on its side. The western slope rises very gently but the eastern side is a precipitous cliff.

Koarvikodds (= "curving claw") is worthy of its name, having the shape of a trough viewed end on, a bold design that is without equal in the Muotka region. It is a cold and barren fell. It has no smile and offers no comfort. Its greyish-blue scree strewn sides bestow a sombre appearance on it; the shattered bedrock at the crown slanting towards the southeast looks particularly forbidding. It is as though it bore some sort of a grudge against its surroundings. But if you have the time, go right up to the summit, to the edge of that mighty

'trough'.

The climb is far from difficult unless one attempts to scale the eastern slope. Only near the higher peak is it necessary to cross piles of broken rocks, after which you come out on the bare top which is of smooth, solid rock. When you reach the summit you suddenly see the reason for the fell's sloping profile. During some ancient movement of the Earth the piles of shattered stone have been thrust up and placed on a slant, so that they are now more vertical than horizontal.

Sitting on the rather severe fell summit you can see out in all directions over charming scenery. The almost perpendicular eastern flank of the fell's nearest neighbour is reflected in the waters of Peäldujavri; looking across from Koarvikodds the eastern slope is a formidable, solid wall. In the north from Soarvekielas to Honkavuoma there is a chain of fells of approximately similar height which from the western edge curls like a ruff.

Northwest of Koarvikodds the scenery becomes so picturesque that many people, even non-artists, feel an urge to take up a brush and palette. A line of six or seven spaced out fells gives the appearance of different coloured layers. Close by lies Kalgoaivi, with its two summit brooks, brownish grey, almost right at one's feet. Green sloped, broken ridged Urrek, and behind it Urroaivi, faithfully mimic the shapes of Kalgu's summits and slopes. And then in the distance as far away as one can see, at about three leagues, smoky grey sacred Ailigas is outlined against the sky. Towards the west and southwest one can also make out gracefully undulating chains of fells. The highest of these are the rounded-topped Kaisavarri fells some one and a half leagues away. Kaisavarri and Jorba-Kaisavarri reach 544.6 metres.

PEÄLDUJAVRI AND PEÄLDOAIVI

Lake Peäldujavri is located slightly over a league away from the main road, right under the Peäldoaivi fell. This is no exaggeration — it really does lie at the foot of the fell, since the latter rises straight off the lake's northern shore, its steep face strewn with rocks. Nowhere does the side of Peäldoaivi drop precipitously but it is so steep that virtually no-one in their right mind would dream of going up it. The lower slopes are densely clothed in thickets of shrubs and long-trunked fell birches which make the going very difficult along the lake shore.

The rambler would do best to follow the trail, which itself stays close to the river's course, to the place at which one Lahtinen has built a small cabin and then gradually turn right right under Lake Harrijärvi, following the brook valleys plunging down the fell. It is best to climb up to the bare fell top where there are plenty of level fell heaths to make walking a pleasure.

Peäldoaivi has two high summits, together with a whole bevy of lower peaks popping up in various direc-

The unusually coloured Lappish violet seeks shade from the sun's heat and shelter from the wind by snuggling under other herbs or boulders.

Reijo Juurinen

The redwing, which builds its nest close to the ground, sometimes chooses imaginative sites.

Hannu Hautala

means 'a loop'. The Kiella waterway in fact seems to be a loop just thrown down on to the fell chain.

The Kiella and its small tributaries for the most part flow through birch woods topped by bare summits. Sometimes the flow is rather gentle, but elsewhere — where the gullies are steep — the water broils and foams its way along. Scots pines appear on the eastern slope of the Kiella valley at Urroaivi and Sudenulvomatsobma, but they do not form forests until much further downstream, where the waters of the Radnojohka and Stuorravdsi, flowing from the west, join the current.

STUORRAVDSI

One of the most interesting sights in the Muotka country is the Stuorravdsi rift valley. Some people opine that this has the dimensions of the Kevo canyon (see p. 244) and, while this may be a slight exaggeration, this, the mightiest ravine in the Muotkatunturi region, is certainly worth exploring.

This gorge is at its deepest and narrowest in its central section, near Keätkepass, where the northern bush-covered flank rises to about 200 metres and the southern wall is a solid wall of rock over 100 metres high. This more than 100 metre deep, often steep, gorge continues for a considerable distance. Especially charming are the six clearwater pools that run, like a string of beads, along the bottom of the ravine.

In places the horns of the gorge are pulled out, so that the distance between them is increased and their steepness decreased. Before long, they close in on each other again to form an even narrower pass. Right at the upper reaches of the brooks at the western end of the gorge two fell sides thrust out towards each other in the form of a series of narrow steps. Avdsegasoaivi and Njurgum with their grey slopes form an appropriate 'Devil's gate' to the western end of the pass. But surprisingly the gorge comes to an abrupt end here. Fell slopes surround it, one to the north, the other to the south, and the end of the ravine spreads out into an area of flattish peatlands dotted with fells and small lakes.

MUOTKA HIKING ROUTES

No marked trails exist in the Muotka area, but the area in general is so well defined that the hiker is able to find his way around with ease; the same goes for the skier. Only rarely are the slopes too steep to climb or the jumbles of boulders too treacherous to clamber over with a full back pack. The same goes for the rather infrequent waterways — the Kiella and Peäldujuuha in their lower reaches.

The Muotka area can be highly recommended as a place for trekking and rambling for those possessing the requisite stamina and skills at surviving in the wilderness; and above all, for those who appreciate the tranquillity and loneliness of the wilds. KKe

tions and between the peaks there are numerous large saddle-like depressions. In the northwest the chain of fells continues with, however, the highest peaks (Toanganoaivi and Jeägeloaivi) standing only a little above 450 metres, despite their rather severe countenance.

From Peäldoaivi the best view is to be had over to the northwest, and conversely in the eastern and southeastern sectors where the village of Kaamanen and Muddusjärvi lake are distinguishable from their surroundings. This almost right-angled sector also presents a mosaic of pools and smaller lakes gleaming proudly when one arrives at the right time of day under the proper lighting conditions.

KIELLAJOHKA

The Kiellajohka (Kielajoki) is the main thoroughfare through the Muotka area and a route into the heart of the fell lands down a wooded valley. The river's catchment area encompasses the greater part of the Muotkatunturi fell chain. The word "Kiella" in the Same language

The Arctic Lemming

The only indigenous vertebrate species unique to Fennoscandia is a tiny creature called the Norway lemming. Its range extends from southern Norway to northernmost Lapland and then eastwards into the Kola Peninsula. There are none to the east of the White Sea, where, however, the Siberian lemming and another species with a distinctive collar-like band around its neck are well established. The Norway lemming's limited range has led experts to speculate that it is a relict species that survived the Ice Age by spending the winters on the unfrozen coast of Scandinavia or on mountain peaks rising above the ice sheet.

A colourful little rodent

The Norway lemming's multicoloured coat sets it apart from our other small rodents, which have plain coats. It is a member of the vole family, whose dark fur is usually good for camouflage purposes, but can one say that about the Norway lemming's coloration? Well, yes and no. In summer, and especially in autumn, it blends well with the background on Arctic heaths and rocky hill slopes, but has to cross white snow plains during its spring migrations. However, ostentatious colours can also be a warning that an animal is aggressive while it is on its migration, and although this is unlikely to deter large predators it may work on some of the smaller ones.

The Norway lemming is most famous for its periodic migrations, about which the most remarkable beliefs have taken root in the popular imagination. Before examining their migrations in any further detail, however, it would be appropriate to take a look at what they eat, because that has a lot to do with their wanderings.

Moss and sedge on the menu

Norway lemmings spend their winters on dry heathland and rock-strewn slopes, where they eat whatever parts of sedges and grasses that have remained green. They also eat moss but are fussy about this and usually stick to types like Dicranum and Polytrichum. They never touch Sphagnum. Another essential requirement is generally a thick protective blanket of snow. When the snow thaws in spring, the lemmings' winter burrows are flooded out and the animals head for their summer pastures. When their numbers are low — which is the normal situation — they probably spend the summer close to their winter homes, perhaps along the banks of the nearest stream or on the edge of a patch of bog. Their summer diet consists of sedges and grasses and, to a certain extent, mosses.

Thus the lemming changes its habitat to suit the season. This is obviously dictated by necessity, because its winter grounds are usually so dry in mid- and late summer that they can not provide enough fresh food. On the other hand, staying in the winter habitat even if the summer is wet would deplete the food stocks there so much that there would be little left over for winter. Short-distance migration of this kind is apparently an aspect of the animal's normal rhythm of life, although it must be conceded that we know rather little about its behaviour in the periods between conspicuous migrations.

In years of major migrations, hikers in Lapland can not fail to notice huge patches of ground covered in lemming droppings. The animals have adapted to food with a very low nutritional content, such as moss, but compensate for this by eating huge quantities and having fast-acting digestive systems. For all that, they do not use anything like all of the nourishment in what they eat. Other voles obtain about twice as much energy from sedges, but do not eat moss. To ensure that they get as much as they need of essential nutrients (like nitrogen and phosphorus), lemmings have to eat a lot. Their digestive systems are adapted to this rapid throughput, and

thus they waste energy and create remarkably large quantities of droppings for their size.

When lemming populations are large, they often consume food in their winter habitats so vigorously that it simply runs out. A feature of their lifestyle is that they destroy considerable quantities of plants that they do not eat. Thus Arctic heaths can look rather mutilated after years in which lemming populations explode. In particular, the development of the mossy vegetation under the snow in the places where they spend the winter depends on the level of the population. A team of botanists from Oulu University have been studying moss growth in Kilpisjärvi since a major lemming migration in 1970.

Reproduction

Before a major wave of migration takes place, the lemmings must reproduce vigorously for a couple of years — also in winter — and manage to rear a high proportion of their young to maturity. This seemingly happens only when both food and snow conditions are optimal. They need a really thick blanket of snow to reproduce successfully in winter, even when food is abundantly available. Under a thick blanket of snow, the temperature remains stable around 0°C. The food situation is likely to be good if summer conditions have been good the previous summer or for several summers and moss biomass has been accumulating well. In years when there is both plenty of snow and abundant food beneath it, lemmings can reproduce even in February, when the Aurora Borealis illuminates the frost-gripped landscape.

A lemming's gestation period is three weeks. The young are weaned at two weeks and are capable of reproducing themselves at less than three weeks of age. A litter can contain as many as 11 young, although the average size is 6-8. Winter litters are generally smaller, containing 3-4. A female can bear litters every three weeks or so.

Mauri Rautkari

Strong reproduction characteristically takes place in winters preceding summers when the lemming population peaks. The population can be quite modest the previous summer, but a large number of births during the winter can fuel a considerable migration only a few months later. If the population is already fairly high at the onset of winter and reproduction is strong during it, there can be a real peak and a strong wave of migration.

What causes migrations?

Nobody has an absolutely certain answer to that question. First of all, a spring migration is of considerably shorter duration than an autumn one — only 2-3 weeks compared with as much as 2-3 months. Of course, this does not mean that an individual animal is on the move for so long, just that the phenomenon of movement can be observed during the period in question.

How long a wave of migration lasts, especially in autumn, depends on the density of the population. The biological research station in Kilpisjärvi has observed four autumn migrations. The most recent major one, in 1970, actually began in late June and lasted until well into the autumn.

By contrast, in 1978 — when the lemming population was moderate — the autumn migration did not begin until about the middle of August.

Spring and autumn migrations differ in several other respects as well. A spring migration is a sudden event triggered by natural conditions and all animals set off more or less simultaneously, but an autumn migration takes place in distinct stages. The first to depart are the breeding males. This is due to the females who, when they are no longer in heat, behave aggressively towards males wanting to mate with them. Rather than biting back, the males consider it more expedient to head for their winter grounds, where there are few lemmings in summer. The females set off once they have weaned their litter, and young individuals once they have reached the age of about 1 ½ months.

The relationship between the density of the lemming population and the duration of migrations may also indicate something about the cause of large-scale migrations. Lemming habitats, especially winter ones, are patchy rather than continuous areas. Good winter habitats are not found everywhere. The best places are soon filled, and the larger the lemming population at the end of the summer, the more there are in search of a good winter berth at the beginning of the autumn.

Peak migration years

There have been three spectacular waves of lemming migration in Finland this century. The first, and probably the largest, was in 1902-03, when the animals swept south as far as the Gulf of Bothnia coast. The next began in 1938 and saw them advance deep into central Lapland. In 1942 and 1946 they further expanded their range as far as southern and south-eastern Lapland, but the southern populations gradually disappeared after that.

Local migrations were observed in northern regions of Lapland in 1959 and 1960. The next major one began in 1970 — and actually in 1969 in some of the northernmost parts of the province — and lemmings were running down the streets of the capital Rovaniemi that autumn. In a way, the events of the preceding migration period were repeated in 1974, 1977-78 and again in 1982-83, when local populations and migrations were observed in many parts of Lapland.

It has been predicted that the lemmings born in southern Lapland during the most recent wave of migration will eventually disappear. It seems highly improbable that the populations that came into being during the last phase of migration could have lived a sedate and unobtrusive life for over two decades and then suddenly erupted in a population explosion just as the northern wanderers approached in autumn 1970. One can only guess when the next major wave of migration will begin. However, I dare to wager that the next to encompass the whole of Lapland will not begin until the next millennium, although there will certainly be local movements before that in the northern parts of the province.

I have not gone into the details of migrations in this article, because I hope that readers are already aware that lemmings do not commit suicide by plunging into the sea, and that each individual migrates alone and not in a herd. HH

The Waders' Remarkable Relationships

In the avian kingdom, monogamy is the basic form of partnership from which all other variations have evolved. A male and a female form a stable pair and retain their relationship throughout the hatching period, and often for at least part of the period until the young leave the nest. Both take turns at hatching the eggs and feeding the chicks. Faithfulness to the partner is also the general rule: if both survive the winter, they usually mate again the following spring. Thus the same

birds can nest together year after year.

Of the many species of waders Lapland, perhaps the finest example of monogamy is provided by the whimbrel, whose tittering, bubbling cry perpetually resounds across the Arctic bogs and upland heaths. Two birds, quite identical in appearance, are constantly bustling about the nesting site. If people come too near the nest, the mothers dash, neck outstretched, through the tussocks, fly agitatedly around and in ev-

ery way try to draw the intruders off. Whenever a predator like a crow or a rough-legged buzzard happens to fly over the area, the mothers join forces in a furious assault on the enemy, which soon flees. Male and female whimbrels share their family chores very fairly.

Although the basic pattern of monogamy is the same with many species, there can be considerable differences of detail. The snipe, which nests on bogs and in dense thickets of

willow scrub along streams everywhere in Lapland, practises a very nominal form of monogamy. The female can mate with several males initially, but then settles down in a partnership with only one. But when she has laid all her eggs, it is her partner's turn to sow his wild oats. He leaves his mate to hatch the eggs on her own and sets off in search of new conquests, even outside his own territory. However, just when the eggs are about to hatch, the male regains his sense of pa-

Jorma Luhta

Ruffs' silent jousting is a unique spectacle. The males have different colours and those with white collars have a special position as the "advertising signs" at the venue where the courting rituals take place.

fairly early stage and leaves the male to provide for the family alone. A good example is the black-bellied dunlin, which lives in the upland bogs of northernmost Lapland. The female's interest in looking after her young usually disappears within a few days of their having been hatched and soon after that she departs on her southward migration. The wood sandpiper and the greenshank are two other waders that follow the same established practice. The result is that as often as not there is only one parent, a male, fussing over the chicks.

Females with harems
In the cases of at least three of Lapland's waders, the male is left practically alone to look after the chicks once they have hatched. At the same time, the female has evolved into a bird that is both bigger and more ornate than the male, and she can mate with two or three partners in succession.

That the red-necked phalarope and the dotterel have reversed their traditional sexual roles has long been known. However, it is only in recent times that years of studying colour-ringed birds have begun to reveal some of the exciting details of their nesting habits.

In the closing days of May, the red-necked phalarope arrives in the bog ponds of Lapland at the end of its long migratory flight. Courting rituals are soon in full swing, and it is always the female that takes the initiative. She approaches every available male, fawningly swims rings around him and does everything she can to attract his attention. Furious battles occasionally break out between females in heat when several of them surround the same male.

Once she has conquered a male, the female red-necked phalarope jealously guards him from other females. Now, for a couple of days, the pair are inseparable, and every time she lays an egg the female leads the male to the nest. However, as soon as all the eggs have been laid, she abandons him and leaves him alone to hatch the brood. If there is still an unattached male in the vicinity, either a surplus individual or one that has lost his nest, the female is immediately ready for a new conquest and soon lays a new clutch of eggs. After that the females congregate in an idle flock and when summer is still at its height head south for their "vacation"!

As for the dotterel, it has long been known that the bird placidly hatching in brushwood on bleak hill slopes is a male. The females of this species, too, are bigamous when the opportunity presents itself: if there are free males available, she lays two clutches by two males. The difference compared with the red-necked phalarope is that a female dotterel may help, at least to some extent, to hatch the second clutch.

Polygamous males rarer
And what about the opposite trend of development, males ignoring their responsibility for their offspring and mating with several females if they get the chance? Examples of this are also known, although not among our Lapland waders. However, in some species of Arctic sandpipers such as the curlew sandpiper, which regularly migrates through Finland, the male is definitely monogamous. He excavates courting pits in his territory and entices females to them. He impregnates the females, but does nothing after that to take care of his offspring. The male departs early on his migratory trip, leaving the females and chicks to fend for themselves.

The ruff's mixed marriages
The fourth main form of partnership is one in which males and females do not enter firm partnerships. Instead, they get together only to mate, often at special courtship sites.

The best representative of this behaviour among our waders is the ruff, which is an odd bird in other respects as well. In their spring jousts, the colourful males resplendent in their handsome erectile neck feathers defend their individual little territories (a square metre or so in size) on the courting site, hopping about, bowing and puffing up their collar feathers, and occasionally skirmishing.

Colour is added to the spectacle by the fact that the males all look different — with black, yellowish, white and multi-hued collar feathers, and neck ruffs in an infinite variety of colour combinations. Some males have permanent territories of their own, whilst others go from site to site trying to occupy a permanent patch of their own on its periphery. Males with white collars are in a privileged position, because they enjoy free access to the centre of the courting site. They simply stride into a territory, irrespective of whose it is, and make out with the waiting females.

When the smaller and less colourful females appear at the courting site, the males all vie with each other to coax them. As a general rule, however, only the older and stronger worthies who hold the middle ground get to mate and those in the peripheral territories have to do without. Here, too, the white-collared males are an exception. They sometimes manage to mate while territory-holders are showing other competitors the door.

The ruffs' mating lasts but a moment and no lasting ties develop between the males and the females. A high-ranking male can mate with several females, just as a female can choose several partners on her various visits to the courting site. It is unlikely that the males even know where the nests are located, and they set off south soon after midsummer. The females do not leave until late summer.

The Temminck's stint and its double dealing
The Temminck's stint indulges in complex mating relationships that fit into none of the four categories described so far. Its nesting customs could be described as a mutual form of bigamy, which means that both the male and the female

rental responsibility. He even hatches for brief spells while the female forages for food, takes care of the first two chicks to hatch, but leaves the two others for his mate to look after. After this the partnership is dissolved, with each partner taking charge of two young. The reason for this family breakup is probably the fact that, unlike other waders, both male and female snipes feed their chicks. It is probably more convenient to have only two rather than four fledglings competing for the titbits brought to the nest.

In the cases of several other monogamous waders the female abandons her chicks at a

Tapani Räsänen

change partners between two consecutive nestings.

Hardly the size of a chaffinch, the Temminck's stint is the smallest species of wader found in Finland. It nests both on the low-lying shores of the Gulf of Bothnia and near water bodies on sandy heaths in Lapland. When it migrates back from southern climes in late May or early June, the male establishes a permanent territory, ownership of which he proclaims by means of a delicate insect-like chirping. While doing this, he either perches on the highest spot in the area, such as a rock or the top of a bush, or slowly performs a courtship flight above his territory, his wings held upwards in a V-shape and quivering and his tail feathers spread. Whenever a female enters his territory, he runs around her, eagerly chirping and flapping his outspread wings. When the female flees, he pursues her in a dizzyingly complex flight pattern.

Partnerships last a few days, during which the female lays her four eggs in one of the hollows scraped out by the male. Immediately afterwards, the female goes her own way and leaves the male to look after the nest. However, he does not get down to hatching at once, but resumes his chirping act and usually entices another female to lay her eggs in his territory. In the meantime, his first partner has found an-

The sparrow-sized Temminck's stint has very unusual mating habits. Each female mates with two males in succession and each male with two females.

other mate and laid a second clutch of eggs in his territory. A female's two clutches can be separated by no more than a few hundred metres of ground, but because some of them disappear altogether from the area after they have laid their first clutch, it is probable that the second is laid a long way away.

Thus each male impregnates two females, who lay their eggs in his territory, and each female lays a clutch in the territories of two males. The first clutch is hatched by the male and the second by the female. Each rears the chicks alone.

For this double nesting method to succeed, it is essential that a female mating for the first time choose a male who does not already have a nestful of eggs in his territory, because no bird can hatch two clutches. That nesting takes place at the same time within the loosely-knit communities, usually consisting of only a few pairs of birds, guarantees that the system generally works. However, it sometimes happens that two females lay their clutches in the territory of one and the same male, whereby one inevitably remains unhatched.

Many factors behind adaptation

Why have waders' mating customs developed in so many different directions? Why do some species adhere to traditional monogamy, whilst others have adopted variants on the theme of bigamy and polygamy?

It is impossible to give an exhaustive answer to these questions. But what is obvious in any case is that all of the various arrangements are natural selection's response to different environmental conditions and the species' different lifestyles. They must be understood in the same way as the even greater variety of adaptations involving choices of nesting places, times, numbers of eggs or egg colouration.

Since the most common pattern is one of monogamy and equal sharing of the work involved in hatching eggs and rearing young, it must be the one that suits most species best. The advantages of two birds sharing the work of looking after a clutch are obvious. First of all, it gives both the birds and their brood a better chance of surviving, because it is more difficult for an enemy to surprise a bird on a nest when the other is keeping watch nearby. In inclement weather — not uncommon in Lapland, where snow can sometimes blanket the land even in summer — two parents can take turns at hatching, whereas it would be virtually impossible for one to obtain sufficient food for itself without leaving the eggs for too long. Likewise, two birds can keep their chicks warm and defend them much better than one. Fidelity has a general advantage, too. Studies have shown that partners that have mated in previous years and are accustomed to each other's ways are more successful on average in rearing broods.

When, however, the combined benefits of those factors are slight, it may be better for one of the parents to leave the family at an early stage and either begin its southward migration or try to mate with another partner. In the former alternative, competition for food is reduced and this may be a greater advantage than two

parents sharing the work of rearing the young. Likewise, if one of the parents finds a new mate, the larger number of offspring has a clear advantage from the viewpoint of the survival of the species.

Whether the bird that is freed from parental responsibility is a male or a female depends on many factors. If, for example, terrain with abundant food and good nesting conditions is available only patchily, the territories claimed by males can vary considerably in quality. The better the territory, the greater the likelihood that a female will accept it and that a brood will be successfully reared. In order for the males that have managed to lay claim to choice territories to be able to hold onto them, they must defend them effectively. That is probably why natural selection has favoured those males that devote more time to defending their territories than to their young.

When, on the other hand, a female manages to lay two clutches of eggs in succession and is able to find a second available male, natural selection has favoured her being freed from family responsibilities, in addition to which she has developed into a bigger and more colourful bird than the male. There appear to be three factors in a line of development towards polygamous females: the food situation, the duration of the nesting period and the ratio of males to females.

Food plays a central role: a female is able to lay two successive clutches only when food is abundantly available during the egg-laying period; waders' eggs are, incidentally, very large in relation to the female's body weight. Another factor that inhibits polygamy on the part of females is the duration of the nesting period; the summer is so brief in Lapland that there is simply not enough time for most birds to lay and hatch two clutches. Nor is there much point in leaving one nest if the chance of finding a second partner is very small. In populations with a preponderance of males or where nesting losses are high, natural selection has tended to produce polygamous females. OH

The hiker wishing to hear the bluethroat's richly-nuanced song need not go all the way to Kilpisjärvi. It lives in the bogs of southern Lapland's forest zone, but it is only in the high fells further north that its pealing voice truly comes into its own. That is where the Finnish population of this species is strongest, with about ten nesting pairs per square kilometre in the Kilpisjärvi area. In small bogs, willow thickets along streams and birch groves near lakes, the population density can rise to nearly 50 nesting pairs per square kilometre.

To be able to hear the clinking of reindeer bells and rapid series of "tacs" in the male bluethroat's song, one has to head for its nesting area in early June. By listening to different males, a trained ear can recognize the calls of a good thirty Finnish birds skillfully mimicked by bluethroats. And that total takes no account of the innumerable unknown songs picked up during their winter stay in southern climes.

Founding a family

The males begin arriving in the nesting area in the last week of May. Older ones come a couple of days before those hatched the previous summer. The females migrate a little later. By the time June yields to July, most of the summer exuberance has disappeared from the males' singing and only now and then do they emit brief bursts of notes. While the singing season is at its height, however, the bluethroat can give recitals just as eagerly during the day as at night.

A nesting territory, into which a male entices a female with his songs, is between one and one and a half hectares in extent. He defends it against other intruding males, but nevertheless it is not unusual to see several in an established territory. Most of the superfluous males have not yet succeeded in finding a partner. Males that have settled in a territory of their own can still fly around well outside, sometimes going as far as a couple of kilometres.

The male is not necessarily content with one partner. When

Martti Rikkonen

Lapland's "Nightingale"

the first has settled down to hatching her eggs, the male may, if he is lucky, manage to attract another to mate with.

The birds build their nests on the ground, well concealed at the bases of birch and juniper shrubs, and sometimes beside sedge-covered hummocks. The deep nest bowls are lined with dried hair grass gathered from the forest. Egg-laying begins in the latter half of June. Each day, the female lays one dull green, delicately-patterned egg. There are generally 5-7 eggs in a clutch, with those laid later slightly smaller on average than those laid earlier.

While she is laying, the male stays close to the female. Indeed, so close that it seems as though he is guarding her. He has good reason to do so, because strange males do not hesitate to mate with a female with which they have had no earlier ties.

The female performs her two-week hatching chore without

any help whatsoever from the male. He does not even bring her food, so she must occasionally leave the nest unattended and go foraging. However, the male stays attentively near the nest and warns the female of anything that approaches it. He drops by at irregular intervals to check the situation at the nest and then gets back to his own activities. Nests with eggs in them can still be found as late as the beginning of July.

The family's brief summer

At just under two weeks of age, the fledglings leave the nest and, still unable to fly, disperse through the area around it. Only a week or two later are they able to fly well.

The young are able to fly only about six weeks after the female begins laying. That is a long time in the brief Arctic summer. Females that have left it late to begin nesting or are still feeding a second brood

have an even tougher life as summer draws to a close, because they must also find time to moult before setting off on the long flight to their winter grounds in southern parts of Asia. Thus they may begin moulting while still feeding their young. This is a double drain on their energy resources and can lessen their chance of surviving the strain of their migratory flight.

The young birds remain in the nesting area for a few weeks after their mothers have departed. They, too, moult, shedding their brightly-coloured fledgling's suits and donning the feathers of a young bird. They can spend several days in the same general area. Then one sees them scuttling along paths like mice, with only their red-bordered tails revealing what they are. Most of them have gone by early September and hikers out to admire the autumnal colour display will be very lucky to see one. HP

SAMMUTTI-JÄNKÄ

Lapland's largest bog

East of the road to Kaamanen, Utsjoki and Varanki, where the Scots pine begins to peter out, the Sammuttijänkä peatland complexity begins. The latter has an overall length of 40 kilometres and covers a surface area of practically 70,000 hectares. This complex can thus be considered Finland's largest peatland.

Sammuttijänkä is situated in the palsa mire zone, where it constitutes Europe's most extensive palsa mire. The excellent location between bare fells and forests on the fringes of the tundra and taiga attract an extremely varied avian fauna to Sammuttijänkä. There are more species of waders and waterbirds here than on any other peatland in Finland. At its most extensive the peatland opens out at the region's southern tip. This mighty peatland is divided into sections — Kiesvaaranjänkä, Sammuttijänkä, Ruoptuojanjänkä and Ravgamoorastjeggi, whose tongue-twisting names seem to pose no problem to the Lapp. These, of course, merge into one another

The male red-necked phalarope is the feminist's ideal husband: he alone looks after his progeny, the female leaving as soon as she has laid!

without any clearly defined limits. Eskers covered with birch woods are very common in the bogs of the northern sector of this region, but they do not succeed in interrupting the overall continuity of this large complexity. Only some birch woods flanking streams diminish the view of the peatlands to a size at which the human mind is able to come to grips with it.

Right on the horizon lie the distant fells. This rather brooding landscape may cause the rambler to panic, or at least make him feel rather apprehensive. This feeling is not improved by the knowledge that after forcing one's way through a greyish willow thicket hiding a brook, one discovers that the distance one has covered is negligible. One's fears are, however, groundless. The basic map is just as accurate here, too, and a league (about 10 km) is certainly neither longer nor shorter than elsewhere. The hummock ridges which support large numbers of small shrubs are rather difficult to walk along. But one can usually find a flat space in which to brew up coffee or tea.

BROWN MOSS FENS AND PALSA MIRES

The bogs and mires of this region generally have a very thin layer of peat. This is evident in the lushness of the flora and in species diversity. There are more brown moss fens than treeless Sphagnum bogs. Dry Sphagnum bogs with Scots pines characteristic of southern and central Finland are no longer found this far north. They are replaced by peaty fell heaths and depressions, and by the summits of palsa mires. Against, as it were, all nature's regulations, the main tree species here is the birch. The spruce falls behind as far south as at Saariselkä and the transitional forest Sphagnum mires are formed of birch, grey alder and willow in place of spruce.

Palsa mires occur over the entire area but their total area is rather small and their contribution to the scenery is only a local one. The vegetation of the brown moss fens is at its most luxuriant in the places where nutrient-rich bog water percolates from one peatland area to another and possibly acquires even more nutrients and oxygen through seepage off the heaths.

238

Some of the brown moss fens have a good deal of water lying on their surfaces in the form of pools. Part of the fringes of such fens consist of birch woods in which herbs and willows form a rather dense 'jungle' and whose nastiness is added to by the water that comes lapping up towards the tops of one's rubber boots. A willow, Salix mersinites grows in the form of large thickets here, its short but sturdy appearance being easy to distinguish by the reddish colouration dappling the green of its leaves.

The hiker who has no particular interest in wetland plants may well opt to keep to the sandy heaths, which are intrinsically beautiful rather than educational. Besides, walking along a well-beaten reindeer path is far easier than wallowing in a mire. Since reindeer paths criss-cross about a quarter of this area, and even the lichens are stunted and low-growing, one naturally begins to wonder how on earth these fairly sizable beasts manage to survive here. The answer is that even though winter feed appears to be minimal, there is plenty during the autumn. The birch woods are full of large Boletus mushrooms, which are available by the ton and constitute delicious, filling food by means of which to build up reserves ready for the hard times ahead.

WADER AND WATER BIRD PARADISE

The diversity of waders in Sammuttijänkä is unrivaled anywhere. The number of nesting pairs is also exceptionally high. The commonest peatland birds — green-shank, snipe, ruff — are also abundant here. The dotte-rel, broad-billed sandpiper, and the jack snipe are inhabitants of the wetter areas which in certain habitats are even commoner than the more usual peatland avian species. This is especially true in the central parts of the bog, as well as at the edges of its pools.

The red-necked phalarope forms very loose — dare one call them — 'colonies'. Around the same pool there may be a score or more of pairs. Jack snipes are also social birds and five pairs of them were once found compressed into a minute area on Kiesvaaranjänkä.

Sammuttijänkä's unusual location on the timberline near the bare areas provides it with wader species belonging to both zones. Characteristic waders of the open aapa mires are the spotted redshank and green-shank, both of which are comparatively common here. Southern species are represented by the lapwing, an immigrant from the south which is slowly on the increase, together with Finland's most northerly inclined cranes and curlews. The redshank nests in this area and while it is a relative newcomer to the peatlands of the south, its history here goes back a long way and can be explained by the close proximity of the Arctic Ocean. The purple sandpiper is expected to follow in its footsteps.

The whimbrel and golden plover are denizens of the palsa mires and fell heaths which now also nest on the boundaries of treeless Sphagnum bogs in this area. Most of the ringed plovers here nest outside the bogs on the slowly drying fringes of peatland pools in the summer heat, or even along the reindeer paths on the sandy stretches. If one wishes to encounter the dotterel, it will be necessary to climb up into the fells and to proceed to the most remote corner of these wilds, Kuorboaivi.

Among the birdlife of Sammuttijänkä one encounters the first signs of the tundra fauna. The dunlin and Temminck's stint live in low densities on the bog. Although there are few pairs, a sight of both of these is a daily occurrence. One of the most sought-after and rarest of the tundra species is the 'queen of the palsa mires', the bar-tailed godwit. Meeting this highly decorative bird with the authoritative voice for the first time is an unforgettable experience. On both the eastern and western sides very large lake basins adjoin the peatlands. Towards the east lie Lakes Sammuttijärvi and Iljärvi, which are flanked by more than 30 kilometres of boggy shore; in the west the Kiesvaaranjänkä and Ruoptuojanjänkä mires are separated from the Utsjoki road by Lakes Syysjärvi and Säyts-järvi. The presence of such large lakes in the area explains why there are so many diving ducks here. The situation in the fell birch zone is quite the opposite. The tufted and long-tailed ducks are the most abundant of the waterfowl, the common scoter being not far behind them. The velvet scoter is also reasonably common in this area, although this northern population is rather small in comparison to its Gulf of Finland counterpart. In these parts the scaup is a rarity.

Teals are the most commonly encountered diving ducks. There are numbers of mallards, while the eider is common on the large lakes. The pintail seems unable to reach the same population standards as the other species in these open treeless bogs. Although there is only a scattering of both species, the proximity of the timberline can also be gleaned from the occurrence of both smew and goldeneye. The black-throated diver nests generally on the large lakes, where also the red-throated diver can be found. The Sammuttijänkä region was originally an important breeding ground of the lesser white-fronted

The large cranberry (Vaccinium oxycoccus), found at Inari, is now very rare in Finland. Most of the cranberries growing on palsa mires belong to a much smaller species (V.microcarpum).

Lappish buntings are very common on palsa mires.

goose. Nowadays it has almost completely disappeared, the most recent sightings having taken place at Utsjoki, right next to Sammuttijänkä.

Bean geese are much rarer than they are lower down in the forested zone. But who knows whether these birds are simply staying out of sight in this area. Bean geese become very shy at the height of summer, thousands of them disappearing into the remotest reaches of the aapa mire areas in order to moult on lakes close to, or in, the birch zone. These flightless birds, the so-called 'sattaset', are able to exploit the primary production of a lake by turning it into a new complement of feathers.

Plenty of examples of this type of place to which the geese go in order to moult are known in the Kola and Ruija regions, and since the traditional destinations of these birds are right next to the Finnish border (but on the wrong side), i.e. on the southeastern side of Lake Pulmankijärvi, it seems logical to assume that the bean goose occurs on the Finnish side of the border, too. For some unknown reason, in spite of a diligent search at Utsjoki, the bean geese have not disclosed their whereabouts.

LAPPISH BUNTINGS AND WHITE-TAILED EAGLES

A large proportion of the abundant birdlife of Sammuttijänkä consists of perching birds. Far and away the commonest species here is the Lappish bunting. This bird characterises the entire region from the fell birch woods of the 'skaidi' to the open mires and palsa bogs. Common on the open mires, too, are the meadow pipit and yellow wagtail. The northern limit of the range of the whinchat and the southern limit of the red-throated pipit meet in this peatland area. Here the latter species can almost be said to be common.

The fell birch heaths harbour large numbers of bramblings, redwings, redpolls, and here and locally too fieldfares. On the Scots pine heaths there are unusually large populations of hole nesting birds like the spotted flycatcher, redstart and pied flycatcher. The less common Siberian jay, pine grosbeak and Siberian tit may remain undetected by the hiker who goes rushing forward with his head bent. In the wetter birch woods one can encounter the bluethroat which is at its densest in the willow thickets growing along brook courses. Here it is joined by the reed bunting and sometimes also by the sedge warbler. It pays to climb up to the treeless zones at higher elevations, where one can encounter the shore lark, one of the birds that will be high on the ornithologist's list of priorities. At the same time one should keep one's eyes peeled in areas covered with stones and shattered rocks for the snow bunting and ptarmigan.

In 1970 local populations of the Norwegian lemming, grey-sided vole, northern red-backed vole and root vole reached a peak, so that by July of that year birds of prey seemed to onlookers to be perpetually on the wing. How did all these red-legged buzzards and short-eared owls manage to discover this rich source of sustenance? The most vigorous reaction to the unprecedented abundance of food, however, was observed among long-tailed skuas. Even at Sammutti, where for some years the species had not be seen at all, several dozen pairs suddenly appeared. It appears that voles do not regulate the breeding populations of other predators. For instance, the hen harrier, which nests on the ground, feeds its young on the nestlings of waders and small birds, as well as on moulting passage migrants, while the merlin takes its prey in the air — a medium likely to produce few small mammals outside bats! The great grey shrike seems to depend mainly upon insects to feed both itself and its young. As one might predict, the populations of these do not seem to expand at all in 'good vole years'. The peak year — 1984 — for this species was in fact rather a poor one for vole-hunting, but by contrast was noteworthy for the wealth of insects that were flying about.

Birds of prey here include a few from the south: peregrine, goshawk and osprey. Several golden eagle territories are known here to ornithologists. When rumours were going about a few years ago that white-tailed eagles had taken up residence in the fells, there were those who laughed and doubtless others who thought about ornithologists going into straight-jackets. But little by little it was revealed that the extent to which the white-tailed eagle now breeds on inland lakes like Iijärvi and Inarijärvi had been vastly underestimated. Now it is known for sure that this huge bird not only lives in this area but also breeds regularly here — though how it manages to do so nobody knows. The start of its breeding season in March and April, when the land is still covered with snow, would appear to be the worst time of year for a species obtaining most of its food from the water, and usually salt water at that. The white-tailed eagles solve the wintering problem by migrating north to the Arctic Ocean near the warming Gulf Stream. PK

Fell Birch Pest

Sooner or later anyone who wanders in northern Lapland will come across extensive areas of "ghost forest" composed of dead fell birch. These typically occur on exposed fell summits, their white bark in tatters, whipping to and fro in the wind. In places, trees have sprouted afresh, but hundreds of square kilometres have become open tundra. Especially large areas of devastation can be seen in the Kevo Strict Nature Reserve at Utsjoki, and in Pulmankijärvi.

Such damage is caused by the larvae of a geometer, the autumnal moth *Epirrita autumnata*, which literally stripped the trees of their leaves in 1964-65. The rather drab adult moth (seen at right) flies late in the autumn (in Lapland September and October), ovipositing on birch, where the eggs remain over the winter. In spring the familiar green looper caterpillars, or spanworms, emerge, and begin nibbling at the leaves from early summer onwards. As each larva consumes only a few leaves, the 1964-65 outbreak must have comprised astronomically large numbers of them. The moth is distributed over the whole of Finland, but it is a serious pest only in the extreme north of Lapland.

Epidemic years

Like many northern animal species, the autumnal moth is subject to great annual variation in abundance. Normally there are only a few caterpillars. In the mid 1960s, however, the summers were exceptionally cool, killing off, entomologists believe, large numbers of the enemies — insectivorous birds, parasitic insects, and pathogens — of autumnal moth larvae. The cold weakened the birches so much that they were unable to survive the loss of so many leaves.

Following this 'peak', the local autumnal moth populations 'crashed' and the moths have remained scarce ever since. Large-scale autumnal moth damage, like that caused by *Operophtera brumata* on the Norwegian coast, is a cyclic occurrence which, unlike that of voles, is impossible to predict.

Nature altered

Nutrients, light and temperature relations, and the flora and fauna, were all affected by the trees' deaths. Excessive amounts of caterpillar droppings and later vast quantities of rotting wood caused the soil to become unusually fertile, producing a prolific growth of flowering herbs. This was short-lived, however, excessive dryness and lack of shade leading to a take-over by dwarf birch and other small shrubs.

For a while reindeer were provided with plenty of lush grasses, but the latter were soon driven out by the encroaching tundra flora. Together with overgrazing of the lichen growth in winter, this resulted in hundreds of reindeer dying — despite emergency feeding measures by desperate reindeer

Pertti Kalinainen

Pirkka Utrio

The autumnal moth is a variable greyish-toned insect that flies in the autumn. It is common over the whole country.

herdsmen. All in all, the fell birch calamity of 1964-65 has been northern Lapland's greatest single catastrophe of the present century. The caterpillars consumed the leaves of something like 5000 square kilometres of fell birch woods: in Utsjoki commune alone 600-700 square kilometres of birch died and became open tundra. Even human impact pales into insignificance alongside such natural devastation. SK

Palsa Bogs

Palsa, like "sauna", is one of the few Finnish words that have made their way into the vocabularies of other languages. It is the name that the people of the North have given to peat mounds that rise from the surrounding flat bogs. Their hearts are a permanently frozen mass of peat, small ice crystals, ice layers and, sometimes, frozen sand and silt.

Palsa mounds are a feature of all permafrost areas in the circumpolar regions from Alaska and Canada through Iceland and Scandinavia to northern Russia. In Finland, they occur in the northern parts of Lapland.

Unusually large or otherwise exceptional palsas along the Kilpisjärvi road in western Lapland include those at Markkina, Iitto and Peera. There are many large ones in Enontekiö to the east of the River Lätäseno. Sammuttijänkä, a large bog complex near lake Iijärvi in the northern part of Inari, is well dotted with them. The Piesjärvi palsas near Ailgastunturi Fell in Karigasniemi and those on Linkkiaapa Bog to the north of the Paistunturi Fells are among the finest examples in the Utsjoki district, the northernmost bulge of Finland.

Shape and size

The palsa mounds that occur in Finland vary from less than a metre to seven metres in height. Their diameters vary from 25 to 50 metres. Some are almost conical in shape, others long narrowish ridges with rounded or flat tops. There are also groups of mounds with water-filled depressions between them.

A single bog usually contains several palsas. They are separated by flat expanses of peat, which supports normal bog vegetation like cotton grass, sedges, stunted shrubs and sphagnum moss. Palsas in different stages of development are often found on the same bog: low ones that are just beginning to grow, tall mature ones, and old ones that have passed their prime and begun to crumble at the edges. Some have already suffered their final collapse, leaving only fairly circular ponds surrounded by raised rims of peat.

Palsas rise steeply from the surface of a bog and are often surrounded by deep, almost moatlike bogholes. Anybody hiking across bogs would be well advised to beware of these,

Reijo Juurinen

Development of a palsa

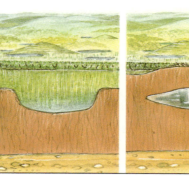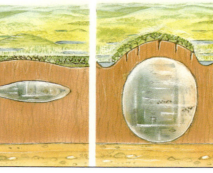

Teuvo Berggren

This palsa has partially thawed. Its edge has collapsed and is falling into the water.

because they can contain 1 ½ — 3 metres of soft muddy peat.

The surface of a palsa is often covered by shrubs like crowberry, bog whortleberry, cowberry and stunted birch, together with haircap mosses and lichens. Lashed by wind and rain, the mounds often develop bald patches, whose reddish-brown colour is visible from afar. The exposed peat surfaces weather into irregular angular shapes. Cracks penetrate to the frozen interior, which in Lapland is 55-70 cm below the surface when the thawing season ends in October. The cracks widen as the palsa grows in height. Eventually, large clods

of peat fall from the sides of the mound and into the water below. As it sheds its flanks, the mound loses thermal insulation and its frozen core begins to thaw.

How they develop

Many theories have been advanced to explain how palsas come into being. One of the earliest had it that they were merely relicts of a dense peat layer, most of which had been weathered away. That, however, is easy to refute, because the peat in the rest of the bog is actually deeper than on the palsa itself, where it has almost ceased to grow any deeper.

The explanation in vogue today is that frost penetrates a bog only in places where the insulating blanket of snow is thin. As the water below the surface of the peat freezes, it expands and creates a bump. Water from the surrounding bog accumulates around the frozen spot and is itself frozen, further fuelling the incipient palsa. The brief summer does not fully thaw the frozen water and peat, and that part of the bog surface remains raised. Now more exposed, it has an even thinner snow blanket the following winter and the frost can penetrate deeper beneath the surface. Year after year, the palsa grows taller and taller. (The diagram above is indicative only; the ice is not "clean", but a mixture of water, peat and sand.)

Snow seems to play a decisive role. On the flat bogs of Lapland, the wind blows it into

drifts of varying depth. Where the blanket is thin, the cold can penetrate to a considerable depth. Snow insulates well, whilst peat conducts heat very poorly. In normal circumstances, ground frost penetrates no more than 40-50 centimetres into the peat, but the ground under a palsa can be frozen to a depth of over 10 metres.

Temperatures inside palsas and the influence of snow depth on their development have been studied in the Utsjoki district. The snow was shovelled away from certain spots on the surface of a bog several times in the course of a winter. This enabled the ground frost to penetrate almost a metre into the peat. The frozen mass did not thaw completely the following summer and an artificial palsa came into being. Seven yers later, its core was still frozen and it rose about 30 centimetres above the surface of the surrounding bog. Time will tell whether it can grow into a full-sized palsa, of which there are several natural ones on the same bog.

The thickness of the peat layer is also a critical factor. The thermal conductivity of dry peat is a lot less than that of sand or gravel. If the peat in a bog is at least half a metre deep, it can be enough — all other conditions being favourable — to allow palsas to form and prevent the heat of the summer sun from penetrating to and thawing the frozen core.

Age

Once a palsa begins rising above a bog, conditions on its surface change completely. First of all, the vegetation changes, something that is also reflected

in the composition of the peat. By carbon-dating the peat at the interface between the two layers, one can accurately estimate when the palsa came into being.

Most of the palsas in Lapland are less than 2,000 years old, and some only a few centuries. New ones are still coming into being today. Some studies have produced estimates of as much as 4,000 years for the age of the peat on the surfaces of the oldest mounds, but here it should be borne in mind that erosion has probably stripped away the youngest peat from the top.

The collapse of old palsas does not necessarily mean that the climate has become warmer or moister. It is simply a normal part of their cycle of development.

Dry peat

Immediately a palsa begins rising from a bog, its surface dries out and the peat layer has to all intents and purposes stopped growing. Conditions on the top of the mound are very bleak: dry and warm in summer, dry, windswept and very cold in winter. But the thick layer of snow that accumulates around the sloping sides of the mound keep them moist for a large part of the summer.

Because the peat around the sides of a palsa is often cracked and only sparsely covered in vegetation, it suits cloudberries ideally. That is why local residents in Lapland know that the bogs that give them the richest pickings of the delicious golden berries are also the best places to find those strange frozen-hearted mounds, the palsas.
Matti Seppälä

Reijo Juurinen

KEVO

The mighty rift valley of the Kevojoki, which has ice age origins, bisects the western uplands of Utsjoki. Almost every hiker arriving for the first time from Petsikko or Outakoski at the Njaggajärvi lakes experiences a feeling of awe, and in some cases of extreme vertigo, as he gazes down into the ravine. The walls rise to a height of more than 100 metres above masses of rock rubble that seem to be on the verge of burying the lakes and the river channel, with its surprisingly small amount of water, below them.

The fell terrain of western Utsjoki makes for easy walking, even for the novice hiker, so long as he is able to skirt the deeper river valleys and the Säytsjärvi — Savdsajärvi — Aksujärvi mires and palsa bogs on either side of the Kaamosjoki river.

Here the fell caps may be so close and of such equal height and so similar to each other that the precise plotting of one's position on the map is next to impossible. The height of the land between the fells here remains at around 200-300 m. From this elevation the higher peaks thrust up prominently to about the same extent again.

In the gullies scarring the landscape the rivers and streams seem about to dry up. This is not just a figment of the imagination: these silvery ribbons may indeed at the height of summer dry up completely. They are fed in the spring by the melting snow. Some of the valleys have a ravine-line form, broken rock lining their walls. These "miniature Kevo's" include the steep-sided valleys of the minor rivers of the Leämmasjoki, Koahppelasavdsejoki and Tsuoggajoki.

Variations in the bedrock are rather small in this region, most of the fells being uniformly based on granitic rocks on whose shear faces light and dark layers alternate. On the sheared surfaces brownish-red structures of circular cross section are visible; such granite is considered a semi-gemstone.

The brambling, which calls in the birch forests, the willow warbler, which secretes itself in the willow thickets, the meadow pipit with its streaked breast, the constantly moving redpoll, the northern yellow wagtail, the redwing bold almost to the point of foolhardiness, and the wood sandpiper calling its warning cry from the crown of some birch tree on bog or mire, serve to enliven the fellscapes during the summer months. Perhaps, however, the memory of that willow grouse abruptly taking wing and setting the rambler's heart beating wildly will be recalled most vividly of all.

The original wildlife of the western Utsjoki region has managed to hold on to its characteristics, even though the area's original inhabitants, the Teno Lapps have been exploiting it for various purposes since time immemorial. The oldest permanent settlements were established along the waterway routes, the main ones being the Outakoski, Nuvvus and Talvadas cattle farming communities.

Dick Forsman

KARIGAS-AILIGAS — PIESJÄRVI MIRE

Multi-peaked Ailagas, Lapland's holy fell, is a spectacular sight even for the modern visitor. Its protuberances are in fact rather rounded. The highest point, topping 620 metres, lies in the southwest. The view down towards Karigasniemi can teach the rambler a great deal about the area's geology and habitats. In the Inarijoki valley, ice age moraine heaps divide dark green Scots pine forests. At an altitude of around 300-500 metres the forests become birch dominant. On the western edge of Ailigas the birch woods thin out to nothing at around 400 metres, where they are replaced by the dwarf shrubs, bilberry and dwarf birch. At the summits there are stony areas entirely devoid of vegetation in which only the most hardy of fell plants are capable of surviving. The vegetation at such elevations includes the mountain heath and wild azalea, as well as the ptarmigan berry, the ground-hugging fell willow, and the mattress-like white-flowered diapensia.

The stone faces are patterned by large numbers of different crustose lichens. Cetraria species are intermingled at high altitude with so-called reindeer moss (the lichen Cladonia). Snow bunting and stone chat nest among jumbles of rock. Up on the fell heaths one may well bump into the fearless orange-breasted dotterel, which raises more of a fuss about the arrival of a group of reindeer than the sudden appearance of a human interloper in its territory.

Far up in the north lies the impressive massif of Pastutunturi, in the east the Luomusjärvi (Luobmosjavrrik) lake chain, whose virtues are extolled in certain travel brochures. Much closer, on the eastern side, lies the Piesjärvi peatland, with its patches of palsa bog; this is a famous avian wetland belonging to the Utsjoki district. Ornithologists estimate that Utsjoki's last pair of lesser white-fronted geese nest here. Other species breed here regularly, including the bean goose, long-tailed duck, tufted duck, scaup, jack snipe, broad-billed sandpiper, bar-tailed godwit and red-necked phalarope.

FELLS NEAR THE PIESJOKI AND AKUJOKI

North of Ailigas the esker gradually descends to the rather narrow Piesjoki valley, where here and there grow low, very flat-topped junipers which have been pressed down by the weight of the winter snow. In the midst of the birch woods there are waters collected from the small tributaries and water coming from the Viertsakaljänkä bog during the summer. Some of the water also comes from the Piesjärvi basin.

On both sides of the Piesjoki estuary opens out the Teno valley which is a traditional agricultural area featuring dairy and beef cattle. This eastern rim of the valley marks the beginning of the lichen-covered heaths that are the common grazing ground of the reindeer belonging to the Paistunturi reindeer herdsmen's association. Far away towards the south the small village of Rovisuvanto can just be made out. Even as recently ago as the 1950s the Tenojoki waterway constituted almost the only route to Utsjoki church and Nuorgam. The road opened

Dick Forsman

The rough-legged buzzard is the commonest bird of prey in Lapland's fell zone. Its breeding habits are keyed to small mammal populations, including those of the grey-sided vole (opposite).

in the summer of 1983 running through Nuvvus naturally helped freight transportation but at the same time perhaps radically changed the whole atmosphere of the original Teno valley.

A unique collection of plants inhabits the sandy banks of the Tenojoki. On warm days at the beginning of July these flowery meadows are alive with butterflies, especially fritillaries, yellows, and browns of the genus Erebia.

As one progresses upstream the river meanders wildly, making large, sweeping turns so that in some places the flow is towards the south! In a couple of the rapids the black and white form of a dipper may be seen diving through a curtain of water to its nest. Mounds, which are the nests of rough-legged buzzards, dot the cliffs; they are occupied only in the best lemming and vole years.

Stuorra Piesvarri dominates the uplands between the Piesjoki and Akujoki rivers, its granulite crown rising to just short of 500 metres above sea level. Otherwise this fell looks just like the rest, its slopes covered with dwarf shrubs and scatterings of stones. Neighbouring fells are a few dozen metres shorter. The fell flora here is rather monotonous, consisting of such plants as mountain heath, ptarmigan berry, and diapensia, as well as local species of woodrush, grasses and clubmosses.

On the eastern side of Piesvarri, enclosing the River Siedgajoki there are dense stands of grey sallows in which bluethroats and Lappish buntings sing. At the height of summer if the mosquitoes and gnats are to be avoided it is best to climb up towards the windy summits of the fells. Around the houses situated to the northwest of Lake Akujärvi there are small strips of meadowland containing bulbous buttercup, yarrow, chickweed, and annual meadow grass, as well as less familiar plants like Rhinanthus groenlandicus and a variety of Anthemis with extra-large (one is tempted to say 'economy size') inflorescences, which have been brought there by the Lapps.

THE PAISTUNTURI FELL GROUP

On the eastern quarter of the headwaters of the Akujoki one cannot fail to notice Tseävrreskielas, from which it is but a short haul up to Kamaoaivi, in the northwestern corner of Kevo Strict Nature Reserve. At least from the floral aspect, one's anticipation will have increased as one stands now, virtually on the roof of Lapland, in the Paisutunturi uplands. However, the dwarf shrubs which rustle and shiver beneath one's feet as one walks promise no unfamiliar floral surprises. The large composites of a species of yellow-flowering Pilosella resemble those of Arnica. It is easy to overlook the fact that the soil here is

Pekka Nurminen

At one thousand years old, far and away Finland's oldest plants, these junipers can be seen at Kevo.

infertile and very acid. Hopes are raised by the sight of a couple of patches of mountain avens on the western slope of Kamaoaivi. In the brook gully on the fell's driest side there is a sprinkling of the red-flowered moss campion, Silene acaulis. Some of the sandy places are occupied by a growth of the willow Salix reticulata.

At the highest point on the very dry and stony ground, we are standing at an elevation of precisely 640 metres. The most startling component of the sparse vegetation up here is a golden-yellow clubmoss. While, owing to the graceful way in which the summit curves downwards, one is unlikely to suffer from vertigo, there is a very real danger of feeling totally isolated from the world, an impression that is not helped by dwelling on the consequences of breaking an ankle on the scree.

At the timber line the varied form of the fell birches arrests the attention. Some of them are single-trunked, others having several main trunks. Regrowth of the former is slow and uncertain, so that this morphological variety suffers greatly after an attack by the autumnal moth. Little by little the landscape takes on the appearance of a true tundra, cool winds blowing across it from the Arctic Ocean.

The hiker cannot fail to be impressed by the large amount of crowberry, which year after year produces masses of rather dry berries that have long been of economic importance to the Lapps. The latter are able to produce an extremely fine flavoured wine from their juice.

The northernmost peaks of the other fells in the Paistunturi cluster offer a variety of what an artist might call scenic experiences — a sort of Arctic hors d'oeuvres. In places among this stony wilderness dwells the yellowish-brown lemming (also called the Norway lemming), whose life may be abruptly terminated by a bite from a mother stoat. On the horizon circles that reindeer herdsman's arch-enemy, the golden eagle. A little further on a pair of ravens examine the corpse of a reindeer from high up.

Many kinds of ice formations are to be found in the ground giving rise to various kinds of surface patterns in these uplands. They include stone circles, polygons, flow hummocks, and erratic pits. At the summit of Stuorra-Mavdna the rambler may well ponder on the almost mushroom- and castle-shaped rocks known as tors, which from a distance resemble glacial 'erratics' but which have actually formed on the site by weathering of the bedrock. These are pieces of granulite which may well date from the Tertiary. On the fells of the Maunatunturi group one may also be intrigued by irregularly shaped rings of stones — these are not natural but have been put there by people. They are the one-time "keätkeporas" or meat stores of Lapps living in the fells.

JESKADAMTUNTURI FELLS – KISTUSKAIDI

Over the Lappish village of Talvas hovers the ghost of 'reindeer emperor' Kadja-Nilla, who is these days remembered as a charitable person. The boat makers of the Niilijoki are extremely proud of their craftsmanship. At the top end of the village, on the island of Teppana, sandy spits are constantly changing their form and position, giving the border guards of both Finland and Norway a headache: for the fifth time this century it has been necessary to decide which of the two countries adjoining the Teno should acquire the few extra hectares of soil. On the southern side of Nuvvus-Ailigas from the Nuvvusjoki estuary there is a road winding away towards the eastern fells as a pale strip across the landscape. Going down the reindeer path it is easy to reach Linkinjänkä, where the entire bog seems covered with snow when the Arctic cloudberry is unfurling its white blossoms.

Further east there is a wasteland caused by the autumnal moth in the 1960s. Here and there new shoots have sprouted on the fell birches, but fallen, rotting trunks are much more common. At Erteggvarri there is a stone 'reindeer wall' in contrast to the usual wooden fence. From a distance this appears to be some sort of bizarre fortress in the wilderness. In good lemming years one may spot a snowy owl sitting on a snow drift on a north-facing slope. This pale and highly personable bird brings to mind the "Woller period" of the 1800s, when the eggs of the snowy owl fetched a fair price. Reindeer herdsmen constituted highly suitable 'agents' as they already despised this pillager of ptarmigan and willow grouse.

In the north appears a set of what may loosely be described as foot hills fronting the Gaissatunturi fell cluster. These minor fells are almost identical, being distinguishable from each other by name alone! Deep down in the valley there is a lake with the tongue-twisting Lappish name of Koahppelasavsdejavri, which is really water backed up behind end moraine. This is one of the best locations in these remote reaches for the brown trout.

The lower trunks of the fell birches gleam whitely in their nakedness, tattered strips of bark hanging from them. By contrast, the upper section of each trunk is almost completely covered with mats of a dark lichen. The latter growth is an indicator of the average depth of winter snow, the lichen occurring only on parts of the trunk remaining above the snow surface. On sunny days on the slopes a notcuid moth with very pale hindwings is frequently to be seen on the wing, when it may well be mistaken for a large fly.

The last landmark before the great Teno valley is the craggy silhouette of Kistuskaidi. Alongside its perpetually moist, dark coloured walls the granulite foundation is broken, plunging into the chasm of the Gaissatunturi fells. The bedrock here contains of an abundance of hornblende; it is much broken and saturated with water. This is the habitat of the dwarf azalea, a species of Rhododendron. The saxifrages Saxifraga aizoides and S.oppositifolia, as well as a species of stonecrop, Rhodo-lia rosea, also constitute part of the flora.

Above the rapids tourists fish for salmon. The black and white costume of the ring ouzel may startle the unwary. Away towards the west, behind the stream dams, the Norwegian 'fjellstue' is clearly visible from here.

INTO THE KEVO VALLEY

One is not permitted to leave the trail running through Kevo Strict Nature Reserve (in contrast to the situation in a national park). Along the trail one passes through extensive areas devastated by the autumnal moth, the orchard-like leafy greenness of the fell birch groves gone perhaps for centuries.

Just before the chain of Njaggaljärvi lakes the trail switches to the western bank and at the ford you will need to look for a convenient length of fallen birch to employ as a staff. As the channels broaden into a lake, large areas of jumbled stone begin to appear on the eastern bank. In this rocky wasteland grows a Dryopteris fern whose distribution is otherwise confined to Greenland and the Urals. Here it seems as though this stout little plant is attempting to bind the jumble of stones together.

At the Njaggaljärvi lakes it is easy to forget that one is in a river valley, or at last walking past running water. Down this chain of lakes grey rocky walls rise almost vertically, so that the general impression imparted is that of a fjord. In these cold depressions grayling, brown trout and whitefish swim nonchalantly. In places long tongue-like eskers covered with Scots pines remind one of the Ice Age. When stopping for a welcome drink of tea or coffee, it is well worthwhile keeping one's eyes and ears open, as one sits practically invisible in this landscape. The wood sandpiper may flit along the shore, the tips of its rigidly held wings almost touching the water, its territorial cry ringing out repeatedly. The feeling of the wilds is intensified by the piercing call of the black-throated diver echoing the length of the labyrinthine valley. After a patient wait, one notices the water surface being quietly broken by the bewhiskered visage of an otter. The notes of the cuckoo, heard here well into the summer, echo across the 'skaidi', while the repeated melodious refrain of the song thrush acts almost as a landmark for the hiker.

FROM THE KAMAJOKI TO THE FIELLUKEÄDGGEJOHKA FALLS

From the Ylä-Njaggaljärvi camping site one must make one's way up a slope strewn with rock rubble. Slowly the bluishness of Njaggala disperses and in the west the attention is arrested by fell birch woods that have died before their time as a result of an outbreak of the autumnal moth. Their ranks have so to speak parted to make way for a vanguard of dwarf birch which has now established a firm footing in the original habitat.

We now come to another ford, a little easier to cross than the first. On the cliffs on the eastern bank there is a small colony of house martins closely scrutinised by a merlin that, when the necessity arises, can move in for the kill with the swiftness of an arrow. From the leafy 'jungles' of the canyon the wren's tinkling song abruptly rings out in competition with that of the Arctic warbler. Many flowers decorate the banks under the cliffs. Saxifraga aizoides, which hangs down from the rocks, has already fruited. One of the first to flower in spring, this plant covers moist rock faces in a purple cloak when the temperature at night falls below freezing point and there are mounds of snow still lying in the valley.

The bedrock tends to be poor in plant nutrients, water percolating down through the slopes dissolving minerals as it trickles down crevices in the rocks. This has the effect of enriching the lower parts of the slopes so that they support many extremely demanding plant species. Additionally, the growing period here in the kingdom of 'Ultima Thule' is an extended one. But the sheer cliff faces remain free of snow in the winter and hence exposed to extremely low temperatures. At most, they are coated with a thin layer of ice. During the daytime sheer walls warmed by the sun's rays reflect thermal energy, but during the night hours the warm air disperses into the wilderness and the bottoms of the valleys cool rapidly. In summer the ravine is a windless sun trap, in winter a highly efficient deep freeze unit. The flowers hanging on the cliffs die off more quickly than those in the valley. At the end of summer, the flowering species are limited to harebell, golden rod and rosebay willowherb, or fireweed.

Crossing the Kevojoki is most easily accomplished in the area of the small pools and the route then turns up towards the upper slopes of Rodosroadja. One may wonder why this visitors' trail does not go over the top of the fell, where there is such a splendid view of the scenery over the Paistunturi fells and Fallak. The sheer walls of the main valley also grow steeper on the western bank, the edge of the ravine extending for a kilometre or two. Finally the trail runs down into the valley through dead birch woods and living juniper clumps to the cauldron-shaped camping site at Fiellokeädggejohka. There is a ceaseless background noise of babbling water as the waters of the Fiellujoki tumble almost 25 metres in a miniature Niagara into the Kevojoki river. It is sometimes rather difficult to sleep here because of the constant murmuring of the water. From time to time the camper may poke his head out of his tent to see who is approaching, but time and again he will find that it was only the Fiellu talking to itself.

Under the waterfall a few Angelica archangelica, a relative of the wild angelica, and the 'olbmoporramrass' beloved of the Lapps, rear their stately heads. Linnaeus in 1732 in his 'Memoirs of Lapland' wrote "The people of Lapland collect the shoots of archangelica just as they are about to burst into flower, tear the leaves from them, scrape the surface off the stem, and offer them as they are to guests." This plant imparts a particularly pleasant flavour to salmon soup and fried reindeer meat. Cough mixture can be made by soaking the leaves in water for some time. Recently 'olbmoporramrass' has been used by the liquor and wine industry.

Within the next few years it is probable that the hiker will be able to visit the country behind the falls as the long-planned "western corridor" to the Fiellujoki river valley would take visitors on to the unlocked huts of Njavgoaivi and Kuivi.

OVER FIELLOKEÄDGGESKAIDI TO LUOMUSJÄRVI

Almost directly opposite the Fiellukeädggejohka river mouth opens out to the south the almost moon-shaped entrance to a canyon along the bed of which flows a shallow river, the Tsieskadasjohka. The path following the double slope of the Fiellokeädggeskaidi disappears periodically into small ravines before literally bumping into the end wall — the so-called "Kevo wall" — marking the valley's abrupt termination. When viewed from a distance the waters of the river seem to descend a series of cliffs into the fell itself as though into the jaws of a devil. At this stage it is a good idea to dump one's pack and take a look to the rear. The river in its giant groove-like valley is hidden in places behind by large boulders but appears in other places as a long shimmering ribbon. The view is spectacular. One can only concur with geologist Erkki Mikkola's laconic statement that "The Kevojoki valley is Finland's greatest and wildest canyon and almost the only place worthy of this title."

After the "Kevo wall" the valley is no longer as startling, becoming much tamer. The feeling of safety is also increased by a pastel-coloured birch wood above which the Suohppasoaivi and Tuolba-Njavgoaivi trail runs. Reindeer herds come up to these green meadows to graze in summer. Everywhere one finds their criss-cross of tracks, eaten grass, and hoof prints on banks that have subsided after the ice has melted.

In the vicinity of the Luomusjärvi lakes there are several Arctic fox summer mounds. From the Ruktajärvi unlocked hut the final trip is very pleasant from the sandy spur at Luomusjärvi. This place is often called Utsjoki's Punkaharju. The Arctic tern which comes curving and diving over Lake Nurttahjavri remains impressed on the memory as we descend into the Luomusjoki valley. The car park serves to remind us that we have left the real wilderness behind and that the Karigasniemi high road is not far away. UL

Kevo Strict Nature Reserve

Utsjoki, 710 km², in the birch zone of Lapland. Under National Board of Forestry management. The main point of interest is a large canyon, down which a trail runs (40 km).

Aimo Holtari

Life on the Rocks

One of the distinctive geological features of Finland is how close the bedrock is to the surface. The loose soils overlaying it are very thin, less than a hundred metres in maximum depth and often virtually nonexistent. In fact, one per cent or so of the country's total land area is more or less exposed rock. Bare rock pavements and gently sloping cliff faces make a pretty bleak environment, in which common forest species live only sparsely. But the larger the area the bare rock covers and the more fractured it is, the greater the variety of specialized species make it their habitat.

We make our first new acquaintances right on the surface of the rock. Only on the undersides of stones and in the deepest recesses of caves and cavities can we see the rock's nat-

ural colour; elsewhere, it is covered by a living skin composed of dozens, and perhaps hundreds of different lichens and mosses. The variety of species is rather poor on granite, gneiss and quartzite, the most common types of bedrock in Finland. It usually consist of scab- or leaflike lichens hugging the surface of the rock, but the more nourishment the rock provides, the greater the diversity of lichens and mosses. The odd fern, such as one of the polypodies or a member of the rather hirsute Woodsia genus, adds further variety.

Cliffs and ravines

The variety of life increases quite a lot if a rock face is almost vertical and high as well. A tall, sheer cliff may attract a peregrine falcon or a gyr falcon to nest; but the bird that will

most commonly take wing from one is a buzzard, which will then wheel screechingly above the intruder for a long time afterwards. Towards the end of winter, when the snowdrifts are at their deepest, cliff faces offer a home to many a raven family. Large cracks and cavities in the base of the cliff can provide wolverines and wolves with shelter, and bears with dens in which to hibernate.

But it is botanists who are most strongly attracted to rock faces. Even in the heart of the forest zone, many Arctic upland species have found permanent sanctuary on rock faces and ledges. Weathering of the stone keeps their habitat constantly young and competition for space is not as severe as on forest land.

The orientation of a rock face determines what kind of growth habitat it is. One facing south is dry and hot in summer, but very cold in winter; very little insulating snow clings to a

A rugged rock slope supports many lifeforms. Lichens thrive on sunny surfaces, mosses in damp, shaded ones. Water-filled hollows support algae. Stoats hide in cracks and hollows, whilst ravens nest on rocky crags and ledges.

sheer rock face and what little there is melts away on the first sunny day in spring. The daytime temperature in early spring can be as high as twenty degrees Celsius, but night can bring as many degrees of frost.

Among the plants that one is likely to find on cliffs facing south are meadow grass sticking out in bluish-green tufts, saxifrage firmly anchored in cracks, and some ferns.

At the base of a cliff, where a protective layer of snow accumulates in winter, many southern plants find a suitable habitat. Debris and soil falling from the cliff and the nutrients leached down by water make the base of a cliff an exceptionally rich substrate. Bird cherry, currant bushes and aspen grow near the bases of cliffs much further north than one would expect to find these species. The deciduous belt is often very narrow. Further down, boulders form a bleak rocky slope.

In contrast to such extremes, cliffs facing north are completely different. The heavy blanket of snow that covers them in winter does not thaw until well into the summer, and even when it does the cliff remains moist, shaded and cool. The flora is entirely different, too. Varieties of lichens that thrive in bright sunlight are absent altogether, and lichens in general are far fewer than on rocks facing south. Mosses and algae form the dominant species in the vegetation that clothes the rock. Northern species like saxifrage are the dominant species among flowering plants. Ferns are also common. The vegetation at the base of a northern cliff resembles that found in meadows or near snowlines. Its

The gyr falcon is one of our rarest nesting species. The steep rocky crags of Lapland give it a secure nesting place.

Dick Forsman

paucity is not due to a lack of nutrients, but to the short growing season caused by late-melting snow.

The walls of ravines comprise sunny southwards-facing walls and cold, moist northern-facing ones. Very different plants can grow quite close to each other. One deep ravine in Värriötunturi Fell is home to both wild strawberries, a southern field plant, and brook saxifrage, a tiny flower usually found in cold streams of meltwater.

If its walls contain calcium, ravines support an enormous range of flora, and quite a few animals as well. In such places, dozens of species that flourished during the final stages of the Ice Age live on in the middle of a forest sea.

These sheltered places in the rock also support many species of spiders and moths.

Bleak pavements

Where ravines are oases of life, large rock pavements and boulder fields are very much a barren wilderness. The combined strength of frost and water has created areas, sometimes many square kilometres in extent, that are strewn with angular rocks. Especially in wet weather, when one's boot can easily slip on the moss and lichen skins that coat the rocks, these places are quite dangerous for hikers.

Nor do they offer the hiker much to see. Snow buntings and wheatears are common residents, and the occasional stoat may be glimpsed in cracks and cavities in the rock, but all of these have to range beyond the rock field to find enough food. Sometimes, tiny patches of ground with enough soil to support grasses or shrubs lie between the boulders. Occasionally, too, an astonishingly bright red fireweed growing out of a cavity brings colourful relief to the grey drabness.

But the most distinctive plant of the stony wastelands is rock brake, a fern with leaves somewhat resembling those of a carrot. It is rare and grows thinly. At one time it was a protected species, but the inaccessibility of the places where it grows and the tenacious grip that its roots ensure protect it just as well as any official regulations. SV

The uplands of western Lapland used to be the domain of the snowy owl. The large white bird was once fairly common in many parts of this spacious treeless landscape. In years when voles were plentiful, it was seen just as often as rough-legged buzzards and skuas. Nowadays, however, the eye searches in vain for its beautiful white shape outlined against a hill slope.

Due to their lifestyle, these birds have always been erratic in their appearances. As predators that live on lemmings and voles, they have adapted to following their prey wherever they go. When the lemming population collapses in the owls' nesting area, they head elsewhere en masse to avoid death by starvation. They keep going until they find an area with a thriving vole population. Their migrations can take them thousands of kilometres away from their former nesting places, to regions as far away as the Azores and Bermuda. The migrant's lot is not an easy one and it can be presumed that many, especially young birds, perish on the way to their remote destinations.

Snowy owls have been found nesting virtually everywhere in the northern hemisphere. Just how far they range in search of food is not exactly known, but it may be that they even change continents between successive nesting seasons. They have been observed on small islands in the Bering Straits, which may indicate fairly regular passage on their part between Alaska and Siberia. They have also been seen on islands in the Atlantic and Arctic oceans, and it is possible that birds from Fennoscandia migrate to northern Canada by way of Iceland and Greenland. The fact that separate sub-species have not evolved on different continents (the birds are the same everywhere) also indicates that individuals from widely separated parts of the world meet and interbreed every now and then.

A gloomy history

The snowy owl probably nested regularly in Lapland until the

late 19th century. Then, however, a passion for egg collecting (in the name of science!) swept Lapland, with fateful consequences for many of the rare species living there.

Wealthy collectors, especially in England, obtained vast quantities of eggs through their agents. The actual collecting was done by locals, who were handsomely compensated for their efforts. Those who knew the locations of nests guarded their secrets jealously and were careful not to damage them so that they could gather another harvest the following year. A bird need not be a goose to lay golden eggs!

Dick Forsman

The Snowy Owl

At the same time that egg-collecting was at its height, around the turn of the century, there were several good nesting years in a row for the snowy owl. There were probably many hundreds of nesting pairs in western Lapland. In 1907 alone, one resident of the Könkämä-enovarre area had collected more than 800 snowy owl eggs for sale! With such intensive collection continuing year after year, it is obvious that few snowy owls grew to maturity in those districts.

A hatred of predators that swept the nation from the late 19th century onwards also took its toll. Migrating owls were particularly vulnerable to hunters, because they often sought prey near buildings and, as denizens of the wilderness, were quite fearless. Not even those that remained in the Arctic fells all winter were safe, because ptarmigan hunters saw them as competitors and persecuted them mercilessly. Nature conservation was unfortunately an unknown concept at that time.

Why did they disappear?

The usual explanation advanced to explain the owls' disappearance is a combination of egg-collecting and persecution, but is it enough? It is obvious that every egg collected and every bird killed is a drain on the population that can not be borne for very long. But a vagrant like the snowy owl is not as vulnerable to such depredations as species like eagles or swans, which remain faithful to the same nesting area once they have selected it. Even if all the snowy owls in a particular area were exterminated, the next migration would replenish the population. The species is still well represented in the Swedish and Norwegian parts of Lapland, although these areas have just as grim a history of persecution as Finland.

It should also be borne in mind that their migrations regularly take snowy owls through Finnish Lapland, where they are often seen in winter. But when spring arrives and it is time to nest, they depart for more clement regions. Thus it would seem that our part of Lapland is no longer the same place to them that it was around the turn of the century, even if the Arctic fells are unchanged and voles still abound in peak years. DF

Nature's Winter Coat

A snow blanket's tale begins when tiny droplets of cold water freeze and form crystals around solid particles in a cloud. The crystals grow, begin falling and on their way to the ground are changed in ways that are determined by the prevailing temperature, humidity and wind conditions.

Snow that falls as flakes in a light breeze forms an airy layer, because the crystals touch each other only at the points of their radial arms. By contrast, the needlelike crystals that fall in a strong wind lie side-by-side and form a dense layer. Since snow falls under many different conditions in the course of the winter, the blanket that covers the ground contains clearly distinct layers.

The lower layers are gradually compressed under the weight of those overlying them. Temperature and moistness levels also differ markedly from layer to layer and this, too, causes changes. Since snow generally contains considerably more air than ice, it insulates heat well and the heat emitted by the ground is conducted only very slowly to the cold ambient air. The surface of the snow reflects most of the radiation energy reaching it and efficiently radiates the energy that it absorbs out into space. In fact, the coldest part of a snow blanket in frosty weather, especially during a cloudless night, is its surface.

Snow is usually saturated with water vapour. Because the capacity of air to absorb water vapour increases as its temperature rises, water molecules rise and condense on the surfaces of the colder snow crystals higher up. Large crystals grow at the expense of smaller ones and at the same time become simpler in structure. The snow closest to the ground is transformed from large, often pillar-like crystals to a brittle layer.

Plants and snow cover

A layer only half a metre deep is enough to ensure that the temperature below it remains stable within a range of only a few degrees. Trees and shrubs that grow above the snow are in danger of dehydration in winter, whilst those beneath the snow suffer hardly any evaporation. However, the thermal insulation that snow gives also has its disadvantages, because plants breathe, i.e. consume energy, throughout the winter. The higher the temperature, the harder they breathe.

Plants' ability to endure cold improves in autumn as gradually hardening frosts toughen them. Once a protective blanket of snow has fallen over them, plants like bilberry shrubs lose some of their resilience to frost and if the snow is removed, e.g. by foraging reindeer, they may freeze to death. Exposed mosses and lichens, by contrast, are very resistant to frost. The bilberry shrub is very sensitive to cold and thus grows on patches between trees, where there is a thick blanket of snow in winter, whereas the similar cowberry (or red whortleberry) shrub copes well close to the bases of firs, where there is relatively little snow in winter. Bilberries do not thrive well on hummocks, either, because the snow is often blown off these. It is probable that also other factors than the thermal insulation provided by snow account for the patchy way in which various plants grow. To take one example: the ground around hummocks and tree bases freezes to a greater depth than in spots where the snow is deeper.

The surface of snow poses a danger to plants not only because of its coldness, but also because the wind in open areas blows sharp-edged crystals, which can damage delicate buds, across the surface. This may be the reason why lonely firs growing on the slopes of Arctic fells are often of an unusual shape: the branches closest to the ground are long and vital, but there are none at the same height as the snow surface. There are branches higher up, too, but they are mainly on the leeward side of the tree.

Sub-snow activity

To living creatures, a snow mantle means first and foremost a scarcity of food. Still, many creatures, including some of the smallest animals, spend an active winter under the protective white layer, where the temperature is just below freezing. Several beetles and spiders are on the go all winter, and the latter even reproduce then.

Favourable weather brings life onto the surface of the snow as well. Springtails (or collembolans) only a few millimetres in length are sometimes so numerous that they can darken a snow slope. One also sees spiders, snow flies and various other insects going busily about their business.

Moles and voles mainly spend the winter in their meandering tunnels on the borderline between the ground and the snow. Their little world is a gloomy one, because not even at midday can light penetrate half a metre of snow. The tiny mammals rely mainly on their sense of smell to inform them of what is happening in their surroundings.

The wood lemming spends the whole winter under the snow and even the Norway

Tapani Vartiainen

lemming comes to the surface only very rarely. By contrast, the bank vole and the grey-sided vole are often seen scuttling across the snow, leaving easily recognized lines of tracks behind them.

Field voles and Siberian voles move about on the surface of the snow a good deal less than bank voles, but all the more in tunnels under it and leading to holes on the surface. Field voles are particularly active in keeping their air holes open. They often pop up to the opening — even in severe frost — as though to sniff the air — and become easy prey for ravens and owls.

Voles' best protection against cold is their nests, which they build on the surface using grass, moss and feathers. A bare snow burrow is a bleak environment for small mammals, because the snow walls quickly absorb the heat radiated by their bodies.

Voles that eat the leaves and bark of deciduous trees and shrubs benefit when the snow blanket thickens both through the additional thermal insulation that it provides and because they are able to reach more food reserves without having to emerge from the safety of the snow.

Waders and floaters

Foxes hunt voles hiding beneath the snow by using their acute senses of hearing and smell to locate their prey and then digging rapidly to catch them. Smaller and more agile predators like stoats and weasels go right into the voles' tunnels in pursuit of them. They can also chase voles across the surface of the snow and mercilessly accumulate an underground food reserve, for example in a burrow that they have

"conquered". Stoats (or ermines when they are in their winter coat) spend more time on the surface than weasels, because their bigger size gives them a better ability to endure cold. Mink and pine martens also prey on voles. Pine martens avail themselves of the relative warmth of the snow by taking their daily naps in hollows under it.

For larger animals, however, a deep carpet of snow mainly means difficulty in getting about. An elk's feet exert a pressure of over a kilogramme per square centimetre, and thus this animal usually has to wade up to its haunches in snow. Of course, its long limbs are an advantage in such conditions. When the snow is exceptionally deep, elk follow the same routes and leave distinct "ruts" behind them.

Reindeer (both domesticated and wild animals) belong to the same genus, but are distinct sub-species. Their feet exert a surface pressure of 140 — 180 grammes per square centimetre, so they do not sink nearly as much as an elk.

By choosing well where they go animals can make it easier for themselves to move about in snow. A good example of this is the wolf, who often uses lakes and their shores, where the ice is only thinly covered by ice. A wolf exerts a surface pressure of only about 100

Unlike the heavier brown hare, the mountain hare can run lightly on the surface of the snow. When the snow is soft, it spreads the toes of its hind legs to make a "snow shoe".

grammes per square centimetre, but its relatively short legs mean that snow as shallow as half a metre can severely hamper its mobility.

As opposed to these waders, there are also "floaters", animals with limbs adapted to enable them to dash about on the surface of the snow with a minimum of difficulty. These include the mountain hare and the ptarmigan. The mountain hare spreads the toes of its large hind feet as wide as the softness of the snow requires. If, however, the snow is very soft, it reduces the amount of energy it needs by following the same route and making paths.

Stout, springy feathers that grow on them in autumn make a willow grouse's feet look like a hare's hind legs and enable it to walk on soft snow without sinking. Its close relative the ptarmigan, which lives on open hill slopes, also has "snow feet".

The deeper the snow becomes, the higher up bushes and trees willow grouse and hares can reach to collect food. They are also able to get at the top shoots of birch branches bent down by the weight of the snow on them and shrubs exposed from the snow by foraging reindeer. Creatures with white fur or feathers are also harder for predators to spot.

Only mammals the size of or bigger than a hare are able to survive unprotected in severe frost. The mountain hare often digs a snow burrow beside the hollow in which it rests, but unlike the brown hare rarely sleeps in it. Its burrow serves primarily as a place of refuge when predators approach. AM

Martti Rikkonen

UTSJOKI, THE FAR YONDER

The asphalt road running north from Kaamanen divides the Utsjoki fell country in two. A vast wild tract spreads across its eastern flank, concealed from the gaze of motorists by its flatness. This fell wilderness is bordered in the west by the magnificent Utsjoki valley and in the north by the massive Teno valley. In the east lies the border with the Kingdom of

Martti Rikkonen

256

Even in winter the hardy ptarmigans do not descend from the windlashed fells.

Norway, a border which cuts arbitrarily through the fell country with the hill tops and fell tops as its benchmarks. To the south the terrain gradually slopes downwards and merges with the hill and peatland country of Inari.

The eastern Utsjoki fell country wears a general expression of monotony and arctic gloom. The landscape is composed of birch covered skaidi lands, mires stretching far into the distance and gently climbing fells. This wilderness is around 250 — 300 metres above sea level. Riverbeds run from it and fells soar out of it. Great river valleys that have carved their way deep into the flat fell country have created topographical variety. Fell birch is the most visible type of vegetation here; the coniferous zone can only be found in the southeast corner. But the birch does not reign supreme everywhere. Above two to three hundred metres the birch gives way to a sparse vegetation. The most interesting place to ramble is the northern part of this region where the landscape of the Utsjoki fells is at its finest — in turn the river valleys, skaidi's and fells ensure an ever changing topography.

The spirit of the wilderness is easy to find in the eastern fell country where no groups of travellers have been to trample down paths from one fell to another.

THE TENO VALLEY

Following the lower runs of the Teno river, it is pleasant to explore Finland's largest range of valleys. Many of the fells reach right down to the banks of the Teno river, forming a handsome backdrop to the river valley. The best view is naturally from on high but climbing to the fell tops can easily remain just a dream. The highest fells descending into the Teno valley, Karnjartsohkka, Luovos-varoaivi and Juovvoaivi, thrust more than 300 metres from the valley floor. Even before Vetsikko, the northwards descending valley slope changes to a steep cliff which continues for a league and a half beyond Vetsikko. The plaintive mewing of the rough-legged buzzard conveys the message that the 150 metre high walls are the domain of more than just human travellers.

The Teno river has carved its bed through the

overlying deposits covering the valley floor. Between Utsjoki and Nuorgam the Teno river swirls with many rapids. At Alaköngäs the river is at its most furious just before calming itself into a kilometre long stretch of quiet water. Well before Alaköngäs the Teno flows calmly in many stretches, depositing sand to form low sandbanks and meadowy and bushy islands.

THE PULMANKI RIVER AREA

From Nuorgami southwards you can speed along the Norwegian gravel road as far as the southern tip of the Pulmankijärvi lake. On foot, however, you appreciate the landscape more. From the Teno valley you should climb about 200 metres to Stuorrakeädgevarri, where you can wander through the birch woods skirting Kuhkesjärvi lake. The terrain descends almost imperceptibly but on nearing Pulmankijärvi lake the road falls quite sharply to the village of Niemelä. From the road along the west bank you get a splendid view of the east bank rising steeply out of the water. Despite the steepness of the slopes the maximum depth of Pulmankijärvi is only 35 metres. The lake bottom is, however, below sea level, as the lake surface itself is only 15 metres above sea level. The shores are intact and there are no islands whatsoever on the lake. The fjord-like nature of the Pulmanki valley is unusual in Finland. During one phase of the development of this valley the continental glacier moulded the bedrock fracture into a U-shaped valley. During the melting of the continental glacier, the Pulmanki valley formed the upper end of the Teno fjord. This phase left its mark by the fluvial terraces on the slopes of the valley. The flounders that live in Pulmankijärvi testify to the proximity of the sea. It's easy for this flat sea dweller to find its way to the lake, as the lower waters of Polmakelpa and the Teno river descend very gently.

At the mouth of the Kalddasjoki river it is worth taking a look at the massive stratified delta formation caused by the glacial river. You get a good view of the area by climbing up the riverside as far as Kalddasluobbali. Because of its terraced structure, the land seems to rise like a staircase. The Kalddasjoki river has cleaved a channel, forming at its centre an erosion valley several dozen metres deep. On the southern side of the river the ridge of the flat Stuorraskaidi spreads out and slopes steeply downwards towards Pulmankijärvi lake. Pools dotted here and there and oblong moraine hummocks, called drumlins, in the Roavvetsohkka area break the monotony of the characterless skaidi scenery.

The Pulmanki valley offers the most attractive route along the ridge of the skaidi. The rambler following the course of the river bed may be surprised to see an identical river bed suddenly appearing behind the river. In its lower reaches the Pulmankijoki river flows at a very leisurely pace and with the passage of the years has carved itself a very winding bed. Its wildest meanderings are on the lower side of Luossajoki, where you can follow the river for 6 kilometres but only travel two as the crow flies. On this stretch it is worth travelling along one of the higher terraces, from where you can really appreciate the

work this river has done to carve out its route. The Pulmankijoki has eaten 30-50 metres deep into the overlying glacial river material covering the valley floor, exposing several former river beds at different levels.

In the Pulmanki valley the rambler can light a tar-scented camp fire despite being well north of the coniferous belt. Nowadays the pinewoods of Pulmanki cover several hectares, although up to the last century there were still more. The sale of wood to the residents on the coast of the Arctic Ocean has taken its toll on the forests. The secret behind the success of the Pulmanki pines lies in the sand and gravel formations of the Ice Age which have created suitable thermal conditions. Conversely, peatlands are unsuitable for pine in deepest Lapland.

At the mouth of the Luossajoki river you can descend to the gravelly spots at the riverside where the rare bush heather grows. After crossing the Pulmankijoki river you can climb up Roavvevarri to study the scenery. The spirit of the Pulmanki valley with its summer greenery differs from the brownish skaidi and fell land. The Askasjoki and Moresveijoki river valleys also extend their green fingers towards the areas of decimated birch. The landscape looks inconsolable as the regeneration of birch simply has not succeeded. In the worst affected areas the dead, ghostly birchwoods gradually become treeless fell land. The attacks by autumnal moth larvae in the river valleys have countered the local weather conditions, which favour the growth of birch.

Tsuomasvar looming in the eastern sky, warrants closer investigation. Although its 435 metres seem fairly modest on the map, the climb to the top will set your heart beating. To the south there is an unbroken view over the shimmering waters to the strangely shaped Kolmmesjärvi lake. While Tsuomasvarri is the place from which to get a good view, above all it is an oasis for rare plants. The lush greenness of the slope already catches your eye. But only on the shining white mountain aven heathlands and the moist patches where water trickles does the real worth of the fell country unfold. Many rare species of saxifrage flower by the sides of the brooks and near the trickling water. Carex species, Gymnadenia conopsea and net-leaved willow grow on Tsuomasvarri. Many of these species are confirmed calcifuge plants and thrive on the gabbro and ultra-basic rocks of Tsuomasvarri.

After the Tsuomasvarri detour the journey continues south following the Pulmankijoki river. The Askasjoki river joins the Pulmankijoki river from the west, plunging down as a rushing waterfall from the skaidi. From here onwards the journey is accompanied by the song of the river as the upper courses of the Pulmankijoki river are far from peaceful. Over a distance of a couple of leagues the land descends about 200 metres. We leave the last pines behind at Moresveiskaidi. The odd pine growing here and there testifies to the fact that the conditions for successful growth do not suddenly disappear. The pine tree forming the furthermost sentinel stands proudly at an altitude of 200 metres only half a league from

The colourful and fearless dotterel is one of the species found on the fell heathlands.

Puolbmakkeäsjärvi lake. A little further south on the eastern side of the river there is a charming resting place on the centre of a moraine hummock at the edge of a shimmering pool.

Approaching Puolbmakkeäsjärvi the traveller may well start to rub his eyes — signs of war in the middle of the wilderness? An aircraft hulk sprawling in a small pool is a reminder of the tumult of nearly five decades ago which spread right into deepest Lapland. During the war many planes ended up in the desolation of the mires and fell lands. Crashed planes can also be found at Fällijärvi, on the slopes of Aldovarri, and on the terrain around Tsiegnalisjärvi. The long and narrow Puolbmakkeäsjärvi lake is surrounded by birchwoods. The banks on the western shore rise to steep cliffs towards the northern tip of the lake. If you so desire you can even take a bath in the hollow of a brook descending from the cliff. You can also harden the soft butter in your rucksack in the snow at the side of the waterfall. Striking onwards from the waterfall towards the lake you will find Adolf's Hut which was built for research purposes. The name stems from one of the old German aircraft wrecks from which the chair for the hut was taken. The visitors book tells us that the pilot whose journey ended here sits in this chair at nights and continues his flight. If the hut happens to be occupied, its probably best to leave this modest shelter for the use of the researchers.

Striking southwards from Puolbmakkeäsjärvi you ascend 300 metres almost without noticing it. Widespread juniper thickets decorate the landscape around Njallajärvi lake. The wanderer might be surprised to see clusters of pine saplings far from the nearest seed bearing tree. Human hands might have assisted the appearance of these little copses along the old reindeer trail.

Dick Forsman

Pertti Kalinainen

This land between Stuorra-Tievja and Kurboaivi separates the singing waters of Pulmankijärvi from the waters of the Näätämöjoki river area. We are now at the source of the Pulmankijoki, just a short climb to the fell highlands.

KUORBOAIVI-NJALLAVARRI FELL HIGHLANDS

Between the Pulmankijoki and Vetsijoki river valleys lies a league wide fell area, the finest part of east Utsjoki for ramblers. The land is mostly hard without any great undulations to make the choice of route difficult. From Kuorboaivi to Njuohkarggu the felltops are broad and the slopes gentle. The absence of trees is due to the area's northern and eastern location.

The ascent to the broad summit of Kuorboaivi is easy from any direction. Although the slopes rise a mere 150 metres above the mire, the massiveness of this fell dominates the landscape. All around, flat lands with mires, lakes and chains of lakes unfold. You would have to go a long way to find fell country as high as this. Kuorboaivi is at its best with the eagles wheeling in the blue sky and the swans swimming on the distant lakes. This is when the joy of the wilderness floods the soul of the traveller.

From Kuorboaivi the fell ridge continues via Koallakuoddetsohkka to Aksonjunti and Kalddoaivi. The plain-

The only place in Finland where the rare bush heather grows is on the shores of Pulmankijärvi lake.

260

tive call of the golden plover from morning to night grates on the ears in the desolation of the uplands. The vegetation beaten down flat to the surface of the land only stretches out in the indentations. On these wind-lashed lands, the protection of the snow and the micro-climate create the conditions for survival. The black crow-berries, black bearberries and creeping azalea have adapted to the barren soil and trying conditions. With the exception of the golden plovers and the long-tailed skuas this ridge appears deserted, but the keen-eyed traveller will see that snow buntings, meadow pipits and wheat-ear also dwell here.

Urraoaivi rises on the northwest side of Kalddoaivi, at 450 metres it is the highest fell in the eastern Utsjoki wilderness. The Uhtsib fells on the west of Kalddoaivi are divided by the tapering, partly barren Kalddasjoki valley. On one side of the watershed shimmers a lake cleft by a narrow esker. The map shows that the "lake" is in fact a group of four lakes.

From the upper course of the Kalddasjoki river you cross Pajanvadda to the gently climbing Njuohkarggu on whose terrain you might encounter an arctic fox. From the summit a splendid view unfolds over the verdant area around Vuognoljärvi lake, an area which has been spared the ravishes of the autumnal moth. From there you can descend to the valley of the Vuognoljoki, Njuoh-karjoki and Loktajoki rivers which cuts through the barren ridge area. Here you can find luxurious hut accommoda-

tion, either at the reindeer round-up station or in the border guards' hut at Vuognoljärvi lake. Owing to the lack of coniferous trees there are very few huts indeed in the eastern Utsjoki fell area. The reindeer herdsmen, fish-ermen, ptarmigan hunters and bordermen have erected a few huts in the area out of birch and peat. In un-favourable weather, these places with their stoves or open fireplaces offer a more comfortable alternative to a tent.

On the northern side of Njuohkar valley the fell becomes steeper and the landscape becomes injected with a certain degree of life. There are plenty of places from which to get a good view. In good weather the rambler will be rewarded beyond his expectations. Where Vuognolvarri meets Keinodakoaivi you can see the blue chain of the Vuognoljärvi lakes. The valley, speckled with pools, offers a scenic route to Irdoaivi and Uhtsa Tsahp-pesjärvi. From Njuohkarjärvi you can just as easily wan-der northwards on the eastern side of the Koahtejärvi and Farppaljärvi lakes. In August, the fens on the upper lands can sometimes be so yellow with the arctic cloudberries that the wanderer can eat his fill in a moment. It would not however be a good idea to pick too many, as cloudberry picking is an important source of income for the locals.

The Kuorbo Njallavarri area comprises small lakes, pools and marshes which offer a fascinating variety of birdlife. In addition to the long-tailed ducks and red-throated divers you can also find arctic tern, common scoter, velvet scoter and scaup. On the shore you can hear the piping of the ringed plover and Temminck's stint. Of the great number of waders inhabiting this area the most famous are the wood sandpiper and whimbrel, while the most interesting is the bar-tailed godwit. This red-breasted wader nests in small numbers in northernmost Lapland, but in the northeastern parts of Utsjoki it is a relatively common sight. The birdwatcher will also be enthusiastic about the spotted redshank, redshank and snipe here. During light night excursions above the marshes you might hear the rattling mating call of the jack snipe.

From Uhtsa Tsahppesjärvi we take the trail leading to Piedtganamvarri. In the west-northwest, the fell land rises again. Njallavarri is the last to disappear from sight as we descend to the Teno valley through the Piedtganamvarri birchwoods.

THE NÄÄTÄMÖJOKI RIVER AREA

The southeastern corner of eastern Utsjoki pushes deep into the Inari district and into the northern coniferous zone, the taiga area. A Scots pine-covered lichen area spreads out on the northern side of the Sevettijärvi road which, as you go northwards, gradually turns into a birch area. Beyond the Näätämöjoki river, pines disappear completely from the landscape. Here the limit of the pine zone is located quite a lot further north than anywhere else in the world. North of the Näätämöjoki river lies a separate area of low fells where bare tops, apart from at Isokivennokka, are few. The peatlands and hills on the eastern side of Näätämöjoki river are unique, but these are spurned by travellers because of the difficulty of the terrain.

Access to the Näätämöjoki valley is easy if you approach it via the Sevettijärvi road. Before leaving it is worth calling at the border guard station as the knowledgeable border guards can give good advice. The well worn trail from the border guard station to the Näätämöjoki river crosses the summit of Puollimvarri with its exposed rocks and multitude of pools. On the northwest side of the hills we descend to the sandfields of the river valley. In addition to the sandfields, the Näätämöjoki river has other glacial formations. An esker chain runs along the southern riverbank between Saarikoski and Niloskoski. In places the river has eroded the esker to form steep cliffs. The finest esker scenery is at Harrisuvanto and Niloskoski. The ridge of the steep esker is nearly 30 metres above the river. In places on the river side of the main esker there runs a secondary esker separated by a deep trench with, on the other side, huge esker pits.

The Näätämöjoki is a wide and powerful river. Several rapids boil between Opukasjärvi and the Finnish border. Crossing the river might cause some unexpected difficulties. If you are not offered the chance to cross the river with assistance from the border guards at the lower course it is better to travel up to Opukasjärvi lake. Salmon enjoy this fast flowing river. The Näätämöjoki is

the third most important salmon river in Finland, the first and second being the Teno and Tornio rivers. Two thousand tons of salmon are taken from the Finnish side every year.

The northern side of Näätämöjoki is excellent for travelling. The relatively clear pine wood zone border is a few kilometres distant from the river. Further north, fell birch and dwarf birch dominate the area. The Villavaara slopes rise as far as the bare montane zone. One particular characteristic of the northeastern Inari fell region is the amount of exposed rock. This is particularly evident on the eastern side of the Opukasjärvi-Laavvuvaara-Kuollepastimtsielgi line. Between Rousavaara and Villavaara the wanderer might come across moraine hummocks whose restless, broken tops and freakish height disparities will certainly catch his attention. Dotted unevenly about the landscape are steep, cracked hummocks anything up to 10 metres high.

The landscape becomes somewhat more hospitable in contrast to the moraine lands of Opukasjärvi. The lake itself has fine sandy beaches, if cold waters, to tempt the swimmer. On the northwest side of the lake are extensive sandfields which reach as far as Iisakkijärvi lake. You can form an idea of the flatness of the land from the massive gravel and drift sand stratifications. In places the rocks have pushed their way up to the surface. The bedrock in this area primarily consists of basic rock types, mainly amphibolite rock. You cannot fail to notice the great amount of purple moor grass, cinquefoil, fragrant orchid and yellow mountain saxifrage.

We leave Näätämöjoki at Opukasjärvi and push onwards to the Silisjoki river bend, leaving the hilly country at the mouth of the Poaskijoki river. A strange-looking area greets the traveller here and it is best to skirt it via the northern side. It is worth climbing the Ladnapuoldsa esker without a backpack, the ridge of this esker rises nearly 40 metres above the Poaskijoki river. From up here you get a view over a terrain broken by dozens of esker pits resembling an area which has suffered heavy bombing. The largest of these pits is more than 30 metres below the level of the ridge. From the highest point on the esker unfolds a vista over an area without fells extending for a league or more. In the west, countless pools and ragged-shored lakes shimmer, forming the blue labyrinth of Ordavääri.

Extending from Ladnapuoldsa westwards there is a dismal fen area above the upper courses of the Tuolpuoja, Vaijoki and Karpulijoki rivers. The area consists of flat peneplains where flood waters persist for a long time. Because of the slow running waters, the area is dominated by the characteristics of still-water countryside — lakes, pools and submerged fens with rushes. Between the marshes are islands of firm land with birch thickets. The landscape is deeply furrowed from west to southwest, which determines the route to be taken. The best way to cross the marshes is to follow the tracks trampled down by the reindeer. This country is a paradise for birdwatchers, but the rambler will be happier skirting it via Stuorra-Tievja and Kuorboaivi. HK

Salmon and Trout

One of the most perfect achievements of nature, purposeful to the last detail and surpassing even the most beautiful of human creations, is a Nordic salmonoid fish, a salmon from one of the great rivers or a trout from a wilderness lake or brook. That is probably the sentiment of any angler who succeeds in landing a strong, self-confident trout. Just taken from the water in spring, a trout clad in its spawning costume glitters in the sun like a living jewel. The dark, almost black colour of its back blends into mossy greens, which in turn proceed to the silvery sheen of the fish's flanks. On the upper sides of the flanks, dark, then electric blue and finally purple-red spots add further richness to the colour scheme. Lower down, towards the belly, the colour gradually changes to gold or a soft cream-yellow. There it is, the pearl of the northern wilderness, a living gem, that mysterious denizen of clear cool waters, the trout.

The northern game fish zone

Most anglers in southern Finland mainly try for perch and pike, but the further north one goes the more important salmon and trout become — in spite of the fact that nearly all of our northern rivers have been destroyed as far as salmon fishing is concerned. But the rivers Näätämö and Teno are still in their prime. Noble game fish — whitefish, char and grayling, in addition to salmon and trout — are also important components of professional fishermen's catches in the large lakes of central and northern Finland. Has random fortune smiled on the lakes of the north, or have the lakes of southern Finland deteriorated to the point where noble species no longer dominate? That the lakes in the south have been altered by human activity is indeed true, but to understand the whole truth one has to take a look at how these species have spread down through the millennia.

As the last Ice Age was drawing to a close about 10,000 years ago, an ice sheet still covered the northernmost parts of Fennoscandia, but its edges were receding rapidly. Huge lakes of cold water formed close to the edges of the glaciers and frigid rivers flowed out of them and onto the new land emerging from beneath the sea. Lakes that have long disappeared spread between hills and eskers and mighty rivers drained their waters into the sea.

As land was uplifted in the region that is today Denmark and southern Sweden, the Baltic was cut off from the world's oceans and became the vast Ancylus freshwater lake. Meltwaters from the glaciers made the salinity of the White Sea far lower than it is today. From those two large water bodies, several species of freshwater fish with a high tolerance for cold began migrating up rivers.

Among the first were perch, pike, burbot, minnows, trout, whitefish, grayling and char. Atlantic salmon migrated up rivers flowing into the Arctic Ocean to the north. One after the other, however, the fish succumbed to exhaustion. Sometimes there were waterfalls too steep for a perch or pike to jump, sometimes the river

263

flowed too fast, or the water was too cold, or the upland summer too brief for young fish to mature. The only species that made it to the uppermost headwaters were trout, grayling, char and whitefish, which are quite at home in cold bleak waters. The result was the northern game fish zone, the waters of which the species

Reijo Juurinen

have divided among themselves to suit their respective characteristics. The subsequent warming of the climate and stocking by humans have changed the pattern somewhat, but the game species still dominate in the north.

The salmon

The largest and most beautiful of them all is the Atlantic salmon. And the finest of all the Atlantic salmon in Europe is, they say, the one that lives in the River Teno, which forms a long stretch of the border between Finland and Norway. Of course, international frontiers mean nothing to the salmon, which swims a thousand or so kilometres up the river. To the people who live along the river, the salmon have always been an important source of supplementary income. And ever since the 1850s, when English gentlemen discovered the Teno, hopeful anglers have been heading north every season in

search of the King of Fish.

The value of the Teno was recognized very early on, and the first fishing agreement between the Norwegian and Finnish authorities dates from 1873 and is still in force. Another agreement that helps preserve salmon stocks in the Teno is one signed in 1984 to restrict net fishing of this species in the

Brook trout spend all their lives in streams or small rivers.

North Atlantic.

The Teno salmon's journey to the spawning beds begins far away in the North Atlantic. Shoals that have gorged themselves on the fatty herrings that swim in the waters off Iceland, but reduced to a tenth of their original number, turn their snouts north-east and east. After a long journey, they recognize the smells of their home rivers. Its degree of acidity and various substances that have dissolved into it give every river and tributary a characteristic aroma, which the fish remember. Of the Teno's 45 tributaries up which salmon migrate, many have their own populations precisely adapted to conditions there.

The first wave of large plump fish reaches the river during the spring spate in May. The second arrives when summer is at its height. Most of the second

wave consists of grilse, which have spent less than a year in the sea and weigh two or three kilos. A local catching one of these seems only bored at the bother involved, but a tourist is content to catch any fish. Indeed, the locals are not too impressed with the fish that come in the third wave, either. These are called "salmon legs" in the Teno area and can weigh up to six kilos. However, the next in size, a "real salmon" weighing anything up to fifteen kilos thrills anybody, local or outsider, but the fulfillment of many a life's dream comes only when one catches one of the "big salmon", which are the last to swim up the river. These whoppers with their hooked jaws can reach weights of forty kilos (90lbs!).

Spawning begins sometime in October or November. Having found a suitable redd, as a spawning bed is called, among gravel in running water, the male entices a female to the spot. Indeed, a handsome specimen can have a whole harem. The female lays her eggs in a depression that she scoops out of the river bed and the male fertilizes them. Besides the master of a particular spawning bed, the eggs may also be fertilized by parr, young salmon which have not yet migrated.

Buried under gravel as much as half a metre deep, the roe mature all winter and hatch in spring. The hatchlings, alvins, remain hidden in the safety of the gravel for up to two months, emerging only when the nourishment in their yolk sacks is exhausted. Now grown to the status of fry, they seek shelter under a stone and establish a territory, where they obtain food and which they defend against any other members of their species entering it. At first they eat microscopic organisms, then water insects and finally small fish.

During the next 2 – 5 years in the river, the growing fish, now called parr, undergo physiological and behavioural changes, which transform them from aggressively territorial loners to migratory and social shoal fish. They also acquire the ability to live in salt water and a new name: smolt. When the spring

floods are in spate, the smolts swim down to the sea, and on the way meet their older relations coming upstream to spawn. The full cycle has been completed.

Trout

In the view of many, the trout is an even better fish than its big cousin the salmon. It inhabits all major river and lake systems in the northern wildernesses and because there are populations in everything from vast lakes to tiny forest streams, it offers anglers a huge diversity of forms and is easier to catch than salmon. Although it is nowhere the dominant species, it is always a prized catch. Nobody who has ever caught one in a quiet wilderness lake or river will wonder why. There are three sub-species of trout in Finland, and colour patterns within these can vary quite considerably. One variety, sea trout, migrates back and forth between rivers and the sea. Lake trout, which are slightly smaller, spend most of their lives in lakes, but usually migrate into inflowing or outflowing rivers to spawn. The smallest of the three sub-species found in Finland lives and breeds entirely in rivers and streams.

A trout snaps at a fly or spinner just as eagerly as a salmon, although for different reasons. Anglers catch salmon during the spawning season, when the fish do not actually eat. Why they are attracted by lures is a mystery, and there are almost as many theories to explain it as there are researchers and anglers. Trout, on the other hand, are simply in search of food, for which reason baits are designed to resemble natural prey as closely as possible. If they are rising for flies, this is the best bait; when they are swimming deep, one can use a replica of an insect larva or a spinner resembling a small fish.

To many, however, nothing beats the sense of achievement that comes from luring a brook trout in a small wilderness stream with a small fly. Many are happy to pay a lot to enjoy that experience and all that goes with it in the waters of northern Finland. EKa

Aimo Holtari

WESTERN
LAPLAND

FROM YLLÄS TO OUNAS

Journeying from Kittilä northwards you encounter the real fell country for the first time at Sirkka. Here the road sneaks between Levi and Kätkä and then branches northwestwards towards Muonio. Along this stretch you encounter the most favourable views of Outa-Lapland — that is, if you are merely satisfied with the view from a windscreen. Beautiful, untouched parts, park-like ancient pinewoods and forests of moss-bearded spruce shading the hill slopes venture right up to the roadside. The fell country of west Lapland extends in a south-north direction for nearly 100 kilometres. It is not

Veikko Vasama

267

however an unbroken tract of wilderness, rather a broken fell chain in parts branching into two. It begins at Kolari Yllästunturi fell and ends at Ounastunturi fell in Enontekiö. Firmly joined to its flanks are Aakenus at Kittilä and in the east, already somewhat further afield, Kätkä and Levi.

The western Lapland fell country belongs to the Karelidic folds of 1800 million years ago. These residual hills have withstood the weathering and erosion and have remained standing like knots in old planks. On the other hand the Ounas ridge has survived the passage of years with little damage through being in the watershed area; it divides the watercourses of the Tornio and Kemi rivers.

The fell lands of western Lapland do not form a particularly coherent region. In terms of landscape they can be divided into various fell chains bordered by wilderness tracts, mires and lakes, but more and more nowadays the wilderness seems to be broken by highways. Nonetheless, the rambler can, with patience and determination, still find the genuine wilderness experi-

ence in the fells of western Lapland, while on the other hand the wide-ranging tourist facilities and plentiful accommodation are a boon to the ordinary traveller.

PALLAS — OUNAS

The 500 square kilometre national park was made a nature protection area in 1938, making it the second oldest national park in Finland. The Pallastunturi fell group dominates the southern part of the park, the continuation of which is a group of different barren tops beginning from Keimiöntunturi fell climbing from the shores of Jerisjärvi lake. The bedrock of this area is amphibolite, crystalline slates containing hornblende. The mainly quartzite Ounastunturi rises on the northern side of the Pahakuru labyrinth. Viewed from the side, the Pallas silhouette undulates attractively but on the wide summit area of Ounas you already encounter the fells.

The coniferous woods begin where the barren top ends. On many of the slopes there is no actual birch zone at all. The bare tops of Pallas are surrounded by lush forests with thick mossy carpets or even lusher spruce copses. The Pahakuru gap is broken by spruces against the skyline. The Ounastunturi fells are already surrounded by pine forests with lichen underfoot. Although many regard the national park as hallowed and untouchable, it should be remembered that the herds of three Reindeer Owners' Associations graze here. This composition may also represent the highest degree of idealism in the diversity of usage of our forests. Despite this protection, and also thanks to it, the genuine original inhabitant can take full economic advantage of the area through his reindeer.

A WINTER'S JOURNEY IN THE FELLS

The Ylläs-Ounas region presents a real challenge even to the determined wanderer. Summer or winter, you can don your rucksack and set off to spend a week in the fells. A signposted network of trails and huts covers the entire fell ridge. Under no circumstances is it obligatory to keep to the trails, but you should obey the rules regarding camping and firelighting here in the national park as well as elsewhere. Because this area, which is Finland's second highest fell area, is a favourite haunt for skiers, we will concentrate particularly on the winter season in the fell country. The first snows begin to fall on the slopes of Pallastunturi fell in September, but the permanent snow cover usually comes around the end of October and the beginning of November. At the beginning of December the snow comes up to the knees of a small man and the Kaamos season begins. For a good four weeks the sun disappears below the horizon and reappears at Ylläs on 29.12 and in Pallas on 8.1 and three days later in Hetta. Although it snows a great deal in January and February, in Muonio for example the snow drifts at the beginning of March are on average 60 cm deep.

The birch sheds its autumn leaves against a cottage wall at Keimiönniemi Jerisjärvi.

In spring the ptarmigan wears a mixture of winter and summer plumage.

ALONG THE TRAILS

The trail network which cuts across the whole of the Ounas ridge begins from Ylläs. Ylläs is the southernmost large fell, with its highest point being 718 metres above sea level. In good weather you can see for miles in every direction from the fell summit. Far to the west you can see the Kingdom of Sweden. In the south and east an enormous patchwork of aapa mires and woods. From this point we can make our final decision about our route and imagine what the future holds as we point our skis downwards towards the north. Before us is the slightly lower fell chain of Kesänkitunturi, Lainiotunturi, Kukastunturi and Pyhätunturi fells. The signposted route follows the western part of this stretch.

After Äkäskero there is a group of at least three open stretches of water, the lakes of Äkäsjärvi, Jerisjärvi and Särkijärvi. The lakes of Pallasjärvi and Vuontisjärvi belong to the same series on the other side of the national park. They are all clear water lakes with relatively barren vegetation. Apart from the usual fish these waters contain whitefish and trout, not to mention salmon. The traveller in search of a dose of culture should stop at Keimiöniemi on the north of Jerisjärvi lake. The row of ancient fishermen's huts conjure up the past, but the identical museum still flourishes today. The glass fibre boats encrusted with whitefish scales on the gravelly shore, the fishing nets and the happy faces at the window of the hut prove that the local fishing tradition is still going strong. The hotel built for skiers near the Pallas travel centre was constructed before the national park was established. The building was destroyed in the last stages of the war, but a new one was built immediately on the declaration of peace and has since been renovated. In the grounds you can nowadays find an information centre for the national park where visitors are plied with written and pictorial information about local wildlife.

From the heart of Pallas our route lies practically straight through the national park northwards. Before us lies the highest point in western Lapland, Taivaskero, also known as Himmelriikki (807 metres). Around us are a host of other peaks and just as many steep sided canyons. Up and down the slopes our trail continues as far as Pahakuru. Between the two massive fells lies a valley formation of rocky ravines, pools and woods. Verdant and romantic in all respects but somewhat problematic for the careless map-reader before his skis begin to slant upwards properly on the Outaka slopes. Then at last we are on the flat Ounastunturi fell going towards Pyhäkero. Before us are just low lying lands and a short sweep over the ice on Ounasjärvi lake to the Enontekiö village, Hetta.

WHERE SOUTH AND NORTH OVERLAP

Two diametrically opposite worlds meet in the Pallastunturi-Ounastunturi fells. More or less as one continuous bridge, the fell ridge attracts many northern, even arctic species. In contrast, on the flanks of the same top just a hundred metres lower down in the shade of a pleasant coniferous forest, you can find certain southern species in numbers just as great as on the shores of the Gulf of Finland. The plants at the limits of their range in this dividing zone include diapensia, mountain avens and Ranunculus nivalis. In the nearby copses the southern forces are represented by meadow-sweet, ostrich fern and moschatel.

In the same way, from the two sides of the coniferous zone can be heard the best spring concert performed by snow buntings and bullfinches, ptarmigan and song thrush, dotterel and wren. The brambling caps it all of course, at this latitude he finally gets the upper hand over his southern competitor, the chaffinch.

The open wilderness provides just the right conditions for some of our noble feathered friends. The eagle is a regular visitor to the park. Sometimes the white-tailed eagle, which used to nest permanently in these regions up to the 1960's, can be seen here too. Nowadays there is little chance of finding a white-tailed eagle's eyrie in the national park — this information is for those illegal egg collectors hoping for ill gotten gains! It is possibly due to these people that the only nesting place for the gyr falcon in Pallas-Ounas has been quite deserted in the last few years.

The four-legged fauna of the national park includes the occasional bear and wolverine. As in all areas where reindeer husbandry is practiced, the fox is rather plentiful and its tracks can be found on the barren tops. After a successful breeding season the Arctic fox may occasionally visit this far south.

The shoreline spruce woods of the river Pyhäjoki which flows into the Pallasjärvi lake may well be the only place on earth where you can come across nine of Finland's ten species of vole in one day. Naturally this only happens when the migration of the abundant Norway lemming from higher up hastens towards the hollows of the ancient spruce woods. When they reach the favourable mossy slopes the lemmings stop to hibernate and have their young. In spring, when they begin to feel the floodwaters, they bounce to the frozen surface of the snow and recommence their journey, but its here at Outa-Lapland that they live their finest moments. In the heart of winter the spruce woods on the fell slopes appear feeble, as if in deep slumber under the snowy mantle. If you investigate this white world closely you will discover otherwise. The absolute silence rings in your ears only momentarily. The first to break this silence is the shy Siberian tit. A little later you hear the shrieking of the great spotted woodpecker muffled in this kingdom of snow covered branches. Then you see rather than hear a soft flapping through the frosty trunks — a Siberian jay, the friend of the Koilliskaira traveller. Ringing above you is a completely unnatural trilling, you prick up your ears — what can it be? On hearing the warbling once more you already know which spruce crown to look at, realiz-ing that the season of hope and love for the woodpecker starts as early as January.

When the short Kaamos day begins to darken you thrust the tips of your skis yet again into a tangle of spruce trunks — a lot of white snow falls on your shoulders but something red has also fallen out of the tree. Down the trunk and into the arms of the snowdrift a small ball of fur flashes past. It was not a midget squirrel but a red-furred bank vole. Or a grey-sided vole. Or was it a northern red-backed vole? They all go to the branches of the conifers to search for food. And as the small creatures which decorate the snowdrifts in every direction will tell you — the vole population is now in strength.

A few winter months later you ski the same course in the Pallas spruce woods. This time however at midnight, as there is enough light to see by all through the day and night. In place of the deep midwinter silence you hear the babbling of a brook that has pushed its way through the snowdrift. Another tinkling accompanies this symphony, the mating call of the hawk owl. The plentiful supply of food has triggered off the stripy breasted owl's mating instinct. All winter long it has been catching the small rodents that have strayed on to the snowdrifts and now its foodstore begins to contain other voles and also lemmings. In the hollows of decayed trunks and even in the lichen-covered spruce branches lie yellow-black mottled tidbits.

The hawk owl rushing to find a furry bundle as a courtship gift is by no means the only enemy of the lemmings which crowd onto the surface of the snowdrifts. A true taiga resident, the great grey owl is also on the prowl. The snowy owl too often lands on the Pallas peaks. And as spring advance other long distance hunters find their way to these surroundings, from the merlin to the rough-legged buzzard, and the kestrel to the long-tailed skua. The wilderness is alive. AK

The Pallas-Ounastunturi National Park

Enontekiö, Kittilä, Muonio, 500 km²
Established: 1938
Under Finnish Forest Research Institute administration

Connections: Roads from many directions go to the national park and its surrounding areas. Suitable departure points for a tour are the Pallaskero Tour Hotel, Raattama village, or Enontekiö Hetta to where there is a bus connection.

Services: Information centre at Pallas. The tour route Pallas — Hetta (64 km) starts there; alongside this route are tenting areas and places for cooking and several unlocked huts. The southern tour route to Ylläs (70 km) also goes from Pallas. Private accommodation can be had in some houses in the surrounding villages. There are also many camping sites, holiday villages, youth hostels and hotels in the area.

Further information: National Park wardens, tel. 9696-51011 Enontekiö, information centre, tel. 9696-2451 or the Finnish Forest Research Institute, North Finland District, tel. 960-15721 (Rovaniemi).

Hunting the White Grouse

Hannu Hautala

Residents of the three northernmost municipalities of Enontekiö, Inari and Utsjoki still have the right to hunt willow grouse and ptarmigan for sale. They are also allowed to trap these birds so coveted by gourmets and enjoy a longer season than elsewhere in Finland. Their rights are based on tradition and the recognition that livelihoods in the north still depend more on the bounty of nature than is the case further south.

As recently as a few decades ago, the white grouses of the north provided many people with their main source of income. Hunters spent the winter in their peat huts in the hills and patrolled their traplines. A hunter could catch up to a thousand birds in a good season.

Things have changed a good deal since then. Only a handful of professional hunters remain, and most of them have to turn to something else, such as fishing, berry-picking or reindeer herding, in the off-season.

Two prized preys

The two birds that attract the hunters are both members of the grouse family, and very similar to each other. But one, the willow grouse, remains fairly scrupulously below the treeline, whilst the ptarmigan prefers barren stony hill slopes. Both species sometimes mingle in hillside willow groves and thickets, but otherwise keep to their respective habitats. With the exception of their black tails, the two species are completely white in winter, although the male ptarmigan can be easily distinguished by the black mark running from its bill to its eye.

The willow grouse is slightly larger than the ptarmigan and is endowed with a sturdier bill. Both have much more colour in summer, the willow grouse in its mottled brown plumage and the ptarmigan in slightly greyer hues.

The easiest way to distinguish between them is by means of their voices: the willow grouse emits staccato "ko-pek-pek-ko" series of sounds, whereas the ptarmigan alternates between drumming "aar-aar-ka-ka" sounds as though from the

Jorma Luhta

depths of its throat and a hasty "kar-r-rk" when alarmed.

Traps

Traps are usually set for willow grouse, although the occasional ptarmigan can wander into them near the border of the treeline. The hunters' strategy is based on the birds' winter feeding habits. The birds nibble twigs and the tips of deciduous tree branches which protrude from the snow on hill slopes.

Aware of this, hunters build curving fences of tightly spaced twigs, which stand out as dark lines on the snow and attract the birds flying overhead. In the middle of the fence, they leave a gap, with a snare the width of a hand above the snow. In former times, the snares were made of linen thread or hairs from a horse's tail, but the most common materials today are nylon fishing line, brass wire or thin steel cord. Technological development alters even the most traditional of livelihoods.

Trappers have to be experts on the birds' habits and movements, in addition to having the stamina to survive in the harsh Arctic environment that is their workplace, often for many days at a stretch.

During the gloomy winter period, their days are short, although snowmobiles nowadays speed up travel. The actual handicraft work, assembling the fence, has to be done from skis or by wading through the snow. Even when the weather is good, an experienced trapper will be lucky to get more than a few dozen fences in place in a day. After that, he goes on until he has set as many as five hundred in all. There is no legal limit to the number of traps; but how many a man can tend is another matter.

Hard work can overcome even poor luck. It may take weeks to catch one's first bird, but then there is another, and maybe even five or six on a morning when fortune smiles. Restaurants pay handsomely, but more than recoup their costs when the fist-sized birds are served up on silver trays.

Trappers used to sell most of their catches to customers in Sweden and Norway, but now there are enough buyers for the increasingly scarce birds at home.

Stuffed ptarmigan and willow grouse are popular as decorations in restaurants and hotels and are often taken home by foreign tourists who consider them exotic souvenirs. This, too, helps augment the hunters' incomes.

Sometimes a run of luck can continue and catches increase, but the trappers have to be on their guard. Crows and ravens, stoats and foxes soon learn where the traps are and plunder them if they get a chance. When he finds no more than a bundle of feathers in his snare, the hunter can forget any ideas of taking a day — much less a weekend — off.

When the season closes at the end of March, the total bag may well be under a hundred birds. Not much for a large family to live on all year round. Declining bird populations in recent years have thinned the ranks of the hunters as well.

Even after a bad summer, the winter catch can be good if one is lucky enough to come across a remote treeless bog, where migrating birds can sometimes assemble in their hundreds in late autumn.

Shooting

If there is any time left after tending his traps, the hunter can also shoulder his shotgun and ski off to the hills in pursuit of ptarmigan.

Those are bleak hunting grounds. The ptarmigan is most at home near bare hill summits or on slopes that the piercing wind has stripped of snow. The hunter has to drive himself against wind, up and down slope after slope, with the rocky ground mercilessly scratching his skis.

He has a good idea of where he is likely to find the birds, but may have to look in several places before he comes across any. Here and there, marks in the snow reveal where some creature or other has dined fairly recently. Now, however, nothing moves.

The short winter day draws to a close and the weary hunter heads back, disappointed that he has had no luck. But then, just as he reaches some shrubs on the edge of the treeline, three fine ptarmigan flash into the air. Although just as white as their surroundings, their flying figures stand out clearly. The hunter wheels on his skis and heads towards the spot, but the birds are gone when he gets there.

The same pattern may repeat itself several times. Hope grows and is dashed — time and time again. Gaining a living from Nature is never easy. Hunters sometimes have their day, but this is not it.

There is nothing more to do but go home and tell about the day. "Now I know where the birds are," says the ever-optimistic hunter. AK

Plants of the Cold

Dick Forsman

1. The depth of the winter snow cover in the fells is a key factor in deciding what vegetation grows there. Diapensia (Diapensia lapponica) grows on wind-swept slopes where little snow gets lodged; a thin coating of ice is usually all that protects it from cold.

Late winter is the most crucial time; in the daytime the sun may raise the temperature of the ground to twenty degrees, at night it may be twenty degrees below zero. The low profile growing habit of diapensia, its thick root and leathery, closely set leaves are adapted to such extremes, and this tiny plant cannot be found in any other set of growing conditions.

2. Like diapensia, moss campion (Silene acaulis) is one of Finland's easily distinguished tussock type plants. This form of growth is admirable for a plant that needs to absorb all the heat it can get. Moss campion grows on calcium-rich fell heaths, as well as on sandy patches and shores. Its flowers contain large amounts of nectar. Moss campion is one of the most obvious insect pollinated plants of the bare fell tops.

3. Allied to the common buttercup, Ranunculus glacialis is able to survive at higher altitudes than any other flowering plant in the Alps (4275 m) and in Fennoscandia (2370 m). It also occurs at the extreme latitude of 12°N. Its distribution is limited to the topmost summits of the fells, where it grows next to meltwater streams and on patches of ground that are snow-covered for most of the year.

Reijo Juurinen

Arno Rautavaara

Reijo Juurinen

4. This dwarf species of willow (*Salix herbacea*) is the exact opposite of diapensia in choosing to grow in moist hollows which in winter are covered by 1-2 metres of snow. As the snow melts . slowly there, the dwarf willow's growing season is exceptionally brief. It has to hurry: flowering as soon as it is exposed, the tiny shrub produces its reddish seed pods within the short space of 5-6 weeks.

5. Though relatively rare, mountain avens is Lapland's most well-known fell plant. The calcium-rich soil it requires occurs in abundance only in the fells of northwest Enontekiö.

As the leaves of this plant are very durable, they have been searched for by palaeobotanists in post glacial deposits in Europe as far north as South Sweden and the Karelian isthmus. Between its present range and the nearest site at which re-

mains have been found, however, there is a large gap. It is possible that the glaciers retreated so swiftly that other plants were able to conquer exposed areas before mountain avens had a chance to establish itself. In this case, the Fennoscandian fell populations must have arrived from the east rather than the south.

6. Purple saxifrage (*Saxifraga oppositifolia*) is one of the first

plants to flower in spring. Like mountain avens, it requires a calcium-based soil. At the edges of melting Norwegian glaciers purple saxifrage is one of the first plants to become established. This makes it likely that in the early post glacial period it occurred in many parts of Finland. With the growth of thicker, stronger vegetation and the build up of detritus in the soil, it disappeared from all except its present localities. SV

Reijo Juurinen

Dick Forsman

The Fells in Colour

The season called "ruska" is when Lapland erupts in a riot of colours. Birches glow in yellows offset by red hues varying in intensity almost from tree to tree. Slender aspens on fell slopes become red pillars of fire, stunted birch shrubs fringing bogs smoulder in many shades of dark red, which are rivalled only by those of the bilberry carpets covering the heaths. Bog whortleberry shrubs and the dense thickets of downy willows on bogs and along rivers and creeks add many blue and bluish nuances to the firelike riot of colour. The brightest element of all comes from black bearberry shrubs, now probably the reddest there is. Those are the main colours in the palette, but every species of plant adds its own nuances to the splendour of the autumnal display.

The dark green of softwoods does nothing to lessen the wealth of colour, but all the more to set it off. Close to their northern limit, individual Scots pines and spruces resemble charred blocks in a huge conflagration and in places where softwoods dominate, the general blaze is replaced by islands of fire in a sea of green.

Lapland's quick change

Although the variety of plant species is much poorer in Lapland than further south, the autumnal colour display is incomparably more splendid there. One reason is the rarity of softwoods, but even more important is the speed at which autumn arrives. The autumn colours are very beautiful in the south as well, but every species prepares for winter at its own pace, over a three-month period from August to October. In Lapland, it all happens in two or three weeks.

But some plants in Lapland begin their change before the others. Bog sedges begin turning yellow and brown well be-

fore the end of August, deergrass tussocks flare in a yellowish gold and some dwarf birch shrubs are a crimson red, although most are still green.

Many parts of the world don colourful autumn garbs as though having a final splash out before the relative drabness of winter descends. In the case of Lapland, it is the Fell birch that plays the leading role.

Fell birch is a distinct subspecies of downy white birch that at some point after the Ice

Age acquired some genes from the ground-hugging dwarf birch. The two species still hybridize and their descendants are fertile. However, they blossom at such different times that this does not happen often. Hybridization has given the Fell birch a much richer gene pool. One of the characteristics that it has received from dwarf birch is the richness of its autumn red colour. There are startling differences between individual trees in this respect; where one is a

brilliant red, its neighbour can be a pallid yellow.

What causes the colours?

In contrast to what is generally believed, frost does not make plants change into their autumn colours. As the daylight period shortens, plants begin preparing for the advent of winter by breaking up the more valuable substances in their leaf cells and transferring them to living cells in the trunk and roots.

Veikko Vasama

and even cell membranes change their structure. All these changes are intended to improve plants' ability to tolerate cold. A plant that can survive only a few degrees of frost in summer — and it sometimes has to so far in the north — can easily cope with dozens of degrees below zero by the end of October.

If a plant cell freezes, it dies. Everyday observations might make one think otherwise, because branches can be frozen to the core in winter. What matters is that whereas a birch can freeze, its cells must not!

There is plenty of space between individual cells, and in winter these spaces are filled with water and air. In heavy frost, the water in these spaces turns to ice. The more severe the frost, the more water is transferred from the cells into the spaces between them, where it freezes; at the same time, however, the freezing water yields heat and softens the impact of the frost. The more water oozes from cells, the thicker their fluids become and the more frost they can stand.

Still, there is a limit to what cell fluids can bear. Somewhere between 40 and 60 degrees below zero Celsius, either the fluids freeze or the cells have lost so much fluid that they are no longer capable of recovering when the thaw finally comes.

Reawakening

Everything happens the other way round in spring. Plants awaken just as slowly as they prepare for their winter sleep. They begin doing so in the darkest heart of winter, although months will pass before there are any outward signs of change. We have all seen it with our own eyes: birch branches placed in a vase in autumn will not produce leaves, nor will willow catkins open, but in early spring, although the branches look the same, they will break into rapid growth. That is because they have awakened.

Thus the autumn colours are not a sign of death, but of life. As Yrjö Kokko wrote: "It is not autumn that is coming to the Arctic fells on the threshold of autumn, but spring." SV

The most precious substance of them all is chlorophyll, the green substance that captures energy from sunlight. Leaves contain so much chlorophyll in summer that it blankets out the other pigments that are also there: yellow carotenoids and red and bluish-red anthocyanins. These continue to be produced as the plant proceeds to dismantle its summer growth mechanisms, and at the same time as the green fades, the other colours gain in intensity.

The show is different every year. A great deal depends on the weather. The fells appear to be ablaze when a warm summer is followed by a dry autumn with bright days and clear, chilly nights. On the other hand, if the summer has been cool and brief and the autumn is rainy and warm, plants delay their winter sleep and their colours are subdued. Even when all other conditions are right for a magnificent display, the result may be disappointing: an autumn storm can strip the leaves away in one fell swoop.

Greater cold tolerance

The colour extravaganza is only a side-show. What really counts is preparing for winter and storing the nutrients that will power the following spring's growth. Plant cells undergo major changes in autumn as they change over from their summer growth phase to a more restful state. Sugars and proteins are stored in cells, cell fluids thicken

WESTERN
LAPLAND

When, a long time ago, the cairn marking the confluence of the boundaries of three separate countries was erected in western Lapland — at the tip of what Finns call 'the arm' of their country — the aim was to place the border line exactly on the great divide separating the sources of streams flowing in radically different directions. All the slopes shelving away towards the Arctic Ocean would belong to Norway, while the springs of brooks flowing south would be divided between Finland and Sweden. Luckily for us the red line now marked on maps was not drawn on a geological basis, for the northwestern tip of our country contains a residue of the Köli region of large

fells thrust up thousands of millions of years ago. The latter in a less condensed form dominate the scenery in the adjoining territories of Sweden and Norway. This, the most barren and elevated corner of the 'arm' of western Finnish Lapland, is known to Finns as Yliperä.

ON THE VERGE OF THE ARCTIC

The tourist motoring at speed along the way of the four winds will not come to the higher fells until he gets to Kilpisjärvi. Here the entire scene is dominated by Saana-tunturi fell. In the left foreground the topmost cove of Lake Kilpisjärvi reflects roundish peaked Pikku-Malla, a kind of warden over Mall, Finland's oldest strict nature reserve. Before heading off into the wilderness, we can well devote a whole extra day to exploring the Malla landscape. This is especially recommended to those who are unable to embark on major hikes lasting a few days, or even a couple of weeks. Moreover, Malla Strict Nature Reserve in effect is Yliperä in a nutshell.

The twisted white-trunked fell birch forms forests whose upper limit lies at 700 metres. Seepage of mineral-rich water down the flanks of fells ensures that on both the Salla and Malla sides the shores of Lake Kilpisjärvi are clothed in luxuriant vegetation.

Perhaps the most commonly observed birds of the fell birch woods are the bluethroat and brambling. The former sings as though it would outdo the nightingale, while the brambling's buzz-saw cry rings out day and night. It is true that there are many other bird species nesting in these birch groves, but the redpoll is the species that most readily comes to mind. Alongside a few species of tits, the redpoll is one of the few small birds to spend its entire winter living on its wits at Yliperä. When there are a lot of seeds on the fell birches, it is possible for flocks of redpolls up to several hundred strong to survive here.

Extremely calcium-rich areas occur on Saana, Malla and other higher fells and here very demanding plants are able to grow. If, for example, we set off along the Pikku-Malla trail above the timber line at the beginning of summer — this would be just after 24 June — we will come across eye-catching heaths whose white colour is contributed by mountain avens and Cassiope tetragona; whose purplish colouration is due to mountain heath and moss campion; and whose bright red hues, like rubies in a crown, are provided by wild azalea.

In the Kilpisjärvi area in winter the average snow depth is about a metre, but the distribution of the snow is very uneven. Wind-battered slopes remain almost completely devoid of snow, whereas in protected hollows three metre drifts are not at all uncommon. These drifts remain as white streaks from spring until autumn. At their sides there is little vegetation, perhaps just a few mosses clinging to stones and hither and thither a flowering Ranunculus glacialis, a pale relative of the common buttercup. With luck, one may also discover the purple saxifrage. In passing, it should be mentioned that here we have two of the plant world's heroes: Ranunculus glacialis holds the record among vascular plants for

altitude, both in the Scandinavian fells and in the Central European Alps. The purple saxifrage is the most northern known plant, flourishing even in the distant parts of Greenland.

In the places where snow remains for well into the summer you will find the original home of the Norway lemming (or just plain 'lemming' if you prefer it). These lemmings spend a very secretive existence nibbling away at mosses and making their tunnels under several metres of efficiently insulating snow.

Oblivious to the lemmings, in both the fell birch woods and on the bare areas right up to where the briefest dwarf shrub ekes out a precarious existence, there dwells the grey-sided vole. He is a short-tailed fellow with a wonderful fur coat, reddish-brown at the back and silvery-grey on the sides. By nature he is a mischievous chap who gains frequent mention in the visitor's book in some of the cabins where he is accused of being the 'mouse that kept me awake', as he has roved about at night inside a haversack in a quiet corner of the cabin. One wonders whether the mild words used to record the event ever bear any relation to reality. Like many similar species, grey-sided vole population numbers vary in the extreme, reaching a peak every few years. The significance of this small rodent to large numbers of predators is much greater here than it could ever be in the south. When grey-sided voles become common, the Yliperä predators get together for a full-scale banquet. At such times both the rough-legged buzzard and the long-tailed skua rear a family of young. In years when the vole is scarce, both of these birds appear to disappear completely off the face of the earth.

In the past Arctic foxes ranged fairly commonly over almost all of northern Finland, and sometimes even further south. Nowadays in the Finnish fells there are just a few dozen individuals, most of which inhabit the bare fell summits of Yliperä. The Arctic fox is also at the mercy of the grey-sided vole, the most recent statistics revealing that reproduction in the Arctic fox is only successful in peak vole years. In intermediate years, the foxes all but disappear.

Among the more determined cliff-nesters are the raven and rough-legged buzzard, but the Pikku-Malla cliff also accommodates one of this area's specialities, the ring ouzel. This is a parson-like bird, jet black with a white bib.

Among the game birds the most Arctic are the ptarmigan, which spends its whole life on the topmost peaks of the great fells. In the depths of winter it seeks out the 'eaves' of cliffs and on wind-swept slopes makes use of dwarf shrubs covered with ice like miniature caves. Ptarmigans as a species have acquired their own ecological niche for which there are no other contestants. Only one species seems intent upon its removal, and that is the gyr falcon. Like its prey, this hawk also spends the winter in the fells. It slices through low-hanging clouds at a speed approaching that of the celebrated peregrine and rushes down on its victim. At the moment Finland's entire gyr falcon population amounts to around twenty pairs, so that this bird is worth looking out for at Malla Strict Nature Reserve in the depths of winter.

A SUMMER HIKE TO HALTI

Many summer hikers trek over the bar fell summits carrying a back pack in order to experience the bounty of the fells, and in order to prove — at least to themselves — that they are capable of surviving in the most rugged parts of the Finnish wilds without any external assistance. Before we set off along the trail, I'd like to say a couple of words about equipment. The weather at Yliperä changes with startling rapidity from one extreme to the other. It may snow whatever the month. This means that, aside from summer gear, one should also carry a warm pullover and gloves. Even more to the point is efficient waterproofing, which will insulate against cold sleet even at the height of summer — while incidentally drenching the wearer with sweat from within!

The cabin network here is nowadays fairly compre-

hensive, with both locked cabins, needing to be reserved in advance, and unlocked huts open to whoever chances by. The latest map will show their locations and the keys where necessary can be obtained before setting off, but it must be remembered that at the height of the tourist season (see below) most of the cabins are full. Carrying one's own tent, if possible, makes one entirely independent.

As regards food, everyone should take what suits their taste and in the appropriate quantities. It must be added that while there are still large numbers of salmonid fish in the water bodies at Yliperä, depending on the time, place and fickleness of the fish, even experienced anglers may go away disappointed. Thus, it is certainly not a good idea to plan your diet around the prospect of catching fish wherever and whenever you choose to throw in some encouragement.

Telephones have now been installed in many of the cabins, serving to radically increase the hiker's safety,

A relative of the rhododendrons, the wild azalea is a bush of small stature but startling presence. Reijo Juurinen

The trap-like flowers of lousewort literally have to be broken into by bumble bee pollinators, which thereby damage the blooms.

but the old adage still holds true: Don't go off into the fells alone. Even an inexperienced companion may prove to be worth his or her weight in gold.

If the outward trip is to be made in as straight a line as possible towards Finland's highest point, then the departure point could well be the yard of the recreation centre or the tourist hotel. Our first objective is the Saarijärvi fell hut.The round trip to Halti is about 12 leagues (100 km) and especially for novices the first kilometre up to the timber line is particularly gruelling. Fortunately the rest of the trip is a bit easier.

Ahead lies a narrow path and after the initial ascent the ground is surprisingly level up as far as Lake Saanajärvi, where there is a relatively new cabin managed by the Finnish Forest Research Institute. This accommodation is intended only for daytime use — as a turning point for shorter hikes, or as protection from bad weather — but it is not made for overnight stays.

According to the visitor's books, even on this initial section of the trail hikers have encountered some of the animals of the bare fell summits. The meadow pipit will hardly cause comment; the stonechat will come in for a

bit more attention, while the Lappish bunting with its ringing voice will steal the show. However, it is the golden plover which is one's constant companion. The black patch on the breast of this 'wader of the dry country' was acquired — according to folklore — long ago when it ventured too close to a wooden ladle that was being tarred by a Lapp. Known as the "bitjuus" to the Lapps, the species was previously a bird of omen. Everbody was well aware that if, on waking, you did not eat something before you heard the call of the golden plover from outside your tepee, you would not get any milk from your reindeer. So the experienced wife always carried an amulet round her neck made out of dried meat, which she would nibble at even before her eyes were fully open in the dawn. Today's rambler will see the golden plover in a different light: as a companionable guardian of the trail whose plaintive piping accompanies him almost ceaselessly, however fast he walks. Where one bird leaves off, the next starts up.

On the western shore of Lake Saarijärvi there is a fell cabin constructed by the Finnish Travel Association. Reservations for this cabin should be made in advance at the start. At times this hut is packed to capacity. On the lake's eastern shore there is also a small hut belonging to the border guards, but the door of this is kept permanently locked. The landscape opening out east of Saarijärvi aptly reflects the nature of Yliperä at its most authentic — in bad weather a thoroughly depressing spot, but when the weather clears an idyllic place full of fresh promise. This is the domain of the Arctic fox and the snowy owl, which later will take to the wing for a brief period, only to settle lazily on a hummock at the first opportunity.

If you want to go on along the fairly easy trail from the Saarijärvi cabin, you should strike out in the direction of the Norwegian border and Tuolihuippu. A deviation of just a few hundred metres to the right will put you almost immediately into very difficult terrain and directly in line with the slithering screes on the eastern flank of Kuonjar. Against, as it were, all the rules when the national boundaries were laid down, you will find a brook under Tuolihuippu which, while originating in Finland, stoically flows away towards the Arctic Ocean. From the lowest of the fell's saddles you proceed on down to Kuonjarvankka. Here there are easily navigated brookside meadows right up to the Kuonjar cabin. The scenery is already extremely rugged: on the right stands Kuonjarvarri fell with its white dolomitic crown. Over on the left the southern flanks of the Kahperusvaara fell group can be made out thrusting up into the clouds.

In front of you the Kahperuslaakso valley is a flattish affair covered in a stand of soft dwarf shrubs which rustle quietly as you walk through them. When the weather is very good you can see over a great distance, so that there is little chance of getting lost. When the clouds are low and the land drenched in drizzle, you will have need of a compass, however. Head straight for Kahperusladnja and just as your left boot begins to crunch on masses of stone fragments that have cascaded over the years down the fell side, your descent into the Meeko paradise begins.

On the right, Saivaara fell, and behind it Porovaara, hove⁻ into view. To the left stands Meekonvaara fell, recognisable by its cliffs. On the opposite side of the lake stretches the several kilometre long bastion of Anjalonji. Between these runs a green valley, a chain of pools like a string of pearls running down its length for about ten kilometres.

At the latest at this stage, it is a good idea to stop for a longer period. Apart from excellent camping spots, there is the "Mieko cabin" standing on the bank of the Pierfejoki river, in addition to a couple of locked cabins lying slightly further north and belonging to the National Board of Forestry. The former is an unlocked hut; keys to the latter are only obtainable in advance, which means giving some thought to the planning of your trek before setting out. In addition to these cabins, there are a couple of smaller huts belonging to the authorities and not intended for public use at all.

This 'village' shares its location with the small Meekonjärvi lake whose name, roughly translated into Finnish is "Määkijäjärvi" (literally "bleater's lake). The name seems to refer to an event in which in addition to luckless Lapps, a couple of goats also drowned in the pool, presumably bleating piteously as they vanished into its depths.

Towards the east behind a willow thicket coming up to head height glimmers Lake Skadjajärvi, on the north shore of which can be found some sod-roofed huts. The latter are monuments to one Aslak Juuso who used to spend his summers fishing here and about whom more details are given on the last page of this chapter. While — even by southern standards — Juuso was a millionaire, his 'summer house' was basic in the extreme. Year after year the 'Yliperä patriarch' would make his way through these familiar reindeer grazing grounds, living on salted winter fish from Skadjajärvi, and delighting in the views that today's hiker only glances peremptorily at before switching his attention elsewhere.

Saivaara fell, resembling a collapsed tam-o'-shanter, rises up on the southern side of Lake Skadjajärvi. Permanent residents of this fell include the rough-legged buzzard, which nests on its cliffs, and Janne, its guardian. The latter is believed to be a four-footed earth spirit. Many is the traveller who has suffered at his hands (the legends would have us believe) and he also appears to have taken affront at the newish Meeko cabin, from which, through the medium of a storm he whipped up, he knocked out a couple of stout logs not so long ago! Saivaara's summit can be reached from at least two different routes, the easiest of which would seem to be the one on the eastern side. In good weather one can spot most of the higher points in the terrain from Saivaara's peak, even Halti, a couple of leagues away to the north. In fact, in every direction there is something of interest. Beyond a couple of lakes and the strips of dry ground between them over towards the east stands Porovuoma, narrowly fringed with fell birches. On the

Rhodiola rosea, a member of the stone-crop family, has rose-scented roots. It is rare even in the fells.

southern shore of Lake Jogasjärvi can be made out the region's oldest unlocked cabin, the so-called 'maahistupa' (literally 'earth spirit's cabin'). Lake Porojärvi boasts a much newer cabin. When going towards Halti under the Meekonpahta cliffs, one is obliged to scramble over broken rocks, but after a few hundred metres of steep slope there is easy walking down the Vuomakasjoki river. If there is only a little water in the river, the latter can be crossed making use of stones, with scarcely a boot heel getting wet. In wet weather the safest crossing place is the northwestern corner of Lake Vuomakasjärvi. Here our hero may need to wade out in water up to his knees, but the chances of the current sweeping him away are negligible. Further up, the current is quite strong in the places marked on the map as fordable!

The Pitsusjoki river babbles along its deep channel in a canyon, round about the halfway point of which there is a spectacular waterfall where the water level drops a matter of 17 metres. In the late glacial period, the water was fairly high even this far up in the fells and the brown trout was the first of the salmonid fishes to ascend the river. With a drop in the water level, the trout's escape route was effectively cut off and other cold water fishes were prevented from proceeding further upstream. Hence, in the waters above the falls there are now only lonely brown trout.

On the northeastern shore of Pitsusjärvi there is a partly open hut and this is a good place in bad weather at which to kick one's heels while waiting for better conditions, before tackling the last leg. From the shores of Lake Koutajärvi, Halti with its annoying tracts of broken stones begins. So long as the cloud cover remains high, Finland's highest point — 1328 metres — and a visitors' book tucked away in the spot high above the last vestiges of melting snow will be found without any problem.

There are few species of organisms on Halti. Apart from a scattering of lichens, the plant world is represented almost entirely by Ranunculus glacialis. In the summer the birdlife is confined to ptarmigan and snow bunting; in the winter it is reduced to the former species alone. Aside from the occasional roving wolverine, the Halti mammals are restricted to grey-sided voles on the slopes living up to their reputation of being the sole fur-bearing animal capable of surviving at these altitudes. Even the Norway lemming has, literally, to look up to these hardy voles, its range beginning somewhere lower down the slopes.

FISHING TRIP

If your schedule, your food supply, and above all your own enthusiasm — not to mention your physical condition — suffice, you can turn east along the border. A good ten kilometres further on you find yourself at Lake Somasjärvi, whence you can follow the course of the Valtijoki as far as Lake Porojärvi. This particular route is highly popular with fishermen.

In the western parts of Yliperä there are a many good fishing places. On account of its scenery, Urtasvankka, west of Lake Vuomakasjärvi, is to be heartily recommended. An especially charming chain of lakes serves to put the finishing touch to a vista of peaks rising to more than 1000 metres: Kovddoskaisi, Urtaspahta, and finally Loassonibba. The "Urtas" part of the name of dominant Urtaspahta stands for one of the umbelifers, Angelica archangelica, which the ancient Lapps were able to make use of. Today that head-high plant clothes the slopes of Urtaspahta wherever there are hollows that have been enriched by water with high mineral concentrations seeping in. On the nearby patches of broken rocks one can also find Oxyria digyna, a relative of the sorrels. The leaves of this latter plant are picked off by the reindeer herdsmen. At home an infusion is made from the Angelica and Oxyria which is then stored in a bottle. Drunk with milk and sugar this herbal concoction still tastes delicious the following March.

The only problem for the hiker here is that the trail ends at Lake Lossujärvi. On the far shore of this lake there lies another country, and while one would very much like to take a short cut to the nearby highway, a distance of a mere ten kilometres, one has to remember that crossing the border is not officially permitted at this particular point (despite the general lack of formalities in this area). You can either return by the same route, or hike south from Loassonibba. In the first case plenty of new experiences await you. If the sterility of a landscape is measured in terms of the number of stones in it, then the setting of Lake Koddejärvi must be a serious contender for a Finnish record. As far as the eye can see there are stones and boulders, in the shade of which even the merest of dwarf shrubs, let alone the primordium of a tree, fails to make an appearance. In the midst of this lunar landscape small clearwater lakes glisten whose surfaces lie almost precisely at 1000 metres, and whose shores in places are still dotted with snow patches at summer's end. The lakes are inhabited by hungry, undernourished thin little brown trout which have great difficulty with obtaining enough food to enable them to maintain a precarious hold on existence.

The 'ordinary' hiker will probably be satisfied with going on from the Saivaara trail to Lake Siedjonjärvi, Kutturankuru and Lake Terbmisjärvi. The terrain is very stony but with a distinct charm. On the final evening of a hike in the fells one could well sit, for example, on the steps of the locked hut at the mouth of the Salmikuru ravine and admire the almost 500 metre high cliffs reflected there in the quiet waters. The track from Terbmis to Tsahkajärvi is well beaten and other hikers are constantly coming towards you, whether you are coming or going.

THE YLIPERÄ YEAR

In the great fells there tend to be large numbers of people at two distinct times of year: at midsummer and in the late winter. Between these two 'seasons' there are eight months during which few outsiders are to be seen in the terrain. Naturally, Yliperä offers plenty of experiences and excitement to naturalists twelve months of the year.

The large numbers of summer visitors have a way of disappearing after about the middle of August. By that time the splendour of the flowers has died down, birds getting ready for their migratory flights seem suddenly at a loss for words — or more correctly a song — fish stop eating (at least spoons and bait), and what is even more frustrating for the outdoorsman, the summer holidays have come and gone.

The last snow of summer falls at the end of August and the first snow of winter descends at higher elevations the following day. Then the autumn russet begins.

The first splashes of colour appear alongside the trails towards the end of August. The brilliance of the tones depends on the weather. If the autumn nights are warm under a sky curtained by cloud, the days grey and wet, the preparation by plants for their winter sleep is a dull affair. Sudden night frosts and bright days seem to encourage the landscape to ripen like a fruit, bedecking it in rich hues. Once seen, a true Lappish russet is not easily forgotten. At Yliperä the russet time arrives during the first half of September. It then depends on subsequent air movements how quickly this blaze of colour becomes converted to a monochrome patchwork of

Dick Forsman

While in good years a familiar sight on the high fells, when voles are scarce the long-tailed skua is scarce too.

black and white.

A relatively permanent snow cover blankets the fells in October. Lake Kilpisjärvi remains uncovered for quite a while, but the smaller lakes and pools fairly soon develop a crust of ice thick enough to bear the weight of the heaviest hiker or skier.

On 29 November the permanent winter twilight — the period of 'kaamos' — officially begins at Yliperä. At that time the sun does not rise above the horizon, even at midday. However, there is no permanent night. In the midst of this wild landscape, the northern lights, or 'aurora borealis' add their own bizzare form of kaleidoscopic shimmering.

In the fell birch zone one sinks into soft snow up to the knees, but on the bare summits the snow is soon hard enough to bear one's weight. The best way of getting about now, of course, is on skis and the daily distance covered should be geared to the number of twilight hours dispensed by the short day. Spending Christmas at a Lappish hotel in authentic Father Christmas country becomes more popular every year. By contrast, the fells lie silent. And yet the visual experiences offered by the pastel shades of these fairy tale conditions cannot be appreciated at any other time of the year. With the ending of the twilight period on 13 January, winter is still in its preliminary stages. Extremely severe frosts, biting cold winds, and snow storms continuing unabated for

several days serve to put the rambler to the test. Very few outdoorsmen actually experience the depths of winter in this region first hand.

A permanent inhabitant of the region, the raven, is already rearing its young when the first migrants appear in April. The snow bunting arrives from the south as the snow melts off the road verges, while other small birds like the redbreast and hedge sparrow appear from quite the opposite direction. The migratory flight of these follows the Norwegian coast where, thanks to the Gulf Stream, conditions are much less severe than in continental Finland. From the coast they fly along the valleys thrusting deep into Finland.

At Yliperä the best skiing conditions occur in early May. In the daytime the sun shines so warmly that even swimming trunks with longer legs sometimes seem too much to contend with! The slight night frost each day makes the surface of the snow iron hard, so that one can even hike over it wearing a back pack. Even though the sun does dip down below the horizon, there is no true night at this time of year. The naturalist in particular will want to go out to see how things are at night, as now the brightly attired willow grouse begins to display in the fell birch woods, giving vent to his monotonous chant of "kopek-kopek-kope-kop-ko-peko-pe-pe-pe", while above the tree line the ptarmigan conducts its own seasonable displays with considerably less pomp and circumstance.

Two of western Lapland's most famous fells, Pikku-Malla (left) and Salla, viewed from Lake Kilpisjärvi.

On 22 May a two-month period begins in which the sun on cloudless days does not disappear from view even at midnight. The snow collapses and melts, brooks and streams become choked with water, and lakes lose their covering of ice. Lake Kilpisjärvi is generally ice free from as 'early' as midsummer (24 June). By contrast, ice may remain on the highest pools well into July.

Spring is at its most vigorous in June. The dwarf birch shoots burst open the minute the snow has uncovered this hardy little shrub. Near cold patches of snow, the purple saxifrage, diapensia and Ranunculus glacialis open their flowers. Bird music rings out on both sides of the tree line. Spring at Yliperä, though, is very fickle. Just when, under the influence of soaring temperatures, the wild azalea is in full bloom and the redpoll has a full clutch of eggs in its nest lined with the down from a willow grouse's breast, the fells are sudenly blanketed in a fresh fall of snow 10 centimetres thick. The reproductive efforts which have just been made have to be remade all over again. Perhaps at the next attempt the young birds will have time to hatch before the Arctic weather again vears sharply in the opposite direction. Cold weather kills off insects, or makes them torpid, so that insectivorous birds suddenly find themselves deprived of their food supply. This means that if the young nestlings do not succumb to the cold, they die of hunger. At this stage the physical condition of the parent birds is too poor to enable them to attempt to rear yet a third brood, in which case the populations of these birds crash. It takes a long time for them to recover, as the following spring may well be just as unaccommodating.

YLIPERÄ PEOPLE

Among the thousands of tourists visiting the upper fells each year there are just a handful of local inhabitants. In the neighbourhood of this 'neljäntuulentie' ("way of the four winds") there are both Same (or Lapp) people, and pure Finns. The most authentic of the Lappish villages is located at the end of a roadless waste at Lake Raittijärvi. Another very ancient settlement occurs on the Swedish

Mauri Rautkari

side at Kotlalahti, one of the bays on Lake Kilpisjärvi. Immediately behind the Norwegian border, by the Galg-gujärvi lake, dwells the Båli clan. Nowadays all of these inhabitants have 'proper' square houses instead of poly-gonal tepees, many of them boasting a vehicle at the end of the road, and a few of them even equipped with a washing machine, or at least a battery-powered portable radio. Despite all kinds of development, the reindeer of the three countries graze in the fells acting and looking just as they did a hundred years ago. Today, too, the reindeer herdsman makes his lean-to on the bare fell tops just as his ancestors have always done. To him a trip to the remotest reaches of Yliperä is just another routine task.

One of Yliperä's legendary figures a few years ago was Aslak Juuso — already mentioned — who chose to live in the kingdom of the earth spirits and whose de-scendants still take their reindeer up to the remote country around Halti. As a person with a debt to nature, Aslak respected his surroundings above all else. He unfailingly accepted into his domain all those fell hikers, ramblers and naturalists who shared his sentiments. His lean-to was always open in all senses of the word and it was his habit to wish guests on their way with a phrase for which he became famous: "May you arrive in good health." Even though these parting words seem to be synonymous with 'Have a good trip!' many people who understood Aslak's philosophy of life saw in them something deeper: "If you live properly and respect Nature as you walk in the fells, you will be healthier — even in the south." AK

Malla Strict Nature Reserve

Enontekiö, 30 sq.km, under Finnish Forest Research Insti-tute management. This reserve lies in the floristically rich region of Köli. Hikers wishing to use the trail through it (11 km) must notify the warden, the Kilpisjärvi recreation centre, or the tourist hotel, of their intention in advance.

Birds in Snow Grottoes

A skier in a tranquil landscape can experience a startling event when a bird, or even a whole flock of them, suddenly bursts into flight from almost underneath his skis. Some members of the order of birds that we call Galliformes have understood the insulating power of snow and burrow into it to escape the sharpest sting of the Arctic night. The gallinaceous birds that live in Finland are the capercaillie, the black grouse, the hazelhen, the willow grouse and the ptarmigan.

Snow conditions vary considerably from one winter to the next. If a thick blanket forms early in winter, gallinaceous birds immediately begin burrowing into it for the night. A capercaillie needs 25 centimetres or so, but will settle for less if necessary. All a hazelhen needs for comfort is 20 centimetres.

Building the grotto

Most years, however, the snow blanket accumulates gradually and frosts alternating with temporary thaws create crustlike layers in it. Although gallinaceous birds are strong diggers, they rarely even try to penetrate the snow beneath a hard crust, but require at least a couple of centimeters of soft snow. When the soft snow overlaying a hard crust on the ground is shallow, black grouse sleep either in open pits in the snow or on a branch on the surface of the snow. They use a snow pit only once.

When the snow is shallow or covered by a hard crust, the birds carefully choose where they dig their grottoes. Black grouse usually do so beside hummocks, stumps or fallen trees, where the snow is both deeper and softer. When there is plenty of easily diggable snow, they are not so choosy, but still prefer forest edges and bogs where the snow is deep. Hazelhens prefer small forest clearings.

The birds dig their overnight abodes either at the end of a short walk or plunge straight into the snow from a branch or wherever they happen to have perched. When there is a deep soft layer and there is no danger of ramming into a stone or rock buried beneath it, black grouse and hazelhens usually just dive straight in. A willow grouse feeding on the snow usually walks some distance before burrowing in, as does a capercaillie, which picks pine needles as it struts along. Its size probably makes it wary of diving. Diving straight in has one clear advantage, because it leaves no footprints for predators to spot.

Those birds that really burrow in first excavate a tunnel varying in length from 20 or so centimetres to a couple of metres. Those dug by black grouse usually have curves or bends, even if the snow is of consistent softness. This is possibly a device to confound predators that rely on their sense of smell. The tunnel is usually sealed by the snow that the birds kick backwards when they enlarge the grotto in which they sleep.

Inside the snow

One would expect the birds to dig in as deeply as possible and sleep in the snuggest layer, but they do not. All a black grouse has above its head is ten centimetres or so, no matter how deep and soft the snow is. One explanation put forward is that too much carbon dioxide would build up in a cavity any deeper. However, a much more likely explanation is that shallow digging is a precaution against predators. Although snow efficiently muffles sound, birds only ten centimetres below it can hear approaching predators (or skiers) well enough, and burst into flight straight through the thin roofs of their grottoes.

Snow is a good insulation material, but still conducts heat five times as efficiently as air. Therefore it is important for the birds to have as little direct contact with it as possible. That is why the snow grottoes are spacious in comparison with the birds' size, especially overhead. Pieces of down sticking to their floors and walls show that the birds puff up their feathers, at least sometimes. This gives them extra thermal insulation.

The temperature of the air above the bird reaches a fairly high level, often above zero in the cases of capercaillie and black grouse. A hazelhen's grotto may be only a couple of degrees below zero even when the air temperature outside is a numbing minus 40. The heat from the birds bodies is transmitted to both the surrounding air and the snow, which crusts during the night. But the snow does not melt, and the birds' feathers are dry when they set about their daily chores in the morning.

Most gallinaceous birds, especially the willow grouse and the ptarmigan, have physiques and metabolisms well adapted to cold. Both can survive the night in a shallow open pit or on the surface of the snow; in fact, the windswept hill slopes where the ptarmigan lives rarely have soft snow deep enough to dig even an open pit. A ptarmigan excavates a roofed grotto only when the temperature drops below minus ten.

Although the black grouse is not all that sensitive to cold either, it spends the night in covered grottoes, snow conditions permiting, if the air is any colder than two below, and sometimes even in warmer

A story written on snow: black grouse dive straight into their grottoes for the night, but usually take a little stroll before they fly away in the morning.

Reijo Juurinen

Martti Rikkonen

Its whiteness makes a willow grouse virtually undetectable even in an open snow pit.

weather. In fact, they have been known to excavate roofed grottoes in above-zero temperatures, when the surface of the snow is thawing. This is probably to escape the wind and the attentions of predators. Hazelhens and capercaillies also sometimes dig in when the weather is mild.

Birds take quite a risk by entering their grottoes in mild weather. If a sunny day in early spring is followed by a very cold night, the birds can be trapped in the deadly embrace of an ice crust, although reports of such deaths are relatively rare.

Snow conditions largely determine at what times of day and for how long the birds forage for food. When black grouse cannot dig into their snow grottoes, they are active more or less from dawn to dusk. But when they can build grottoes, they switch their metabolisms onto "economy", feeding for only an hour or two in the morning, after which they retire to their grottoes and remain there until the next day, i.e. over 90% of the time. Since this saves so much energy, all they need to sustain them until the next morning is a few catkins.

Also capercaillies, hazelhens and ptarmigan spend most or nearly all of the day in grottoes when the snow is soft. In early spring they sometimes pop into them for a rest during the day.

Tales of gallinaceous birds spending several days continuously in their snow grottoes during spells of severe frost or blizzards abound, but that they really do so often is unlikely, because their systems are attuned to daily feeding. Their bodies can store only very little energy.

Some small birds, such as snow buntings, bullfinches, great tits and, especially, mealy redpolls, can also dig into snow when the weather is cold. Their grottoes differ from those of gallinaceous birds in that the tunnels leading into them are generally left open Small birds build their grottoes much more randomly than gallinaceous species, probably because the smallness of their bodies and the inferior insulation properties of their plumage reduces the amount of thermal shielding that they can get from snow. Some small species, such as goldcrests, occasionally spend the night in ready-built grottoes that they find in the snow. AM

THIS IS FINLAND

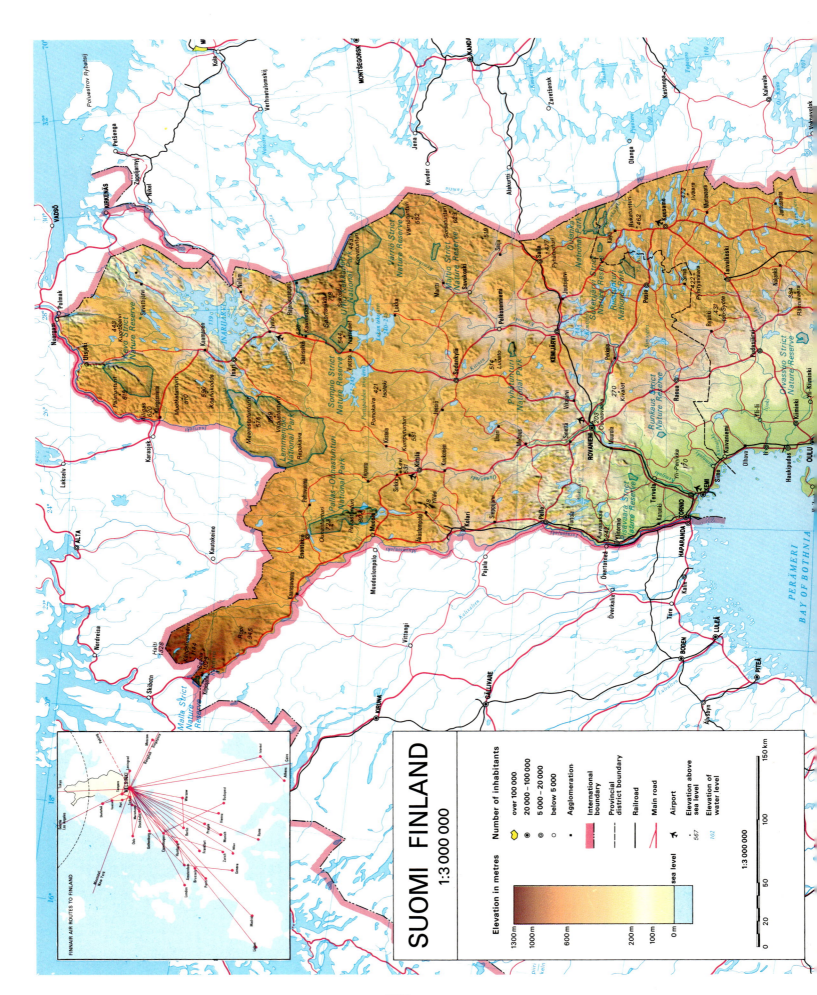

SUOMI FINLAND

1:3 000 000

Number of inhabitants
- ◉ over 100 000
- ◎ 20 000–100 000
- ○ 5 000–20 000
- • below 5 000
- ⬡ Agglomeration

International boundary
Provincial district boundary
Railroad
Main road
✈ Airport
· Elevation above sea level
567
102 Elevation of water level
sea level

Elevation in metres

1300 m · 1000 m · 600 m · 200 m · 100 m · 0 m

1:3 000 000

0 · 20 · 50 · 100 · 150 km

FINNAIR AIR ROUTES TO FINLAND

PERÄMERI
BAY OF BOTHNIA

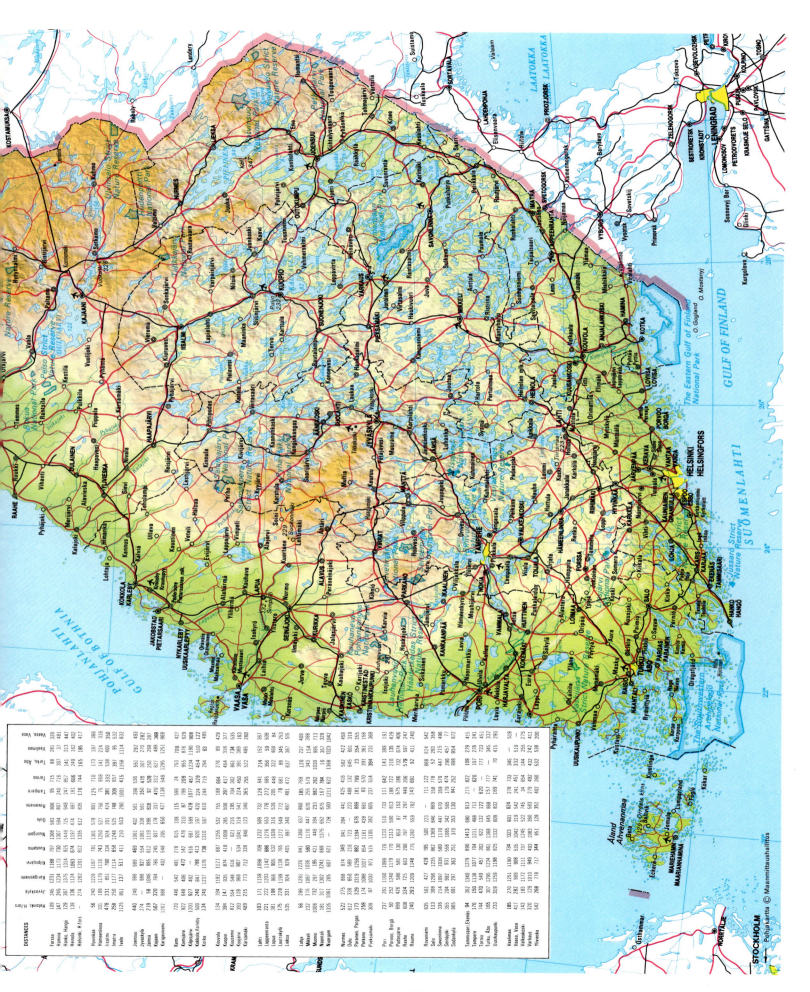

The last snow remains on the northern bank of the river Saikkalanjoki at Mouhijärvi.

The summer brings stooks to the south side of the river to feed the cattle over the winter.

Lying at the eastern limit of Western Europe, Finland is a frontier country standing close to the Soviet Union. Here the technological 20th century meets a wilderness of forest and Arctic wasteland. Indeed, two-thirds of Finland is covered by lakes and forests, and the snows that fall in November do not melt until April or May. But it is this austere beauty which inspired the music of Jean Sibelius (1865—1957) and the clean lines of the architecture and furniture of Alvar Aalto (1898—1976) and Eero Saarinen (1910—61).

Most of Finland is low-lying, although it rises to over 1000 m (3300 ft) in the north in Lapland, and there are extensive peat bogs and swamps. The extensive forests, from which one-fifth of Finland's main export — paper — is produced, consist mainly of spruce where the soil is clay and fragrant Scots pine on the drier sands and gravels; the slender birch thrives almost everywhere.

At the end of the last great Ice Age when temperatures rose, the vast ice sheet retreated and left immense quantities of glacial debris on the ancient granite bedrock. Thousands of lakes were formed in the process. As the ice melted, the sea level rose. But, relieved of the weight of ice, the land is today rising at a rate of as much as 800 mm (30 in) each century along parts of the west coast on the Gulf of BOTHNIA, an arm of the BALTIC SEA. As a result, land is being gained from the sea at the rate of 1 km^2 every ten years. Lapping the shores of this land of lakes, even the Baltic resembles a lake: it has virtually no tides and is not very salty.

Across the Gulf of Bothnia, and forming Finland's western boundary, lies Sweden; the eastern boundary of the country is shared — for 1269 km (about 790 miles) — with the USSR. The Soviet city of LENINGRAD, on the Gulf of Finland, lies only 300 km (190 miles) from the Finnish capital, HELSINKI. Norway, reach-

The hay has been carried away; the scenery has acquired autumn colours.

Snow covers the valley again. The river bank thickets delineate the river's course.

CLIMATE

The Finns experience great extremes of climate between winter and summer. The citizens of Helsinki in the south may sometimes have to endure winter cold as low as –30°C (–22°F) in January, and yet find themselves

ing across the top of Scandinavia, forms the northern boundary of Finland. One-third of Finland lies inside the ARCTIC CIRCLE.

basking in temperatures as high as 30°C (86°F) in July. Summer days are long and light, but in the winter the days are short and gloomy. Inside the Arctic Circle the sun can shine at midnight for two months in the summer but some winter days see only an hour or two of daylight.

Autumn is short and spring comes late; frosts in early summer are a widespread hazard. It is not suprising that Finland is sometimes known as the 'land of three winters' — autumn winter, high winter and spring winter. During the long, harsh winter everything freezes, even the Baltic; March is a brilliant month, with dazzling sun on ice and snow.

Thanks to the influence of the Gulf Stream, Finland has a much more hospitable climate than most other regions at the same latitude. Helsinki, for example, lies only a little further south than Anchorage, Alaska, while Rovaniemi in Lapland is a good

deal further north than Fairbanks.

The mean temperature in Finland is higher than in other countries lying between 60° and 70° N, the difference ranging from –6 to –13 degrees C in February and from 14,7 to 17,8 in July. The Great Lakes in North America, which lie between 42° and 48° N, have almost the same mean temperature as Finland (–3 to –15 °C) in January, whereas July in southern Finland is as warm as England, Holland and

Matti A. Pitkänen

FINLAND AT A GLANCE

Area 338,145 km² (130, 557 sq miles)

Population 4,938,000

Capital Helsinki, population 490,000

Government Parliamentary republic

Currency Markka = 100 penni

Languages Finnish, Swedish

Religion Christian (92 % Lutheran, 1 % Greek Orthodox)

Climate Temperate, with cold winters. Average temperature in Helsinki ranges from –9 to –4°C (16—25°F) in February to 12—22°C (54—72°F) in July

Main primary products Timber, cereals, potatoes, livestock, fish; copper, zinc, iron, chromium, lead

Major industries Forestry, timber products including wood pulp and paper, machinery, shipbuilding, clothing, chemicals, fertilisers

Main exports Paper, machinery, ships, timber, chemicals, clothing, wood pulp, petroleum products

Annual income per head (US$) 11,007

Population growth (per thous/yr) 4

Life expectancy (yrs) Male 72 **Female** 77

Midnight Sun	District and latitude
May 17—July 27	Utsjoki 69° 52′
May 22—July 22	Ivalo 68° 40′
May 30—July 14	Sodankylä 67° 25′
June 6—July 7	Rovaniemi 66° 30′
Polar Night	**District and latitude**
Nov 25—Jan 16	Utsjoki 66° 52′
Dec 3—Jan 9	Ivalo 68° 40′
Dec 18—Dec 24	Sodankylä 67° 25′

LKA/Hannu Hautala

Snowy solitude: this is what the motorist faces in the North.

Belgium (mean temperature 16 to 18 °C) and in northern Finland a little colder (mean temperature 12 to 15).

The midday temperature is, on average, 2—5 degrees higher and the minimum night temperature that much colder than the mean, which is roughly the same as that at 8 in the morning or 8 in the evening.

An endless day (left) and night represent the extremes of Lapland's climate.

LKA/Teuvo Suominen

However, averages should be taken for what they are: averages. As in most parts of Europe, the weather in Finland can be fickle. One has to be prepared for it. If you intend to spend a lot of time outdoors and have not taken along proper clothing and gear, you will have no difficulty finding what you need in Finland's well-stocked speciality shops or department stores.

Midnight sun
Around Midsummer in northern Finland, the sun is constantly over the horizon and does not set for several weeks. In Utsjoki

this "longest summer day" lasts for over two months. Even in more southern places, the night does not get dark at all, the days being separated by a couple of hours of twilight.

Winter darkness (Polar Night)
Since northernmost Finland is within the Arctic Circle, the sun does not rise at all during the "kaamos" period. This lasts for nearly two months in Utsjoki. The winter days are short all over Finland and the sun is very close to the horizon even at midday. By mid-April, however, it is above the horizon for 14 to 15 hours in southern Finland and 16 hours in northern Finland. Even the "kaamos" is not as unmitigatedly gloomy as it sounds, because there are long periods of twilight.

Lake and sea temperatures
The water in the lakes is rather warm in summer because they are shallow. To some extent this also applies to the sea. Thus in July the temperature of the water in the larger lakes is 18° to 20°C in southern Finland and 16° to 18°C in the north, while

the smaller lakes are even warmer. Around the inner islands and the lakes of southern Finland the water is as warm as the northern coast of Spain, and around the outer islands and in the lakes of northern Finland the same as in the coasts of Cornwall, Kent and Holland.

Wind conditions at sea
The mean wind velocity in summer is about 12 knots (Beaufort 4) during the day and about 8—10 knots (Beaufort 3) at night. Winds stronger that 22 knots or more (Beaufort 6 or more) occur in 5 per cent of the whole summer time. (For the sake of comparison, the corresponding frequency is 7—11 per cent in the North Sea.) In autumn the frequency is close to 20 per cent.

Snow conditions
In southern and central Finland the snow comes to stay at the beginning of December and melts in open places in mid- or late April, and in the forest (70 per cent of the total land area) at the beginning of May. In northern Finland the snow comes to stay about five weeks earlier and melts about three weeks later than in the south.

THE OUTDOORS LIFE

If you go on a hike, always tell somebody where you are going and when and where you hope to arrive.

Never go into the wilderness alone unless you are an experienced outdoors person, in which case you will make sure to have good maps and a compass.

Suomen Latu (Fabianinkatu 7, 00130 Helsinki) is an organization devoted to promoting hiking and skiing. It publishes useful information on these subjects in English and several other major languages.

Beware of fire
Exercise extreme caution if you light a fire outdoors. During spells of very dry weather, the authorities prohibit outdoor fires altogether, either in all of Finland or in certain areas. This is announced in newspapers and on radio and TV. Ask a local if you are in doubt. Fires can be devastating.

Footwear
Much of Finland is boggy, and you will always have to cross wet patches on a hike, so rubber boots are the height of fashion, especially in Lapland.

Bugs
In summer, do not underestimate the mosquitoes and blackflies, especially in Lapland. If you intend spending a long time outdoors, take plenty of repellent oils and sprays. During peak periods, you would be well advised to wear a hat with a gauze veil. You can buy one in a sports goods shop.

Wilderness cabins
Lapland is dotted with "wilderness cabins", some of which

must be booked in advance, but most of which are open to anybody wishing to use their facilities. They are marked on good topographical maps and usually spaced a day's hike or so apart.

They contain dry kindling, a stove, bunks and essential tools and utensils. The principle is that you leave them at least as tidy as you find them, making sure that there are matches, dry wood, etc., for the next visitor (whose life may depend on it).

Access to the environment

Based on both ancient custom and current law, everybody enjoys what are called "Everyman's Rights". What this means is that — with certain restrictions —

Nature can be good to man: delicious mushrooms and salmon wait to be picked and caught.

everybody has the right of access to and to enjoy the natural environment. You cannot light a fire nor put up a tent without the landowner's permission. Crops, farmyards and fenced-in areas are off limits, but otherwise go where you want and experience the delights of Finnish nature. Berries and mushrooms are yours for the picking, and, provided you have a licence, catch as many fish as you can.

Fishing

You need two licences. A general government one is obtainable at any post office for a small fee and is valid for a calendar year. In addition to that, you will need another licence for whatever area or water body you fish in. Enquire locally.

International borders

If you plan a hike in Lapland, remember that you can cross the border only at official crossing points. To cross in terrain, you need special permission from both countries and the red tape involved is probably not worth it.

There is an exclusion zone, usually about 3 kilometres wide, along the Soviet frontier. You need police permission to enter this zone, in which photography is forbidden.

Motoring

To drive in Finland, you need an international licence. Traffic is right-hand. Horns are used only when necessary. The main roads are surfaced and kept in good condition all year round. Keep your lights on, at least dimmed, at all times outside cities. Seat belts are compulsory for all passengers, front and back.

IF YOU DRINK, DON'T DRIVE!
IF YOU DRIVE, DON'T DRINK!

Winter motoring

In Finland studded tyres are not compulsory in winter, but are allowed from 1 October to 30 April, and at other times when justified by weather conditions. In December, January and February it is highly recommended to use at least snow tyres, i.e. tyres that cope with mud and snow conditions on all motor vehicles under 3.5 tonnes. Both a caravan and the car pulling it must have the same type of tyres. It is advisable to carry snow chains for a caravan, jumper leads, a towrope, a shovel, a bag of sand and a spray to prevent

LKA/Reijo Juurinen

A wilderness cabin at its best: well-equipped, clean and cozy, ready to receive its visitors.

A light tent, a lean-to, gives shelter to the hiker resting beside an open fire.

LKA/Jorma Luhta

dampness in electric equipment. Watch the elks and the reindeer. The warning signs are these:

If you drive in remote areas in winter, have some food and blankets in the car and something to get a fire going. In the event of a breakdown, stay with the car until help arrives.

LKA/Pauli Nieminen

In the frontier zone, a visitor will come accross signs warning of the nearness of a foreign country.

Maps and charts

You will find a comprehensive range of maps at the Map Centre of the National Board of Survey, Eteläesplanadi 4, in Helsinki (quite close to the colourful Market Square). Bookstores and filling stations all over Finland also sell maps.

NATURAL BOUNTY

In the autumn and summer there is a harvest of wild berries and mushrooms, simply waiting to be picked. Finland's natural bounty also includes a wealth of game birds and wildfowl, and the lakes and rivers are rich in pike, perch, powan, trout and salmon, although pollution — caused by waste from wood processing, fertilisers and acid rain — is becoming a problem. Almost every Finnish family has its hunting

paper, wallboards, laminates and prefabricated timber components, as well as chemical products, all of which swell the export market.

Not only has the timber processing industry advanced recently. The complete revision of industry which followed the last war led to investment in metallurgy, electrical manufactures and engineering, which now employ most of the country's industrial workers. For example, there is a new state-owned iron and steel complex in the north at Rautaruukki. Shipbuilding has boomed, prompted in the 1950s by Finland's need for an effective fleet of icebreakers. Icebreakers are now built for other countries too, including an entire fleet for

A familiar sight on the Finnish waterways: a chain of log bundles is being towed to the paper mill.

The pride of the Finnish shipbuilding industry, a luxury cruiser from the Wärtsilä shipyards.

ported: Finnish banking representatives work in all the world's major banking centres, and Finnish design of clothing, glass, porcelain, sports equipment, kitchenware and electronic goods has not only made for a good export trade but influenced design elsewhere.

Finland's trading links with the USSR are strengthened by its need for Russian energy supplies. Only one-third of its energy needs can be supplied by domestic sources. It has already developed almost all possible hydroelectric power, and readily available peat has a limited use. Finnish nuclear reactors are producing power, and the Finns seem to have no qualms about establishing more of them. But meanwhile the energy gap is closed by imports of crude oil and natural gas from the USSR, and of coal from Poland and West Germany.

In the areas where seasonal unemployment is worst (the construction industries suffer es-

LKA/Rauno Pelkonen

Wärtsilä Marine

and fishing enthusiasts, and some 70,000 licences to shoot elk are issued every year to keep down their numbers, because of the damage they cause to crops and young trees. Bears, which were once hunted, are now protected. Wolves come out of the forests, and often make local headlines; their victims are usually the reindeer.

Finland still lives to a large extent by its forests, although the picturesque days of the seasonal employment of hordes of lumberjacks, and large-scale floating of logs down the rivers, are over. Now skilled workers are employ-

ed in the forests all year, although felling still takes place mostly in winter; huge rafts of logs are sometimes floated across the lakes, but much of the timber is moved by lorry.

Most of the forests are privately owned and held in small lots, and widespread education in forestry has improved yields enormously. Continuous surveys of forest areas, both by air and on land, ensure that the timber is not cut down faster than it is replaced. Advances in forestry are matched by those in the factory. New processes and diversification have led to new types of

the Russians to use in the Arctic. Shipyards in Helsinki and Turku also build ferries and cruise liners, and recently mustered the expertise of several nations to build the P. & O. cruise liner *Royal Princess*.

Entire industrial plants have been exported from Finland, including power stations and factories for processing softwoods. The biggest of these undertakings has been the construction of an iron and steel complex in Soviet Karelia, with a Finnish labour force who camped on site and travelled home for weekends. Finnish skills are also ex-

pecially from the long winters), new industries and public works have been set up to ease the situation. Financial support is provided on a graduated scale, so that most goes to the needy north-east and the least to the wealthier south-west. Developments are complemented by an elaborate conservation programme, with 22 national parks and over a thousand protected areas, as well as controls on industrial pollution. More Finns are building summer homes, and the people have not lost their appreciation of their country's exceptional landscape.

INDEX

of species, people, and points of interest

301